Advanced Malware Analysis

D1401233

About the Author

 **Christopher C. Elisan** is a veteran of the security industry, having started his career straight out of college in the 1990s. He is a seasoned reverse engineer and malware researcher. He has seen malware develop from the DOS days to the more complicated and sophisticated malware we see today. He is currently the Principal Malware Scientist and senior manager of the Malware Intelligence Team at RSA, The Security Division of EMC.

Elisan is a pioneer of Trend Micro's TrendLabs, where he started his career as a malware reverse engineer. There, he held multiple technical and managerial positions. After leaving Trend Micro, he joined F-Secure. He built and established F-Secure's Asia R&D and spearheaded multiple projects that included vulnerability discovery, web security, and mobile security. He then joined Damballa, Inc., as a senior threat analyst specializing in malware research. Elisan graduated with a Bachelor of Science Degree in Computer Engineering and holds the following industry certifications: Certified Ethical Hacker, Microsoft Certified Systems Engineer, Microsoft Certified Systems Administrator, Microsoft Certified Professional, and Certified Scrum Master.

Elisan is considered one of the world's subject-matter experts when it comes to malware, digital fraud, and cybercrime. He lends his expertise to different law enforcement agencies, and he provides expert opinion about malware, botnets, and advanced persistent threats to leading industry and mainstream publications, including *USA Today, San Francisco Chronicle, SC Magazine, InformationWeek, Fox Business,* and *Dark Reading.* He is a frequent speaker at various security conferences around the globe, including RSA Conference, SecTor, HackerHalted, TakeDownCon, Toorcon, (ISC)² Security Congress, Rootcon, and B-Sides. He also authored *Malware, Rootkits & Botnets: A Beginner's Guide.*

When he is not dissecting or talking about malware, Elisan spends time with his kids playing basketball and video games. He also enjoys watching with his family the Atlanta Hawks beat the hell out of their opponents. If time permits, he lives his rockstar dream as a vocalist/guitarist with his local rock band in Atlanta.

You can follow him on Twitter: @Tophs.

Advanced Malware Analysis

Christopher C. Elisan

New York   Chicago   San Francisco
Athens   London   Madrid   Mexico City
Milan   New Delhi   Singapore   Sydney   Toronto

Cataloging-in-Publication Data is on file with the Library of Congress

McGraw-Hill Education books are available at special quantity discounts to use as premiums and sales promotions or for use in corporate training programs. To contact a representative, please visit the Contact Us page at www.mhprofessional.com.

Advanced Malware Analysis

Copyright © 2015 by McGraw-Hill Education. All rights reserved. Printed in the United States of America. Except as permitted under the United States Copyright Act of 1976, no part of this publication may be reproduced or distributed in any form or by any means, or stored in a data base or retrieval system, without the prior written permission of the publisher, with the exception that the program listings may be entered, stored, and executed in a computer system, but they may not be reproduced for publication.

All trademarks or copyrights mentioned herein are the possession of their respective owners and McGraw-Hill Education makes no claim of ownership by the mention of products that contain these marks.

1 2 3 4 5 6 7 8 9 0   DOC/DOC   1 2 1 0 9 8 7 6 5

ISBN   978-0-07-181974-9
MHID   0-07-181974-6

Sponsoring Editor Meghan Riley Manfre
Editorial Supervisor Stephen M. Smith
Production Supervisor Lynn M. Messina
Acquisitions Coordinator Amy Stonebraker
Technical Editor Jong Purisima
Project Manager Sonam Arora,
         Cenveo® Publisher Services

Copy Editor Kim Wimpsett
Proofreader Barnali Ojha
Indexer Jack Lewis
Art Director, Cover Jeff Weeks
Composition Cenveo Publisher Services
Illustration Cenveo Publisher Services

Information contained in this work has been obtained by McGraw-Hill Education from sources believed to be reliable. However, because of the possibility of human or mechanical error by our sources, McGraw-Hill Education, or others, McGraw-Hill Education does not guarantee the accuracy, adequacy, or completeness of any information and is not responsible for any errors or omissions or the results obtained from the use of such information.

To my family, Kara, Sebastian, and Noah,
for their love, support, and understanding,
and to all security practitioners who always
strive to be better than they currently are.

Contents at a Glance

Part IV   **Appendixes**

Contents

Foreword

The threat of malware is everywhere. Individuals, organizations, businesses, and governments are being targeted. The motivation of these threats has evolved from simple nuisance to information theft and espionage. Because of this, the role of malware in cybercrime and digital fraud is bigger than ever. Malware has become a standard part of the arsenal an attacker deploys for malicious campaigns against targeted entities.

The consequences of these attacks are not confined to the destruction of digital assets alone. With everything around us being controlled by digital assets that are connected with each other, a destruction or failure caused by malware can translate to destroyed infrastructure and even loss of human lives. Imagine a destruction of our power production, transmission, or distribution infrastructures, the result of which could be devastating.

Malware threatens our national security. The theft of military secrets, defense and military strategy, and plans for new weapons can give adversaries an advantage. Compromised weapon control systems might have catastrophic consequences.

Understanding a malware's main directive gives us the ability to mitigate its threat and strengthen our defenses against future generations of similar malware attacks. It helps us build better solutions that minimize the proliferation of malware and helps us detect and respond to compromises. Malware analysis is an indispensable skill for security professionals who are tasked with battling advanced threat actors head on.

Malware analysis requires, aside from understanding the concepts of malware and the different tools available, a lot of patience and perseverance. It is often considered a challenging topic to tackle, but it is an exciting one. This book will walk you through the exciting paths of analyzing malware. It starts with introducing the different malware concepts and taxonomy, and progresses to hunting down and collecting malware samples, and finally how to analyze them effectively by using the right tools the right way.

Amit Yoran
President, RSA

Acknowledgments

First, I would like to thank God for this blessing. Second, I would like to thank all the people who were involved in one way or another in the creation of this book: Amanda Russell, Brandi Shailer, Melinda Lytle, Wendy Rinaldi, and Amy Jollymore. Special thanks go out to Meghan Manfre for seeing the book through; Meghan's support, patience, and understanding were instrumental in finishing this book. And thanks to Jong Purisima for sharing his views and expertise as technical editor of this book.

Thank you to Amit Yoran, President of RSA, for writing the foreword of this book. I really appreciate him taking time out of his busy schedule to share his thoughts about this book. A big thank you goes out to my colleagues, Rotem Salinas and Ahmed Sonbol, for their contribution in the laboratory part of this book.

Specifically, thanks to Rotem Salinas for sharing his knowledge in malware analysis through the following labs:

- ▶ Manually Unpacking a Packed Malware
- ▶ Analyzing a User Mode Rootkit
- ▶ Analyzing a Kernel Mode Rootkit

Also, thanks to Ahmed Sonbol for sharing his experience in Cuckoo through this lab:

- ▶ Installing and Configuring Cuckoo

Rotem Salinas is a security researcher on RSA's FirstWatch Team. His work focuses on reverse engineering malware and research-oriented development of tools for this purpose. You are most likely to find him coding in Python, C++, Assembly, and .NET. Rotem has spoken at security conventions such as RSA Conference 2015 and RSA Global Summit 2014.

Ahmed Sonbol is a senior technologist at RSA, The Security Division of EMC. He focuses on malware analysis and reverse engineering. Ahmed has years of experience in writing log and network parsers for different RSA products. He holds a Master of Science Degree in Computer Science from Northeastern University in Boston and a Bachelor of Science Degree in Computer Science and Automatic Control from Alexandria University in Egypt.

About the Technical Editor

Jong Purisima has been around threats and malware since he analyzed his first malware in 1995. He started his affiliation with the computer security industry by being part of the Virus Doctor Team at Trend Micro, where he analyzed malware to generate detection, remediation, and customer-facing malware reports. Throughout his decade-long stint at Trend Micro, he wore various hats, but the common theme was to deliver technologies, services, and solutions from TrendLabs to Trend Micro customers. Jong then joined Webroot Software as a core technology product manager, managing Webroot's anti-malware and URL filtering engines, as well as OEM relationships. He then later joined GFI Software's Security Business Unit as an anti-malware lab manager, leading a global team of 100 in the sourcing, processing, and publishing of anti-malware signatures for the VIPRE product line.

He currently works as a product manager in Cisco's Security Business Group. During his free time, Jong keeps himself busy as an amateur handyman, and loves woodworking and taking road trips, during which he stops and takes photos at "Welcome to _____!" state signs with his family.

Introduction

This book is a labor of love. I hope that it adds value to your endeavor of becoming the best malware researcher that you can be.

Why This Book

This book was written to be an essential resource when it comes to malware analysis. It is presented in an easy-to-read and easy-to-understand format to allow novice malware analysts to ease into each topic without overwhelming them and to give more seasoned malware analysts a chance to review the concepts before getting into the nitty-gritty details of malware analysis. The book is also rich in practical and easy-to-follow tutorials so each topic learned can be applied immediately in a real-world scenario.

Who Should Read This Book

This book was written for self-guided IT professionals who are responsible for securing enterprise networks and systems and those who tackle malware on a regular basis; security professionals, malware analysts, and researchers who want to advance their skills in malware analysis; students who are taking technology courses and want to learn how to analyze malware; and anyone who has the patience and perseverance to educate themselves about malware analysis.

What This Book Covers

This book covers different malware concepts and the technologies these malicious software use to achieve their directive. The book then discusses how to hunt down and collect malware samples from different sources. Once malware samples are on hand, the book then shows how to set up your malware analysis lab, which ultimately leads to malware analysis by using the right set of tools the right way.

How to Use This Book

This book can be read from cover to cover. This will give you the most benefit because the book is written in such a way that the succeeding chapters build on top of the previous chapters. But this does not mean that this is the only way to read this book. Although the chapters are interrelated, they can be read separately without reading the previous or next one and still have the chapter's main idea and concept understood. Each chapter can stand on its own independently but also enjoys interdependency with the other chapters. Therefore, if you are already familiar with a specific chapter's subject matter, you can skip that chapter without sacrificing the book's continuity. And since the chapters are independent of each other, this book can be used as an excellent reference for malware analysis.

How This Book Is Organized

This book consists of 13 chapters and three appendixes divided into four parts.

- ▶ Part I: Malware Blueprint
- ▶ Part II: Malware Research Lab
- ▶ Part III: Malware Inspection
- ▶ Part IV: Appendixes

Part I: Malware Blueprint

Part I discusses the different malware concepts and the technologies malware uses to achieve its goal. It consists of five chapters.

- ▶ Chapter 1: Malware Analysis 101
- ▶ Chapter 2: Malware Taxonomy
- ▶ Chapter 3: Malware Deployment

- ► Chapter 4: Protective Mechanisms
- ► Chapter 5: Malware Dependencies

Chapter 1 is an introduction to malware analysis. It discusses what malware analysis is and how important it is to have as a skill in the fight against malware proliferation.

Chapter 2 discusses the different types of malware and how they are categorized. It shows the different ways malware can be clustered together and how each clustering method can be advantageous to researchers.

Chapter 3 shows how attackers deploy malware. It presents the different technologies that are used or abused by attackers to have their malware reach their target entity.

Chapter 4 discusses how malware protects itself from security products and the prying eyes of malware analysts and researchers. Different malware protective mechanisms are discussed to give you an understanding of how each one works and how to beat them.

Chapter 5 discusses the different things that malware depends on to operate or function properly. You will learn that malware, like any other software, has dependencies that are vital for their operation. This chapter gives you an idea of how to stop malware by simply removing or messing around with one of their dependencies.

Part II: Malware Research Lab

Part II is all about setting up the lab for malware analysis. It consists of three chapters.

- ► Chapter 6: Malware Collection
- ► Chapter 7: Static Analysis Lab
- ► Chapter 8: Dynamic Analysis Lab

Chapter 6 discusses how to collect malware from different sources and how to set up an automated system for malware collection.

Chapter 7 teaches you how to set up a fully functioning and effective static analysis lab.

Chapter 8 teaches you how to set up a fully functioning and effective dynamic analysis lab.

Part III: Malware Inspection

Part III delves into the nitty-gritty details of the malware. It consists of five chapters.

- ▶ Chapter 9: The Portable Executable File
- ▶ Chapter 10: The Proper Way to Handle Files
- ▶ Chapter 11: Inspecting Static Malware
- ▶ Chapter 12: Inspecting Dynamic Malware
- ▶ Chapter 13: Tools of the Trade

Chapter 9 introduces you to the Portable Executable (PE) file. It discusses the format of the PE file and goes into detail about what makes the PE file what it is.

Chapter 10 educates you on how to properly and correctly handle files, especially those that are deemed malicious and suspicious. In this chapter, techniques are introduced to make sure that no unwanted infections will happen during the course of malware analysis.

Chapter 11 discusses the different techniques and tools used to analyze malware while it is at rest.

Chapter 12 discusses the different techniques and tools used to analyze malware while it is running on a target system.

Chapter 13 discusses the different tools that malware analysts and researchers use to effectively analyze malware. In this chapter, different tool combinations are used to solve the most common use cases that analysts and researchers face on a regular basis.

Part IV: Appendixes

- ▶ Appendix A: Tools List
- ▶ Appendix B: List of Laboratories
- ▶ Appendix C: Volatility Framework Basic Plug-ins

Appendix A contains a list of all the tools that are used in this book.
Appendix B contains a list of all the laboratories in this book.
Appendix C contains a list of Volatility Framework basic plug-ins.

Malware Blueprint

Malware Analysis 101

S o you want to learn how to analyze malware? Well, you picked up the right book. But before I go into the meat of analyzing malware, it is important to know and understand several things that will be key in effectively analyzing malware.

This chapter will get you started on the right path to malware analysis by establishing the needed foundational knowledge to effectively analyze malware.

The chapter will tackle the two types of malware analysis, as well as its purpose, its limitations, and the malware analysis process itself. The chapter will then conclude by discussing what is needed to become an effective malware analyst.

Malware Analysis

Malware analysis is the process of extracting information from malware through static and dynamic inspection by using different tools, techniques, and processes. It is a methodical approach to uncovering a malware's main directive by extracting as much data from malware as possible while it is at rest and in motion.

LINGO

*A **malware at rest** is a malware that is not running in a target environment, while a **malware in motion** is a malware that is running in a target environment.*

Data is extracted from malware through the use of data extracting and monitoring tools. The techniques and processes needed to successfully gather data from malware differ depending on the malware's capability; they adapt to the changing malware landscape. This is why malware analysis is considered an art. The tools are your paintbrushes, the techniques and processes are your drawing style, and the malware is your subject. How effectively you use those tools and how well the techniques and processes are applied and refined will reflect how well the malware subject is pictured. It's a picture you create to show the malware's true identity stripped of all its protective mechanisms and revealing only its darkest and deepest malicious directive. The artist becomes better at her craft through practice and by gaining knowledge, skills, and experience as time goes by. The same concepts apply to the malware analyst and researcher. With continuous practice and exposure to different malware, the malware analyst becomes more knowledgeable, skillful, and experienced.

Malware Analysis and Reverse Engineering

I always separate malware analysis from reverse engineering, although many consider reverse engineering as malware analysis. The way I see it, the two require two different sets of skills. Malware analysis is more about the mastery of different tools, techniques, and processes to extract as much information from malware without disassembling or decompiling it and to make malware function in a controlled environment for the purpose of monitoring and collecting data that can be used to understand the malware's true directive.

LINGO

Disassembling is the process of breaking down a binary into low-level code such as assembly code, while decompiling is the process of breaking down a binary into high-level code such as C or C++.

Malware reverse engineering, on the other hand, is the process of breaking down malware into low-level lines of code, usually assembly code, to fully understand its function. It requires that you can read and understand low-level code. This is where knowledge of assembly language becomes crucial. It is needed to decipher and read low-level code. Without this knowledge, it will be impossible to trace each line of code's execution flow let alone understand what each line of code actually means.

Malware reverse engineering complements malware analysis. It is usually the last resort when malware analysis fails to extract the needed data from malware to paint an accurate picture. As we will discuss later in the "Limitations of Malware Analysis" section, reverse engineering is an important activity that serves as an addition to the malware analysis process.

NOTE

A combination of malware analysis and reverse engineering usually exposes new malware techniques that are otherwise not visible through malware analysis alone.

Types of Malware Analysis

As previously defined, malware analysis is the process of extracting information from malware through static and dynamic inspection by using different tools, techniques, and processes. Given that inspection or analysis can take place regardless of whether the malware is static or dynamic, it is only appropriate that the two types of malware analysis are called static analysis and dynamic analysis.

LINGO

Static malware is malware at rest. *Dynamic malware* is malware in motion.

Static Analysis

Static analysis is the process of extracting information from malware while it is not running. Typically, malware is subjected to different static analysis tools, which will be detailed in succeeding chapters of the book that are designed to extract as much information as possible from the malware. The information that is collected can range from the simplest, such as the malware's file type, to the most complicated, such as identifying maliciousness based on non-encrypted code or strings found in the malware. Static analysis is the easiest and least risky malware analysis process. It is the easiest because there are no special conditions needed for analysis. The malware is simply subjected to different static analysis tools. It is as easy as clicking some buttons or using a command line. It is less risky because the malware is not running during static analysis; therefore, there is no risk of an infection occurring while analysis is taking place.

Another thing that makes static analysis less risky is the availability of tools in other operating system, such as Linux, that can be used to statically extract information from Windows files. Statically inspecting a malware in an operating system where the subject malware is not intended to execute eliminates the malware's ability to run and wreak havoc in the system.

But not all static analysis tools that Windows offers have a counterpart or equivalent tool in other operating systems. This leaves the researcher no choice but to use those Windows-based tools. If this is the case and just an added precaution, Linux-based systems can still be used to run Windows-based static analysis tools by using WINE in Linux. WINE is short for Wine Is Not an Emulator. WINE makes it possible to run Windows programs under Linux-based systems, such as Ubuntu and Debian. WINE acts as a middleman and translator between the Windows-based program and the Linux-based operating system.

TIP

Using WINE in Linux to run Windows static analysis tools also means that the subject malware can run using WINE. Utmost care must still be practiced at all times even if the malware's capability is limited because of the absence of some aspects of Windows that the malware needs to achieve its directive.

Static analysis is considered to be a low-risk, low-reward process. It is low risk, but it yields less promising results because information gathering is based solely on what can be seen while the malware is inactive. The information gathered is limited and does not reveal that much about the malware's directive. Most of the time, malware reveals its true nature only while it is running.

Dynamic Analysis

Dynamic analysis is the process of extracting information from malware while it is running. Unlike the limited view static analysis provides of the malware being analyzed, dynamic analysis offers a more in-depth view into the malware's functions because it is collecting information while the malware is executing its functions and directives.

To conduct dynamic malware analysis, two things are needed:

▶ Malware test environment

▶ Dynamic analysis tools

A malware test environment is a system where malware is executed for the purpose of analysis. It is designed to satisfy most, if not all, of the conditions for a malware to run. It must consist of an operating system that the malware is written for and must have most, if not all, of the dependencies the malware needs to execute properly.

Dynamic analysis tools, also known as system monitoring tools, are the ones monitoring the malware test environment for any changes made by the malware to the target system. Some of the changes that are monitored and recorded include changes in the file system, modifications in configuration files, and any other relevant changes that are triggered by the malware's execution. The dynamic analysis tools also monitor inbound and outbound network communications and any operating system resources used by the malware. With these tools, the analyst is able to understand what the malware is trying to do to the target system.

A fully implemented malware test environment with the appropriate dynamic analysis tools is also known as a malware sandbox. A malware sandbox is where an analyst can run and observe a malware's behavior. A malware sandbox can be a single system or a network of systems designed solely to analyze malware during runtime.

LINGO

Malware sandbox, malware test environment, and *dynamic analysis lab* are different names given to a system where malware is executed for the purpose of analysis.

Unlike static analysis, dynamic analysis is a high-risk, high-reward process. The risk of infection or something wrong happening is high because the malware is running; the reward is high because the malware reveals more of itself during execution. But do not let the high-risk part of dynamic analysis scare you because this is manageable and just takes common sense. There are precautions that can be taken to minimize if not completely eliminate any risk of infection. One of them is to make sure that the system used for dynamic analysis is fully isolated from any production systems and network. I'll talk more about dynamic analysis precautions in Chapter 8 once we start explaining how to build your own dynamic analysis lab or malware test environment.

Purpose of Malware Analysis

Malware analysis is an important skill to have in today's interconnected world. It is a nice skill to have for anyone who uses a computer and an essential skill to have for information security professionals. With the influx of malware, malware analysis has become an indispensable tool for information technology professionals. This is because it has an important purpose, which is to understand malware for the purpose of stopping it.

From this understanding of malware behavior, you can accomplish many things, such as formulating a solution to prevent the malware from spreading further or compromising new target systems, detecting the malware's presence on compromised systems, and remediating the infection caused by the malware by completely eradicating the malware's hold on the infected systems.

Aside from formulating a solution for the specific malware, data collected can be used to gain a deeper understanding of malware in general. It gives researchers the knowledge to come up with proactive solutions to combat the onslaught of malware. And in some cases, these data can be used to formulate actionable intelligence that can be used by different law enforcement agencies to investigate and capture the people behind the attack.

Prevent the Spread of Malware

Preventing the malware from spreading further is usually made possible by understanding how the malware gets into the system. If you understand the infection vectors used by malware, you can intercept or block the malware's main infection method of compromising the target system.

LINGO

Infection vector refers to the technology used by attackers to deliver or deploy malware into a target system.[1] The most common technology used is e-mail.

Preventing the spread of malware is a good first step when malware is discovered in a target system. It is like first-aid: Stop the bleeding first while waiting for the paramedics to arrive.

Identifying the malware's infection vector is easier said than done. In most cases, it is hard to determine how the malware got in. In cases like this, the only way to prevent the spread of malware is to understand how it infects other systems. Does it require a network share? Does it rely on a specific e-mail client to spread? The information to answer these questions can be pieced together from the data gathered during malware analysis.

Detect the Presence of Malware

The data collected from malware analysis can be used as signatures or fingerprints to detect the malware in the network and in the host. When it comes to detecting the malware's presence in the host, the following are the most common:

▶ Host changes

▶ Code snippet collected from the malware code

Host changes made by the malware can be used to spot malware infection or detect the presence of malware, especially if the detection technology used to look for possible infections is a system scanner. A system scanner is any tool that scans the whole system for changes in the file system, registry, or operating system configuration files.

For example, a researcher analyzed a malware that drops a copy of itself in the Windows Startup folder with the name IAMNOTAVIRUS.EXE. The researcher adds this data to a signature database that is used by a system scanner. If during a routine scan, the system scanner finds a file in the Windows Startup folder named IAMNOTAVIRUS.EXE, it will recognize this as a match in its signature database, and it will alert the user of an infection.

Using a code snippet to create a malware signature is the most common practice in the industry. File and memory scanners utilize this kind of signature database that contains malware code snippets. This is the foundation of antivirus (AV)

---

[1] *Malware, Rootkits & Botnets* by Christopher C. Elisan, published by McGraw-Hill.

products. The catch here is that the code snippet must be from an unencrypted malware code; otherwise, it will cause a lot of false alarms.

LINGO

False alarms are divided into two types: false positives and false negatives. **False positive** means that the scanner identified a benign file to be malware. **False negative** means that the scanner identified another malware with a different malware name.

TIP

The best code snippet signature is from an unencrypted malware code.

The file and memory scanners scan every file in the system and those that are loaded in memory for a possible match in its signature database. If there is a match found, it alerts the user of an infection.

LINGO

Signature database, scan patterns, and antivirus definitions all mean the same thing.

When it comes to detecting the presence of malware in the network, the most common indicator is its network communication. The data collected from network sniffers such as Wireshark is a good source for detecting the presence of malware while it is traversing the network or while it is communicating to the different network resources it needs.

For example, during dynamic analysis, say a researcher was able to collect domains communicated to by the subject malware. These domains, upon further research and analysis, are determined to be network resources being used by malware, so they can be used to spot systems in the network that are possibly infected by malware. Any system that shows any sign of communication to and from these domains can be flagged as a possible compromised system.

These are just a few examples of how data from malware analysis can be used to detect the presence of malware. The main idea here is that every footprint the malware leaves behind can be used as an indicator of its presence in the host and in the network.

Remediate the Malware Infection

After the presence of malware has been detected, the next step is to remove it from the system. This is where the data regarding host changes becomes really important. If the analyst or researcher is able to identify the host changes, there is a chance that it can be reversed and the operating system restored to a "pre-infected" or clean state. This is the ideal scenario. In most cases, infection is hard to reverse. The malware has embedded itself so much into the system that removing it will corrupt the operating system, rendering the system unusable. This leaves system administrators little choice but to restore the system using a backup or to completely rebuild the compromised system from scratch.

Clean tools use host changes to reverse the effect of malware. There are usually two types of clean tools: generic and specific. Generic clean tools reverse host changes that are common to most malware, while specific clean tools are tailored to reverse changes done by a specific malware family or its variant. Specific clean tools are often created for malware that is involved in an outbreak or has affected numerous systems worldwide.

Advance Malware Research

Data gathered from malware analysis helps researchers determine new techniques malware uses to compromise the target system, new malware technologies being used by the attackers, and new vulnerabilities being exploited by malware. These data sets are used more to beat the malware by understanding the current threat landscape and to predict how it will look in the near term and long term. This enables researchers to come up with new ways of preventing, detecting, and remediating malware infections. Academia is full of research papers discussing new ideas on how to stop malware, and most of these papers are good examples of how data gathered from malware analysis can be used to further advance research on the war against malware.

Produce Actionable Intelligence

In addition to using this gathered data for advanced malware research, law enforcement agencies have special interest in malware analysis data if it is enough to produce actionable intelligence that can be used as evidence against threat actors. In some cases, threat actors are sloppy enough that data collected from malware analysis can link them to an attack campaign.

LINGO

Threat actors are also known as attackers.

Limitations of Malware Analysis

Although malware analysis is key in understanding malware's true nature, it also has its limitations. In static analysis, data gathering is effective only if the malware is in its true form free from any type of encryption or obfuscation. This is why malware decryption, deobfuscation, and unpacking are big. They totally eliminate or at least minimize static malware protection that hinders static analysis. To mitigate this limitation, encrypted malware is subjected to different tools and methods that help reveal the decrypted malware code before being subjected to static analysis.

LINGO

Encrypted malware is a catchphrase that includes not only encrypted malware but also obfuscated and packed malware.

Dynamic analysis is all about making the malware successfully execute in a controlled environment. Therefore, its limitation is because of the different malware dependencies that enable it to run successfully in a target system. They are the following:

▶ Program dependencies

▶ User dependencies

▶ Environment dependencies

▶ Timing dependencies

▶ Event dependencies

If one of these dependencies is not satisfied, the malware may not execute any or all of its functions. If the malware does not run because of an unsatisfied condition or dependency, no data will be collected during dynamic analysis. If the malware does run but some of its routines or functions are dependent on some of the factors mentioned, no data will be collected from those functions, which can result in an incomplete picture of the malware's behavior. This is the main reason why some malware analysis systems produce little data compared to other analysis systems. The malware analysis system that can satisfy more malware dependencies will produce more malware analysis data.

For example, automated dynamic analysis systems, also known as automated malware sandboxes, can record only the malware behavior that the malware exhibits during the short amount of time it is running. Some functions that require special conditions, such as a user logged in to Facebook, an e-mail client running, network connection conditions such as home network versus corporate network, or even those that require hours to start executing their directive, will not be executed by the malware; thus, no visible behavior can be observed, resulting to zero data gathered for those special functions. If the analyst opts to not use an automated sandbox but instead use more of an interactive malware environment that she has control of and can be active as long as needed, it will still be hard for her to see all possible execution paths of the malware, especially if she does not have knowledge of the triggers or dependencies.

NOTE

Reversing, a short term for malware reverse engineering, uncovers these special conditions and helps improve malware sandbox implementations.

The Malware Analysis Process

Malware analysis is an art. Depending on the researcher's knowledge and skill, she might approach analyzing malware using different techniques and methods. The approach an analyst takes is often influenced by the experience she has gained through years of analyzing different kinds of malware. One researcher's approach might differ slightly or greatly with another researcher's but yield similar results. One thing is certain, no matter what techniques and methods a researcher or an analyst employs, the malware analysis process can be represented succinctly, as shown in Figure 1-1.

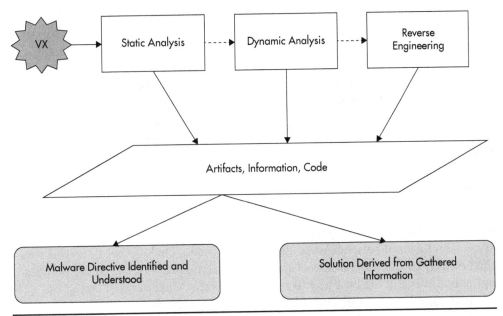

Figure 1-1 *Malware analysis process.*

Figure 1-1 shows that the malware file, represented as VX (which is a common term used in the industry to symbolize virus in the past and now malware as a whole), is subjected into static analysis. The data, which can be used to generate usable information, gathered from static analysis is collected and added to artifacts, code, and other information collected about the malware. The end goal here is to identify the malware's main directive and to create a solution for the malware to prevent it from spreading, detect its presence, and remediate, if possible, the malware infection. In most cases, static analysis is not enough, so the malware is subjected to dynamic analysis, where malware undergoes further scrutiny while it is running on a target system. The data gathered from dynamic analysis is added to the data collected from static analysis. If the data gathered from both static and dynamic analyses is enough to produce actionable intelligence to prevent the spread of malware, detect its presence, and possibly remediate compromise systems, then the analysis process usually ends. But if the malware proves to be difficult and static analysis and dynamic analysis yield poor results, reverse engineering is done to get to the bottom of what the malware really is.

> **TIP**
>
> *When analyzing malware, there is no need to choose between the two types of static analysis or dynamic analysis. They complement each other and should be done one after the other.*

As previously stated, the first step in the analysis process is to subject the malware to static analysis. If the collected information is enough to understand the malware and formulate a solution for it, then subjecting the malware to dynamic analysis becomes an optional or nice-to-have task. But this is rarely the case. Almost all the time, dynamic analysis is needed to collect more information to determine the malware's directive and formulate a solution based on dynamically gathered data from the malware sandbox. But if static and dynamic analyses prove to be not enough to understand the malware because of its complexity and sophistication, then reverse engineering becomes the last resort.

Manual Malware Analysis

During the early years of malware, when everything was still called viruses, malware analysis was mostly done by hand. A handful of tools, a single isolated system, and a lot of patience were all that was needed. During that time, this was the best way to analyze malware. Fast-forward to the present, and in my humble opinion, this is still the best way to analyze malware. Most of the techniques, methods, and concepts are still the same. The tools are better, and the test environment has expanded. The single system is now an isolated network of systems and, if needed, has a restricted Internet connection. When I was at Trend Micro, we used the term *infect machine* to describe the single isolated system used to analyze malware during the DOS era and the term *superlab* to describe the network of systems used to manually analyze modern malware that you see today.

Performing manual malware analysis is always required, especially if the malware is noteworthy. This gives the analyst time and total control of the environment where malware is being executed for the purpose of analysis.

LINGO

Noteworthy malware *is malware that exhibits new technology or is currently found in the wild.* **In the wild** *describes malware that is currently and actively infecting systems.*

The beauty of manual malware analysis is that the researcher has full control of the timing. The researcher can choose how long a malware must be executed and not be limited by time constraints used in automated malware analysis systems. In automated malware systems, the execution time for malware can range from 30 seconds to a few minutes. This is not helpful, especially if the malware has a sleep function. A sleep function is a malware routine that allows it to be dormant for a period of time before it starts executing. It can be minutes, or it can be days. A malware with sleep function is the attacker's defense against automated malware analysis.

Manual malware analysis also enables the researcher to be more interactive with malware. The researcher can execute programs and even log in to banking sites, web-based e-mails, or social media. This is helpful especially if the malware has program dependencies or works only when a user tries to log in to an online resource. This is mostly true for keyloggers. The information-stealing routine of a keylogger gets activated if the malware believes that the user is logging in to a website that it is targeting to steal credentials from.

TIP

Just to be clear, when logging in to a supposed banking site, do not use a real banking site and do not use a real login credential. An internally controlled fake bank site must be done for this. For webmails and social media, a dummy account will work.

Automated Malware Analysis

As the years go by, the onslaught of malware has become alarming. The number of malware samples seen every day is astounding. Figure 1-2 shows that the number of malware discovered by mid-2014 already exceeded that discovered in 2013.

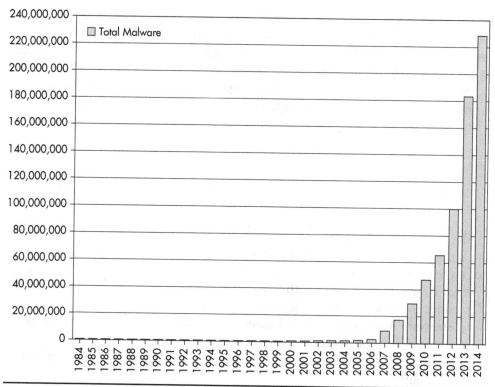

Figure 1-2 *Number of malware discovered from 1984 to 2014. (Source: AV-Test.ORG.)*

As of June 16, 2014, the number of malware that has been discovered is about 230 million. This equates to about 1.4 million unique malware samples per day, and that is already about 50 million more than all malware discovered in 2013. Note that this is discovered malware. It does not account for malware that has not been discovered yet. There could be millions more out there that is still enjoying the luxury of not being found.

With this fact, manual malware analysis is not feasible anymore. It does not scale to handle this amount of malware, and even if all the researchers in the world combined to tackle this amount of malware on a daily basis, our efforts would still not be enough. This is why the process of malware analysis became automated. Manual malware analysis is now called upon only when a malware is considered noteworthy or if the automated malware analysis systems are not able to produce any results.

An automated malware analysis system consists of multiple malware test environments or malware sandboxes. Malware samples are thrown at these sandboxes, where the malware is executed and monitored for a specific amount of time. As mentioned in the previous section, this can range from 30 seconds to a few minutes. The more sandboxes there are, the more malware the automated system can process. The processing is done in parallel, so if an automated system has 10 sandboxes and each is configured to run malware in 30 seconds, then it can process 10 malware in 30 seconds, which equates to 28,800 malware processed per day (assuming an ideal situation where each system is utilized and there is no downtime).

LINGO

Automated malware analysis systems are also known as *automated sandbox systems* or simply *sandbox*. The term sandbox is widely used to describe automated systems because it is expected that a sandbox is always part of an automated malware analysis system.

Static analysis complements dynamic analysis. I cannot stress this enough, but unfortunately some automated malware analysis systems do not utilize static analysis and proceed directly to dynamic analysis. In my humble opinion, this is a waste of sandbox resources. Static analysis is still needed not only to gather static information from malware but also to provide intelligence to the whole automated malware analysis system. One of the ways it does this is by determining whether the malware needs a special sandbox implementation. For example, if the analyst has different sandbox flavors and implementations, it is important to know which of those flavors and implementations will work well for the malware. This intelligence can be provided by static analysis. So instead of subjecting the malware blindly to the next available sandbox, the automated system, through the intelligence provided by the static analysis, can assign the malware to the appropriate sandbox, thus increasing the chances of a successful dynamic analysis session. Figure 1-3 shows an automated sandbox implementation taking advantage of static analysis.

Before going into a detailed discussion of the automated sandbox implementation shown in Figure 1-3, it is important to note that not all files subjected to malware analysis, be it manual or automated, are malware. Most of the files are suspicious files that end up being proven to be a non-malware or benign file. This is the most important use case of malware analysis: to determine whether a file is malicious and, if it is malicious, gather as much data as possible to generate important information and actionable intelligence that will enable the analyst to prevent the spread of, detect the presence of, and remediate infection caused by malware.

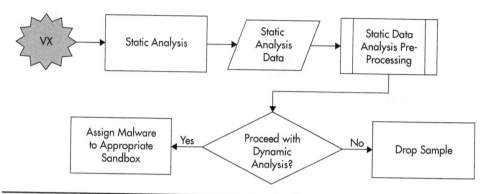

Figure 1-3 *Automated sandbox implementation taking advantage of static analysis.*

In a typical scenario, a suspicious file is subjected to static analysis first. In this stage of the analysis process, all data that is collected from the file is processed. A typical static data analysis pre-processing determines the following:

▶ Has the file been processed before?

▶ Does it match any known benign files?

▶ Does it match any known malicious files?

▶ Does it require any special sandbox implementations?

The first two are the most common reasons for a file to be dropped and not processed by the automated malware analysis system anymore. Answering the first two questions is made possible by identifying duplicate files and having a whitelist database as part of the automated malware analysis implementation. A whitelist database is a database of file hashes that are known to be benign. The hashes usually come from files of different operating systems and popular software.

> **TIP**
>
> *A whitelist database is not perfect, so it is always advisable to use other indicators of being benign to reinforce file determination.*

The third question also causes a file to be dropped, especially if there is an exact match or duplicate that has already been processed. An exact match here can be an exact hash match; i.e., the files have the same MD5 hashes.

NOTE

A typical automated malware analysis system drops files that are duplicates regardless of whether they match a whitelist or database hash of known malware.

But when it comes to matching with known malicious files, some implementations use malware families and classes.

LINGO

*A **malware family** is a group of malware that behaves in the same way. A family can be divided into different variants, especially if a new generation has different functionality than the previous ones. For example, the Conficker family of malware has three known variants: Conficker.A, Conficker.B, and Conficker.C.*

LINGO

*A **malware class** or **malware type** is a group of malware with similar malicious behaviors or directives. For example, a malware that deletes all files on a hard disk and another that formats the hard drive can both be classified as a Trojan because of their destructive nature.*

If a file matches a family of malware, an automated sandbox can be configured to not process it anymore because indicators of compromise (IOC) were already collected from previous family members.

LINGO

***Indicators of compromise (IOCs)** are host and network footprints of malware that can be used to determine whether a system has been infected or compromised.*

An automated sandbox can also be configured to process the file to determine whether it is a new variant or whether it has new features that were not present in other family members that were processed before.

If a file matches a malware class, the sample is seldom dropped. The malware class usually helps to determine what to monitor or look for during dynamic analysis. In some cases, it can be used to determine a specific sandbox implementation. For example, if a sample has been determined statically to have mass-mailing capabilities, it can be thrown into a sandbox that has different mail clients installed.

The main idea here is throwing the suspicious file deemed to be malware into a sandbox implementation that satisfies all of its known dependencies to get the most promising results during dynamic analysis. Having this kind of intelligence provided by static analysis data enables you to save time and sandbox resources.

This makes a lot of difference in terms of resources and cycle time, especially if you are processing hundreds of thousands of suspicious files on a daily basis, and improves the efficiency of the whole automated malware analysis system.

> **NOTE**
>
> *Static analysis can easily be beaten by packed and encrypted file. This is why file unpacking and decryption are important in the fight against malware.*

Static analysis also determines whether a file is packed and encrypted. If this is the case, appropriate actions are taken to statically unpack or decrypt a file so static analysis data can be gathered. If this is not possible, no static analysis can be done, and the file is subjected to the next available sandbox where the researcher can attempt to capture memory images of the unpacked file and then subject that captured memory image to static analysis. This is an example of dynamic analysis feeding samples to static analysis for the purpose of system improvement.

In most cases, regardless of whether the file is packed, dynamic analysis yields promising results because the dynamic analysis system does not care whether a file is packed. The file will still function, and the dynamic analysis system can still capture data from the running file. But there will always be files or samples that will not yield any data through static and dynamic analyses. A well-designed automated system will flag these samples for review by malware researchers and analysts, and whatever is learned from these samples is then applied as new technology to the automated malware analysis system so it can tackle those file samples the next time around. This is how an automated malware analysis system evolves. As new malware employs evasion techniques to avoid data being gathered from them through static and dynamic analyses, the researchers take a closer look into those samples with the purpose of understanding the evasion techniques and finding ways of thwarting these newly discovered malware technologies.

The Effective Malware Analyst

The main goal of this book is to help you become an effective malware analyst. To do that, I have identified three characteristics that will help you achieve that goal.

▶ Familiarization with malware
▶ Familiarization with analysis tools
▶ Patience

Familiarization with Malware

To effectively analyze malware, you must first be familiar with what it is. An analyst must be familiar with how malware behaves, how malware operates to stay persistent, how malware protects itself, and how malware manipulates the target environment for it to execute its directives.

In reality, malware analysis may not reveal all the information about the malware because of the known limitations of malware analysis and because of the sophistication and difficulty level of the malware. The analyst may get only bits and pieces of data that she needs to connect together and make sense of. In cases such as these, familiarization with different malware characteristics enables the analyst to recognize and make an educated guess on how the malware behaves given a collection of data extracted from the malware during static and dynamic analyses. This is helpful especially, as stated previously, if the malware is extremely difficult to analyze and there is only a short amount of time available to understand what the malware is doing.

Familiarization with malware enables the malware researcher and analyst to formulate information from bits and pieces of data and not come out empty handed. This comes with experience and education. The malware can then be tested again to either prove or disprove the conclusion drawn by the researcher or analyst from the bits of data gathered.

> **TIP**
>
> *Reading malware blogs, white papers, and detailed malware technical reports helps in increasing familiarity with different malware characteristics.*

Part I of the book is all about malware. It is designed to serve as an introduction to novice researchers and analysts and a refresher to seasoned professionals. I will discuss the different classes of malware, how malware is deployed, how malware protects itself, and what the different dependencies are that malware has for it to function as designed by the attacker.

Familiarization with Analysis Tools

An effective malware analyst is someone who has the right skills and has the right tools. It has to be both. An analyst with skills but without the proper tools is like a carpenter trying to hammer a nail using a screwdriver. An analyst without skills but with the proper tools will not know what to do with them. Since you picked up this book, I would say that you are already working on your skills. To sweeten the pot, I will throw in the analysis tools as well.

This book will discuss the tools needed to analyze malware. I will start by showing how to set up a malware research lab and then go through the different static and dynamic analysis tools that will help you in becoming an effective malware analyst.

Patience

Malware analysis is not for those who get frustrated easily. As a malware analyst, you have to understand that analyzing malware will not always go the way you want it to go. There will be hiccups along the way. There will be unforeseen circumstances and challenges that might slow you down. Your limits and patience will be tested. But the key here is to recognize that this will happen, and you have to prepare yourself for it. There will be instances wherein nothing is going right and no data is being extracted from the malware. If this happens, you need to pause for a bit and give yourself some time to relax and then start tinkering again. Do not be afraid to try different things, different tool combinations, or different methods. Malware analysis is an art after all.

> ### TIP
>
> *It is important to remember that malware analysis is not a set process, wherein you just follow a series of steps and arrive at your destination. Nothing is set in stone. Every malware analysis case can be different. The best thing to do is to recognize patterns of analysis so you can apply them as a mental template when faced with a malware analysis problem.*

Recap

Malware analysis is a fun and exciting activity. The joy of discovering a new malware technology and using it against the malware can be an overwhelmingly good feeling. This chapter introduces malware analysis to the reader. It is aimed to warm you up before your journey into malware analysis. It serves as a brief introduction into malware analysis.

In this chapter, I discussed the two types of malware analysis, which are the following:

► Static analysis

► Dynamic analysis

I then proceeded to discuss the purpose of malware analysis, which includes the following:

► Preventing the spread of malware

► Detecting the presence of malware

► Remediating the malware infection

► Conducting advance malware research

► Producing actionable intelligence

Understanding how the malware operates enables you to achieve all of these. You also recognized the fact that malware analysis has its limitations, which I described so you fully understand what malware analysis can and cannot do.

I also touched on the two types of malware analysis process, which are the following:

► Manual malware analysis

► Automated malware analysis

I gave an overview of each process and discussed how each of them can be used to your advantage in solving the malware problem in general.

Then I concluded by discussing the characteristics or needed knowledge, skills, and attitude of an effective malware analyst. I summarized them as follows:

► Familiarization with malware

► Familiarization with analysis tools

► Patience

Now let's begin.

Malware Taxonomy

The first part of your journey into malware analysis is to understand the nature of malware, including why it exists and what its purpose, directive, and primary function are. Understanding all of these topics will help you get to the core of the malware's behavior, which is the main goal of analyzing malware.

The first step in accomplishing this is to understand the different classes of malware. This is where malware taxonomy comes into the picture. Malware taxonomy is the process of classifying malware into different groups using a systematic approach based on its characteristics or attributes. It results in well-organized groups of malware with recognizable relationship patterns. Becoming familiar with these patterns enables you to identify specific malware that belongs to a certain class. It also leads to the discovery of a new and unknown class of malware, especially if the characteristics or attributes of the newly discovered malware do not fit any of the known classes. Familiarization with different classes of malware helps you predict malware behavior based on patterns of characteristics or attributes that are revealed during the stages of analysis. If this gathered data is similar to a certain class of malware, it will be easy for you to conclude what the malware's main directive is. In this instance, you save time and effort by not going through the other steps of analysis because what you need to know was already revealed by the patterns you found.

In this chapter, I will discuss the different classes of malware and how each class differs from the others. I will highlight the main functionalities and directives so you can better understand each malware class.

Malware Classes

Malware has been classified in different ways. Classifications include target operating system (OS), such as Windows, OS X, or Unix; target device, such as mobile devices or desktop devices; vector dependencies; spreading mechanisms; type of victims; and more. Each of these taxonomy methods serves a purpose. It may be a specific purpose or something that covers a wide range of needs. An analyst who wants to eliminate or mitigate a malware's infection vector might be interested in classifying malware based on vector dependencies and spreading mechanisms, while someone who wants to build a computing infrastructure might be more interested in classifying malware based on target OS, target device, and type of victims the malware is after. In most cases, an understanding of all these classes is needed to secure an organization.

In this book, I will classify malware based on its behavior. The categories are as follows:

- ▶ Infectors
- ▶ Network worms
- ▶ Trojan horses
- ▶ Backdoors
- ▶ Remote-access Trojans
- ▶ Information stealers
- ▶ Ransomware
- ▶ Scareware
- ▶ Fakeware
- ▶ Greyware

It is important to note that malware does not neatly fall into just one category. The attackers do not write malware to stick to one class alone or follow strictly the description of a specific class. This is not their concern. Their main concern is for malware to execute based on their directive. If achieving the attacker's directive means creating a malware that infects files to spread, which is classified as an infector, and with backdoor capability, then so be it. In reality, therefore, most malware will exhibit two or more of the behaviors in the previous list. This reality can pose a challenge in classifying malware. To solve this, researchers and the industry at large moved to classify malware based on class priority. The classes listed previously are based on priority, with infectors being the highest priority and greyware being the lowest. This is the common practice in the industry.

To better illustrate this, let's take two imaginary malware as an example: first a malware that spreads via e-mail that also has the ability to infect files, and second a malware that is destructive that also has a backdoor capability that provides access to a compromised system. Based on class prioritization, the first example of the e-mail malware is classified as an infector, while the second example is classified as a Trojan.

TIP

Malware classes can be considered as attributes or characteristics and tagged as such. If one malware exhibits two or more class behaviors, it can be tagged with those classes.

When it comes to classifying malware, it is always good to tag it with all the classes it belongs to, especially in a malware database. Based on the e-mail malware example, the malware can be classified, or tagged, as an infector and a network worm. This makes it easy to query for malware based on class behavior. In this scenario, the prioritization is not an issue. Instead, the main issue is to tag the malware with all the class behaviors it is exhibiting. This is useful when it comes to profiling malware.

Infectors

A malware that spreads by attaching a copy of its malicious code to a target host is known as an *infector*. Its main directive is to populate by infecting other computer files that are usually of the same file type. The first infectors were called *computer viruses*. Named after their real-world counterparts that spread from one human host to another causing an epidemic within a small community, these computer viruses instead infect files causing a system-wide infection within the compromised system. In the old days, computer viruses were considered to have reached pandemic proportions if computer systems from different geographical locations became infected because of removable media usage such as floppy disks.

Before the term *malware* was coined, all malicious programs were collectively called computer viruses. Computer viruses are self-replicating programs that spread from one host to another. They were mainly file and boot sector infectors. But because of advances in technology and the ability to spread to other systems through other means that are much more efficient and faster than file and boot sector infection, infectors have vanished into the annals of malware history.

Infectors are rare nowadays, but it is still important to know about them, especially if you are going to deal with malware that has been armored by tools such as binders and joiners, which I will discuss in detail in succeeding chapters.

LINGO

Binders and *joiners* are malware tools that enable a malware to attach itself to a benign file.

Infectors are divided into the following types:

► File infectors
► Boot sector viruses
► Multipartite viruses

File Infectors

File infectors defined the computer virus era. All widespread computer viruses during the DOS era were file infectors. File infectors attach themselves to host programs, and then these infected files serve as the virus carrier to other systems. When an infected file is executed, the virus code in the infected file gets executed first, and after that is done, the execution flow is then passed to the code of the host program. As far as the victim is concerned, the program did what is supposed to do but unknown to him the virus code was executed first.

> **LINGO**
>
> The changing of execution flow from virus code to the host code is also referred to as **passing control**.

Before a host becomes an infected file or a virus carrier, file infection has to take place. File infection can occur in two ways.

- ▶ Through direct infection
- ▶ Through memory infection

Direct infection occurs when a virus actively looks for files in the system to infect. Depending on the search parameters of the virus, it might search for files in selected folders such as the operating system folder, the programs folder, or the current folder where the virus was executed; or it can search for files in the whole system.

Memory infection, on the other hand, occurs when a host file is executed and is loaded in memory. In this form of infection, the virus does not actively look for files to infect; rather, it sits in memory waiting for a host file to be executed. Once a host file is executed, the virus attaches itself to the host file's code in memory, and when the operation is complete, the virus code is saved to the file on disk.

> **NOTE**
>
> Direct infection occurs when the host files are static, while memory infection occurs when the host file is running. As a result, direct infection has the potential of infecting all malware-supported file types in the system, even those files that have not been executed for a long time.

There are different types of file infectors.

▶   Executables

▶   Macros

▶   Scripts

Executables   In the early years of malware, almost all infectors were executables. They were either a COM file or an EXE file. Some of them infect exclusively their own file type; i.e., COM infects COM only, and EXE infects EXE only. But there are those that infect all file types regardless of what the original malware's file type is; i.e., COM infects both COM and EXE, and EXE infects both COM and EXE.

Regardless of what file type the computer virus is, it follows certain patterns when it comes to infecting or attaching its code to the host file. These patterns of infection serve as a way to classify viruses and file infectors.

They are the following:

▶   Overwriting viruses

▶   Companion viruses

▶   Parasitic viruses

An overwriting virus is the most destructive of all file infectors because, as the name suggests, the virus overwrites the host code with its own. This results in the total destruction of the host file. There is no way to recover from this infection unless there is a backup of the overwritten host file. Figure 2-1 shows the results of an overwriting virus infection.

Figure 2-1 shows two different scenarios. If the size of the host file is bigger than the overwriting virus, the resulting file is the overwriting virus plus the remaining bytes at the end of the host file. The virus simply overlays itself on the host file. If the size of the host file is equal to or smaller than the overwriting virus, the resulting file is the overwriting virus itself, an exact copy, because it has completely overwritten the host file.

In some cases where performance is a must, such as it was during the DOS era, the overwriting virus, regardless of the size of the host file, simply replaces the host file with its own copy and changes its name to that of the host file. Although this improves the malware's performance, it also has a drawback. Replacing the host file with a copy of the virus can lead to easy detection via optical inspection by simply listing the files in the directory. For example, say an overwriting virus

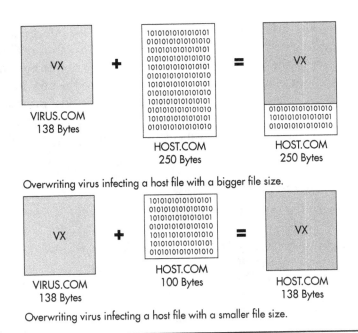

Overwriting virus infecting a host file with a bigger file size.

Overwriting virus infecting a host file with a smaller file size.

Figure 2-1 *Overwriting virus infection.*

with a file size of 470 bytes infects a folder of several thousands of files that originally have different file sizes. Listing the files in this folder will show all of them having 470 bytes each, which will arouse suspicion. In addition, assuming the malware does not have a routine to retain the original date of the infected host files, the infected files will have similar timestamps, which will definitely scream infection. These telltale signs are so obvious that optical inspection makes it easy to spot the virus.

Another telltale sign of an overwriting virus infection is that every time an infected host file is executed, it will not function as expected because the virus code completely destroyed the original program or host code so there is nothing to pass the control to after the virus code has executed, which is often silent. As far as the user is concerned, nothing happened. This will raise the level of suspicion that something might be wrong.

NOTE

The only way to recover from an overwriting virus infection is by restoring the affected files from backup.

Companion viruses are the second type of executable file infectors. Companion viruses are interesting because they are the only ones that do not really attach their malware code to the host file. I often refer to them as an exception to the rule. But even without attaching companion virus code to the host file, the virus code is still executed first, and control is still passed to the host program code for it to execute its function and not raise suspicion. The virus is able to do this, without the need to attach its code, by using the operating system's rules and capabilities, which are the following:

► File type execution hierarchy
► Ability to set a file's attribute to HIDDEN

File type execution hierarchy, on the other hand, deals with deciding which files with the same name but different executable extension get to be executed first. In DOS and Windows, this hierarchy exists. The order of execution based on filename is COM, then EXE, and then BAT. For example, if there are three files with the names HELLO.BAT, HELLO.EXE, and HELLO.COM in the same folder, typing **HELLO** only without any extension at the command line will execute HELLO.COM. Deleting HELLO.COM and typing **HELLO** at the command line again executes HELLO.EXE. Deleting HELLO.EXE leaves the user with HELLO .BAT, so typing **HELLO** executes HELLO.BAT. Evidently, taking advantage of file type execution hierarchy works best in command lines, which is why companion viruses were highly successful during the DOS era but not in modern operating systems.

> **TIP**
>
> *Make it a habit to type the entire filename when executing a file at the command line.*

Figure 2-2 (a) shows an example of a companion virus renaming a target host file's extension and setting its attribute to HIDDEN. For example, when VIRUS .COM infects HOST.COM, the virus renames HOST.COM to HOST.CON (note the *N*) and sets its attribute to HIDDEN. Then the virus renames itself to HOST .COM. So when the user executes HOST.COM, he is actually executing the virus, and then after the virus executes, it passes control to HOST.CON, which is the real HOST.COM. This scenario is applicable to COM files because COM is highest when it comes to file execution hierarchy.

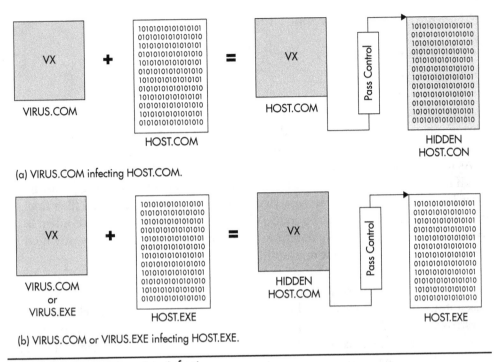

(a) VIRUS.COM infecting HOST.COM.

(b) VIRUS.COM or VIRUS.EXE infecting HOST.EXE.

Figure 2-2   *Companion virus infection.*

Figure 2-2 (b) shows how VIRUS.COM or VIRUS.EXE deals with an EXE file. Instead of renaming and setting the attribute of the target host file (HOST.EXE), the virus renames itself and sets its attribute to HIDDEN. As a result, the virus becomes HOST.COM with a HIDDEN attribute. So when the user types **HOST** at the command prompt, he is actually executing the virus because of the COM's highest hierarchy and not HOST.EXE. Once the virus is finished executing, the virus passes control to HOST.EXE. This scenario is the main reason why it is always suggested to type the whole filename including the extension when executing a program at a command line.

The third type of computer virus, parasitic virus, is the most definitive executable virus of all because, technically speaking, this virus attaches itself to the host file during infection and still lets the host file function as intended. This is the classic form of file infection. A parasitic virus takes control of a target host file's first instruction by replacing it with a jump or a pointer to the virus code. To pass control back to the host file after the virus executes, the virus saves the location of the host file's real first instruction.

There are two types of parasitic viruses, as shown in Figure 2-3.

► Prepending
► Appending

A prepending parasitic virus attaches itself to the top of the host file. In this type of infection, there is little need for file instruction manipulation because the virus code is on top of the file, so the virus code gets executed first.

As for an appending virus, the virus code attaches itself at the end of the file. If parasitic virus is the classic form of file infection, an appending parasitic virus is the classic form of parasitic virus infection. It hijacks the host file's first instruction to point to the virus code. After virus execution, it passes control back to the host program code. As mentioned, the virus is able to do this by saving the location of the host file's first instruction.

Macros   What is a macro? A macro is a set of instructions that performs a specific task automatically. The task can be a series of mouse movements, clicks, and keystrokes that follow a specific pattern that can be repeated in an automated fashion. Macros can be constructed using an application-specific macro language. A macro language is a form of scripting that enables a user to program tasks to

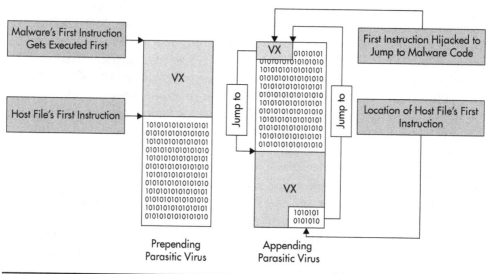

Figure 2-3   *Parasitic virus infection.*

run automatically. This is utilized mostly in word processors and spreadsheets to automate tasks such as formatting text and crunching numbers.

An application-specific macro language is essentially a programming language. And if there is an opportunity to program or write instructions, there is always the possibility to write a virus. It didn't take long for virus writers to use macro languages for their creations. This resulted in a new form of file infectors called *macro viruses,* which are viruses created from an application-specific macro language.

The most popular macro viruses have been written mostly using the Microsoft Office macro language. It produced the following macro viruses:

- ► Single-platform macro virus
  - ► Microsoft Word macro virus
  - ► Microsoft Excel macro virus
  - ► Microsoft Access macro virus
  - ► Microsoft PowerPoint macro virus
- ► Cross-platform macro virus

Single-platform macro viruses infect only the same file type the macro is written in. For example, a Word macro virus will infect only Word document files and nothing more. Cross-platform macro viruses, on the other hand, have the ability to infect other Office file types. This is possible because in Microsoft Office, Visual Basic for Applications (VBA) is the macro language used across Office documents.

Cross-platform macro viruses infect not only other Office document file types but also executables.

Scripts   Since a macro is a scripting language, it is not far-fetched to use other scripts as platforms for viruses. The only difference between a macro virus and a script virus is that the script does not need to be embedded in a file. It can be embedded, or it can be a stand-alone script.

The most utilized scripting languages to write script viruses are Visual Basic Script (VBS) and JavaScript. VBS is supported by Windows, so there are no special dependencies needed for it to run properly. As for JavaScript, it usually works as part of an application such as a web browser and a Portable Document Format (PDF) file. Therefore, for it to function as intended by the virus writer without revealing its true nature, the virus takes advantage of vulnerabilities present in the application where JavaScript is implemented.

NOTE

Any file format that uses or can interpret scripts has the potential to be infected.

Boot Sector Viruses

A virus always wants to get control of the system's execution flow first, even before the operating system. One way to achieve that is to infect the boot sector of the disk.

The boot sector is located at sector 1 of each volume. As defined by Microsoft,[1] the boot sector is a critical disk structure for starting a computer. It contains executable code and data required by the code, including information that the file system uses to access the volume. The boot sector is created when a volume is formatted. At the end of the boot sector is a 2-byte structure called a *signature word* or *end-of-sector marker*, which is always set to 0x55AA.

For example, a Windows 2000 boot sector consists of the following elements:

▶ An x86-based central processing unit (CPU) jump instruction

▶ The original equipment manufacturer identification (OEM ID)

▶ The BIOS parameter block (BPB) data structure

▶ The extended BPB

▶ The executable boot code, also known as the *bootstrap code*, that starts the operating system

Similar to a file infector, a boot sector virus works by taking control of the boot sector's first instruction. It does this by hijacking the x86-based CPU jump instruction and pointing it to the malicious boot sector virus code. Once the virus code executes, it passes control back to the original boot sector code. The location of this can be found in the hijacked x86-based CPU jump instruction. Executing the original bootstrap code or executable boot code is crucial so that the system will boot properly. Since a boot sector contains only 512 bytes of code, there is not enough space for a boot sector virus. A boot sector virus, therefore, often utilizes other sectors of the disk to hide its code.

Multipartite Viruses

Multipartite viruses are viruses that infect both files and boot sectors. This type of virus has a file infector and a boot sector infector component. It does not matter

---

[1] Microsoft Technet: http://technet.microsoft.com/en-US/.

whether the boot virus or the file virus counterpart is executed. Both parts usually follow the same formula; that is, the virus looks for host files to infect and then looks for boot sectors to infect. If the virus supports Master Boot Record (MBR) infections, it looks for a fixed hard disk and attempts to infect it.

The Master Boot Record, as defined by Microsoft,[1] is the most important data structure on the disk. It is created when the disk is partitioned. The MBR contains the following:

► A small amount of executable code called the *master boot code*

► The disk signature

► The disk partition table

At the end of the MBR is a 2-byte signature word or end-of-sector marker, which is always set to 0x55AA.

NOTE

0x55AA marks the end of a master boot record, an extended boot record (EBR), and the boot sector.

LINGO

*Nowadays, **multipartite** refers to viruses that are capable of multiplatform infection, not just boot and file infections.*

Network Worms

A network worm is a type of malware that replicates or spreads via a network with little or no user intervention using widely used network services such as Internet browsers, e-mail, and chat, among others. Worms usually rely on social engineering to spread, while the most advanced worms exploit software vulnerabilities to infect other systems. The reach of the network worm when it comes to potential victims is massive. Everyone who is online or connected to any network such as the Internet is a potential victim.

Network worms changed the game when it came to the speed and coverage of infection. Before the advent of network worms, malware infections were limited to file infections, which spread slowly. And if they did spread, the coverage was usually just a small geographical area. But network worms spread widely and quickly across networks with no geographical boundaries, giving meaning to the term *malware outbreak*. What took days or even months for a typical malware to spread across different geographic location takes only seconds for a network worm to accomplish.

LINGO

Malware outbreak describes a worldwide malware infection occurring in a short time.

Network worms are further classified based on their network-propagating features.

- ► Mass mailers
- ► File-sharing worms
- ► Instant messaging (IM) worms
- ► Internet Relay Chat (IRC) worms
- ► Local network worms
- ► Internet worms

Mass Mailers

Worms that spread via e-mail are called *mass mailers*. Social engineering is usually this worm's most potent weapon. It fools the user into downloading and executing an e-mail attachment, which is the worm itself. Or if the e-mail is not carrying any file to avoid anti-spam solutions, it persuades the user into clicking a link, which oftentimes leads to a download site that installs a malware onto the user's machine.

File-Sharing Worms

A file-sharing worm spreads through publicly facing file-sharing folders by dropping a copy of itself into a folder using an enticing filename that users will likely download to their systems and execute. File-sharing worms usually take advantage of file-sharing peer-to-peer programs to spread.

A few example of enticing file names are below.

- ► MSOfficeCrack.EXE
- ► FreeAntivirus.EXE
- ► PopularGameUnlockedVersion.EXE

IM Worms

Instant messaging worms spread through IM. The worm utilizes the infected system's installed IM software by sending messages to the user's contact list. The message usually contains a malicious link pointing to a drive-by download site. In some cases, instead of sending a malicious link, the IM worm initiates file transfers to the target victims in the contact list. Since the file transfer is coming from a known contact and the file has an enticing name, there is a big chance the target victim will accept the file transfer, download it, and then execute it. IM worms are good at exploiting trust because the target user thinks the link or file is coming from a friend.

LINGO

The server component is the one that is deployed by the attackers to compromise a system, while the client component is the one that the attackers use to control the server component in the compromised system.

IRC Worms

IRC worms spread through IRC channels by sending messages containing malicious links or instructions that the receiver or target victim should type in return for something such as "free software" or "ops channel privilege." The links point to a website that serves the worm, while the instruction that the target victim is being socially engineered to type results in a series of commands that can infect not just the target victim's system but also the other users in the channel.

IRC worms also utilize direct client-to-client (DCC) file transfer requests. The worm usually sends the requests to users joining the channel. These files, like any other socially engineered malicious files, have enticing names to increase their chances of being executed in the target system.

Local Network Worms

Local network worms spread within the confines of a local area network (LAN). A local network worm spreads by scanning for write-enabled share folders in servers or hosts connected to the network. Once it finds these types of share folders, it drops a copy of itself there using enticing names, as usual. The worm also searches for public folders in the network and drops a copy of itself there.

Another way this type of worm spreads, without using shared folders, is by exploiting vulnerabilities found in an OS or other software used in a corporate environment. Successful exploitation often leads to machine compromise. Instead of scanning for folders, the worm scans for software used in host machines connected to the local area network.

Internet Worms

Internet worms spread to other system by scanning the Internet for vulnerable machines. Oftentimes, Internet worms use vulnerable browsers to infiltrate target systems. An unpatched system that is connected to the Internet always runs the risk of being infected by an Internet worm.

> **NOTE**
>
> *An unpatched system is a good way to collect malware samples just by connecting to the Internet.*

Trojan Horse

A Trojan horse, also known simply as a Trojan, is a destructive malware in disguise. It passes itself as a harmless, legitimate program that is enticing to the user. It can disguise itself as a game, a tool, or even popular software. The main idea is to convince the user to run it.

The main directive of a Trojan is destruction of files or the system. The end result is usually loss of files and an inoperable system. The only way to recover from a Trojan is by restoring from backup or reinstalling the whole system.

Backdoors

Backdoors enable an attacker to gain access to a compromised system, bypassing any form of digital safeguards and authentication, usually through the use of vulnerable and undocumented OS and network functions. The access can be an open shell with root permission.

An important characteristic or attribute of a backdoor is stealth because its success lies in it being hidden and undetected. Once it is discovered, it is "game over" for the attacker.

Remote-Access Trojan

A remote-access Trojan (RAT), also known as remote administration Trojan, is a malicious system administration tool that has backdoor capabilities, enabling an attacker to gain root access to the compromised machine through a stealthy malicious program running in the system. Unlike a backdoor that typically uses

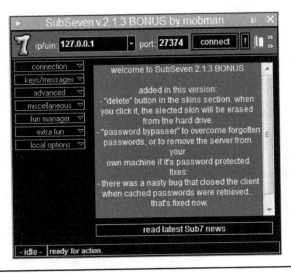

Figure 2-4   *SubSeven by mobman.*

a shell, a RAT uses a client-server model. A RAT has a user interface (UI), also known as the client component, that the attacker can use to issue commands to the server component residing in the compromised machine.

Looking at the RAT's user interface, you can immediately determine what the attacker can do to the compromised machine. The UI is so revealing that it is easy to analyze the malware. But the challenge here is obtaining a copy of the client component, which is usually in the attacker's possession. Most of the time, researchers and analysts are left only with the server part, which is extracted from the compromised machine.

One of the most popular RATs was SubSeven by mobman, as shown in Figure 2-4.

Information Stealers

An information stealer, as the name implies, is a malware that steals information. The stolen information could be a password, financial credentials, proprietary data, intellectual property, or anything that is reserved for somebody else's eyes and not the attacker's.

Information stealers are further classified into the following:

▶   Keyloggers
▶   Desktop recorders
▶   Memory scrapers

Keyloggers

Keyloggers capture keystrokes in a compromised system. The captured keystrokes can be stored locally for future retrieval, which was true for early keyloggers, or sent to a remote server to which the attacker has access.

Desktop Recorders

Desktop recorders work by taking a screenshot of the desktop or the active window when the conditions are met for the malware to capture such information. Usually, the conditions are event driven, such as a mouse click or keyboard press, or is determined by a certain time interval. Desktop recorders are oftentimes used to get around virtual keyboards utilized by some online banks.

One disadvantage of desktop recorders is the amount of data they store. The file size of each screenshot quickly adds up.

Memory Scrapers

Data and code when in memory are decrypted, which is the only way they can be processed. Memory scrapers take advantage of this fact by stealing information in memory while it is being processed. Memory is always the best place to grab data because everything is decrypted.

Ransomware

Ransomware is a malicious program that holds data or access to systems or resources containing that data hostage unless the victim pays a ransom. This type of malware is a form of virtual extortion that can be any of the following:

▶ Data encryption
▶ Data destruction
▶ User lockout

Data Encryption

In this type of extortion, the ransomware encrypts a victimized user's data. The data can be specific such as documents, pictures, or files with specific extensions, or it can be a lockdown of the whole disk or a certain partition. The main idea here is that the data is held hostage, preventing the user from accessing it. To restore access, the user needs to pay a ransom, after which the data will be decrypted by the malware or the user will be provided with a decryption tool and key. Or a more devious act can be purported by the attacker, such as running away with the money and leaving the victimized user with inaccessible data and a big hole in his pocket.

The most telling characteristic of this type of ransomware is that it has encryption algorithms.

Data Destruction

This is like saying, "Pay up or I will blow up the town." In this scenario, the user is given a time frame to pay or the data or hard drive will be wiped clean. This typically happens after data is encrypted to prevent the user from copying or backing up anything, and then the attackers resort to this type of extortion so they get the money immediately.

The most telling characteristic of this type of ransomware is that it usually has a disk-wipe or data-deleting feature.

User Lockout

Instead of encrypting data, how about just denying the user access to the system itself? This is what user lockout is. The user is locked out and denied login access to the system. This also renders the system unusable because the user is stuck at the login screen. If the user does decide to pay the extortionist, he would need a different system to do it.

> **NOTE**
>
> Not all ransomware can do what it claims to do. Fake ransomware relies on scare tactics to coerce a user into paying a ransom.

Scareware

Scareware is a form of digital fraud. These are malicious programs that are designed to scare users into installing a program and even paying for it. Fake antivirus (AV) programs are the most popular scareware. These are programs that fool the user into thinking that his system is infected with multiple malware and the only way to solve the problem is to install the full version of the program and pay a nominal fee such as $30.

Scareware can victimize the user in three ways. First, it convinces the user to install something into the system, which is most likely malware. If there are User

Account Control (UAC) prompts or requests to grant administrative permission, the user is likely to agree to them. Second, it asks for the user's credit card to "unlock" the full features of the program to make the bad things go away, giving the attackers access to the victim's credit card information that they can use to sell or use for their own purposes. Third, the user's credit card is charged an average of $30 for the software. The attackers just made money on bogus software. In short, the victim installed the malware, gave his credit card number away, and paid for everything.

NOTE

The difference between a ransomware and a scareware is that a ransomware asks the user to pay money to gain access to the user's system or data, while a scareware scares the user into paying money to solve a problem that does not exist.

Fakeware

If other malware such as Trojans use enticing names to get executed, fakeware passes itself along as a legitimate program update. It disguises itself as an update of popular software, including security software. Figure 2-5 shows an example of a fakeware disguising itself as a Flash Player update.

It is always suggested that users update their software to avoid being exploited by attackers. This is the sentiment that attackers are banking on when it comes to fakeware. If users believe a fakeware is a legitimate update, it has a higher chance of being installed on the system.

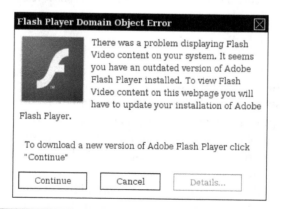

Figure 2-5   *Fakeware disguising itself as a Flash Player update.*

NOTE

The difference between a fakeware and a fake AV program is the part where the user is charged money for installing the software. Even with this difference, it is acceptable that a fake AV program be classified as both scareware and fakeware.

TIP

Always update software using manufacturer-suggested methods such as visiting a specific link manually or using the software's own update features. Treat updates popping up randomly with suspicion.

Greyware

There are files that are not malicious but can be malicious based on how they are used and what effects they have on a user. This is why they are classified as gray-area software or greyware.

The most common greyware types are the following:

▶ Joke

▶ Hacktools

▶ Adware

▶ Spyware

LINGO

Greyware is also known as a potentially unwanted program (PUP).

Joke

A joke greyware is a program designed to fool the user into believing that something is wrong with the system when really there is nothing wrong. The classic joke programs usually invert the display, make the mouse cursor move in the other direction, mess up the keyboard, and even make disc drives open and close. These programs are harmless and do nothing malicious to the system, but they are nuisances.

Joke programs are supposed to be fun, but they have the potential of producing unwanted consequences depending on the victim's reaction. Take, for example, the blue screen of death (BSOD) joke program. This program makes the user believe that the system is not functioning anymore. If the user is not aware that this is a joke, he might resort to formatting the system immediately to fix the "problem."

If the user has backed up of all his files, this is fine. He only lost time in formatting and restoring his system, but if the user has no backup, he just lost all his files because of a simple joke program.

Hacktools

Hacktools is short for hacking tools. These are programs that give users access to a target system. Hacktools are similar to network administrator tools. Most of them function the same way. The only difference is the intent for which they are used. A network administrator tool can be used to manage a network to make sure that everything is running smoothly, but in the wrong hands, that same tool can be used to compromise a network.

Some organizations want hacktools and administration tools absent from all systems connected to their network except for those used by network and system administrators. Think of these like guns. Guns in the hands of law enforcement are used for preserving the peace and for upholding the law, but guns in the wrong hands can have deadly consequences.

Adware

Adware is short for advertisement software or ad-supported software. These are programs that display advertisement pop-ups. These pop-ups are definitely a nuisance because they appear more frequently than they are supposed to, and most of the time, the pop-ups are offensive to some users.

Adware became popular in free software. A developer posts or shares a product for free, but to recover development costs and to generate income, the freeware is most of the time bundled with adware. This gave rise to the term *ad-supported software*. The user can continue using the software as long as the ads are displayed.

> ### NOTE
> There is nothing bad about ad-supported software. It becomes bad or considered a nuisance only when pop-ups appear almost all the time even if the freeware is not running.

Spyware

Spyware is pretty self-explanatory. Some people consider it really bad and would even group it under the category of information stealers. When spyware was booming, almost everybody was calling anything that stole information spyware. There is nothing wrong with this because technically speaking a spyware is an information stealer, but there is a difference between greyware spyware and the information stealers class of malware. Spyware, in the strictest sense, is software that can be purchased for the purpose of spying. This means it is available to anybody who can afford it. On the other hand, the information stealers class of malware is available only to the attackers. Their functionalities are added exclusively to the attacker's malware creation.

The target consumer of spyware usually includes those who want to monitor their family members' activity online, but most of the time it can be used to spy on other people as well. When Internet cafés were becoming popular, most unscrupulous owners would plant spyware in the system that they used for renting out to patrons. This made it a major security and privacy concern that gave rise to a lot of anti-spyware companies in the nineties and early part of the 21st century.

NOTE

Almost all spyware comes with an end user license agreement (EULA) stating that the user must own the computer where the spyware is being installed and that the publishers have no liability whatsoever resulting from the use or misuse of their software.

Recap

Malware taxonomy is the process of classifying malware. Depending on the need, malware can be classified in different ways. But for our purposes, you can classify malware based on its behavior or directive. The following are the different classes of malware that were discussed in this chapter:

- ▶ Infectors
- ▶ Network worms
- ▶ Trojan horses
- ▶ Backdoors
- ▶ Remote-access Trojans
- ▶ Information stealers
- ▶ Ransomware
- ▶ Scareware
- ▶ Fakeware
- ▶ Greyware

Classifying malware enables analysts to come up with well-organized groups of malware with recognizable patterns. Familiarity with these patterns is important to make an educated guess about a malware's main functionality, especially if the data gathered during analysis is not enough to paint a complete picture of the malware. It also makes analysis efficient by enabling analysts to predict malware behavior based on the patterns that are revealed during the different stages of analysis, thus saving time and effort by not having to go through the other steps of analysis.

CHAPTER

3

Malware Deployment

Before malware can do any real damage, it must reach the target system. To reach a target system, the attackers use or abuse different technologies, some of which are legitimate while others are designed purely to deploy malware.

Malware deployment is just as important as the actual capabilities of malware. Without the deployment technology, malware, no matter how sophisticated, will be rendered useless. Think of malware as soldiers. For them to reach their target site, they must be deployed effectively and oftentimes under stealth. This is why capable countries invest in air, land, and sea deployment vehicles for the purpose of successfully carrying soldiers to their target destinations. This is the same concept when it comes to malware deployment technologies. The attackers invest heavily in the most effective and stealthy deployment technology to deliver their malware. One example of this is the exorbitant price of a newly discovered, zero-day vulnerability.

Malware deployment does not concern itself with the execution of malware, although some deployment technology has that capability. It is mostly concerned about malware reaching its intended target. For instance, in the early days of computer viruses, the often-used technology to deploy or spread malware was the floppy disk. The disk carried infected host files, and an infected disk, once placed inside a disk drive, was considered a successful deployment. The malware had reached its target. Infection of the target system was possible because the infected files reached the target, and if a user executed these infected files, the result was a compromised system.

As previously stated, some deployment technology has the capability of automatically executing malware, resulting in deployment and infection. Going back to the disk example, if a disk is infected with a boot sector virus, simply accessing the disk will execute the boot sector virus, causing system compromise. There is no need for a user to execute any infected files to infect the target system.

NOTE

Successful malware deployment does not equal successful malware infection.

The computer virus was successfully deployed using physical media, the disk, to reach its target. The ability to execute the malware once it reaches a target is an added bonus, especially if a deployment technology has this capability. The physical media, and other techniques or technology used to deploy malware are called *malware infection vectors.*

In this chapter, I will discuss what a malware infection vector is and how it is used by attackers to deploy malware to their targets. I will identify the different dimensions of a malware infection vector that serve as a guide to attackers on which specific infection vector to use in their attack campaigns. And most importantly, I will enumerate the most common malware infection vectors that are being used by attackers regardless of whether their campaign of attack is opportunistic or targeted. I will then conclude the chapter by identifying the different characteristics that make a technology suitable for becoming a malware infection vector.

Malware Infection Vectors

An infection vector (or a combination of several infection vectors) is what is behind the spread of malware. It is responsible for the distribution and proliferation of malware. In a threat ecosystem, having the right infection vector is what separates success from failure of malware deployment.

LINGO

A **threat ecosystem** is a collection of different technologies that attackers use to conduct attack campaigns. Each of these technologies supports the malware and each other. If one fails, so does the attack campaign.

There are a lot of infection vectors at the disposal of attackers. I will enumerate these different infection vectors later in the chapter. To help attackers choose which one is best for their specific needs, they consider the different dimensions of each malware infection vector.

Infection vectors are chosen based on the different dimensions they offer. The following are the important dimensions of an infection vector:

▶ Speed

▶ Stealth

▶ Coverage

▶ Shelf life

Speed

The speed by which infection occurs is important to the attackers. Depending on the attacker's intent, she might choose the slow physical media infection vector that relies on physical transport by humans or the faster e-mail infection vector that relies on the speed of different network connections to reach a target. If time is of the essence, the faster infection vector is always chosen. If there is no rush and the target system to be compromised is not connected to any network systems, the physical media might be the better alternative.

The speed by which a malware can reach a target is quite scary. Before everybody was connected to the Internet and everyone had e-mail, malware infection was slow. Almost all malware relied on physical media, and malware infection was not a big thing. A well-known researcher and a personal idol of mine once said in an interview that computer viruses are an urban legend, like the crocodiles in the New York sewers, and one U.K. expert claimed that he had proof that computer viruses were a figment of the imagination.[1] Systems still get infected, but the impact is not as big to garner any attention. There were infections that are well known during those times but not as impactful as the infections that occur when everybody got on the World Wide Web.

With the advent of e-mail and so many computers and devices connected to the Internet, malware now has a faster infection vector in e-mail. This means malware has the ability to reach targets in an instant. With this speed, a malware coming from the East Coast can reach a target on the West Coast, or in any part of the world for that matter, in mere seconds.

The speed and coverage of an e-mail infection vector make it possible to have a worldwide malware outbreak.

Stealth

A successful infection vector is one that cannot be detected easily and can bypass most security solutions. The stealthiest infection vector by far is vulnerable software. A well-crafted exploit can easily bypass most security hurdles and take advantage of the vulnerable software's permissions and privileges. It is always a challenge to detect a zero-day vulnerability. In most cases, it takes a long time to detect the vulnerability and even more time to fix it. This is why zero-day vulnerabilities fetch a big chunk of change in the underground market. Software publishers would rather pay researchers who discover zero-day vulnerabilities rather than know about the zero-day after a massive infection has hit.

LINGO

Zero-day vulnerabilities or *zero-days* are vulnerabilities that have been discovered but are still unknown to the software publisher and to the information security industry at large.

---

[1] 1988 The Game Begins by DaBoss: http://www.cknow.com/cms/vtutor/1988-the-game-begins.html.

In some cases, physical media can prove to be the stealthiest infection vector of all. For example, a target company that does not have any security policy in its endpoints to prevent the use of unauthorized universal serial bus (USB) sticks or external hard drives can easily fall victim to a malware delivered through infected physical media. No matter how state-of-the-art or best-of-breed security solutions are used to guard the network from infiltration and infection, the lowly physical media can easily infect an endpoint, which can serve as the staging ground for further infections within the network.

Coverage

Coverage means the number of targets an infection vector can reach. Is it a single target? Is it in the tens of thousands? Is it in the millions across geopolitical borders? All of these are possible depending on the infection vector chosen.

In an opportunistic attack, the desired coverage is as many as possible. Therefore, an e-mail spam carrying the malware or linking to the malware is often used as the infection vector. Think of the worldwide malware outbreaks that the world saw in the nineties and early part of the 21st century such as the Melissa worm, the ILOVEYOU worm, and MYDOOM, among others. Most of the malware was delivered by e-mail. Anybody who has an e-mail address is a potential target.

> ### LINGO
>
> An **opportunistic attack** is an attack targeting everybody. Whoever stumbles upon the infection vector and becomes compromised becomes the attacker's victim.

In a targeted attack, the desired coverage can range from a single person to a handful of targets. If the target is a specific person or position within a target entity, the malware infection vector needs to deliver the malware to only one target. If the target is a group of employees, the malware infection vector might be crafted to deliver malware to only this small group. For example, an attacker who wants to compromise a small subsidiary that has ten employees will target only those ten employees. In most targeted attacks, the smaller the number of compromised systems, the higher the chance that the malware will stay hidden and not raise any suspicion.

> ### LINGO
>
> A **targeted attack** is an attack focusing on a specific entity chosen specifically by the attacker. Targets are usually executives or important people within an organization.

Shelf Life

Some malware infection vectors have an expiration. Take, for instance, software vulnerability. A patch that closes the software vulnerability can render all exploits that take advantage of it useless. The software vulnerability will not be as successful in deploying malware as it was before the patch was applied.

An e-mail that is captured that delivers malware loses its freshness immediately after a solution to block it gets released.

This is why time is always of the essence when it comes to deploying malware. It is a race between the attackers and the researchers. Once a vector is found out, it is only a matter of time before that specific infection vector is rendered useless, and it is up to the attackers to come up with a new one.

Types of Malware Infection Vectors

An attacker can deploy malware using one or a combination of different infection vectors that includes, but is not limited to, the following:

- ▶ Physical media
- ▶ E-mails
- ▶ Instant messaging and chat
- ▶ Social networking
- ▶ Universal resource locator (URL) links
- ▶ File shares
- ▶ Software vulnerabilities

In analyzing malware, it is also important to determine the infection vector the malware used to deploy itself because it completes the story of how the malware reached the target and it answers the most important question of how a system got infected. This information is valuable to security professionals who are in charge of securing a network or establishing a network perimeter defense. Sometimes this is evident based on the behavior that will be extracted from the analysis, but sometimes it is not, especially if the deployment technology is completely decoupled from the malware. A decoupled deployment technology is an infection vector that is not initiated by the malware but controlled by the actors behind an attack.

LINGO

*A **decoupled infection vector** is a deployment technology separate from the malware itself. Decoupled infection vectors can be used to deploy different kinds of malware and are not dependent on any malware that they deploy.*

For example, an e-mail carrying a malware in the initial stages of infection is considered a decoupled infection vector if the malware does not initiate the sending of that e-mail. Since the malware does not initiate the e-mail, the e-mail won't be part of the analysis because it's not possible to know it was involved. This is similar to how a person carrying an infected disk to a computer won't be seen by analysts after the fact. But if the malware when active sends out more e-mail carrying itself, then that e-mail infection vector is not decoupled because you can see that behavior once the malware is analyzed.

NOTE

Sometimes it is a challenge to determine how a system got infected from the malware alone, especially if the malware was deployed using a decoupled infection vector.

Physical Media

Physical media are the main infection vectors of computer viruses. Since computer viruses are mostly file infectors, the only way they can reach another system is to be manually carried to that system through the use of a disk.

A malware with no capabilities of spreading through any other means than file infection usually uses this infection vector. It is already assumed that the infection vector is physical media since there is no other way for this type of malware to get into another system. But if a malware infects physical media such as the boot sector or sets itself up in the physical media to take advantage of the autorun capabilities of the target OS, then that is clear evidence the malware uses physical media as its infection vector. But what if the malware does not exhibit these capabilities? Is it still possible to use physical media as an infection vector? The answer is yes.

There have been cases where malware that has no routine to infect files or boot sectors is deployed using physical media. For example, someone giving away USB sticks outside of an office building, a school, or anywhere for that matter, can simply put a sophisticated malware on the USB stick hoping that somebody will put it in a system and start the infection process. In this case, the USB stick is a decoupled infection vector because the malware did not put itself on the USB stick; therefore, no traces of this activity will be found during analysis.

TIP

Be wary of free USB sticks even at security conferences; they might be carrying more than what they're supposed to be carrying.

E-mails

One of the fastest ways to reach someone is through e-mail. The same thing goes for malware. Anyone with an e-mail address is a potential target. Lots of noteworthy malware went on to produce worldwide outbreaks because of e-mail; among them are the ILOVEYOU worm, as shown in Figure 3-1, and the Melissa worm.

If during analysis it becomes evident that a malware accesses the default mail client, accesses the user's address book, or uses Simple Mail Transfer Protocol (SMTP), chances are that malware uses e-mail as its main infection vector to spread to other systems.

Even with lots of e-mail security solutions available, the use of e-mail as an infection vector is still popular with attackers because most solutions can be easily bypassed and the e-mail vector is cheap and fast. Plus, there are still lots of users who are easily fooled by simple social engineering tactics. Figure 3-2 shows an example of a socially engineered e-mail vector created for an opportunistic attack.

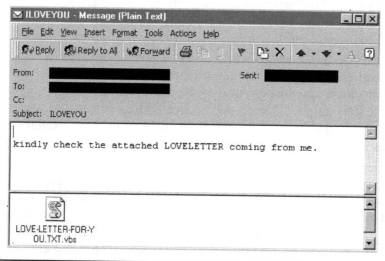

Figure 3-1 *ILOVEYOU worm.*

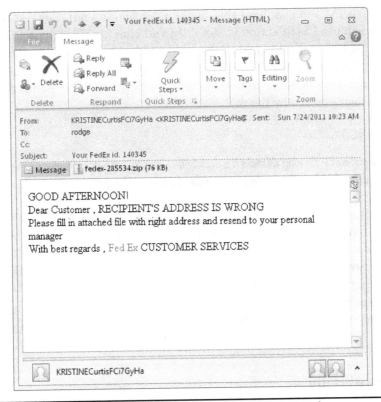

Figure 3-2 *Socially engineered e-mail vector for opportunistic attack.*

LINGO

*There are two types of attacks: **targeted** and **opportunistic**. A **targeted attack** is geared toward a specific company, individual, or entity and usually takes ample preparation from the attackers before it is executed. An **opportunistic attack**, on the other hand, is a form of attack that is waged to as many potential victims as possible. It does not have a specific target. The main goal is to have as many system infections as possible.*

Instant Messaging and Chat

Instant is the magic word when it comes to IM and chat. It's real time. Although e-mail is fast, slow e-mail servers can delay the delivery of a malware or drop the infected message altogether because of non-compliance with e-mail policies or being blocked by mail security products. This is not good for the attacker.

Like e-mail, IM and chat have the capability of sending not only text but also files. But when used as infection vectors, IM and chat usually deliver malicious links pointing to a malware-serving domain or a drive-by download site. In this case, the malware does not necessarily send a copy of itself to propagate. It can be setting up a new malware to be installed on a target PC. It depends on what malware is being served by the malicious link.

LINGO

*A **malware-serving domain** is a domain that links to a network resource that hosts malware. A **drive-by download site** installs malware once a victim visits that site.*

Instant messaging and chat take advantage of trust. A compromised system can make use of the victim's IM account to send malicious links or files to that victim's entire list of friends. The receiving friend will think that the link or file is legitimate because it came from their friend. Some of the target friends won't think twice about clicking the link or downloading and executing the transferred file.

The two popular ways a malware uses IM and chat to spread is by hijacking a user's IM account once the machine is infected and by disguising itself as an IM client.

Social Networking

Social networks are popular. They not only are used to connect with someone but also are used to promote products. The more registered users a social network has, the more valuable it is, and the number of users is directly proportional to its popularity. Some social networks are so popular that the number of registered users actually exceeds the population of some countries, as shown in Figure 3-3.

Social networks offer features that are desirable to attackers. Among them is the ability to send instant messages and post updates in the form of feeds. The feeds can be visible to friends only or to the public. The feeds are desirable to the attackers because the links remain posted until they are taken down; they are just there waiting for unsuspecting users to click them.

Social networks also take advantage of trust. Attackers can post malicious links to the compromised account's wall, and posts can be made to a friend's feed wall. That friend will think it's legitimate, and chances are he will click that link.

A malware that looks for social network accounts or requires a certain user to be logged in to a social network for it to function as intended usually uses social networks to spread. But not all malware that uses social networks to spread will show this feature, especially if the social network is used as a decoupled infection

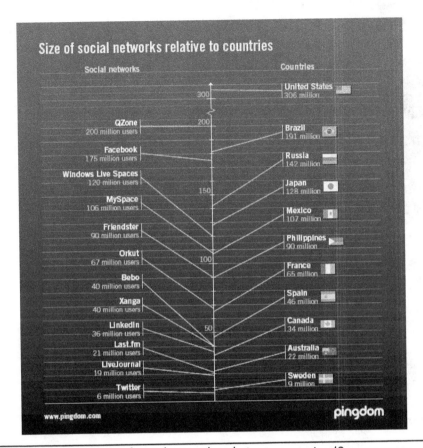

Figure 3-3   *Population size of social networks relative to countries. (Source: www .pingdom.com.)*

vector. One example of this is when the attackers create a social network page about a celebrity, a new movie, a new product, or breaking news. These pages will often attract users to it. The more relevant the subject of the page is, the more users will be drawn to it. Chances are, some of these potential victims will click a link or download a file from that page. Figure 3-4 shows a social network page created by attackers to lure visitors to do what the page says. The result of course is infection.

TIP

Be wary of clicking supposed videos in social network feeds. The malicious ones are not videos but graphic files pretending to be videos with play icons in the middle. They can lead to infection.

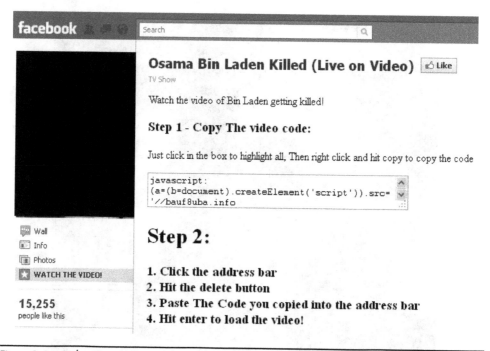

Figure 3-4   *Fake Osama Bin Laden video page on a social network site.*

URL Links

Another way of delivering malware to a target system is through URL links. Attackers use URLs to point to a webpage containing malware or even directly to the malware itself. In the case of the latter, the malware is saved to the file system. In the worst-case scenario, it gets executed immediately, a classic example of a drive-by download site.

A URL link is a special kind of infection vector. It is both an infection vector and a payload of another infection vector. Infection vectors that have URL links as their payload are called *infection-vector-hosting* (IVH) infection vectors and include e-mail, instant messaging, social network feeds, and documents with links.

> **TIP**
>
> When investigating malware that uses IVH infection vectors, be on the lookout for links. These links usually contains new version of the malware or some of its components.

Sometimes static analysis can reveal some of these URL links, especially if the malware is not encrypted. Otherwise, dynamic analysis with network monitoring tools is the only way to reveal these malicious URL links.

File Shares

Peer-to-peer (P2P) file sharing is commonly taken advantage of by malware to get into the system of other users. A malware will drop a copy of itself in the public-facing file share folders. This makes the malware available to all peers that are downloading files. To make sure that other users will download and execute the files, the malicious files use enticing names such as MSOfficeCrack. EXE, DOTAFullVersionNoAccountNeeded.EXE, and more. The idea is to social engineer its way into a target user system by making itself desirable for download.

A malware that looks for common P2P file share folders and drops itself there during execution uses this kind of infection vector.

Software Vulnerabilities

No software is perfect. All software has bugs, and some have flaws. Some are known, while others are not. Some are critical, while others are minor. Depending on the severity of the bug, it can have unpredictable and unintended results. The attackers, with some of them being software developers themselves, recognize the value of an unknown or undiscovered critical bug waiting to be exploited in certain software.

It is important to know the difference between a software bug and a software flaw. A software bug is an issue with a feature that is not functioning as intended, while a software flaw is an error in the design and architecture of the software. A bug can be fixed by a patch, but a flaw can be fixed only by a complete redesign of the software.

The advantage of using software vulnerabilities as an infection vector over other infection vectors is that it significantly lowers, if not totally eliminates, the need for human interaction. Typically, it results in the automated execution of malware, which is what is considered the most effective way of infecting a system. It also takes advantage of software that is whitelisted in the system, thus evading any sort of application control security products.

LINGO

Application control is also known as whitelisting. The concept of this security product or feature is to let only known whitelisted applications to run in a system.

Lots of material covers software vulnerabilities already. With this in mind, I will focus on those that are used to install malware on a system.

To take advantage of software vulnerabilities, the attackers use an exploit. An exploit can be a piece of code or a chunk of malformed data that causes the target software to behave in a way not intended by the software manufacturer. The most common exploit is the one that takes advantage of buffer overflow.

> **NOTE**
>
> *An exploit is not a vulnerability. An exploit is something that takes advantage of a vulnerability.*

Buffer Overflow

Software consists of two distinct components: code and data. Code is the set of instructions that makes use of data. During data manipulation, software often makes use of a temporary data storage called a *buffer*. A buffer is created to hold data and nothing more. But sometimes, because of programmatic error, more data is written to the allocated buffer. This results in data overflowing to adjacent buffers. This condition is called a *buffer overflow*. Attackers take advantage of this by overflowing the buffer with code instead of data. The buffer is overflowed in such a way to transfer the control to that code, thus executing it. The often-used buffer overflows are

▶ Stack overflow

▶ Heap overflow

It is important to note that a buffer overflow can be triggered using a malformed file. The malformed file is the one that is deployed by the attacker. Once this file is opened using the vulnerable application, the data from the malformed file overflows the buffer. Getting hold of a malformed file during malware hunting helps in understanding how the vulnerable application is being exploited.

Stack Overflow   The stack is a last-in first-out (LIFO) data structure. This means the data that is pushed last onto the stack is what is popped out first. It is aptly called a stack because it is stacking data on top of one another. Think of it like a stack of plates. The last plate that is put on the top of the stack is the one that is used first. Because of its LIFO nature, the stack is often used to store temporary variables, making it efficient to use with program functions.

Stack overflow is the result of overflowing the buffers on the stack to get control of the execution flow of the program. This is made possible by overflowing the

Figure 3-5   *What the stack looks like during a function call.*

buffer enough to overwrite the value stored in the return address (RET). To understand this concept, let's look at how program functions use the stack.

A program function is like a small program within a program. It's independent, compartmentalized code that performs specific operations using data passed to it and then returns the result to the main program. Since a function has to manipulate data, it utilizes the stack as a temporary storage for this data. When a function is called within a program, it pushes all the data into the stack, including the return address. To understand what the stack looks like, see Figure 3-5.

The return address is where the instruction pointer is currently pointing when the function is called. This is important because after the function has finished processing, the execution flow has to go back to that return address so the main program can continue its execution flow. This value is stored in RET. When the function finishes, the value stored in RET is passed to the instruction pointer so the main program can go back to its execution flow before the function was called. So if the attacker is able to overflow the buffer and as a result overwrite the value stored in RET with an address value that points to malicious code, the instruction pointer will point directly to the malicious code, resulting in the malicious code being executed.

Heap Overflow   The heap is dynamically allocated memory space. The logic behind this is that the amount of memory needed by a program is not known in advance; therefore, memory has to be allocated as needed and freed up when not needed. The difference between a heap and a stack is that a heap does not have a return address like a stack does. This makes the technique used to control execution flow in stack overflow useless. Overflowing a heap instead results in data and pointers to other data or program functions being overwritten. As a result, the attacker can overwrite these pointers to point to malicious code instead of the original location.

Privilege Escalation

The ability of a software vulnerability to deliver and install malware in a system depends on its getting privilege escalation. Privilege escalation is the process of gaining access to system resources that are accessible only to a superuser or system administrator. With this, the attacker can do pretty much anything with the system, including installing malware.

Privilege escalation is achieved when the exploited, vulnerable software (or some of its components) is already running on escalated privilege or it has access to system resources or functions running on escalated privileges.

Zero-Day Vulnerabilities

The knowledge of a program's vulnerabilities that can be exploited is often kept private by the attacker. This is known as a *zero-day vulnerability*. A zero-day vulnerability is an exploitable hole in an operating system, software, or even hardware that has no solution and has been discovered by those other than the manufacturers or publishers of the vulnerable object. If an independent researcher has discovered a zero-day vulnerability, the next step is to report this to the manufacturer or publisher so a patch or a new minor version can be released that fixes the vulnerability. Some software manufacturers even pay for this kind of information, making vulnerability discovery a good independent business for software hobbyists. But it's a different story if an attacker discovers it. It is usually kept secret to be used in future attacks or to be sold to other cybercrime groups. Keeping it a secret creates immense value because this vector's shelf life depends on how long it is kept a secret and how long before a patch is released to fix it.

There have been cases where a vulnerability has been public already but the patch to fix it was pending release; thus, any malware that utilized this vulnerability still enjoyed some level of success. Unfortunately, the only way to prevent vulnerable software with no available patch or fix from being exploited is to uninstall or not use it, but in cases where the software is vital to an enterprise's operation, this is usually out of the question.

> **TIP**
>
> *A good way to stay abreast of the latest vulnerabilities is by visiting http://cve.mitre.org.*

Potential Infection Vectors

It is important to note that any technology can be used as a malware infection vector as long as that technology possesses one or a combination of the following:

- ▶ The ability to process data from an external source
- ▶ The ability to move data to a chosen destination
- ▶ The ability to share data

Who knows? In the span of your research and analysis, you might discover a new malware infection vector.

Recap

Malware deployment is an important part of the threat ecosystem. As stated previously, it is as important as the actual capabilities of malware. Without the deployment technology, malware, no matter how sophisticated it is, would be rendered useless.

Having familiarity with the different malware infection vectors enables analysts to determine how the malware spreads. This answers the important question of how the victim got infected and also helps security professionals in securing networks.

In this chapter, I discussed what an infection vector is and how attackers use it to deploy their malware. I enumerated the four dimensions of a malware infection vector, which are the following:

- ▶ Speed
- ▶ Stealth
- ▶ Coverage
- ▶ Shelf life

Depending on the attacker's needs, an infection vector is chosen based on these dimensions. It serves as a guide for the attacker on which appropriate infection vector should be chosen to deploy their malware.

I then enumerated the most common infection vectors that are used by the attackers to deploy their malware.

- Physical media
- E-mails
- Instant messaging and chat
- Social networking
- URL links
- File shares
- Software vulnerabilities

An infection vector can be coupled with or decoupled from the malware. A coupled infection vector can easily be revealed during malware analysis because the malware initiates the use of the vector. A decoupled vector is much more challenging to discover; because it is not initiated by the malware, no evidence of it will appear during analysis. The attackers usually initiate the use of a decoupled vector.

It is important to note that most infection vectors used by attackers are legitimate services that are essential to the operation of any network system. These services cannot be blocked simply for the purpose of stopping malware. The key here is to understand how these technologies are being used by attackers to deliver their malware and then find a solution.

Any technology can be used by attackers to deploy malware, which is why I concluded this chapter by discussing the potential of any technology to be used as an infection vector. It actually depends on the following characteristics:

- The ability to process data from an external source
- The ability to move data to a chosen destination
- The ability to share data

Finding out which infection vector an attacker used to deploy malware completes the story of system compromise. And most of the time, it is important to complete the story.

Protective Mechanisms

Deploying malware is a risky business. The deployment technology or malware infection vector can be intercepted, opening up the malware it is carrying to exposure. Once a malware is deployed, it always carries with it the risk of being captured. And once the malware is captured, it can then be analyzed, which is not a good thing for the attackers because this leads to the malware's behavior being understood and the malware technologies being discovered. With all this knowledge, researchers then have the ability to stop the spread of the malware by blocking whatever infection vector it is using and can create a solution for the malware to prevent it from achieving its purpose. To avoid ratting itself out and revealing everything to researchers, the malware must have the ability to protect itself when captured.

Malware employs different mechanisms to protect itself from the prying eyes of researchers and analysts. The protective mechanisms used by malware are designed to evade analysis and detection or at least buy some time long enough for it to achieve its directive. This is of paramount importance, especially if the malware is utilizing a new malware technology or a zero-day exploit. Discovery of this new technology and exploit by researchers and analyst can lead to the development of solutions not only against the current malware but also against future malware creations that will utilize these same malware technologies.

Protective mechanisms are therefore designed to make it difficult for security products to detect the delivery, installation, and presence of malware and for researchers to analyze and uncover malware behavior and new malware technologies. In the case of researchers, the real goal of malware is to make unraveling the protective mechanisms so challenging and time-consuming that it is next to impossible.

In this chapter, I will discuss the different protective mechanisms employed by malware and how malware applies these evasion techniques while it is being deployed and while it is running in a target system. Understanding how a malware protects itself and familiarizing yourself with the different technologies a malware uses to protect itself is key to removing these protective mechanisms so malware analysis can proceed.

The Two States of Malware

As mentioned in Chapter 1, malware exists in two states.

- ► Static
- ► Dynamic

Static malware is malware at rest, which means that the malware is not running or active in the system it is in. Dynamic malware is malware in motion, which means that the malware is running or currently being executed in the system it is in.

> **NOTE**
>
> *These two states are not exclusive to malware. These two states apply to all executables, benign or malicious.*

Malware must be able to protect itself regardless of what state it is in. Attackers know this to be true. A malware before it is executed will always be in a static state first. For it to be able to achieve dynamic state, it must be able to survive in a static state. Survival here means it is not detected by any security products and not easily analyzed by malware analysts and researchers. Once it reaches the dynamic state, the malware can then utilize other protective mechanisms that it is endowed with so it has enough time to achieve its directives.

Static Malware

A malware that is being transported by a deployment technology such as a physical drive or e-mail is a malware at rest. This is usually a good time to capture malware because it is powerless in this state. It cannot do anything to prevent anyone from copying it from the deployment technology and distributing it to other analysts and researchers for further analysis. Whatever protective mechanisms it has that are activated by its malware code are rendered useless. But this does not mean the malware is easy to crack. The attackers have taken this into consideration, which is why static malware or malware at rest also has protective mechanisms built in.

Dynamic Malware

Dynamic malware, or malware in motion, is malware that is currently active or running in a system. Unlike static malware, dynamic malware has all the encoded protective mechanisms available to it; therefore, it can actively defend itself from scanning by security products, from the invasive system-monitoring tools that record the malware's every move, and from the prying eyes of researchers.

A running malware can actively protect itself. It has full access to its codes and features that the attackers built into the malware. It has the ability to react to whatever changes there are in the target system it is running on and to guard against any tools that are used for the purpose of extracting and analyzing it.

Protective Mechanisms

The attackers understand the risk of malware being captured through interception of the malware infection vector used or through extraction from the compromised system. This is why highly funded attackers invest heavily in different evasion technologies to protect their malware. A malware's main goal is to impede detection and analysis. The more time it takes for researchers and analysts to understand malware, the more time the attackers have to achieve their directive. It is therefore essential that malware researchers and analysts understand the different protective mechanisms employed by malware. The ability to recognize and mitigate these protective mechanisms is important so malware analysis can proceed.

LINGO

Malware protective mechanisms are also known as *evasion technologies*.

The attackers choose or create malware for their attack campaign with the goal and expectation that it will be successful. They do everything that is technically possible within their capability to protect their malware creation. A well-funded attacker group might have access to more malware protective mechanisms and technologies, while those that form a rag-tag group might have limited options. Regardless of the funding, the main idea is that the attackers will do everything in their power to protect their malware to achieve success in their attack campaign.

A successful malware is one that has the ability to evade detection and analysis for it to function as intended by the attacker. Evading detection enables it to reach its target and execute unimpeded. Evading analysis enables it to conceal its real purpose when subjected to malware analysis and reversing. To achieve this, the malware must employ protective mechanisms for it to survive long enough to accomplish its directive.

For a malware to be successful, the malware writers must be able to deal with what their creation is up against. The malware faces these two foes:

- ▶ The security product
- ▶ The security analysts and researchers

A collection of security products, consisting of both software and hardware, is what stands between the attackers and the individual or organization they are attacking. As much as possible, they want their malware to be able to evade whatever detection technology these security products are employing. To do this, attackers familiarize themselves with the different technologies used by security products so they can come up with ways to circumvent those technologies. If the malware can evade these technologies, it has a better chance of executing and maintaining a foothold in the target system.

Of course, if there is an infection or system compromise, the system will be scrutinized by incident responders or security professionals within the company or from a third party. A captured malware must have the capability to protect itself from analysis. The main idea here is to buy more time. The more time it takes for analysts to break a malware, the more time the attackers have to do whatever they need to do on the compromised system or network. Malware that requires continuous access will need a strong protective mechanism, while other malware might not need any protection at all such as malware used in a hit-and-run attack that usually lasts minutes or hours. A malware used in these types of attacks usually does not need protective mechanisms.

LINGO

A *hit-and-run attack* is an attack that happens in a short period of time, usually in less time than it takes for the company to deploy a solution to stop the malware.

No matter how many protective mechanisms are used, they can be broken. It just takes time, and it depends on the difficulty level of the protective mechanism being used. The more layers there are, the more time it takes. And if each layer proves to be more difficult than expected, then it becomes more time-consuming.

LINGO

Breaking a malware is a phrase used to describe removing all protective mechanisms employed by malware.

As mentioned, attackers want to defeat the security product and the security analysts and researchers. Almost all protective mechanisms are designed with these goals in mind, which means a malware writer has to consider how to protect the malware whether it is at rest or in motion against security products designed to stop malware and from analysts and researchers eager to dissect the malware to uncover each bit and byte of its functionality.

Static Malware Protective Mechanisms

A static malware is always at the mercy of the analysts. No matter how sophisticated the protective mechanisms its code employs, it is rendered useless because the malware is not executing. The analyst can dissect it and expose its functionality through its extracted malware code.

> ### *NOTE*
> *A malware's source code is a gold mine. It is the key to understanding all of the malware's functionalities and all the technologies it is using. It is so important that competing malware writer groups kill their competition by leaking a copy of the competition's malware source code. If source code is leaked, the malware loses value in the underground market.*

The malware's most important asset is its source code. A malware that is at rest is susceptible to having its code disassembled and reversed. It is therefore imperative for the malware writers to protect the malware code. It is the key to everything. With it, analysts will be able to understand how the malware works and how to stop it. This is why static malware protective mechanisms are all about protecting the malware code. The following are the most common static protective mechanisms employed by malware:

► Entry-point obscuring

► Basic malware encryption

► Polymorphism

► Metamorphism

► Anti-reversing

> ### *LINGO*
> *Malcode is short for malware code.*

Entry-Point Obscuring

An entry point is a pointer to the location of an executable's first instruction. It points to the location where the execution formally starts. For a malware, the entry point almost always points to the start of the malware code. This is especially true for infected host files. Therefore, hiding it is advantageous for the malware because of the following:

► Antivirus (AV) scanners use the entry point to find the malware code and match the malware signatures the scanners have in their databases.

► With the entry point, reversers are able to disassemble and trace the code through the use of disassemblers and debuggers.

Hiding the malware code's entry point protects the malware from both analysis and scanning. The protective mechanism that hides a malware code's entry point is known as *entry-point obscuring* (EPO). The EPO technique is popular with file-infecting malware. This is because an infected file will always have two sets of code: the malware code and the original host file code. The trick is to hide the malware code by pointing to some benign code. To see how this works, you need to understand how a typical infected host file executes, as shown in Figure 4-1.

When an infected host file is executed, the malware code gets executed first. This is because during infection, the malware modifies the target host file's entry point to point to the attached malware code. The main reason for this is to get initial control of the execution flow of the program. After the malware finishes execution, the control is passed back to the original host file code. This gives the impression that there is nothing wrong because the host file is still executed. This behavior of file-infecting malware makes it easy for analysts to locate the malware code because it is always the first code being pointed to by the infected host file's entry point.

But EPO malware does things differently. The entry point does not point directly to the malware code; instead, it points to something different. A good illustration of this is an EPO technique that uses code patching, as shown in Figure 4-2.

Instead of passing control immediately to the malware, the EPO malware lets the host program execute some of its code, and then a few instructions later, a patched instruction passes control to the malware code. And once the malware

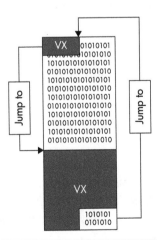

Figure 4-1 *Typical infected host execution flow.*

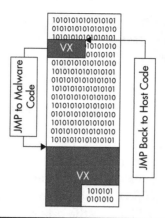

Figure 4-2   *Entry-point obscuring via code patching.*

finishes executing, it lets the host program continue with its remaining code. This technique is especially effective against AV scanners because the scanner is taken to a set of instructions that are not malicious instead of the real malicious code.

Basic Malware Encryption

Encryption is a good way to hide code. It is used in legitimate software to prevent software piracy and cracking. If it works for legitimate software, it will surely work for malware. With EPO, you saw how malware tries to hide the location of its malicious code, but in malware encryption, the malware is actually protecting the whole malicious program.

An encrypted malware has three components:

▶ The encryption/decryption engine
▶ The encryption/decryption key
▶ The malware code

NOTE

An encrypted program does not mean it is malicious. Encryption is a technology used by software publishers to protect their intellectual property, which includes software code. Malware writers and attackers use it for the same purpose. They do not discriminate between technologies; if they can use it to their advantage, they will use it.

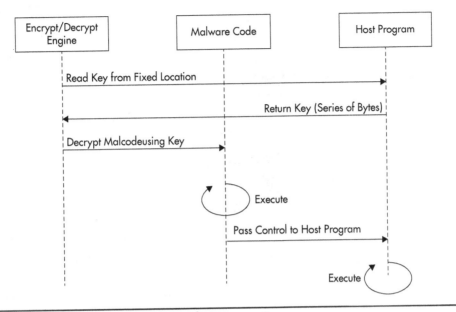

Figure 4-3 *Basic malware encryption during execution.*

When an encrypted malware is executed, as shown in Figure 4-3, the encryption/ decryption engine gets loaded into memory and decrypts the encrypted malware code using the encryption/decryption key. Once the malware code has been decrypted, it then executes its directive. After that, control is passed back to the host program. This is the simplest form of malware encryption.

Basic malware encryption was first used by file infectors to make their infections look different in form and structure from one another. During infection, as shown in Figure 4-4, the decrypted malware code is encrypted by the encryption/decryption engine using a different encryption/decryption key. The new key is usually taken from a series of bytes found in a fixed location of the host file being infected. The location is constant, but the series of bytes found in that location differs for each file. Since the key is different, the newly encrypted malware code looks different from other infections. No two infections are exactly alike. Once malware code encryption is complete, the newly encrypted malware code attaches itself to the host file. The main reason for malware encryption is to avoid detection using a single signature. Instead of AV companies pushing a single signature to detect all infections, it will be forced to push a 1:1 ratio, which does not scale and is a totally ineffective way of solving this problem.

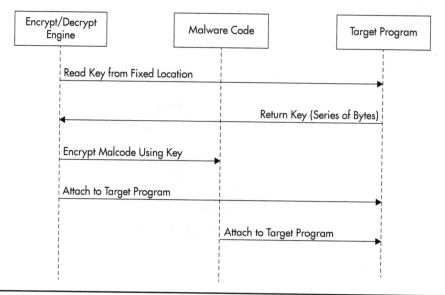

Figure 4-4 *Basic malware encryption during infection.*

Although this protective mechanism seemed cutting edge at that time, the security companies were able to catch up pretty quickly because one of the three components remained constant. The encryption/decryption key was always different per infection, resulting in the encrypted malware code being different as well from previous infections. But the encryption/decryption engine remained constant. Using the encryption/decryption engine codes, security products were able to create a single signature to catch this basic form of malware encryption.

Polymorphism

Attackers recognized that an improvement had to be made from the basic malware encryption that they were using, so they introduced a new malware technology known as the *mutation engine*. The mutation engine, which is part of the malware code, basically alters the code of another application without changing the application's functions. With the introduction of the mutation engine, it is now possible to alter the encryption/decryption engine code without changing its functionality. The three components are now different in every infection. This new form of malware encryption is known as *polymorphism*. As defined by Merriam-Webster, polymorphism is "the quality or state of existing in or assuming different forms." This is exactly what polymorphic malware is.

Still, polymorphic malware has a weakness, as shown in Figure 4-5. A polymorphic malware still needs to decrypt the encrypted malware code in memory, and every time the malware code is decrypted, it is constant. It shows its original form. This makes it possible for a signature to be created to detect the malware code in memory or through antivirus emulation techniques. Polymorphic malware is highly effective in defeating static scanning but not the more advanced dynamic scanning.

Metamorphism

The attackers had to come up with a way to counteract the AV technologies used to detect encrypted and polymorphic malware. And so they did. They introduced a new form of encrypted malware known as *metamorphic malware,* as shown in Figure 4-6.

Recognizing that a paradigm shift was needed, the attackers approached the problem differently. They realized that they had a powerful technology on their side in the form of the mutation engine. Instead of working with the three components of malware encryption, they realized that the mutation engine could simply mutate the whole malware code itself. This freed them from the inherent

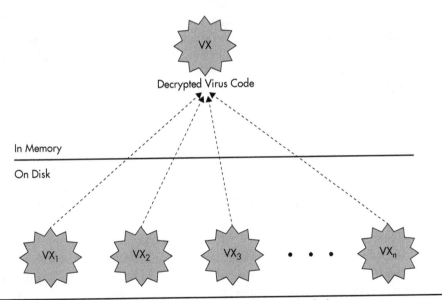

Figure 4-5 *Different generations of polymorphic infections look the same in memory when decrypted.*

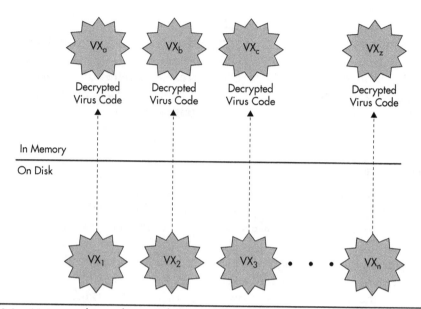

Figure 4-6 *Metamorphic malware infections differ on disk and in memory.*

weaknesses of the basic malware encryption and polymorphic techniques. With metamorphism, each malware infection is totally different, both on disk and in memory. Although almost perfect, metamorphic malware still has a weakness because for it to morph, it needs to analyze its own code and reassemble it to its new form. If the mutation engine can do this, the reversers can do it as well, but it takes a lot of time, and the formulated solution might be complicated for existing AV technologies.

Anti-reversing

A sure way to understand malware is through reversing. No matter the protective mechanism, reversing can shed light on how to beat it. The only enemies are time and effort. Depending on the malware's difficulty level, a reversing session can range from minutes to months. For example, when Ultimate Packer for Executables (UPX) was first used to pack and encrypt malware, it was pretty awesome. It enabled attackers to easily distribute malware with far lesser resistance from security products and the prying eyes of analysts and reversers. Almost all malware used it. But once the packing routine was reversed, unpacking a malware packed with UPX using OllyDbg takes only minutes. Plus, there are a lot of tools available for download that can unpack UPX in seconds.

As a rule of thumb, a malware is deemed successful in implementing anti-reversing techniques when it takes a reverser longer to understand the malware than the malware needs to survive. If an attack campaign uses a malware that needs only a couple of days and it takes a reverser three days to solve that malware, the malware has already won.

The main idea of anti-reversing is to make the reversing process as difficult as possible to the point that it seems impossible to reverse the malware. The most common anti-reversing techniques used to protect static malware are the following:

- ▶ Anti-decompilers
- ▶ Anti-disassemblers

If a reverser or the tools he uses cannot decompile or disassemble a malware, the reverser is denied access to the malware source code, and without the source code, reversing cannot proceed. But there is a drawback in this protective mechanism. It works only for decompilers and disassemblers supported by the malware. This is because decompilers and disassemblers, like other software products, have their own proprietary design, algorithm, and implementation. For example, a malware with anti-disassembler capability can support only the IDA disassembler but not others such as Win32DASM. So if a reverser uses IDA, it might not work as planned, but using Win32DASM might yield the output the reverser desires since the anti-disassembler technology used by the malware does not support Win32DASM. Usually, malware that uses anti-decompiler or anti-disassembler protective mechanisms supports the most popular tool that reversers use. Again, the main point is to make life difficult for reversers. It takes the reversers more time and effort to reverse the malware. And if the malware is able to achieve this, that is, buy more time for the malware to finish its directive, then the anti-reversing protective mechanism has done its job.

NOTE

Entry-point obfuscation, code obfuscation through encryption, polymorphism, and metamorphism also slow down reversing. So, in effect, these protective mechanisms can also be viewed as anti-reversing technologies.

Dynamic Malware Protective Mechanisms

When a malware is in motion, i.e., running in the system, it has the full capabilities of its code. This means, when executing, the malware has available to it whatever protective mechanism it is endowed with by its writer.

The following are the most common protective mechanisms employed by dynamic malware:

▶   Anti-debugging

▶   Anti-sandboxing

▶   Environment lock

▶   Anti-AV scanning

▶   Network behavior protection

Anti-debugging

One of the most effective ways of tracing malware is to use a debugger. This enables a reverser to follow the malware as it executes per line of code, look at the contents of memory and the system's registers, and examine the changes done to the system by the malware. Debugging is an important part of reversing. Without it, it is extremely hard to do a reversing session. This is why an anti-debugging protective mechanism is attractive to attackers.

The main goal of anti-debugging is to fool the debugger into following a dead-end execution flow, making it difficult for the reverser. The more difficult it is, the more time and effort that are needed. Sometimes, this is more than enough for the malware to be successful.

> ### TIP
>
> It is always good to have disassembled code available while doing a debugging session. This is a good way to check for inconsistencies between the disassembled code and the actual execution path the debugger is taking.

Anti-sandboxing

In rare cases, static analysis is enough to extract information from malware that reveals its directive, but in most cases dynamic analysis is needed. As defined in Chapter 1, dynamic analysis is the process of extracting information from malware through the use of system monitoring tools and technologies. Usually, dynamic analysis is done by using a sandbox. A sandbox can be manually driven, or it can be automated. The following are the two most important components of a sandbox:

▶   Sandbox environment

▶   System monitoring tools

The sandbox environment is the system where the malware is executed. During execution, the malware is supposed to do what it was designed to do. The system monitoring tools make sure that everything the malware does on the system is captured and logged for analysis purposes. If the malware does not execute in the sandbox, no information is extracted, and the whole process fails. This is the key to beating a sandbox. The malware must be intelligent enough to know whether it is running in a target system or in a controlled sandbox.

Anti-sandboxing techniques usually cover two things.

▶ Detection of sandbox environment

▶ Detection of system monitoring tools

See Figure 4-7 for an illustration of anti-sandboxing technology in action.

Detection of Sandbox Environment   If a malware knows that it is running in a sandbox or a malware test environment, it does not need to execute, so no information

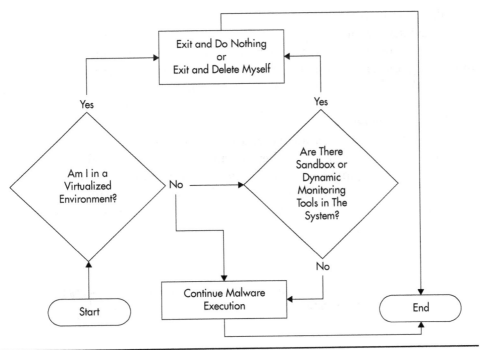

Figure 4-7   *Anti-sandboxing technology in action.*

can be captured during dynamic analysis. Most sandbox implementations are virtual because of the many advantages this offers such as portability and easy restoration. So, for malware to know whether it is running in a sandbox, it needs to know only whether it is running in a virtualized environment. This led to the most popular anti-sandboxing technology: the anti-virtualization technique. This technique simply detects telltale signs common to virtual machines. If the malware senses any indication of it running in a virtualized environment, it will simply exit and do nothing.

> **NOTE**
>
> *Malware programs with only anti-virtualization techniques are often used for opportunistic attacks, which result in more home users being infected because most of them are not using virtualized systems.*

Detection of System Monitoring Tools   Not all sandboxes are implemented in a virtualized environment. Bare-metal sandbox implementations are available as well. This solves the anti-virtualization technique employed by most malware, but it costs more to implement, and restoring images takes longer compared to the virtualized counterpart.

As previously mentioned, a sandbox has two important components: the sandbox environment and the system monitoring tools. Without the system monitoring tools, no information can be extracted from the running malware. In bare-metal implementations, a malware relies on detecting the presence of system monitoring tools. This is the opening the malware writers have to beat bare-metal sandbox implementations.

As with other software, system monitoring tools leave telltale signs or footprints in the system whether they are running or not. The malware writers simply familiarize themselves with these tools and the footprints they leave in the system and arm their malware with the ability to detect the presence of these footprints. If a malware detects the presence of any of these telltale signs, it exits and does nothing.

> **NOTE**
>
> *Some instances of malware, especially malware used in targeted attacks, will stop execution only if they detect system monitoring tools running, because most enterprise production systems are virtualized.*

Environment Lock

Malware is designed primarily to execute to do its job. If it does not execute in the target system, then it has failed. But it must be intelligent enough to know whether it is running in a target system or in a malware test environment.

Most of the time, malware is captured from a compromised system. It is then subjected to static and dynamic analysis to extract information from it. The environment lock feature protects the malware from dynamic analysis. The main idea of this protective mechanism is to have the malware execute only in the environment it initially compromised. Getting that malware out of that environment and have it execute in any other system, be it a sandbox or just another system, will not work. This is because during its first execution on its target system, the malware takes environment-specific markers—such as the hardware ID, media access control (MAC) address, or anything that is unique to the system—as variables or encryption keys and mutates itself by using these keys, which then become the conditions for its execution. The resulting mutated malware will run only in the first compromised system and nowhere else. If the malware is moved to another system and the system-specific markers do not match, it will not be able to decrypt its code in memory and execute. Capturing a malware with an environment lock feature and subjecting it to a sandbox for dynamic analysis will not yield any result. This virtually defeats dynamic analysis.

Anti-AV Scanning

The malware's foremost nemesis has always been the AV product, and malware writers know that their creations can be beaten if AV is able to scan and detect them. Detection depends on the signatures the AV product has. It can specifically detect and identify a malware if there is a signature that matches the malware's characteristics. For malware that is totally new and not covered by any specific detection, the AV product uses heuristic detection. Depending on how the heuristic signature is written and the number of malware samples that a heuristic signature is based upon, it can be effective or not. And to ensure that the system is always protected, real-time scanning is always enabled. This is an AV feature that lets it reside in memory, keeping a watchful eye on the file system on disk and the programs loaded and executed in memory.

A malware can arrive in a target system in different ways; it depends on the deployment technology used. The malware can be downloaded from the Internet or can arrive as an attachment in e-mail. If this is the case, the malware typically undergoes static scanning. Obviously, static scanning is easy to defeat given the available static malware protective mechanisms the attackers use. So, almost all the time, malware gets into the system undetected. Once the malware is executed in the target system, the AV product uses dynamic scanning to inspect the malware during runtime. Depending on the current signature database of the AV product, the malware might get detected using specific or heuristic detection. But before any signature matching takes place, the AV scanner must be able to find the malware code. It does not matter whether it's static or dynamic scanning; the scanning flow is the same, which is to find the right entry point to the malware code. The only difference is that in dynamic scanning, the memory image of the malware is the one that is being scanned. Given that the scanning flow is the same, some code obfuscation techniques that worked in protecting static malware also work in protecting dynamic malware. The most effective protective mechanism techniques that usually work for both states of malware are entry-point obscuring and metamorphism.

Another anti-AV scanning technology used by malware to protect itself from scanning is to simply turn off the AV product altogether and deny access to AV vendors' websites. The same concept as the one used in detecting the presence of system monitoring tools is applied, but this time, the presence of AV products is the one being detected. Once detected, the malware turns off the AV product. This works only if the malware is totally new and not detected by the installed AV product. Given the protective mechanisms available to attackers, this is not hard to do.

An easier anti-AV scanning alternative is to use a security product's "Do Not Scan List." The malware simply adds itself to that list so every time a scan is performed, the security product will skip the malware. Again, this works only if the malware is new and not detected when it first compromises the target system.

Network Behavior Protection

With the rise of botnets and the agility it offers to attackers, most malware used in attack campaigns must have the capability to communicate to the attacker. Communication can be one-way or two-way. One-way communication means the malware can accept commands or directives only from the attackers, while two-way communication means the malware not only has the capability to accept commands but also can post status updates or any other information that the attacker needs.

When a malware is running in a compromised system, the most common way it communicates to its command-and-control (C&C) is through the use of domains.

LINGO

Command-and-control *is also known as* ***CnC, C&C,*** *or* ***C2.***

Every time a malware communicates, it leaves network traces. Network logs can see what domains it connects to, and network sniffers can tell what data it is sending and receiving. Because of this, domains that are used as C&C are collected and can be added to a blacklist to be used to detect the presence of malware in the network. An endpoint that attempts to communicate to any of these known malicious domains will be flagged and disconnected from the network for analysis purposes. This effectively kills what the malware is trying to do. No matter how good the malware is at hiding or protecting itself in the endpoint, its network behavior is enough to betray it and shout to the whole world of its existence.

Because of this, attackers have devised ways of protecting their malware's network behavior from detection and analysis. The following technologies are commonly used to accomplish this:

▶   Domain fluxing

▶   Internet Protocol (IP) fluxing

▶   Abusing legitimate services

Domain Fluxing   When the first botnets came out, most malware used in these botnets had hard-coded domains; therefore, once these domains were discovered, all instances of that malware could easily be detected using a domain blacklist technology. There was no need to invest time in doing forensics in a suspected infected host or endpoint. The domains decided the endpoint's guilt. And most of the time, this was enough. If the endpoint was not critical, some organizations would simply restore it to an original clean state. This saved them effort and time in restoration.

Attackers understood that this was a major weakness even for the most sophisticated malware, so they came out with domain fluxing. Domain fluxing is the ability of malware to generate unique domain names on regular intervals, usually a day. This is made possible by a domain generation algorithm (DGA) that is coded into the malware. With this protective mechanism, the domain blacklist is rendered useless because whatever is added on a certain day becomes obsolete the next day.

The most infamous malware that utilizes DGA is Conficker. Conficker.A and Conficker.B can generate 500 unique domain names in a day, while Conficker.C can generate 50,000 unique domain names in a day.

It is important to note that not all of these domains are active. Out of the large number of domain names produced, only a handful or even a single one will be active. The rest are NXDOMAINS. This is one flaw of this technique because an endpoint that attempts to connect to massive amounts of NXDOMAINS can trigger a network rule and thus be flagged for suspicious activity.

LINGO

NXDOMAINS is short for non-existent domains.

IP Fluxing   IP fluxing refers to having a single domain name resolve to a frequently changing IP address. This protective mechanism, when combined with domain fluxing, can be a powerful anti-detection and anti-takedown protection. With a rotating IP address, identifying (and taking down) the C&C server is challenging.

LINGO

*IP fluxing is also known as **fast fluxing**.*

This protective mechanism beats IP blacklists but not domain blacklists, especially if the malware does not use this capability together with domain fluxing. This is because this protective mechanism is geared toward hiding the C&C and not the malware itself.

Abusing Legitimate Services   Another way for malware to hide its network communications is by using known and legitimate services within the network. For example, if a network allows peer-to-peer communication within the organization, a peer-to-peer (P2P) malware might be used, so its communication with other peers will not raise any flags. A malware can use social media posts or updates as its command and control; for example, tweets that the malware monitors can appear to be normal musings of the account owner but in fact are commands that the malware can understand and act upon. This is also true for wall postings and updates on other social media networks. A malware can even utilize free hosting services to get updates or commands from attackers. Network rules and policies may not raise an alert to any of these network communications because they are known to be legitimate, and the domains the malware are connecting to are popular domains that are known to be benign. The only way to stop malware that abuse these services is by blocking the services.

When it comes to hiding network activity, malware cannot hide everything. There will be network footprints, and they can easily be identified. The attackers understand this; therefore, malware used for attacks with the directive of hiding and maintaining a foothold on the system will seldom connect to any network resource. These types of malware might connect once a week or even less frequently. This makes a malware's network footprint a drop in the bucket in the daunting world of network logs.

Recap

In this chapter, I discussed protective mechanisms employed by malware. These protective mechanisms are designed to protect malware against its two foes. They are as follows:

- ▶ The security product
- ▶ The security analysts and researchers

I enumerated the two states of malware that the attackers concern themselves with when protecting malware against security products and security researchers. They are as follows:

- ▶ Static
- ▶ Dynamic

I then discussed the different protective mechanisms used to protect malware at each of these states.

The following are the common protective mechanisms employed by static malware:

- ▶ Entry-point obscuring
- ▶ Basic malware encryption
- ▶ Polymorphism
- ▶ Metamorphism
- ▶ Anti-reversing

The following list are the common protective mechanisms employed by dynamic malware:

- ▶ Anti-debugging
- ▶ Anti-sandboxing
- ▶ Environment lock
- ▶ Anti-AV scanning
- ▶ Network behavior protection

Familiarizing yourself with these protective mechanisms regardless of which malware state they are employed in enables you to make adjustments to the analysis process so that analysis can proceed.

CHAPTER 5

Malware Dependencies

A malware's main purpose is to execute effectively on the target system to achieve its directive. If it is not able to do this, then it has failed. This is what you want. You want the malware to fail. This is why there are many safeguards in place to prevent, detect, and respond to malware attack. Organizations invest money in different security products and security teams to make sure that malware will fail if it ever finds itself on the target system.

But when it comes to malware analysis, the opposite is desired. You want the malware to function as intended by the attacker. You want it to execute all the functions it has. The more functions or capabilities the malware exhibits during execution, the better it is for malware analysts and researchers. The more successful the malware is at executing on a target system, the more data that can be gathered, which leads to understanding the malware's behavior and main directive. All of this of course must happen in a controlled environment.

But this is not a perfect world. Malware is not perfect. Although malware is designed to execute (and even if you want it to execute), it might not be able to do so because of some factors. Malware, after all, is software. Like other software, it can have flaws or bugs that might prevent it to execute all or some of its functions. A flawed malware is useless and usually not analyzed further. A malware that is buggy is the same thing and not analyzed further. Although it is tempting to try to fix a buggy malware to see how it works, it is a debatable task. In the industry, the consensus is that this is unethical.

For malware that does not work because of flaws and bugs, it is often named with the DAM or INT extension, such as W32/MalwareFamily.DAM or W32/MalwareFamily.INT. DAM stands for damaged, while INT stands for INTENDED. DAM is usually used for flawed malware because the malware design itself is the main culprit of why it does not work; hence, it is damaged from the get-go. INT, on the other hand, is used for buggy malware. The malware is intended to function in a certain way, but because of a bug or bugs in its code, it is not able to do so.

> **NOTE**
>
> *The distinction between DAM and INT is not always followed in detection names. In most cases, all flawed and buggy malware is just given a DAM extension.*

Malware that does not have flaws and bugs may not run perfectly in the target system. There can be other impediments for malware to execute or function properly as intended by the attackers. In some cases, malware execution can stall or proceed only in parts, meaning that only a few functions execute while the rest do not. And in malware analysis, you want the malware to execute all functions.

The reason for non-execution or partial execution of malware is known as *malware dependencies*. Just like any other software, malware has dependencies for it to function properly. Think of scanning software that has all the bells and whistles to enable a user to scan from any printer or from a mobile device camera, with the scanned object saved directly to a computer. Without the main drivers that enable it to communicate with the hardware used for scanning, the software will not function as intended. Another example is a script that reads social media messages and then displays the messages on a customized user interface. Even if the script is flawlessly written but executed in a system without the library to support the social media protocol, it will not work. This is true for malware, as well. Without the presence of its dependencies, it will not function normally.

In this chapter, I will discuss the different malware dependencies that influence the successful execution of malware. Understanding these dependencies is key to creating an effective, controlled environment for malware dynamic analysis.

Dependency Types

Malware, like any other software, has dependencies for it to function properly. The more sophisticated the malware is, the more dependencies it has. This is true especially for malware used for targeted attacks. For example, a malware that will be used to attack Organization A will be designed to run only in endpoints present in Organization A. The malware is able to accomplish this by adding a dependency that is present only in Organization A's endpoints. An example dependency is a logged-in username. If the username is preceded by ORGA and has the format ORGA\username, then the malware assumes that it is running in an endpoint in Organization A and thus will function according to plan.

> **NOTE**
>
> *Malware dependencies can be intended or unintended. They are intended if the attacker needs them as conditions or triggers, and they are unintended if the attacker designed the malware in a controlled lab and failed to take into consideration that not all the dependencies the malware needs to run are present in a target system.*

Malware dependencies can range from the system's characteristics, as discussed earlier, to user-driven events. They are divided into the following:

- ▶ Environment dependencies
- ▶ Program dependencies

- ▶ Timing dependencies
- ▶ Event dependencies
- ▶ User dependencies
- ▶ File dependencies

Environment Dependencies

If all the systems in the world had uniform environments, malware analysis would be easy. Then again, it would be easy for the attackers too. The way a malware operates is confined within the environment's digital physics. This is true for all software as well. Each environment has its own rules of digital physics. As a consequence of this, a malware written for one environment will not function in another environment. It is as simple as that.

> ### *NOTE*
>
> *Most malware writers design their malware to be environment-agnostic by piggybacking on popular programs used across different environments such as a multi-platform web browser.*

Therefore, for a malware to successfully execute, it must be running in the right environment. Dependency on the system environment is the most critical dependency of all. Violate this and the malware is useless. This is why static malware handling and storage are often done in an environment in which the malware will not run.

Environment dependencies include the following:

- ▶ Operating system
- ▶ System settings
- ▶ Virtualization

Operating System

The operating system (OS) is the link between applications and system hardware. It is a software platform that manages hardware, peripherals, and any other resources the system uses. Without it, no application would be able to run or communicate with any hardware resources such as the keyboard, mouse, and monitor. For an application to function properly in a system, it must be written to run in the operating system that is present on the system. Malware is an application, so it must be written, therefore, to run in the operating system that is running on the target system.

An operating system dependency is quite self-explanatory. The malware has to be executed in the operating system it was written for. But it is important to remember that operating systems are not static; they are dynamic. This means there will be bugs discovered that need to be fixed or features that need to be added to improve the operating system's functionalities. These fixes and improvements come in the form of service packs (SPs).

> **TIP**
>
> *Get the latest service pack or update for Windows from http://windows.microsoft.com/en-us/windows/service-packs-download#sptabs=win8other.*

Different Windows versions can have different service pack levels. In some cases, a malware will run on a Windows system only with the latest service pack, or in the case of older malware, they might run properly only with older service packs installed. This is because service packs introduce several updates and bug fixes that might impact or close the holes that malware exploits to execute properly. Service packs also modify some system structure that renders old malware to be useless because the new structure is unsupported by the malware code. For example, disabling autorun, which is covered under the Security Advisory (SA) 967940 update, has contributed to a decline in the autorun capability exploiting malware and having sandboxes with this update installed will not be able to properly see the autorun capabilities of these types of malware. Therefore, it is important to be mindful of service pack changes that might affect malware execution.

> **TIP**
>
> *Always keep different OS flavors and service packs on hand. You never know when you will need them.*

An executable written for a specific operating system will have a format specific to that operating system. Only the operating system it is written for will be able to understand that specific file format and thus execute the file. This is a good way to determine whether a certain executable will run in a target system. There are lots of tools that can be used to determine an executable's file format. This enables you to know whether the file is worth analyzing in the first place. For example, an executable file determined to be a Linux executable is of no interest to you if you are concentrating on Windows executable files. If this is the case, you do not need to analyze the file further.

In automated malware analysis systems, this is an important process in weeding out files. Executable files or any other file format that is not supported by the automated malware analysis system will not be submitted anymore. These files will be discarded, which saves sandbox resources. Say a system receives 100,000 samples a day, but 30 percent of those samples are unsupported. If each file is processed for 30 seconds in the sandbox, then weeding out those files saves the system 900,000 seconds, or 250 hours.

System Settings

System settings are another important aspect of successfully executing malware. A restrictive setting might not be a good idea when it comes to providing malware with an environment to properly run on. Although some malware is designed to circumvent even the most restrictive settings, it is still a good idea to make a malware test environment more malware friendly. This also includes a more relaxed setting for other key programs that malware utilizes, such as Internet browsers.

> **TIP**
>
> *In some cases, malware will expect a more restrictive setting, especially if it is written for targeted attacks. If this is the case, always keep environment images with restrictive settings.*

You can find the Windows 7 security settings in the Control Panel, as shown in Figure 5-1.

If you want malware to connect freely to the network resources it needs, you will have to turn off or deactivate the network firewall. If you want the malware to do what it needs to do in the host, you need to disable virus protection, spyware, unwanted software protection, and Windows Defender, among others. User Account Control (UAC) will need to be disabled as well so the malware can make whatever changes it needs to the system during installation or infection.

Virtualization

You can implement a malware test environment in two ways: virtualized and bare metal. Most implementations are virtualized because those implementations are cheaper (one machine can host multiple guest OSs) and faster to restore. But with the rise of virtualization-aware malware, they are not always the best choice unless the analyst knows beforehand that the malware being analyzed is not virtualization-aware or virtual-aware.

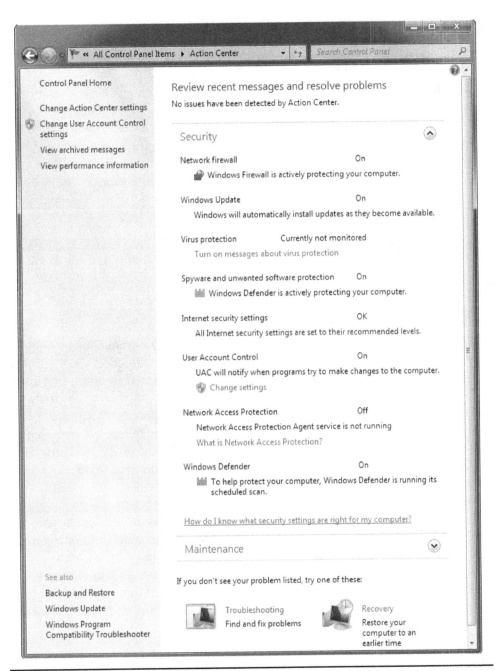

Figure 5-1   *Windows 7 security settings.*

LINGO

Virtualization-aware, *virtual-ware*, and **VM-aware** all mean the same thing.

Although there are tricks that can be employed to fool the malware that it is not running in a virtualized environment, it takes only a short amount of time for the malware writers to circumvent this, especially if the trick is already public. If it is already in the public domain, chances are the malware writers are already working for a solution to undermine that specific trick. Therefore, it is always advisable to have a bare-metal system ready when the need arises.

TIP

When people ask me which implementation I prefer, I always tell them that I run an unknown malware in a virtualized environment first, and when nothing happens, then I use my bare-metal environment.

Program Dependencies

Malware that has specific functions most of the time has program dependencies. Some malware utilizes specific programs for it to achieve its directive. The programs or applications the malware depends on are usually common on systems that are used regularly but not in dynamic analysis systems. This is the reason why malware runs successfully in a victim system but not in a test environment. To mitigate this, the test environment or malware analysis system must mimic a system that is used for everyday computing. Familiarizing yourself with the often-used program utilized by malware will help you in setting up a test environment that is as close to a real-world computing system that is being used regularly.

For example, most mass-mailing worms need the presence of an e-mail client. If no e-mail client is installed, they will not work. The malware will not be able to send copies of itself through e-mail. The most common e-mail client that is often abused by malware is Outlook. Having Outlook installed in a target system will help in satisfying this program dependency. But simply having Outlook may not be enough. In most cases, a mass-mailer malware will need to read an existing address book to know where to send copies of itself. An empty address book will not work; the address book must have entries.

TIP

Put entries in the address book of a malware test environment that point to e-mails that you control. This will help you determine whether the mass-mailer is a success and what kind of e-mail is being sent. This is good for formulating an anti-spam solution.

Attackers understand that not all target systems will have Outlook, especially those systems that are owned by home users. If this is the case, mass-mailers will often utilize Outlook Express, which comes with Windows. To make sure that the malware can successfully utilize it, Outlook Express must be configured, and the address book must be populated. Take note that newer versions of Windows do not have Outlook Express anymore, but if the test environment uses a flavor of Windows with Outlook Express, it must be configured to make the system more malware friendly.

Another popular program that malware is often dependent on is the Internet browser. Everybody who owns or has access to a computer, be it a desktop or mobile device, will always use an Internet browser. This is why the browser is also arguably the most abused program. It is not only used as a dependency but also used as an infection vector for malware. An Internet browser is also a good candidate for exploitation by the attackers, especially if it has lots of vulnerabilities. An attacker can exploit any of the Internet browser's known vulnerabilities and deploy a malware to a target system.

The presence of vulnerabilities is not the only reason why Internet browsers are important to attackers. Going back to program dependency, Internet browsers are our windows to the Internet. Browsers enable all of us to access web-based services such as webmail and social networks. A malware that wants to minimize program dependency on something that is already installed on a possible target system that almost everybody uses finds Internet browsers an attractive candidate. For example, a malware that wants to spam e-mails can hook into an Internet browser so that every time a user logs in to a webmail service, the malware can take over and send spammed copies of itself to the contact lists of the compromised user and even reply automatically to new e-mails that are received. It is therefore important to have an analysis system where malware like this is submitted to have an Internet browser running and logged in to an active and controlled webmail account.

Another example of a malware that finds Internet browsers useful is one that uses social networks as an infection vector. These types of malware rely on a user to be logged in to a certain social network for the malware to function properly. For example, the Trojan known as Febipos takes advantage of a victim's Facebook account once it compromises the target machine. As described by Microsoft, it performs several social network–related tasks such as liking a page, sharing a post, posting messages, joining a group, inviting friends to a group, commenting on posts, and sending messages and links via chat. For malware with similar behavior, it is important to fire up an Internet browser first and then log in to a controlled social network account on the analysis system before the malware is executed.

Aside from e-mail clients and Internet browsers, Portable Document Format (PDF) readers, chat software, and file-sharing programs are among the programs that malware utilizes for its own malicious purpose.

> **TIP**
>
> *Always keep a collection of different versions of often-exploited programs just in case they aren't available for download anymore.*

Having familiarity with how malware uses the different programs it is dependent on ensures that it will execute as intended in the malware analysis system. A good malware test environment must have all or some of these programs installed to increase the chance of the malware executing properly and the analyst collecting data from the dynamic malware.

Timing Dependencies

Timing is everything. This is also true for malware. Depending on the attack, a malware might go dormant for a significant amount of time before striking, or it can strike immediately after it has taken hold of a target system.

Timing dependencies usually have to do with a malware payload. A malware payload is a malware function that reveals what it really is. It can be considered a malware's main directive. For example, a malware with a payload of deleting all files in the system can be considered a Trojan because of its destructive directive. It is important to determine what a malware's payload is because it enables researchers and analysts to come up with preventive measures and solutions to mitigate it.

Execution of a malware payload can be instant, or it can be based on a specific condition such as date and time, which is known as a time trigger. A malware might wait for a certain time in the day to execute its payload. For example, a malware might trigger its information-stealing function every 3 a.m. when nobody is around. Or the malware might wait for a specific date to activate its payload. The Conficker worm actually grabbed headlines years ago that it was going to trigger some mysterious payload on April 1. Nothing happened. April 1 is April Fool's Day after all.

> **TIP**
>
> *To check whether a system is infected by Conficker, use the Conficker Eye Chart located at www .confickerworkinggroup.org/infection_test/cfeyechart.html.*

A timing dependency can also mean dormancy, where the malware sleeps or does nothing for a certain amount of time. This can range from minutes to even months. This is a common evasive technique against automated malware analysis systems. An analysis system gives malware only a limited time to execute. It is usually 30 seconds to 3 minutes. Because of this timing dependency, the malware will not execute, and therefore no malware activity will be recorded. This is why it is wise to have a manually driven analysis system for special malware such as malware with a timing dependency.

A telltale sign that a malware might have a timing dependency is a function that enables it to determine the local system time. In the old days, it was easy to manipulate malware that had timing dependencies. A simple change in the system date and time to coincide with the malware's trigger usually did the trick. Obviously, the malware writers were aware of this. The malware writers knew that system date and time could be manipulated, especially in malware-testing environments. To mitigate this, the attackers programmed their malware to check Network Time Protocol (NTP) servers to determine the real current date and time. NTP synchronizes the time across computer systems. Of course, malware checking NTP servers works only if the compromised system is online.

Event Dependencies

As I discussed in the previous section, the execution of a malware payload can depend on timing. It can be instant, or it might take a longer period of time. The exact time or length of time before a malware executes its function or payload is called a time trigger. But this is not the only trigger there is. There is also another that is based on a specific condition. This condition can be an event or series of events. It is called an *event trigger*.

An event can be anything that goes on inside the system. Some examples are pressing a key, clicking the mouse, moving the mouse pointer to a certain location, putting the system to sleep, shutting down, and starting up. These events can trigger a malware payload. For example, On Windows, a key press combination of Alt+Prtscrn is used to capture the active window as an image in the clipboard. An information stealer malware might use this as an event trigger to save the current clipboard for later exfiltration. A more complex event can be the execution of an Internet browser followed by a series of keystrokes that spells out an online banking site. This event can trigger a keylogger, desktop capturer, or memory scraper with the purpose of stealing banking credentials.

An event can also be outside the system. For example, a social media or website update can be considered an event. If a certain monitored social media site or website posts something that triggers a malware to act, then that posting is considered a malware trigger event. This is especially useful for botnets that are utilized for spamming jobs. A botnet agent can simply monitor a specific product's website for an announcement, and once an announcement is done, the botnet sends out its spam e-mails that could be carrying malware. For example, if the botnet wants to send spam about a new Apple product, it can simply monitor Apple's website for any announcement of a new product and then trigger its spam to potential victims announcing that they have won that new product and all the user needs to do is to click a link to claim the prize or download or double-click an attachment.

Malware that has event dependencies is challenging when submitted to an automated analysis system. The only time an automated analysis system will succeed in executing the malware is when all of the events are satisfied and thus triggering the malware. In actual practice, malware with event dependencies is often analyzed manually to fully understand its capabilities. Only then will those events be added to an automated analysis system.

Spotting malware that has event dependencies depends on the functions it exhibits. Malware that has functions monitoring any system events or external resource such as online feeds will likely have a payload that is event-triggered.

User Dependencies

Some malware depends on targeted users to achieve its directives. It takes advantage of users in two ways, as follows:

▶ Compromise accomplice
▶ Roles and access

Compromise Accomplice

As much as possible, malware writers want their malware to be able to compromise a target without any form of user interaction. The more silent and hidden the malware is, the less chance it has of being detected. But there are cases where malware needs the user to accomplish its task, and as a result, the users become accomplices to the infection of their own systems.

Users being used by malware as unwitting accomplices to its initial stage of compromise is nothing new. Some malware has always been dependent upon the users to do what the malware cannot do such as bypassing security features that only the user can disable. This is especially true when malware needs the user to click buttons for the malware installation to proceed. Scareware such as fake AV malware is notorious for this. Since it has disguised itself as a legitimate security product to fool the user, the user simply clicks whatever the malware wants the user to click to have the fake AV malware installed on the system. This is a good method of bypassing Windows UAC. Socially engineering the user to grant the malware administrator rights is one sure way of getting the malware installed on the target system. For this type of user dependency to be successful, the malware must be able to fool users through social engineering or scare tactics, which are techniques used by scareware, and get them to do anything that the malware or disguised malware wants them to do.

Roles and Access

Malware user dependency is not confined to users clicking buttons or being victims of malware social engineering tactics. Sometimes malware infects a target system based on user roles or a user's position in the company. In this case, a malware targets a system based on what kind of user has access to that system.

> ### NOTE
> *The attackers also use personnel roles to gauge the gullibility of a user. The higher up the person is in the food chain, the more knowledgeable that person is when it comes to security, so utmost care and a much more sinister social engineering technique is often employed.*

The following are the common types of users found in an enterprise:

- ▶ Executives and senior management
- ▶ Technical users
- ▶ HR and finance
- ▶ Marketing and sales
- ▶ Non-critical users

Executives and Senior Management   Systems used by people with high positions within the company such as executives and senior management can contain the most sensitive data about the company. Plus, these users or the systems they use have access to servers that hold lots of information that is vital to the company's business. This can include data that has future company strategy, a release road map of a flagship product, or confidential correspondence with partners, business contacts, and people within the company. Since executives and senior management are the people responsible for steering the company to success through their decision making based on various company or competitor data they have, theft or tampering of these data can be detrimental to the company's business.

Executives and senior management are so important that there is a specific phishing attack geared toward them. It is known as *whale-phishing*. The attack consists of specially crafted e-mails or any correspondence to mislead these head honchos to act on it. The action can result in credential theft or malware installation. It results in credential theft because the content of the whale-phishing e-mail is convincing enough to trick the executives and senior management officials into divulging information such as logon credentials or any other access credentials that will give the attackers access to systems that are reserved for the executives and senior management team only. It results in malware installation because the whale-phishing e-mail can be used as a deployment technology that carries the malware itself or points to a uniform resource locator (URL) where a visit can result in malware installation.

In most organizations that hold sensitive information, executives and the senior management team undergo periodic security training. In some cases, even their immediate family members are briefed about the risk of security and posting information online via social media. For example, say a CEO's daughter posts this in her social media account: "Party at our place. Mom is attending a conference in Vegas." An attacker can use this information to send a whale-phishing attack to the CEO. The e-mail might contain something like, "Thank you for attending our conference in Vegas. As a token of our appreciation, please download the certificate attached in this e-mail." Here is another variation: "Thank you for attending our conference in Vegas. We would really appreciate it if you can provide us with your feedback. Please click the link to take you to the survey. After completing the survey, we will send you a $100 certificate that you can use for next year's conference." There are two things that can happen here. The attachment that claims to be a certificate is malware, and the link that is being passed as a survey is a drive-by download site.

Another way of taking advantage of the information posted by the daughter is through snail mail. Instead of sending a whale-phishing e-mail, a letter is sent through the postal service with a certificate and a note requesting the CEO to visit a certain URL. Another variation of this is that instead of a URL, a USB stick is included as a sign of appreciation for attending, but unknown to the CEO, this USB stick contains malware.

For some reason, most people trust postal mail more than e-mail, prompting the attackers to take advantage of this human behavior.

Technical Users Technical users are attractive targets because they have access to the company's goodies. The research and development department, for example, has access to the most valuable intellectual property of the company such as new concept research, source code, or detailed information about a product's technology. These users also are the ones who get their hands dirty because they are accessing systems with sensitive data all the time. Just think of the following roles in this group, to name a few:

▶ Researcher

▶ Analyst

▶ Developer

▶ Quality assurance

▶ Architect

▶ Engineer

▶ Database administrator

The amount of data these roles have access to can be attractive to attackers, especially if the attack is company espionage.

Another group of technical users is the IT department. This is probably the most important group in this role, especially if the attack is about network compromise and planting a backdoor for long-term access. IT personnel have access to information and details about the organization's network infrastructure. They also have access to other credentials that serve as keys to the kingdom. This makes it attractive to attackers because it enables them to compromise not only systems within the company but also systems of partner organizations if the credentials are available.

HR and Finance Information about company employees resides in systems that human resources (HR) personnel have access to. The information in these systems can include salaries, benefits, performance ratings, and other job-related information. But most importantly, these systems contain personal private information (PPI) that is associated with each employee. Some of the PPI that can be found in an employee information database are Social Security numbers, parents' full names, birthdays, government ID numbers, and any sensitive information that is unique to the employee. The misuse of this sensitive and private information can lead to identity theft. PPI can also be used to blackmail an employee and become the attacker's inside connection to the company. For example, instead of planning for sophisticated malware deployment technology, the attacker can simply ask the blackmailed employee to execute a malicious binary in the company's network.

The financial data of a company reflects how financially healthy the company is. It can also include financial statements that potential investors might be interested in. Financial data is attractive to attackers because it can be used by a competing organization to gauge its competitor's financial capability and plan around it. It can also be leaked publicly, which could be detrimental to the company, especially if there are anomalies found in it.

In some organizations, HR and financial data resides in the same system. Other data that can be useful to attackers consists of the employees' bank accounts, especially those who conduct direct deposit of their salaries. Although it's not common, an attacker can manufacture forged checks using an employee's checking account number and routing information and make it payable as cash.

Marketing and Sales   Systems that are used by marketing and sales contain information about customers. Aside from the customer name, customer information can also contain company name, position in the company, address, e-mail, phone number, and fax number. Attackers can use this information in so many ways; some of them are the following:

▶ **Phishing attack targets**   Attackers can use the e-mail addresses as recipients of spam, and depending on the person's position, a whale-phishing attack can be conducted.

▶ **Spoofed e-mail address**   Attackers can use the e-mail addresses in the From field of their spam campaign.

▶ **For sale**   Attackers can sell the information to third-party marketing entities or to competing organizations.

Aside from customer information, the systems used by marketing and sales can also contain customer leads and marketing strategy. Customer leads are important because they have the potential to become customers. A good way for organizations to get potential customers is through conferences. An organization might offer something for free such as a shirt or stress ball in exchange for scanning the customer's conference badge. A conference badge contains information such as name, company, role, e-mail, and phone number. After the conference, these potential customers will get phone calls or e-mails following up whether their company is interested in buying whatever product or service that organization is offering. As you can see, one conference badge scan can cost the organization a shirt, which if bought in bulk is roughly $8 to $10 each. This is how much the data from one potential customer costs the organization. Ten thousand customer leads can cost $80,000 to $100,000. An attacker who steals this kind of information can sell it for cheap to a competing organization. The competing organization will not only have a copy of the list of potential customers but also save time, effort, and money if the competing organization were to acquire potential customer leads itself through conferences and other means.

Other important information that may be valuable to a competing entity is marketing strategy. This information can be found in systems accessed by marketing and sales.

Non-critical Users   Non-critical users are those who have limited access to any data within an organization. The only data these users have access to is data considered to be in the lowest spectrum of sensitivity. This is something the company does not mind leaking to the public because it has little value or will not affect the company's business in anyway if it gets stolen. One example of a non-critical user is a front-desk employee, who has access only to scheduling data. Attacking this role may lead only to systems with minimal sensitive data or no sensitive data at all. The danger is only when the system's non-critical users use or have access to a network that has systems connected to it that contain sensitive data.

File Dependencies

Malware that steals information, also known as information stealers, is the most common type of malware that has file dependencies, especially malware designed to steal documents. This type of information stealer functions by enumerating files inside the Documents folder or any folder where documents are saved. It then proceeds to compare the names of the documents to keywords that the malware has coded in its code or found in a configuration file that the malware is using. A few example keywords are *financial, salary, report, employee, incentive,* and so on. If a file matches any of these keywords, the malware will send copies of the matching document to a drop zone that is controlled by the attacker.

Another method of picking which documents to steal is through filename extensions. An information stealer, instead of using keywords, will just send copies of all documents that have extensions of .DOC, .DOCX, .XLS, .XLSX, .PPT, .PPTX, .PNG, .JPG, .TIF, and so on. Attackers understand that these files are data heavy, which is why exfiltration of stolen information is sometimes done not in bulk but in a staggered way. The only drawback of this is that once the malware is found and stopped, the attacker is left with corrupted data.

> **NOTE**
>
> *Information stealers also target graphic files, especially if the attack is against a publication company.*

In most cases, this behavior of information stealers can be triggered only by the presence of these files. It is therefore important to have documents and graphic files present in a sandbox environment to entice information stealers to activate their file-stealing capabilities. But be mindful of document sizes also; most information stealers have a checking mechanism. The checking mechanism has to do with size. If the files have 0 bytes, nothing will happen. So, it is important for these dummy files to have dummy information inside them.

During analysis, if the dummy files suddenly disappear, it means that the information stealer has a destructive functionality. This functionality is activated once a copy of the stolen file has been exfiltrated. The information stealer deletes the files from the compromised machine, leaving the victim with nothing.

Recap

In this chapter, I discussed the different malware dependencies and how each affects the successful execution of malware. They are as follows:

- ▶ Environment dependencies
- ▶ Program dependencies
- ▶ Timing dependencies
- ▶ Event dependencies
- ▶ User dependencies
- ▶ File dependencies

Knowing a malware's dependencies is critical to ensuring that it is able to execute all of its intended function in a controlled environment. This is key when extracting information during dynamic analysis. A malware that is running successfully in a controlled environment enables you to capture more data to understand the malware's main directive.

Malware Research Lab

Malware Collection

N ow that you have an idea of the different classes of malware, the different technologies used to deploy malware, the different protective mechanisms malware employs to protect itself, and the different dependencies malware has to execute properly in a target system, you are ready to tackle malware.

The ability to analyze, scrutinize, and examine malware requires the use of computer systems that are set up for the purpose of unraveling the mysteries of malware. These computer systems serve as the malware analyst's research lab, commonly known as a *malware research lab*. A malware research lab is a collection of systems fully under the control of malware researchers and analysts. It is not for production nor does it serve any other purpose besides the research and analysis of malware. A malware research lab consists of different systems that have a special purpose, the most common of which are the following:

- ▶ Malware collection lab
- ▶ Static analysis lab
- ▶ Dynamic analysis lab

A malware collection lab is a system or collection of systems designed solely to collect malware samples from different sources. A static analysis lab is designed to gather data from malware while it is at rest, and a dynamic analysis lab is designed to gather data from malware while it is in motion.

In this chapter, I will concentrate on malware collection. I will discuss the different sources of malware samples and the ways of collecting them from these sources.

The following are the most common sources of malware samples:

- ▶ Your own backyard
- ▶ Free sources
- ▶ Research mailing lists
- ▶ Sample exchange
- ▶ Commercial sources
- ▶ Honeypots

Before malware analysis can begin, you must have malware samples on hand. Malware has to be available. It is therefore important that you first familiarize yourself with the different sources of malware.

Your Own Backyard

Before you look any further, it's always better to look somewhere close to home. Systems that are in "your own backyard" are a good source of malware samples. These are systems you have at home and those that belong to your friends and relatives. Have you ever been called by your non-tech-savvy friends, siblings, cousins, nieces, nephews, aunts, uncles, parents, or even grandparents and asked for help to solve whatever issues they were having with their computers? Probably almost all of us have experienced something like this. And after looking at the problem, more often than not, it was probably caused by malware. So, these systems that are in "your own backyard" are good sources of malware samples.

Not only do you have a good source of malware, but you can see the malware in action in a target environment outside of a controlled malware analysis system. In other words, you are seeing the malware in the wild. Once you have access to an infected system and can see the malware in action, the next best thing to do is to extract the sample from the infected system.

This is easier said than done. Collecting malware from infected systems is different from analyzing malware. In malware analysis, you have an idea which suspicious or malicious binary or process is running; therefore, it is easy to monitor and account for the changes it makes on the target system. In malware collection, you have no idea what binary or process is causing the infection. Finding/extracting malicious files from an infected machine requires a different set of skills. It requires skills in system forensics, which are important skills for a malware incident responder to have.

But sometimes extracting the malware is easy, such as when e-mail is used by the attackers as the malware deployment technology. E-mail is the most common malware deployment technology, and the e-mail attack vector can be carrying the malicious file or a link to a drive-by download site. In cases like this, you can easily extract and collect the malware for analysis purposes.

But if there are no traces of any malware deployment technology and the malware is already live in the system, then you need to use special tools to determine where the malware is hiding in the system so it can be extracted. Although system forensics is beyond the scope of this book, I will list the steps to help you identify and extract malware from an infected system and show some tools you can use during each step.

> ### NOTE
> *The only difference between a live infected or compromised system and a controlled malware analysis environment is that the compromised system is not isolated. You can use the same tools for dynamic analysis as for live compromised systems.*

The following steps will help you identify and extract malware from an infected system:

1. Scan for malicious files.
2. Look for active rootkits.
3. Inspect startup programs.
4. Inspect running processes.
5. Extract suspicious files.

Scan for Malicious Files

The first thing to do when identifying which file is possibly malicious is to use an antivirus (AV) scanner. If the victimized system has an AV product installed and the malware is already active, chances are the AV product installed in the system will not detect the malware. If this is the case, try updating the installed antivirus product's signature database. If detection yields nothing even after the update, you will use other alternatives such as using free online scanning services. The following are some of my favorites:

▶ **Trend Micro HouseCall** http://housecall.trendmicro.com/
▶ **F-Secure Online Scanner** http://www.f-secure.com/en/web/home_global/online-scanner

Free malware detection and removal tools are an alternative to free online virus scanners. Unlike free online scanners, these tools have to be downloaded and installed. They are also AV products. So if the compromised system does not have these tools installed yet, this is a good time to do so. They are as follows:

▶ **Microsoft Security Essentials** http://windows.microsoft.com/en-us/windows/security-essentials-download
▶ **Comodo Cleaning Essentials** http://www.comodo.com/business-security/network-protection/cleaning_essentials.php
▶ **Kaspersky Security Scan** http://www.kaspersky.com/free-virus-scan

Once installed, simply run a full system scan and wait for the result.

Look for Active Rootkits

If the antivirus scanning does not reveal anything, there are a couple of reasons for this. One is that the malware is new, and there is no signature available to detect it yet. The other is that the malware can be employing a rootkit technology. One or both of these reasons can apply to a specific malware that is undetected in the system.

If the malware is new, which is more likely, then it may or may not be using a rootkit technology. If it is not using a rootkit technology, then it makes it easier to determine which binary is the culprit and extract it. But if it is using a rootkit technology, the next logical step is to look for active rootkits in the system.

The following tools are useful in doing this:

► **RootkitRevealer by Microsoft** http://download.cnet.com/ RootkitRevealer/3000-2248_4-10543918.html

► **TDSSKiller by Kaspersky** https://support.kaspersky.com/us/viruses/ utility#TDSSKiller

RootkitRevealer is an advanced rootkit detection utility that runs on Windows XP (32-bit) and Windows Server 2003 (32-bit). Its output is a list of registry and file system application programming interface (API) discrepancies that may indicate the presence of a user-mode or kernel-mode rootkit. RootkitRevealer successfully detects many persistent rootkits including AFX, Vanquish, and HackerDefender.[1] Figure 6-1 shows an example of output from a RootkitRevealer scan.

TDSSKiller by Kaspersky is a rootkit detection utility that detects and removes the following rootkits: TDSS, SST, Pihar, ZeroAccess, Sinowal, Whistler, Phanta, Trup, Stoned, RLoader, Cmoser, and Cidox. It also detects rootkit-like anomalies.

If none of the previous steps reveals anything, then you can follow a series of steps essentially calling for analyzing the infected system itself. You will do this by inspecting all the startup programs and the running processes in the system. Figure 6-2 shows an example of a scan result from TDSSKiller.

> **NOTE**
>
> *Rootkit detection tools are good at detecting known rootkits but may have difficulty in detecting new ones.*

---

[1] Microsoft Technet: http://technet.microsoft.com/en-US/.

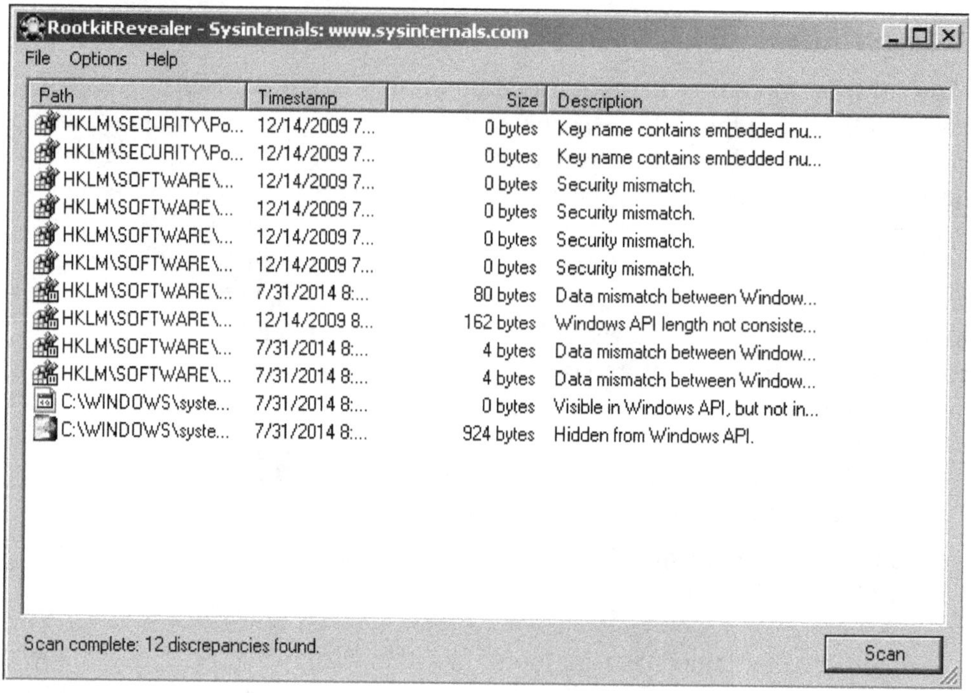

Figure 6-1 *RootkitRevealer scan output.*

Inspect Startup Programs

For malware to continue establishing a foothold on the compromised system, it needs to have the ability to survive a reboot or startup. This a common characteristics across all classes of malware; therefore, the next logical step is to inspect the different programs that start up in the compromised system.

To determine the different applications that start up, you can use the following tools:

► **Autoruns by Microsoft** http://technet.microsoft.com/en-us/sysinternals/bb963902.aspx

► **Autorun Analyzer by Comodo** http://www.comodo.com/business-security/network-protection/cleaning_essentials.php

Both of these tools are designed to display the different applications or programs that start up during bootup. They also hide known benign startup applications, leaving only those that are not recognized by the tools.

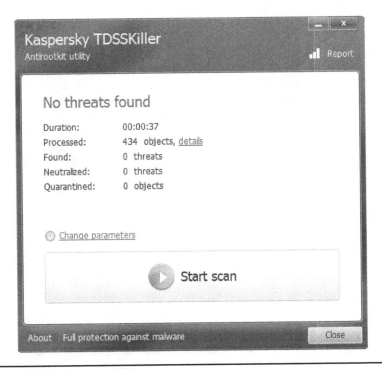

Figure 6-2   *TDSSKiller scan result.*

Microsoft Autoruns, as shown in Figure 6-3, filters the following:

► Empty locations
► Verified code signatures
► Microsoft entries

The Comodo Autorun Analyzer, as shown in Figure 6-4, does not have the same filter granularity as Microsoft Autoruns.

Take note that Autorun Analyzer by Comodo is part of Comodo Cleaning Essentials (CCE), so if you have CCE installed already, simply go to the Tools menu and select Open Autorun Analyzer. Another way of running Autorun Analyzer is to go to the folder where CCE is installed and double-click Autoruns.EXE.

Take note that the tools mentioned in this section concentrate on applications that start up in the compromised system. There are other ways a malware can start up aside from this, one of which is by infecting the Master Boot Record (MBR) or the boot sector. This requires a different set of tools, known as boot analyzer tools.

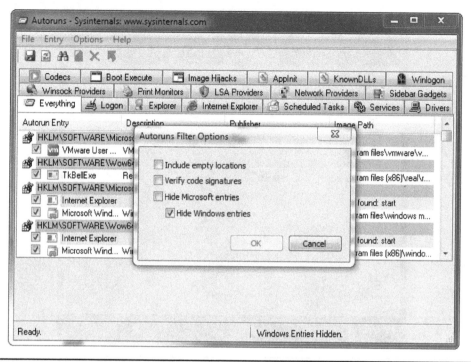

Figure 6-3 *Microsoft Autoruns filter.*

The following are the most common boot analyzer tools:

▶ **GMER**   http://www.gmer.net

▶ **MbrScan**   http://eric71.geekstogo.com/tools/MbrScan.exe

▶ **MBR Backup**: http://www.trojanhunter.com/products/mbr-backup/

▶ **Boot Sector Explorer**   http://www.pendriveapps.com/boot-sector-explorer-backup-and-restore-mbr/

The previous two tools are good for getting an image of the MBR and the boot sector. At Nate's MBR and Boot Sector Analyzer webpage (http://www.aqfire .com/boot/), you can upload an image for analysis.

Another way to image an MBR or a boot sector is by using hex editors. Lots of hex editors are available, but the most popular and a favorite of mine is WinHex. You can download it from http://www.winhex.com/disk-editor.html.

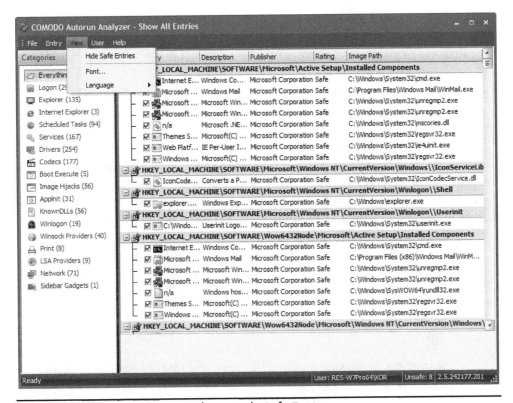

Figure 6-4 *Comodo Autorun Analyzer, Hide Safe Entries menu.*

These are but a sampling of MBR and boot sector tools. There are many more available for download, but please be careful when using these tools. You have to be fully aware of their capabilities and the risks they carry.

TIP

It is good practice to treat free tools as suspicious and analyze them to determine whether there are hidden functionalities that will prove detrimental to the user's system.

Inspect Running Processes

Any software, including malware, running in a system has its own process space. The challenge here is to determine which software is the malware. To do this, you need to inspect a good number of running processes on the system.

To inspect running processes, you can use the following tools:

▶ **Process Explorer by Microsoft** http://technet.microsoft.com/en-us/ sysinternals/bb896653.aspx

▶ **KillSwitch by Comodo** http://www.comodo.com/business-security/ network-protection/cleaning_essentials.php

Both tools give the user the ability to dig deeper into a process. Which tool to use depends on the user's preference. The thing I like about Microsoft Autoruns is the ability to save a process' image in memory, and the things I like about Comodo Autorun Analyzer are its performance graphs and the option to show only unsafe images in memory. Familiarizing yourself with these tools will go a long way in determining a possibly malicious process.

Similar to Autorun Analyzer, KillSwitch, as shown in Figure 6-5, is part of Comodo Cleaning Essentials. To open this tool, go to the Tools menu and select Open KillSwitch. Another alternative of running KillSwitch is to go to the folder where CCE is installed and double-click KillSwitch.EXE.

> ### TIP
> *You must read the terms and conditions of the tools carefully and understand the consequences or effect of using these tools. They might have an unintended effect on the system if used improperly.*

Extract Suspicious Files

Once the suspicious files have been identified by using the different tools and going through the steps listed earlier, it is time to extract the files. In most cases, extracting the files is easier than copying them to external media. But there are instances where the active malware will prevent you from doing this, especially if it has full control of the system. The malware can simply put special permissions on all malware components to prevent them from being copied. If this is the case, one way to extract the malware or suspicious files is by booting the infected system using a different operating system (OS). Good OS candidates are Linux-based distributions such as Ubuntu. This negates whatever special permissions the malware assigned to the malware components, and therefore the files will be easier to extract. How to create an Ubuntu boot disk is described in later chapters.

It is possible that you will end up with a bunch of suspicious files if there is not enough evidence to discount some of them. These extracted files are the ones to

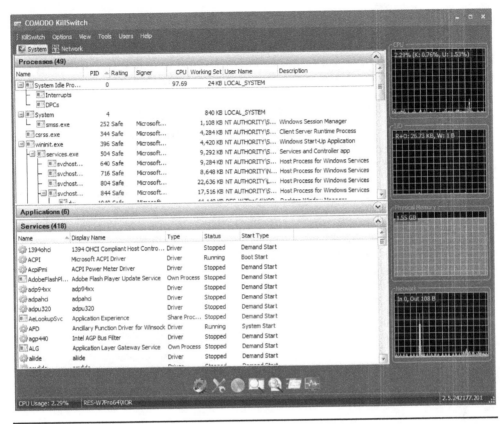

Figure 6-5   *Comodo KillSwitch.*

subject to malware analysis to determine which of them are malware and which of them are not.

The steps just outlined are just a small taste of what is needed to identify and extract malware from an infected system. System forensics is an exciting field that complements malware analysis pretty well. The tools I presented are the most common tools used in system forensics. Experimenting with these tools is a good first step in improving your skills in system forensics.

TIP

To help you start pursuing more knowledge and skill in the field of system forensics, experiment with the tools mentioned in the previous section.

Free Sources

If you don't have the time or energy to devote yourself to helping your friends and relatives with their computer woes, you can always get malware samples from free sources. There are lots of well-meaning researchers who devote time and effort to helping the security community; one of the most awesome things they do is make malware samples available to those who will be using them for research. The following are some of the free sources:

- ► Contagio
- ► KernelMode.info
- ► MalShare.com
- ► Malware.lu
- ► Malware Blacklist
- ► Malwarebytes forum
- ► Malekal's Forum
- ► Open Malware
- ► Tuts4You
- ► VirusShare.com
- ► VX Heaven
- ► Malware trackers

TIP

There is always a risk of infection when using these sources. Please be responsible when clicking links and downloading files. It is always best to access these resources from a machine that is isolated from any production or home network.

Contagio

Contagio is operated by Mila Parkour, a well-known researcher in the security community based in Washington, D.C. Contagio has two excellent sources of malware samples: Contagio Malware Dump and Contagio Sample Exchange.

Contagio Malware Dump

You can find Contagio Malware Dump at http://contagiodump.blogspot.com, as shown in Figure 6-6. This is a good place to discuss and share anything about malware with other researchers. It is a good source not only of malware samples but also other artifacts relating to malware infections and compromise, such as packet captures (PCAPs).

Figure 6-6   *Contagio Malware Dump main page.*

Contagio Malware Exchange

Contagio Malware Exchange, as shown in Figure 6-7, is located at http://contagioexchange.blogspot.com. As explained on the site, this was created to absorb malware samples shared by readers of Contagio. This is meant to be a community-driven malware collection.

KernelMode.info

KernelMode.info, a forum for kernel-mode exploration, is a good source for discussing and exchanging malware samples and anything related to it. Registration is required to join.

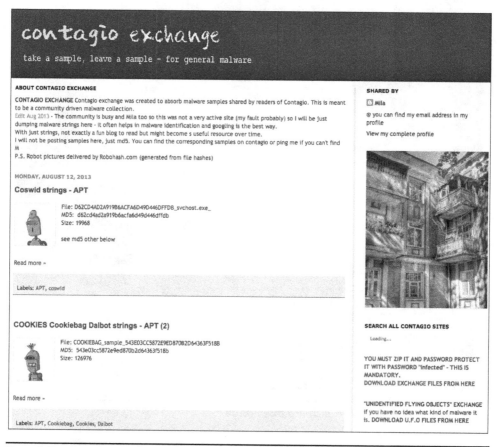

Figure 6-7 *Contagio Malware Exchange main page.*

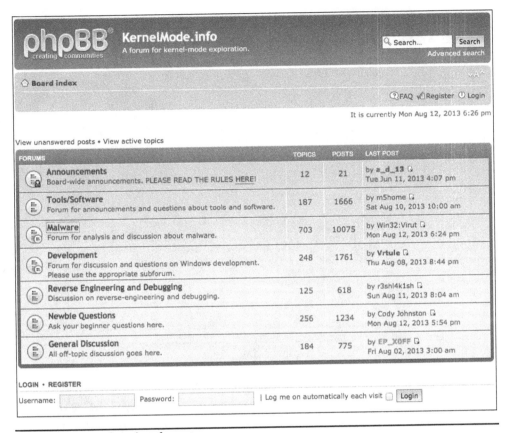

Figure 6-8   *KernelMode.info main page.*

From the main page, as shown in Figure 6-8, clicking the Malware forum leads to topics covering the hottest malware and also to forums where you can request malware samples and view completed malware requests.

MalShare.com

MalShare.com, as stated in its splash page, shares samples collected from online scraping of blacklists and not from any interaction of the owner of the site with customers or clients without their consent. To be able to request samples, the user must have an API key and know the sample's MD5 hash. But before that can happen, you must agree to the legal disclaimer at http://malShare.com. After agreeing to the legal disclaimer, you are taken to http://api.malShare.com, as shown in Figure 6-9, where you can request a sample.

Figure 6-9   *MalShare.com sample request page.*

To get an API key, you must send an e-mail request to api@MalShare.com with the subject "API Key Request." The body of the e-mail must contain the user's name and e-mail address. Figure 6-10 shows what the e-mail request looks like.

Malware.lu

Malware.lu, as shown in Figure 6-11, is a good source for malware samples and malware information articles. It is operated by itrust consulting located in Luxembourg. Registration is required to access the sample repository. To request an account, as explained on the site, send an e-mail to register@malware.lu with the desired username and a short explanation of why you want to have an account.

Malware Blacklist

Malware Blacklist, located at http://malwareblacklist.com, not only contains malware samples but also contains the biggest repository of malicious uniform resource locators (URLs), as shown in Figure 6-12.

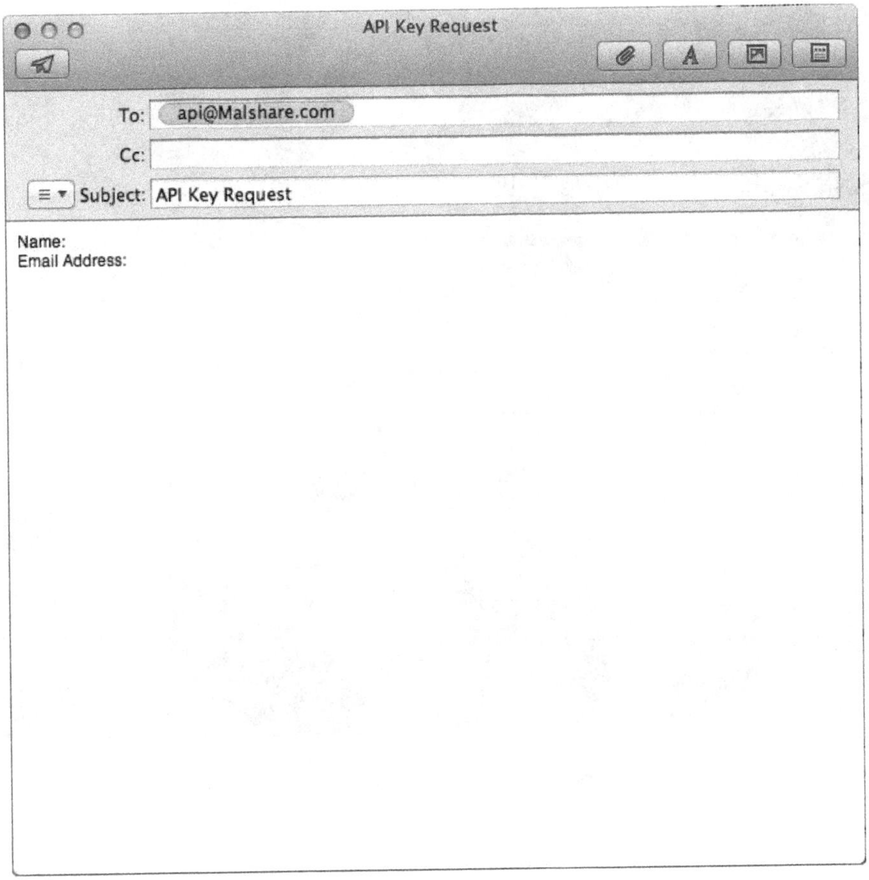

Figure 6-10 *API key request e-mail format.*

Registration is required to download the samples. To register, click Login and then click Create A Free Account. A contact form page, as shown in Figure 6-13, will open. The user must provide all the information asked in the contact form to be able to successfully register.

NOTE

Sometimes there is a limit on the number of downloads a free user can get. The reasons for this can vary. One of the most common reasons is user reputation. A user who contributes more will be able to download more.

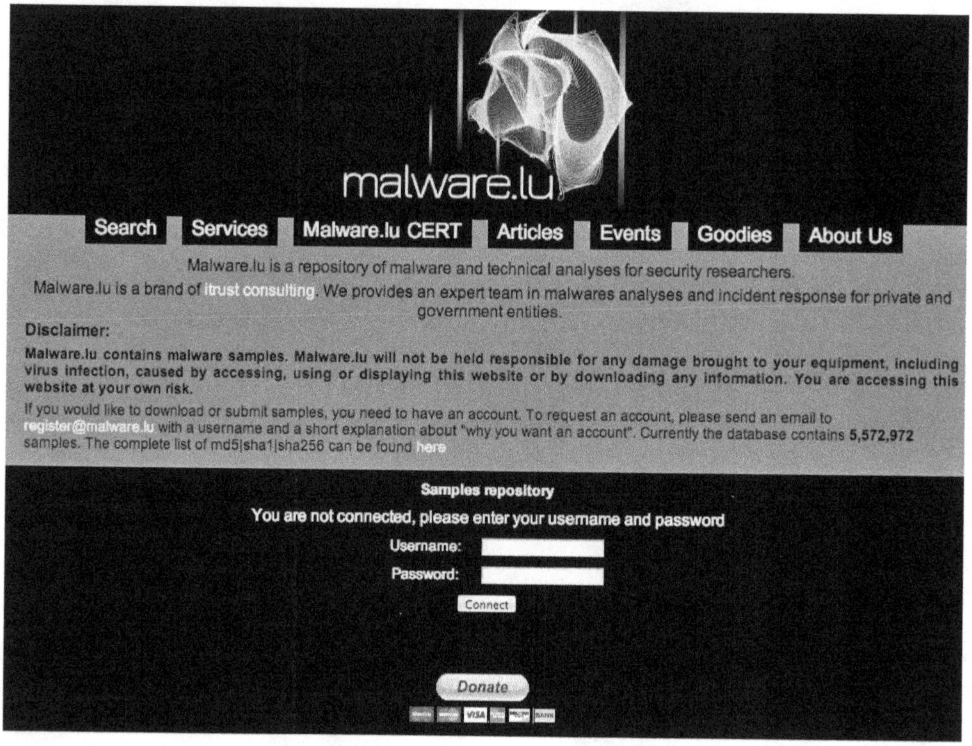

Figure 6-11   *Malware.lu main page.*

Malwarebytes Forum

The Malwarebytes forum is a good source for anything about malware including malware removal. The main forum is located at http://forums.malwarebytes.org. But the main page of interest is the Newest Malware Threats forum. A direct link to this forum is http://bit.ly/13xUEvm.

To gain access to samples, registration is not enough. A registered user has to contact the forum administrators/moderators to ask for access to download samples. This is one way of ensuring that nobody can just download samples and

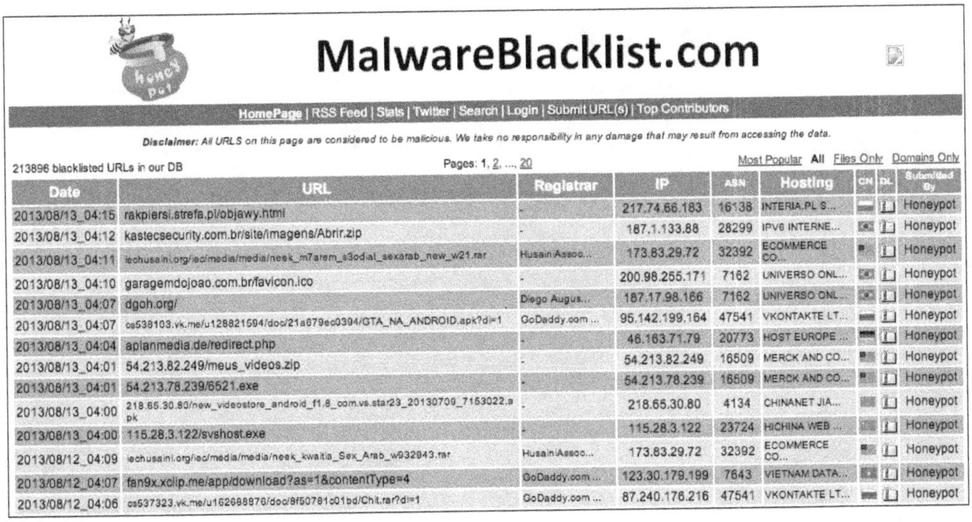

Figure 6-12 *Malware Blacklist main page.*

that only experts who have experience in handling malware will be able to do so. This minimizes the risk of having unwanted malware infection or, worse, an outbreak.

Malekal's Forum

Malekal's Forum is a French forum where malware samples are collected daily and compressed in a single ZIP file that can be downloaded on a daily basis. Malekal's Forum is located at http://malwaredb.malekal.com. You can find the ZIP file containing the daily samples on the lower-right side of the page, as shown in Figure 6-14. Just click the ZIP icon to download the daily collection.

Open Malware

Open Malware is not only a good source for malware samples but a good source for security-related articles. The main page, as shown in Figure 6-15, is located at http://openmalware.org.

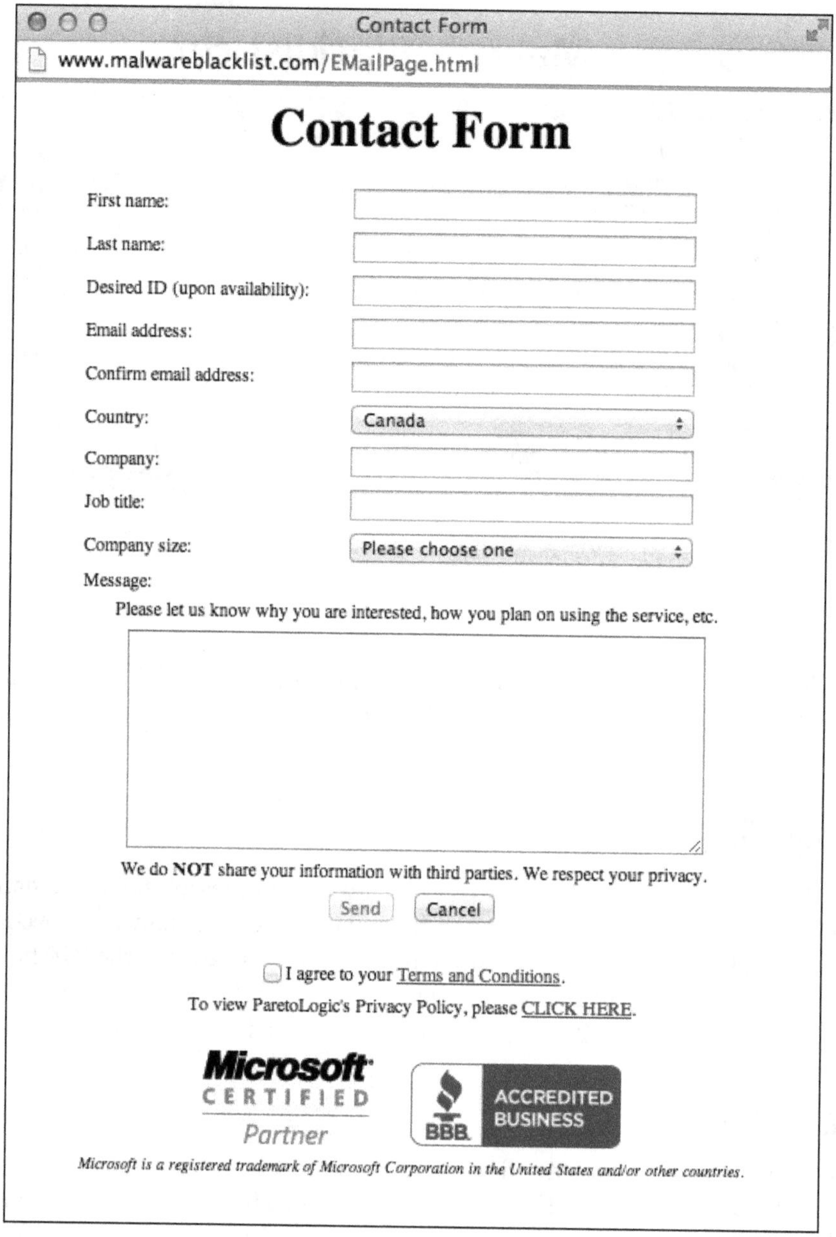

Figure 6-13 *Malware Blacklist contact form.*

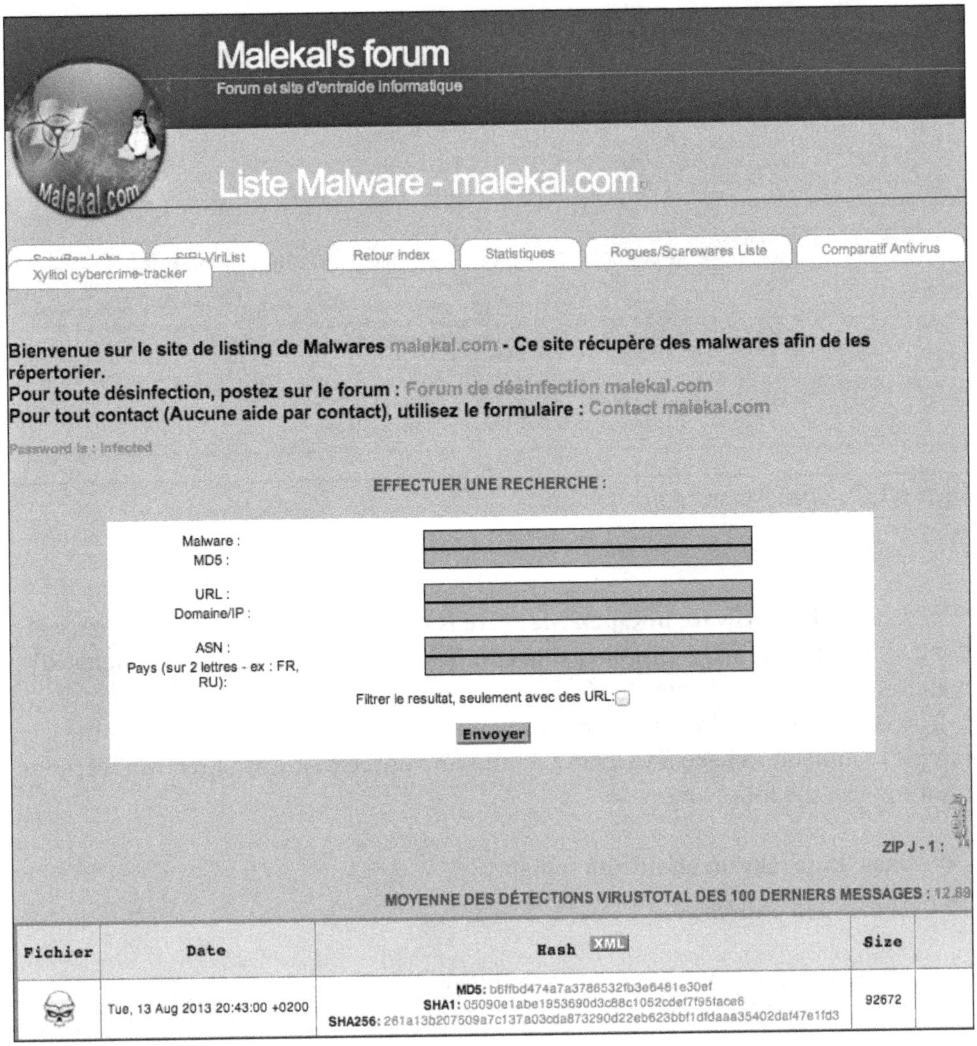

Figure 6-14   *Malekal's Forum main page.*

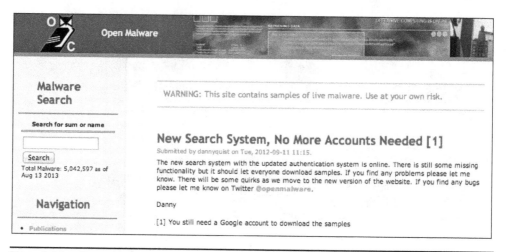

Figure 6-15 *Open Malware main page.*

Searching for malware in Open Malware is easy. You can use a hash or part of the malware name. For example, using Conficker as a search argument yields 20 matches, as shown in Figure 6-16.

You can then download the samples you need. But before downloading the sample, you need to have a Google account and agree to grant Open Malware the right to view the following:

▶ Basic information about the account

▶ The e-mail address

Figure 6-17 shows the splash page that prompts the user to accept these terms.

Notice that in the results page in Figure 6-16, the domain name is http:// gtisc.gatech.edu. This is Georgia Tech's GTISC, which stands for Georgia Tech Information Security Center. Clicking Home on the results page brings the user to http://oc.gtisc.gatech.edu:8080, which is the main page for the search. It does not have any links to any articles. It simply has a search box similar to the one on Open Malware's main page. It has a minimalist design that gets the job done, especially if your main purpose is searching for malware samples.

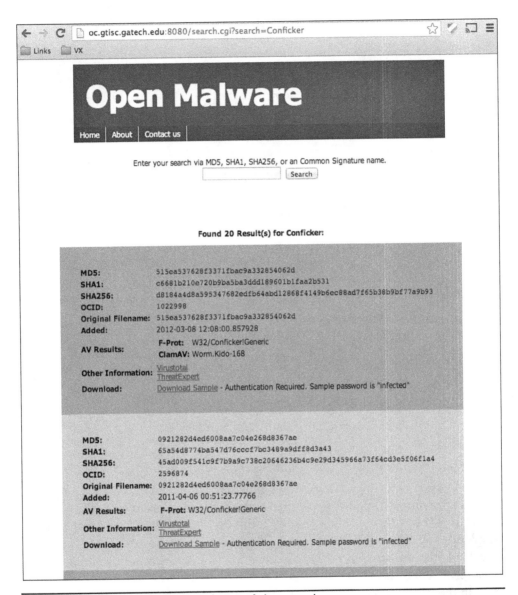

Figure 6-16   *Open Malware result for Conficker search.*

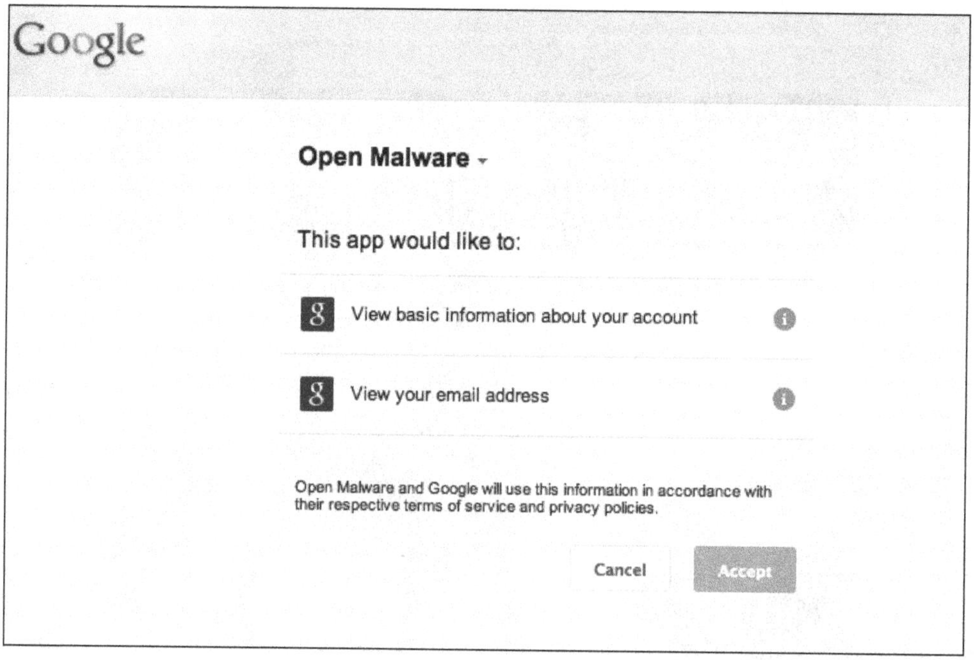

Figure 6-17   *Open Malware splash page that prompts users to give access to their Google accounts.*

Tuts4You

Tuts4You is a forum that caters not only to sharing malware samples but also to educating the user in the art of malware analysis and reversing. This is a good source for anyone who wants to get into battling the malware threat. The forum is located at http://forum.tuts4you.com. From there, you can search for malware samples or any other topics that might interest you. For example, if you want to download StuxNet samples posted by other community members, a simple search for *StuxNet* will bring you to the page, as shown in Figure 6-18, where you can share in the discussion and download the StuxNet sample.

VirusShare.com

VirusShare.com is a no-frills malware sample–sharing site. The most pertinent information about the malware and the download link are right there in front of you, as shown in Figure 6-19.

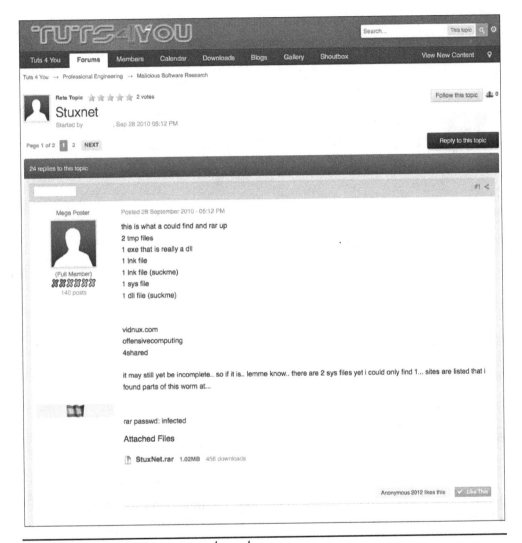

Figure 6-18 *Tuts4You Stuxnet search result.*

Aside from downloading samples individually, which can be done by clicking the download icon in the upper left of the sample information page, you can also download large collections of malware samples. You can find the link to the samples and instructions on how to do this in the "Torrents" section of the page.

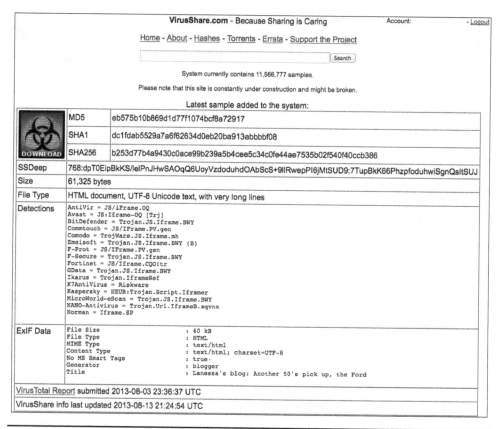

Figure 6-19   *VirusShare.com sample information.*

Registration is needed to be able to download samples. As posted in the site, access to the site is granted via invitation only. You must send an e-mail request to admin@virusshare.com explaining who you are and why you need access.

VX Heaven

VX Heaven, located at http://vxheaven.org, is a good source for classic malware. It contains malware source code, encryption and mutation engines, malware kits, malware simulators, and utilities for malware collection. In addition to those mentioned, VX Heaven contains lots of articles concerning malware technologies.

Malware Trackers

Malware trackers are a good source of in-the-wild malware. An in-the-wild or wild malware is one that is released intentionally or accidentally into the world that has caused infection and compromise or is currently infecting or compromising systems. In other words, these are malware samples that have been used in or are currently being used in an attack campaign.

The following are the most popular malware trackers:

▶ ZeuS tracker

▶ SpyEye tracker

▶ Palevo tracker

These malware trackers are a good source of wild malware and are good sources of command and control (C2) servers, malware download domains, and domain drop zones. In addition to providing this useful information, these malware trackers also provide malicious domains and Internet Protocol (IP) blacklists for download so users can use these blacklists (or *blocklists* as they are referred to by the trackers) to protect systems under their control. Snort rules and IP blacklists for iptables are also available for download.

ZeuS Tracker

ZeuS Tracker tracks the latest active Zeus infections. The main page is https://zeustracker.abuse.ch, but the page where wild Zeus samples can be downloaded is https://zeustracker.abuse.ch/monitor.php?browse=binaries, as shown in Figure 6-20.

> *TIP*
>
> *There is a shortcut to download all Zeus binaries and configuration files in the ZeuS Tracker. The links are https://zeustracker.abuse.ch/downloads/zeusbinaries.zip and https://zeustracker.abuse.ch/downloads/zeusconfigs.zip, respectively.*

SpyEye Tracker

SpyEye Tracker tracks the latest SpyEye infections. The main page is https://spyeyetracker.abuse.ch, but the page where wild SpyEye samples can be downloaded is https://spyeyetracker.abuse.ch/monitor.php?browse=binaries, as shown in Figure 6-21.

> *TIP*
>
> *There is a shortcut to download all SpyEye binaries and configuration files in SpyEye Tracker. The links are https://spyeyetracker.abuse.ch/downloads/spyeyebinaries.zip and https://spyeyetracker.abuse.ch/downloads/spyeyeconfigs.zip, respectively.*

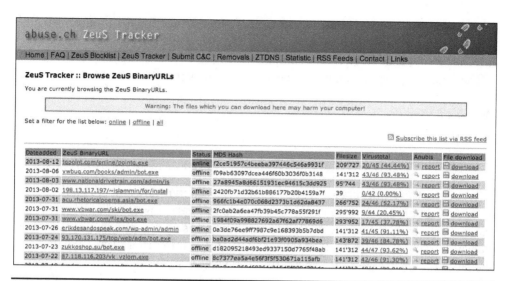

Figure 6-20   *ZeuS Tracker binaries.*

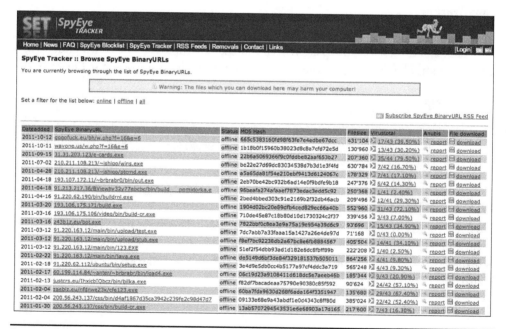

Figure 6-21   *SpyEye Tracker binaries.*

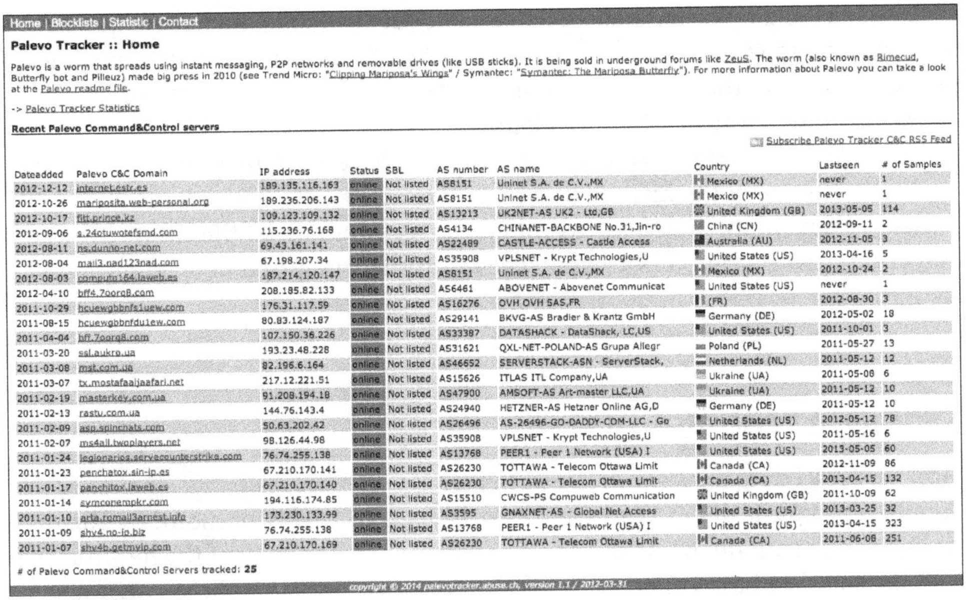

Home | Blocklists | Statistic | Contact

Palevo Tracker :: Home

Palevo is a worm that spreads using instant messaging, P2P networks and removable drives (like USB sticks). It is being sold in underground forums like ZeuS. The worm (also known as Rimecud, Butterfly bot and Pilleuz) made big press in 2010 (see Trend Micro: "Clipping Mariposa's Wings" / Symantec: "Symantec: The Mariposa Butterfly"). For more information about Palevo you can take a look at the Palevo readme file.

-> Palevo Tracker Statistics

Recent Palevo Command&Control servers

Subscribe Palevo Tracker C&C RSS Feed

Dateadded	Palevo C&C Domain	IP address	Status	SBL	AS number	AS name	Country	Lastseen	# of Samples
2012-12-12	internet.estr.es	189.135.116.163	online	Not listed	AS8151	Uninet S.A. de C.V.,MX	Mexico (MX)	never	1
2012-10-26	mariposita.web-personal.org	189.236.206.143	online	Not listed	AS8151	Uninet S.A. de C.V.,MX	Mexico (MX)	never	1
2012-10-17	fitt.prince.kz	109.123.109.132	online	Not listed	AS13213	UK2NET-AS UK2 - Ltd,GB	United Kingdom (GB)	2013-05-05	114
2012-09-06	s.24otuwotefsmd.com	115.236.76.168	online	Not listed	AS4134	CHINANET-BACKBONE No.31,Jin-ro	China (CN)	2012-09-11	2
2012-08-11	ns.dunno-net.com	69.43.161.141	online	Not listed	AS22489	CASTLE-ACCESS - Castle Access	Australia (AU)	2012-11-05	3
2012-08-04	mail3.nad123nad.com	67.198.207.34	online	Not listed	AS35908	VPLSNET - Krypt Technologies,U	United States (US)	2013-04-16	5
2012-08-03	computo164.laweb.es	187.214.120.147	online	Not listed	AS8151	Uninet S.A. de C.V.,MX	Mexico (MX)	2012-10-24	2
2012-04-10	bff4.7oorq8.com	208.185.82.133	online	Not listed	AS6461	ABOVENET - Abovenet Communicat	United States (US)	never	1
2011-10-29	hcuewgbbnfs1uew.com	176.31.117.59	online	Not listed	AS16276	OVH OVH SAS,FR	(FR)	2012-08-30	3
2011-08-15	hcuewgbbnfdu1ew.com	80.83.124.187	online	Not listed	AS29141	BKVG-AS Bradler & Krantz GmbH	Germany (DE)	2012-05-02	18
2011-04-04	bff.7oorq8.com	107.150.36.226	online	Not listed	AS33387	DATASHACK - DataShack, LC,US	United States (US)	2011-10-01	3
2011-03-20	ssl.aukro.ua	193.23.48.228	online	Not listed	AS31621	QXL-NET-POLAND-AS Grupa Allegr	Poland (PL)	2011-05-27	13
2011-03-08	mst.com.ua	82.196.6.164	online	Not listed	AS46652	SERVERSTACK-ASN - ServerStack,	Netherlands (NL)	2011-05-12	12
2011-03-07	tx.mostafaaljaafari.net	217.12.221.51	online	Not listed	AS15626	ITLAS ITL Company,UA	Ukraine (UA)	2011-05-08	6
2011-02-19	masterkey.com.ua	91.208.194.18	online	Not listed	AS47900	AMSOFT-AS Art-master LLC,UA	Ukraine (UA)	2011-05-12	10
2011-02-13	rastu.com.ua	144.76.143.4	online	Not listed	AS24940	HETZNER-AS Hetzner Online AG,D	Germany (DE)	2011-05-12	10
2011-02-09	asp.spinchats.com	50.63.202.42	online	Not listed	AS26496	AS-26496-GO-DADDY-COM-LLC - Go	United States (US)	2012-05-12	78
2011-02-07	ms4all.twoplayers.net	98.126.44.98	online	Not listed	AS35908	VPLSNET - Krypt Technologies,U	United States (US)	2011-05-16	6
2011-01-24	legionarios.servecounterstrike.com	76.74.255.138	online	Not listed	AS13768	PEER1 - Peer 1 Network (USA) I	United States (US)	2013-05-05	60
2011-01-23	penchatox.sin-ip.es	67.210.170.141	online	Not listed	AS26230	TOTTAWA - Telecom Ottawa Limit	Canada (CA)	2012-11-09	86
2011-01-17	panchitox.laweb.es	67.210.170.140	online	Not listed	AS26230	TOTTAWA - Telecom Ottawa Limit	Canada (CA)	2013-04-15	132
2011-01-14	symconempkr.com	194.116.174.85	online	Not listed	AS15510	CWCS-PS Compuweb Communication	United Kingdom (GB)	2011-10-09	62
2011-01-10	arta.romail3arnest.info	173.230.133.99	online	Not listed	AS3595	GNAXNET-AS - Global Net Access	United States (US)	2013-03-25	32
2011-01-09	shv4.no-ip.biz	76.74.255.138	online	Not listed	AS13768	PEER1 - Peer 1 Network (USA) I	United States (US)	2013-04-15	323
2011-01-07	shv4b.getmyip.com	67.210.170.169	online	Not listed	AS26230	TOTTAWA - Telecom Ottawa Limit	Canada (CA)	2011-06-08	251

# of Palevo Command&Control Servers tracked: **25**

copyright © 2014 palevotracker.abuse.ch, version 1.1 / 2012-03-31

Figure 6-22 *Palevo Tracker.*

Palevo Tracker

Palevo Tracker tracks the latest Palevo (also known as Mariposa Butterfly, Rimecud, and Pilleuz) infections. The main page is https://palevotracker.abuse.ch, as shown in Figure 6-22. As of this writing, I did not find any ways to download Palevo samples, but since the MD5 hash of the samples are displayed, they can be used to query other free malware sources that have been discussed previously. Also, the wealth of information available on the tracker page, including the sample's Anubis and VirusTotal report and the availability of blacklists, is more than enough evidence to show how important this malware tracker is.

Research Mailing Lists

One advantage of being a security professional or independent malware researcher who has proven his worth to the community and his peers is the ability to join research mailing lists. Research mailing lists are exclusive mailing lists for researchers where malware samples are shared on a regular basis and where members exchange ideas and hold informative discussions about threats.

To be part of a research mailing list, a candidate has to be invited or sponsored by an existing member and then vouched for by other members of the mailing list. Depending on the research mailing list, there might be other requirements for the purpose of vetting the candidate.

Be aware that almost all research mailing lists have zero tolerance for product marketing. In one of the mailing lists that I am a member of, a new member started sending marketing information about the products of the company he was working from. He was kicked off the list immediately and banned from ever joining again.

Sample Exchange

Most security companies are involved in malware sample exchange or sharing. Sample exchange is done on a periodic basis, usually weekly or monthly. The main idea here is that all members of the sample exchange dump all of the new malware samples that they have collected during a given time period and then organize them in a way that follows the agreed-upon sample exchange protocols; in return, they get access to the samples being shared by the other members.

The main reason why security companies do sample exchange is to make sure all users are protected regardless of who their security provider is. In my opinion, this is a noble activity by security companies since it is more about providing protection than making a profit.

Another advantage of being a security professional is that if you work for a security company that is involved in some sort of sample exchange, then there is no need to exert much effort in other ways of procuring malware samples for research purposes.

Commercial Sources

Malware samples, especially fresh ones, are considered commodities. This is why there are businesses out there that sell malware samples to vetted companies for the purpose of research. These commercial sources of malware usually specialize in the collection of malware in the wild. They build their malware collection with the sole purpose of selling the malware.

Purchasing malware samples from these sources is sometimes the most practical way for a company that is doing malware research to get malware samples. Instead of investing time and money in building systems to collect malware, it is often much more feasible to just buy them. Sometimes the juice is not worth the squeeze; it is like outsourcing the process of building and maintaining systems to collect malware to a commercial source.

Honeypots

Even with the different sources available to get your hands on malware samples, it is always better to learn how to build systems that collect malware. In malware collection, honeypots are the main systems used to collect malware automatically.

As defined in most literature,[1] a honeypot is an information system resource whose value lies in unauthorized or illicit use of that resource. The idea behind this methodology is to lure in attackers such as automated malware. As a consequence, the automated malware used in the attack can be collected and then studied in detail.

There are two general types of honeypots.[2]

▶ Low-interaction

▶ High-interaction

Low-interaction honeypots[2] offer limited services to the attacker. They emulate services or operating systems, and the level of interaction varies with the implementation. The risk tends to be low. In addition, deploying/maintaining these honeypots tends to be easy. With the help of low-interaction honeypots, it is possible to learn more about attack patterns and attacker behavior.

High-interaction honeypots, on the other hand, offer the attacker a real system to interact with. More risk is involved when deploying a high-interaction honeypot; for example, special provisions are created to prevent attacks against systems that are not involved in the setup. They are normally more complex to set up and maintain.

NOTES

Low-interaction honeypots are emulated, while high-interaction honeypots are real systems.

Depending on the need, a honeypot system can be emulated or implemented as a real system. There are pros and cons to this. Low-interaction honeypots have

---

[2] *Malware, Rootkits & Botnets* by Christopher C. Elisan, published by McGraw-Hill.

fewer risks of infection than high-interaction ones. Deployment and maintenance are easier in low-interaction honeypots compared to high-interaction honeypots, making low-interaction honeypots more scalable. But one advantage a high-interaction honeypot has over a low-interaction honeypot is the ability to study the attack in more detail because high-interaction honeypots, being based on a real system, offer full system functionality, making high-interaction honeypots much more expressive. In other words, low-interaction honeypots score high on scalability, while high-interaction honeypots score high on expressiveness.

Dionaea

Dionaea offers both of these advantages: the scalability of low-interaction honeypots and the expressiveness of high-interaction honeypots. Dionaea, as defined by its creator, is a system intended to trap malware that exploits vulnerabilities exposed by services offered to a network with the ultimate goal of gaining a copy of the malware.

NOTES

Before Dionaea, there was Nepenthes. But it is not available in most repositories anymore. Dionaea is actually meant to be a successor of Nepenthes, and it is advised not to use Nepenthes anymore and use Dionaea instead.

LAB 6-1: *Installing Dionaea*

Dionaea can be installed in different Linux flavors as mentioned on its homepage, but in this lab, you will install Dionaea in Ubuntu 64-bit 12.04 LTS.

NOTE

If you are new to Ubuntu, you can visit http://www.ubuntu.com for more details. Also, how to set up Ubuntu will be discussed in the next chapter.

What You Need:
► Ubuntu 64 bit 12.04 LTS

Steps:
1. Install Dionaea dependencies.
2. Compile and install Dionaea.
3. Check for successful installation.
4. Update Dionaea.

Step 1: Install Dionaea Dependencies

Some dependencies are provided by apt-tree, while some need to be installed from source. To begin installing, please open a terminal window in Ubuntu and execute the following commands.

Dependencies Provided by apt-tree

```
$ sudo apt-get install libudns-dev
$ sudo apt-get install libglib2.0-dev
$ sudo apt-get install libssl-dev
$ sudo apt-get install libcurl4-openssl-dev
$ sudo apt-get install libreadline-dev
$ sudo apt-get install libsqlite3-dev
$ sudo apt-get install python-dev
$ sudo apt-get install libtool
$ sudo apt-get install automake
$ sudo apt-get install autoconf
$ sudo apt-get install build-essential
$ sudo apt-get install subversion
$ sudo apt-get install git-core
$ sudo apt-get install flex
$ sudo apt-get install bison
$ sudo apt-get install pkg-config
$ sudo apt-get install libnl-3-dev
$ sudo apt-get install libnl-genl-3-dev
$ sudo apt-get install libnl-nf-3-dev
$ sudo apt-get install libnl-route-3-dev
$ sudo apt-get install curl
```

Dependencies Installed from Source

Create the /opt/dionaea folder, if it does not exist, for dependencies.

```
$ sudo mkdir /opt/dionaea
```

Install liblcfg.

```
$ git clone git://git.carnivore.it/liblcfg.git liblcfg
$ cd liblcfg/code
$ autoreconf -vi
$ ./configure --prefix=/opt/dionaea
$ sudo make install
$ cd ..
$ cd ..
```

Install libemu.

```
$ git clone git://git.carnivore.it/libemu.git libemu
$ cd libemu
$ autoreconf -vi
$ ./configure --prefix=/opt/dionaea
$ sudo make install
$ cd ..
```

Install libev.

```
$ wget http://dist.schmorp.de/libev/Attic/libev-4.04.tar.gz
$ tar xfz libev-4.04.tar.gz
$ cd libev-4.04
$ ./configure --prefix=/opt/dionaea
$ sudo make install
$ cd ..
```

Install Python 3.2.
Install Python dependencies first.

```
$ sudo apt-get install sqlite3
$ sudo apt-get install bzip2 libbz2-dev
```

Download and compile Python.

```
$ wget http://www.python.org/ftp/python/3.2.2/Python-3.2.2.tgz
$ tar xfz Python-3.2.2.tgz
$ cd Python-3.2.2/
$ ./configure --enable-shared --prefix=/opt/dionaea --with-computed-
gotos --enable-ipv6 LDFLAGS="-Wl,-rpath=/opt/dionaea/lib/ -L/usr/lib/
x86_64-linux-gnu/"
$ sudo make
$ sudo make install
$ cd ..
```

Install Cython.

```
$ wget http://cython.org/release/Cython-0.15.tar.gz
$ tar xfz Cython-0.15.tar.gz
$ cd Cython-0.15
$ sudo /opt/dionaea/bin/python3 setup.py install
$ cd ..
```

Install libpcap.

```
$ wget http://www.tcpdump.org/release/libpcap-1.1.1.tar.gz
$ tar xfz libpcap-1.1.1.tar.gz
$ cd libpcap-1.1.1
$ ./configure --prefix=/opt/dionaea
$ sudo make
$ sudo make install
$ cd ..
```

Step 2: Compile and Install Dionaea

Compile and install Dionaea next.

```
$ git clone git://git.carnivore.it/dionaea.git dionaea
$ cd dionaea
$ autoreconf -vi
$ ./configure --with-lcfg-include=/opt/dionaea/include/ \
      --with-lcfg-lib=/opt/dionaea/lib/ \
      --with-python=/opt/dionaea/bin/python3.2 \
      --with-cython-dir=/opt/dionaea/bin \
      --with-udns-include=/opt/dionaea/include/ \
      --with-udns-lib=/opt/dionaea/lib/ \
      --with-emu-include=/opt/dionaea/include/ \
      --with-emu-lib=/opt/dionaea/lib/ \
      --with-gc-include=/usr/include/gc \
      --with-ev-include=/opt/dionaea/include \
      --with-ev-lib=/opt/dionaea/lib \
      --with-nl-include=/opt/dionaea/include \
      --with-nl-lib=/opt/dionaea/lib/ \
      --with-curl-config=/usr/bin/ \
      --with-pcap-include=/opt/dionaea/include \
      --with-pcap-lib=/opt/dionaea/lib/
$ sudo make
$ sudo make install
```

Step 3: Check for Successful Installation

After installing all the dependencies and Dionaea, it is always good to do a quick check of whether Dionaea is running. A quick check is to invoke Dionaea's help menu together with its default values.

```
$ cd /opt/dionaea/bin
$ ./dionaea -H
```

The –H switch displays Dionaea's help menu together with its default values, while the –h switch simply displays the help menu.

Step 4: Update Dionaea

A freshly installed Dionaea does not need to be updated, but as time passes, it is always good to regularly update your Dionaea installation. To do this, execute the following commands inside the clone folder of Dionaea. This is the folder produced by the git clone command in step 2.

```
$ git pull
```

If a message saying "Already up-to-date" is shown, then you're good to go; otherwise, issue the following command:

```
$ sudo make clean install
```

After the update, it is always good to make sure your config file is up to date. To do this, issue the following command:

```
$ cd /opt/dionaea/etc/dionaea
$ diff dionaea.conf dionaea.conf.dist
```

Once you have installed Dionaea, you can visit http://dionaea.carnivore .it/#running for more information on how to use and configure Dionaea.

Recap

In this chapter, I defined what a malware research lab is and the common purpose it serves. The following are the types of labs:

▶ Malware collection lab

▶ Static analysis lab

▶ Dynamic analysis lab

In addition, I concentrated the discussion on one purpose of the malware research lab: malware collection. I enumerated the different sources of malware and showed that not all of them require a lab setup, but it is always good practice to browse online malware sources from a system that is totally isolated and is designed solely for the purpose of collecting malware.

The following are the different sources of malware I discussed:

▶ Your own backyard

▶ Free sources

  ▶ Contagio

  ▶ KernelMode.info

  ▶ MalShare.com

  ▶ Malware.lu

  ▶ Malware Blacklist

  ▶ Malwarebytes forum

  ▶ Malekal's Forum

  ▶ Open Malware

  ▶ Tuts4You

  ▶ VirusShare.com

  ▶ VX heaven

  ▶ Malware trackers

▶ Research mailing lists

▶ Sample exchange

▶ Commercial sources

▶ Honeypots

Knowing the different sources of malware and how to collect them is important in your journey of analyzing malware.

Tools

In this chapter, I discussed and made use of the following tools:

▶ Free online antivirus scanners

  ▶ **Trend Micro HouseCall** http://housecall.trendmicro.com/

  ▶ **F-Secure Online Scanner** http://www.f-secure.com/en/web/home_global/online-scanner

► Free malware removal tools

  ► **Microsoft Security Essentials** http://windows.microsoft.com/en-us/windows/security-essentials-download

  ► **Comodo Cleaning Essentials** http://www.comodo.com/business-security/network-protection/cleaning_essentials.php

  ► **Kaspersky Security Scan** http://www.kaspersky.com/free-virus-scan

► Rootkit detectors

  ► **Rootkit Revealer by Microsoft** http://download.cnet.com/RootkitRevealer/3000-2248_4-10543918.html

  ► **TDSSKiller by Kaspersky** https://support.kaspersky.com/us/viruses/utility#TDSSKiller

► Startup examination tools

  ► **Autoruns by Microsoft** http://technet.microsoft.com/en-us/sysinternals/bb963902.aspx

  ► **Autorun Analyzer by Comodo** http://www.comodo.com/business-security/network-protection/cleaning_essentials.php

► Boot analyzer tools

  ► **Gmer's MBR.EXE** http://www.gmer.net

  ► **MbrScan** http://eric71.geekstogo.com/tools/MbrScan.exe

  ► **MBR Backup** http://www.trojanhunter.com/products/mbr-backup/

  ► **Boot Sector Explorer** http://www.pendriveapps.com/boot-sector-explorer-backup-and-restore-mbr/

  ► **Nate's MBR and Boot Sector Analyzer** http://www.aqfire.com/boot/

  ► **WinHex MBR / boot sector editor** http://www.winhex.com/disk-editor.html

► Process examination tools

  ► **Process Explorer by Microsoft** http://technet.microsoft.com/en-us/sysinternals/bb896653.aspx

  ► **KillSwitch by Comodo** http://www.comodo.com/business-security/network-protection/cleaning_essentials.php

► Honeypots

  ► **Dionaea** http://dionaea.carnivore.it

Static Analysis Lab

ollecting malware samples can be as easy as going online and downloading the samples from a website where malware samples are shared freely, or it can be as difficult as extracting the samples from an infected system using different kinds of system forensics tools. But one thing is certain once a malware sample is collected. The first step in determining its true nature is to have it undergo static analysis.

Static analysis is the process of extracting data from a file while the file is at rest, or static. From this data, information is formulated to determine whether the file is malicious. Static analysis was successful during the early days of computer viruses, but as malware became complicated and able to apply protective mechanisms such as encryption while the malware is static, static analysis usually comes up short when it comes to determining a file's true behavior and, in the case of malware, the malware's main directive. But this is no reason to discount static analysis altogether. Static analysis can still offer a glimpse, albeit limited, of the suspicious file's nature. So, static analysis is still a useful first step in the process of determining the malware's true directive.

The process of static analysis is made possible by different file inspection tools and the system where all these tools are correctly installed and configured. Static analysis is not possible without the right combination of these two.

In this chapter, I will focus on the system where static analysis is conducted. I will discuss how to set up a static analysis lab that will host different file inspection tools.

The Static Analysis Lab

The static analysis lab is a computer system used to analyze files at rest. Its main purpose is to host the different file inspection tools needed by malware researchers and analysts to extract all the data possible from a file at rest.

A static analysis lab does not need to cater to all the different needs or dependencies of malware or any suspicious files that need to undergo static analysis. Static analysis, after all, is the analysis of files without executing those files. Its main concern is to have all the file inspection tools function as intended by the researchers.

An effective and well-configured static analysis lab has the following characteristics:

▶ Can host different file inspection tools regardless of the operating system (OS) the tools are written for

▶ Can mitigate possible infection through hardening the system

▶ Can mitigate the possibility of the lab becoming a staging point by malware and attackers by isolating the lab from any production network

▶ Can go to different online resources anonymously

These characteristics are important to consider when setting up a static analysis lab. They should serve as a guide to ensure that the lab will not cause any unintended infections during its normal operations.

Host File Inspection Tools

A static analysis lab should be able to host different file inspection tools regardless of the OS the tools are written for. This is possible by emulating or virtualizing different operating systems that have useful file inspection tools. In static analysis, there are tools that are on only one operating system but are useful in analyzing files written for another operating system. For example, there are tons of file inspection tools present only in Linux-based operating systems that can be used to analyze Windows files. Also, some scripting languages are easily created and supported in Linux systems that can be used to create scripts to parse a Windows file for the purpose of analysis.

Mitigate Possible Infection

A static analysis lab must be *hardened*. This means it must be secured, with the exception of having a real-time malware scanner enabled, so the possibility of becoming infected is minimized.

A static analysis lab must be treated as a system with operational value. It must be secured as you would an operations system. And since this system will process suspicious and malware files, the only thing that must be excluded when it comes to hardening or securing the static analysis lab is the presence of any endpoint security that will interfere with the static analysis process. One example is a real-time malware scanner that will quarantine or delete a suspicious or malware file that it detects in the system.

> ### NOTE
> *Antivirus scanners are considered file inspection tools and are used in static analysis labs. Some researchers prefer them to be on a separate system, while some do not mind having them in the same static analysis lab as other tools as long as the real-time scanning capability is disabled.*

> ### TIP
>
> *If one of the static analysis tools of choice is an antivirus scanner, it is always good to find a command-line version of the scanner. If there is none, make sure that real-time scanning is disabled, and as an added precaution, set the action to quarantine if a file is detected.*

Mitigate Becoming a Malware Staging Point

This is related to the previous section of mitigating a possible malware infection. But just to be sure that the machine or static analysis lab will not be used as a staging point for malware to infect other systems or conduct an attack, the system must be isolated from any production network.

Every machine gets infected. It is just a question of when. Therefore, isolation is key in mitigating the possibility of becoming a malware staging point.

> ### NOTE
>
> *There is a possibility that some free or open source static malware analysis tools can have hidden code in them that can be detrimental to the system and user. Isolating the lab minimizes the risk of any malicious network-related functions that some of these tools might carry.*

Anonymous Communication

A static analysis lab can also be used to conduct research online or download tools or malware samples from different sources. It is always good to have any malware research lab anonymized in case there is a need to do these tasks. It is a precaution to protect the systems from being blocked by attackers or, worse, become a target of their distributed denial-of-service (DDOS) attack. You also do not want the organization where the malware research lab is located to be tagged by attackers.

> ### TIP
>
> *It is always good practice to anonymize all malware research labs.*

> ### NOTE
>
> *Some researchers prefer a separate system to do online research, but it is still good to have the system anonymized so nothing will be traced back to the researcher or organization doing the research.*

It is also important to consider backup and restoration of the static analysis lab in case of failure. As you know, all computer systems carry the risk of failure one way or another. It is better to be prepared for this scenario so static analysis operation can continue without any significant downtime.

Setting Up the Lab

You can set up the static analysis lab in either a virtual or bare-metal environment. There's no difference between the two since the malware is at rest. It does not affect the efficacy of the tools unless a tool specifically needs a bare-metal environment, which is unlikely for a static file inspection tool. But regardless of the environment, the steps in setting up a static analysis lab are the same.

To set up a static analysis lab, you will be doing the following steps:

1. Choose the hardware.
2. Install the operating system.
3. Harden the lab.
4. Anonymize the lab.
5. Isolate the lab.

Choose the Hardware

An often-overlooked process in setting up a malware research lab such as a static analysis lab is choosing the correct hardware. This is an important choice and must be based on the needs of the analyst. For the hardware, there are two choices.

▶ Desktop
▶ Laptop

Both of these choices have several advantages, but the right choice depends on the analyst. If the analyst wants to set up multiple static lab images that require a lot of storage, memory, and computing power, she might be tempted to choose a more powerful desktop that can expand memory capacity up to 64GB and that can support up to four internal hard drives of 4TB each for her hardware. If she's mobile and travels a lot or is an incident responder who goes to different clients, then a laptop might be the more reasonable choice. Whatever hardware is chosen depends on the needs and circumstances of the analyst. The most important thing is that the hardware has enough space, memory, and computing power to support the static analysis lab and the tools that will be installed.

> **TIP**
>
> It is always good to have external hard drives available for backup and extra storage and to have universal serial bus (USB) sticks for transferring files and for serving as boot disks in case of failure.

In some cases, this is not even a choice. A well-funded malware analyst can have both a desktop and a laptop setup.

Install the Operating System

Although the concentration is on analyzing Windows-based files here, I will not be limiting the discussion to using Windows-based file inspection tools. There are tools offered by other operating systems such as Linux that will prove valuable in static analysis.

With this in mind, I will present two static analysis labs: a Windows-based static analysis lab and a Linux-based static analysis lab. For the Linux one, I will be using Ubuntu.

Windows

When creating a static analysis lab running on Windows, I always opt for Windows 7 32-bit. The main reason for me choosing 32-bit is to cater to most static analysis or file inspection tools that are widely used today. Take note that this is a personal preference; please feel free to use 64-bit if you desire to do so. Most tools will run there too, and it's just a matter of time that all the tools will run seamlessly in 64-bit.

Installing Windows is quite easy and well documented already, so I will not delve into it that much. Instead, I will focus more on solving issues relating to its installation, especially those that are common in installing Windows in a bare-metal environment. Some of the issues are the following:

▶ "A required CD/DVD drive device driver is missing" error
▶ Systems shipped without CD/DVD drives

"A required CD/DVD drive device driver is missing" Error   Most researchers use a Microsoft Developer Network (MSDN) subscription to download various flavors of Windows ISO images and burn them onto a disc. This is a common practice. But using this type of installer disc and not the one provided by the computer manufacturer to set up Windows often leads to an error message that pops up during installation. The error message is "A required CD/DVD drive device driver is missing." This is easily solved by using the installation discs provided by the manufacturer or invoking the restoration procedure using the OS backup that came pre-loaded on the computer's hard disk. But in most cases, the installation discs are no longer available or accessible, and the hard disk has been reformatted to fit the researcher's need, thus losing whatever restoration files that are there. So, the only choice is to use a Windows installation disc burned from MSDN-provided Windows ISOs.

The main reason for the error message appearing during installation is because Windows 7 installation discs do not have all the system drivers for all manufacturers. Windows 7's generic drivers do not work either.

When the disc is inserted and the option to boot using the disc drive is activated, the Basic Input/Output System (BIOS) spins the drive and checks whether the disc is bootable. If it is, it loads the data from the installation disc. Control is then passed to Windows so it can proceed with the installation. Since most of the data Windows needs to continue installation is on the disc, it needs to be able to read the contents of the disc. But then when it tries to control the disc to read data, Windows is not able to do it because it does not have the correct drivers to do it. This is because the BIOS was not able to or does not have the capability to pass the disc driver it used to Windows. As a result, Windows has no interface to control the disc drive, and the error message, "A required CD/DVD drive device driver is missing" appears. For Windows to have the ability to control the disc drive, the user has to provide the driver.

Take note that the driver Windows 7 needs is not the one that comes with or is provided by the disc drive manufacturer but the RAID/SATA/IDE driver of the motherboard. You can download this driver from the computer manufacturer's website, or you can ask the manufacturer to send you a copy on a disc.

The driver files are usually compressed in ZIP or RAR format. Make sure they are decompressed and copy them to the installation disc, a thumb drive, or a separate partition in the hard disk. When Windows 7 asks for the drivers during installation, browse to the folder where the drivers are located, and installation will proceed unless the drivers are wrong. If the drivers are wrong, make sure you find the right one and try again. If everything is OK, you should be good to go.

If after the first reboot Windows 7 spits out an error about the digital signature being invalid or needing verification because it does not recognize the newly installed driver, simply reboot the machine and press the button that will bring you to the BIOS boot option. Once inside, disable the driver signature enforcement capability, save, and reboot again. This should fix the problem.

LAB 7-1: *Extracting and Copying Drivers to the Windows 7 Installation Media*

Some drivers come in an installation package that needs to undergo an installation procedure so the driver files can be extracted. This lab will show how to extract the driver files.

What You Need:

▶ Installation media

▶ System running Windows 7

▶ Copy of the driver

Steps:

1. Download or copy the driver to the system running Windows 7.

2. Double-click the driver installation package to install it in its default location. Figure 7-1 shows an example of installing the driver in its default location of C:\DRIVERS\WIN\AMT.

3. If the driver installer has an option of not installing the driver and just copying it in the default location, you can select not to install it. If there is none, just continue the installation. Figure 7-2 shows a check box that will not install the driver after it has been extracted into the default location.

4. Perform the previous steps for all drivers that are needed during installation.

5. Go to the default location where the drivers are installed and copy them to the installer media or any media that can be accessed during installation.

> **TIP**
>
> Copying the whole DRIVERS folder is easier and does the trick really well when drivers are needed during installation. Just be mindful of the size.

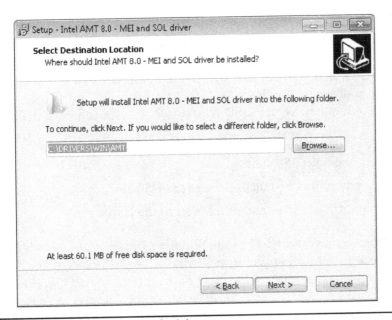

Figure 7-1   *Installing a driver in its default location.*

Figure 7-2   *Check box that can be unselected so driver will not be installed.*

System Shipped Without CD/DVD Drives   Most laptops today, especially the thin and lightweight ones, ship with no disc drives. However, there is an option to buy an external disc drive, but I find this to be bulky, especially if the aim is to travel with the static analysis lab. In cases like this, I use a thumb drive or a USB stick as the installation medium for Windows 7.

To create a thumb drive or a USB Windows 7 installer, you need to do the following:

1. Create a bootable USB stick.

2. Copy the Windows installation file to the USB stick.

3. Copy important drivers and other tools to the USB stick.

A bootable thumb drive that has the Windows 7 installation files should be treated similar to a bootable Windows 7 installation disc. Everything else is the same except the media. It is good to have all the drivers copied into the thumb drive. This makes it easy to install the drivers. For me, I always use a Bluetooth-connected mouse rather than the touchpad because of its sensitivity. Having my Bluetooth mouse driver in the thumb drive enables me to use my mouse immediately while going through the rest of the installation.

It is also good to have all the tools the analyst needs on the thumb drive. This speeds up the installation of tools because they are in one location and also serves as a good backup of all the essential tools needed to conduct static analysis.

LAB 7-2: *Creating a Bootable USB Stick Windows 7 Installer*

In this lab, you'll create a bootable USB stick.

What You Need:

▶ USB stick with at least 8GB of available space

▶ System running Windows 7

▶ Windows 7 ISO/extracted installer files

▶ Driver files and other tools

Steps:

1. Insert the USB stick into the system running Windows 7.

> **NOTE**
>
> *The flavor of the Windows OS running on the system and the Windows installer you are creating must match; otherwise, the USB Windows installer will fail.*

2. Open a command line by right-clicking it and have it run as administrator. An administrator privilege is needed to do the following steps.

3. At the command line, type **diskpart** and press the Return key, as shown in Figure 7-3. DiskPart, as defined by Microsoft, is a text-mode command interpreter that enables the user to manage objects (disks, partitions, or volumes) by using scripts or direct input from a command prompt.

4. Once inside DiskPart, execute the following commands:

```
DISKPART> list disk
DISKPART> select disk 1
DISKPART> clean
DISKPART> create partition primary
DISKPART> list partition
DISKPART> select partition 1
DISKPART> active
DISKPART> format fs=ntfs label=WIN7
DISKPART> exit
```

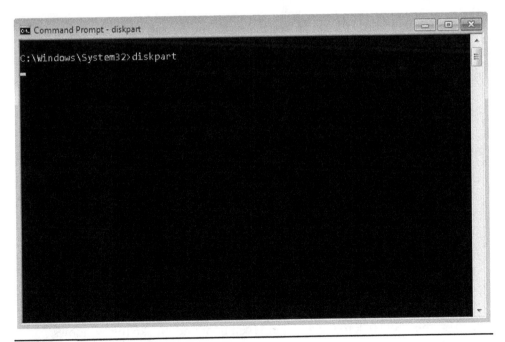

Figure 7-3 *Executing DiskPart.*

NOTE

The assumption here is that disk 1 represents the USB stick. If there are multiple internal hard disks installed or an external hard drive connected, the USB stick will be assigned a different disk number, so please be mindful of that.

The previous command lines result in a formatted USB stick with an NTFS file system and WIN7 as its label. Figure 7-4 shows the whole DiskPart session.

5. Look for BootSect.EXE. BootSect.EXE, as defined by Microsoft, updates the master boot code for hard disk partitions to switch between BOOTMGR and NTLDR. This tool can also be used to restore the boot sector on your computer. It is a replacement for FixFAT and FixNTFS. You can find it inside the boot folder of the Windows installer CD. BootSect.EXE requires escalated privileges. The command line must be running at the same privilege level for this tool to work; you can do this by right-clicking the command prompt and choosing the Run As Administrator option. Figure 7-5 shows the context menu.

NOTE

To make BootSect.EXE work, the Windows 7 machine you are using must be the same version as the Windows 7 installer files where the BootSect.EXE tool is located.

6. Execute BootSect.EXE with the following options. Take note that F: represents the drive of the USB stick. This may be different in your own test lab.

```
Bootsect.exe /NT60 F:
```

Figure 7-6 shows the BootSect.EXE session.

7. Copy the Windows installer files from the installation disc or from the extracted ISO image by using XCOPY.EXE with the following arguments. Take note that D: is the source drive where the Windows installer files are located and F: is the USB stick. This may be different in your own test lab.

```
Xcopy D: F: /E /H
```

Figure 7-7 shows the XCOPY.EXE session.

8. Copy the device drivers and other tools needed during installation to the USB stick.

9. Test the USB stick to see whether it can boot and invoke the Windows installation.

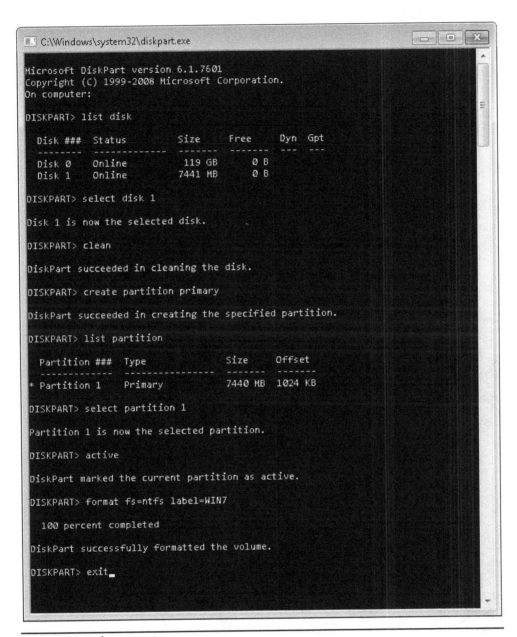

Figure 7-4   *DiskPart session.*

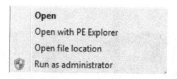

Figure 7-5   *Context menu.*

Microsoft understood that something like this is needed so it came up with a tool that makes the creation of a bootable Windows 7 USB installer much easier. You can download the tool from http://images2.store.microsoft.com/prod/clustera/ framework/w7udt/1.0/en-us/Windows7-USB-DVD-tool.exe. It is called the Windows 7 USB/DVD Download Tool.

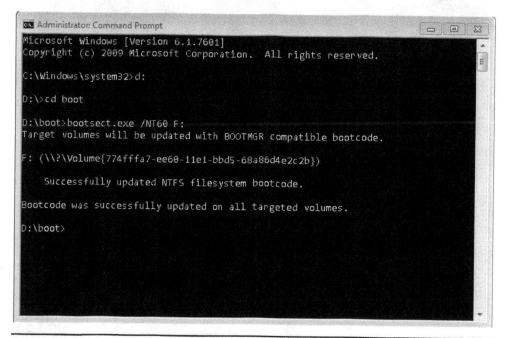

Figure 7-6   *BootSect.EXE session.*

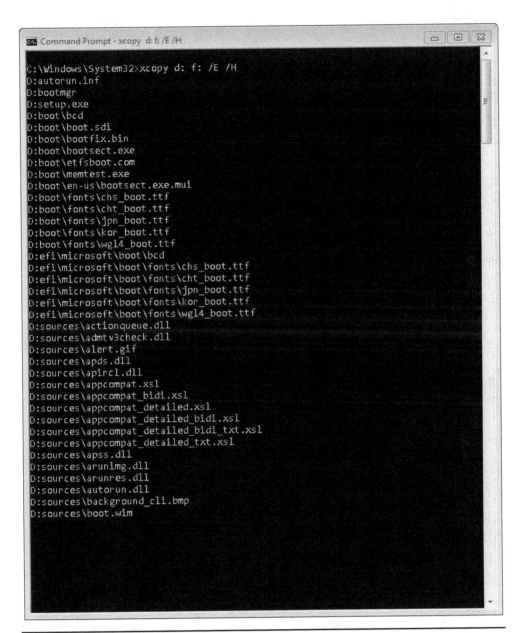

Figure 7-7 *XCOPY.EXE session.*

LAB 7-3: *Creating a Bootable USB Stick Windows 7 Installer Using the Windows 7 USB/DVD Download Tool*

In this lab, you'll create a bootable USB stick using the Windows 7 USB/DVD Download Tool.

What You Need:

▶ USB stick with at least 8GB of available space

▶ System running Windows 7

▶ Windows 7 ISO

▶ Driver files and other tools

▶ Windows 7 USB/DVD Download Tool

Steps:

1. Download the Windows 7 USB/DVD Download Tool from http://images2. store.microsoft.com/prod/clustera/framework/w7udt/1.0/en-us/Windows7-USB-DVD-tool.exe.

2. Install the tool. Take note that the Windows 7 ISO must match the Windows 7 system where the tool is being installed.

3. Execute the tool and follow these steps:

   A. Choose the ISO file.

   B. Choose the USB media type.

   C. Insert the USB device.

   D. Begin copying to create bootable USB device.

   If all steps are followed correctly and the Windows versions match, the creation of a bootable USB device will be successful, as shown in Figure 7-8.

4. Test the USB stick to see whether it can boot and invoke the Windows installation.

Ubuntu

Ubuntu, as described in its official documentation, is a complete desktop Linux operating system, freely available with both community and professional support. The Ubuntu community is built on the ideas enshrined in the Ubuntu Manifesto: that software should be available free of charge, that software tools should be

Figure 7-8 *Bootable USB device created successfully.*

usable by people in their local language despite any disabilities, and that people should have the freedom to customize and alter their software in whatever way they see fit. You can find the full documentation at https://help.ubuntu.com.

For an Ubuntu static analysis lab, I always opt for the version that has long-term support (LTS). As of the book's writing, the latest LTS version is Ubuntu 14.04.1 LTS. LTS versions usually come with five years of security and maintenance updates. Ubuntu 14.04 was released in the summer of 2014, so it gives you until 2019 for updates.

You can download Ubuntu from http://www.ubuntu.com/download/desktop. Installing Ubuntu is simple. All that is needed is to follow the detailed documentation at http://www.ubuntu.com/download/desktop/install-desktop-long-term-support. Ubuntu can be installed using a DVD or USB stick. You can find instructions on how to burn an Ubuntu DVD installer in Windows at www.ubuntu.com/download/desktop/burn-a-dvd-on-windows. You can find instructions on how to create a bootable Ubuntu installer USB stick at http://www.ubuntu.com/download/desktop/create-a-usb-stick-on-windows.

Harden the Lab

A static analysis lab is like any computer system. The only difference is its main purpose, which is to analyze static malware or malware at rest. Therefore, to keep it from being compromised and exploited by attackers, it is a must to harden a static analysis lab, similar to how typical computer systems are hardened. The only exception is the installation of an endpoint security product, which may result in the quarantine of malware samples that will undergo static analysis.

In actual practice, not only is the static analysis lab used to analyze malware, but it is also used to do research about malware and different kinds of threats on the Web. Therefore, it is exposed to the same infection vectors as any other systems are.

To effectively harden a static analysis lab, I always follow these steps:

1. Update and patch.

2. Protect the web browser.

3. Restrict access.

Update and Patch

Hardening the system requires all the essential bug fixes and security patches to be installed. This includes not only the operating system patches but also patches of software installed in the static analysis lab. This ensures that some bugs and vulnerabilities are solved, but you must understand that there will always be bugs or vulnerabilities out there that are known or unknown that are not covered by the latest patches.

> **TIP**
>
> Create a regular schedule of updating patches. I usually make mine Tuesday evening to coincide with Microsoft's Patch Tuesdays. But if you are in a different time zone, you might need to schedule the updating of patches differently.

Windows Update takes care of updating Windows. It displays critical and optional updates that the user can choose to install. Sometimes some of these patches will cause the system to crash; if this happens, you can use System Restore to revert to a known good state before installing the patches. Windows Update makes a restore point before the patches are installed, so you should be covered.

As for the software installed in the system, there are lots of free vulnerability scanners available that are designed to detect vulnerabilities and weakness in the installed software and redirect the user to a patch, usually located on the software manufacturer's site, if it is available.

My personal favorite when it comes to vulnerability scanners is Secunia Online Software Inspector (OSI). It's free, and it's online. You can find it at http://secunia .com/vulnerability_scanning/online/.

> **TIP**
>
> *A good place to keep up to date with the latest vulnerabilities is http://cve.mitre.org/.*

The Windows Update equivalent in Ubuntu is the Update Manager, as shown in Figure 7-9. It takes care of updating the operating system and software installed in the system.

> **TIP**
>
> *To look for the Update Manager or any other application in Ubuntu, simply click the Dash Home icon in the left corner and enter the name of the application you are looking for in the search bar that will appear.*

For the command-line purists, Ubuntu offers an update mechanism by simply using the apt-get command-line tool. This command-line tool handles different software packages in Ubuntu and other Linux-based distros. To update using the command line, issue the following commands:

```
$ sudo apt-get update
$ sudo apt-get upgrade
```

The apt-get update command syncs the package index files with their sources. These sources are usually reached via the Internet. After everything is synchronized, issuing the apt-get upgrade command starts the installation of the newest versions of all software packages installed on the system.

Escalated privilege is needed to accomplish the update, which is the reason for the additional use of sudo in the command line (sudo is short for "superuser do"). Once this command is used, you must input a root or superuser password.

Protect the Web Browser

Your window to the Web is your Internet browser. When doing online research, the chances of stumbling upon a malicious domain or uniform resource locator (URL) are high, especially if the main goal is collecting more data about a certain malware. In some cases, you will need to scour the Web to download a malware sample and its related files, opening the browser to more risks. There are also instances wherein the information that is needed is hosted by a questionable

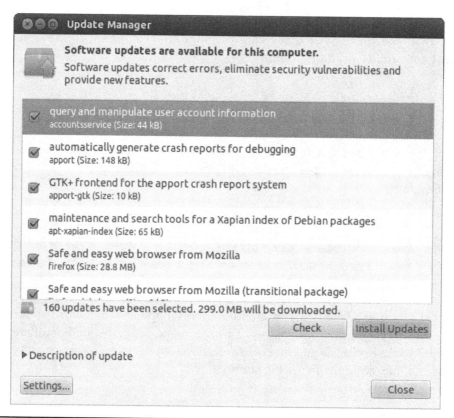

Figure 7-9 *Ubuntu's Update Manager.*

source and there is no certainty that the browser will pass unscathed after the research session. Therefore, it is imperative to protect the browser as technically possible as you can. Fortunately, most browsers have security and privacy features available, and there are add-ons and plug-ins that are designed to secure the browser. A good combination of these two will help in protecting the browser.

> **TIP**
>
> *Restore your static analysis to a clean state every time you do an extensive research session. This ensures that whatever malicious miscreants the system caught will be eradicated. Backup and restoration will be discussed later in the chapter.*

My browser of choice when doing online research using my static analysis lab is Firefox because of the many plug-ins that it has to secure the browser. But please feel free to use any browser of your choosing as long as it is secured and protected. The main idea here is that the browser is protected from the following:

▶ Malicious domains and URLs

▶ Malicious scripts

TIP

Do not use your static lab to log in to any accounts that you do not want to be compromised, such as your regular e-mail account and online banking accounts.

LAB 7-4: *Protecting Firefox Using Built-in Options*

In this lab, you will protect Firefox using its built-in security and privacy options.

What You Need:

▶ System with Firefox installed

Steps:

1. If you have not done so, please download the latest version of Firefox from http://www.mozilla.org/en-US/firefox/new/. As of this book's writing, the latest version of Firefox is 25.0.

2. Choose Firefox | Options | Options. The Firefox menu is on the upper-left side of the browser window.

3. Click the Privacy icon and apply the following options:

   A. In the Tracking section, make sure that Tell Sites I Do Not Want To Be Tracked is selected.

   B. In the History section, choose Firefox Will: Never Remember History. This will restart the browser, so you need to choose Firefox | Options | Options again.

   C. In the Location Bar section, choose When Using The Location Bar, Suggest: Nothing.

When you're done, the Options | Privacy window should look like Figure 7-10.

4. Click the Security icon and make sure the following are checked:

   A. Warn Me When Sites Try To Install Add-Ons

   B. Block Reported Attack Sites

   C. Block Reported Web Forgeries

   When you're done, the Options | Security window should look like Figure 7-11.

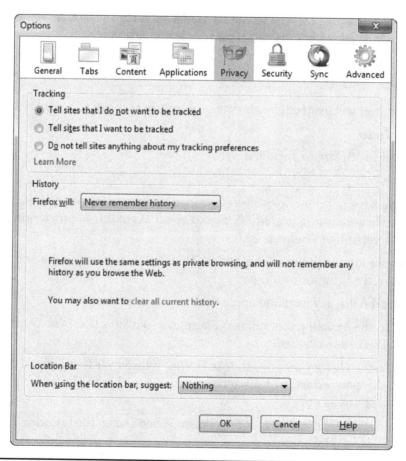

Figure 7-10 *Firefox privacy options.*

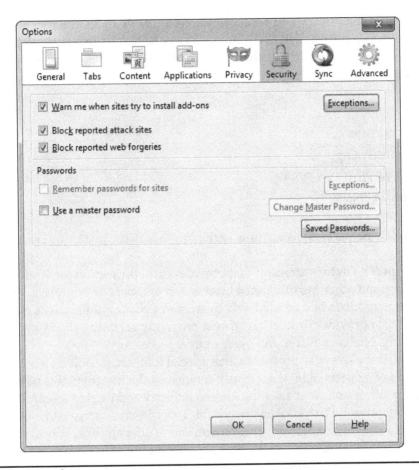

Figure 7-11 *Firefox security options.*

TIP

Click the Exceptions button on the Security tab if you want to exempt trusted sites you know.

5. Click the Advanced icon and, on the General tab in the Accessibility section, select Warn Me When Websites Try To Redirect Or Reload The Page. Review the rest of the tabs and modify them as you see fit.

6. Click OK, and the settings will be applied.

Aside from the privacy and security options available to Firefox users, add-ons and plug-ins can be installed in the browser to enhance the security and privacy of Firefox. Some of the add-ons that I think are useful for these purposes are the following:

- ▶ NoScript
- ▶ BetterPrivacy
- ▶ RequestPolicy
- ▶ Web of Trust (WOT)
- ▶ Adblock Plus

The following paragraphs are how each plug-in is described by its creator or publisher.

NoScript is a Firefox extension that provides extra protection for Firefox, Seamonkey, and other Mozilla-based browsers. It allows JavaScript, Java, Flash, and other plug-ins to be executed only by trusted websites of the user's choice. NoScript also provides protection against cross-site scripting (XSS) and clickjacking. NoScript is free and open source.

BetterPrivacy serves to protect against special long-term cookies, a new generation of "supercookie" that silently conquered the Internet. This new cookie generation offers unlimited user tracking to industry and market research. Concerning privacy, Flash cookies are critical. This add-on was made to make users aware of those hidden, never-expiring objects and to offer an easier way to view and manage them since browsers are unable to do that for the user. Flash cookies (local shared objects [LSOs]) are pieces of information placed on the user's computer by a Flash plug-in. Those supercookies are placed in central system folders and are frequently used like standard browser cookies. BetterPrivacy has the capability to list and manage Flash cookies, that is, to remove those objects automatically on browser start and exit or by a configurable timer function while certain desired Flash cookies can be excluded from automatic deletion.

RequestPolicy is an extension that improves the privacy and security of the user's browsing session by giving the user control over when cross-site requests are allowed by webpages that the user visited.

WOT is a website reputation and review service that helps users make informed decisions about whether to trust a website when searching, shopping, or surfing online. WOT simply shows the website reputations in the form of traffic lights next to search results when a user uses Google, Yahoo, Bing, or any other supported search engine. Clicking the light icon displays more information about the website's reputation and other users' opinions about that website.

Adblock Plus allows the user to regain control of the Internet and view the Web the way the user wants to, that is, without annoying advertisements, tracking, and banner displays. The add-on is supported by more than 40 filter subscriptions in dozens of languages that automatically configure it for purposes ranging from removing online advertising to blocking all known malware domains.

LAB 7-5: *Protecting Firefox Using Add-ons and Plug-ins*

In this lab, you will protect Firefox using available add-ons and plug-ins.

What You Need:

▶   System with Firefox installed

Steps:

1.   Choose Firefox | Add-ons.

2.   Go to the search bar located on the upper right, look for the following plug-ins, and install them one by one:

   A.   NoScript

   B.   BetterPrivacy

   C.   RequestPolicy

   D.   WOT

   E.   Adblock Plus

> **NOTE**
>
> *Read the description of each plug-in to have an idea of what it does and offers.*

> **TIP**
>
> *These are third-party plug-ins, and they may carry certain risks. Make sure you understand the consequences of installing third-party applications, add-ons, and plug-ins.*

Restrict Access

It is always good practice to have the least privilege account running when using a system and give or use escalated or admin privilege only when needed. In the

static analysis lab, the main tips when it comes to restricting access include the
following:

▶ Run under the least privileged account.

▶ Give tools admin access only when needed.

Run Under the Least Privileged Account   Anyone who has experienced or has been
compromised with malware knows the importance of having a least privileged
account currently logged in when the malware is attempting to infect the system.
A least privileged account usually will have no or limited access to resources
that the malware needs to successfully compromise a system. Although it is
possible that the malware has technology to get around this, it is still important
to make life difficult for the malware. And if malware ever became successful in
compromising a system with a least privileged account currently logged in, there
is less damage because of limited access to vital system resources.

Take note that the default account in older versions of Windows such as
Windows 2000, Windows XP, and Windows Server 2003 is the administrator, and
it has escalated privileges. If your desired Windows static analysis lab will use
any of the previously mentioned versions of Windows, it is important to create
a standard user account before doing any form of static analysis just to be on the
safe side.

Give Tools Admin Access Only When Needed   Most static analysis tools will function
without the need for escalated privileges or admin access. Therefore, it is always
good practice to run a static analysis tool under the context of the currently
logged-in least privilege user. The only time a static analysis tool must be granted
escalated privileges is when it requires it to function properly.

Anonymize the Lab

As mentioned previously, you can also use the static analysis lab to do research
about malware and different kinds of threats on the Web. It can also be used to
research information about different threat actor groups. When you do research
online, you leave footprints that reveal a lot of information about the system you
are using, your location, and your overall browsing activities and behavior. This all
can be used to track you. Obviously, you do not want any of your research activity
tracked back to you, especially if it involves researching about the bad guys. You

also do not want the cybercriminals to remember the systems you are using as research systems and get blocked or attacked. Therefore, anonymity is important.

There are different ways to stay anonymous online. Among them are the following:

▶ Proxy servers

▶ Virtual private networks

▶ Online anonymizers

▶ Tor

Proxy Servers

The most common way to stay anonymous online is through the use of proxy servers. A proxy server, also known as a *proxy*, is a system that acts as an intermediary between a computer or a local network and the Internet. In other words, it acts as a middleman between the local systems and the Internet. It does this by intercepting all connections from the local systems and having them all come through one port. The proxy then forwards the connections to the Internet or another network through another port. Since there is no direct access between the local systems and the Internet, it is difficult to identify the exact computer making the connection or request. As a result, the attackers won't be able to put tabs on the system or static analysis lab doing the research.

> ### NOTE
> *A proxy server not only provides security but also provides increased performance when browsing since it caches frequently visited websites.*

It is important to keep in mind that communications from the local systems to the proxy server and from the proxy server to the Internet are not encrypted. So if there is data there that can identify the local system behind the proxy server in any way, it is possible that the cover can be blown.

> ### TIP
> *The best way to protect communication between the local system to the proxy server and from the proxy server to the Internet is by using HTTP Secure (HTTPS).*

Lots of free proxies are available on the Internet. The following are some online resources containing lists of free proxy servers:

▶ **Hide My Ass!**   http://hidemyass.com/proxy/

▶ **Proxy 4 Free**   http://www.proxy4free.com

▶ **Samair.RU**   http://www.samair.ru/proxy/

▶ **Public Proxy Servers**   http://www.publicproxyservers.com/proxy/list1.html

These proxy servers are open to anybody. But since they are free, they may suffer from limited or controlled bandwidth; therefore, they may not be as fast or reliable as you want. And there is a high chance that these proxy servers will permanently disappear without notice, so they might be good only for temporary anonymization. This is why it is important to always have a fresh list of publicly available proxy servers.

> **TIP**
>
> *Free proxies carry several privacy risks. Make sure you understand the privacy policy of the free services before using them. Free services often come with a price, and that price has to do with giving up some of your privacy or information. Use these services at your own risk.*

For those who want a more reliable proxy service that will not disappear without notice, the best way is to subscribe to a paid proxy service. Another alternative, if you have the budget and resource, is to create your own.

Virtual Private Networks

The communication between the local system and the proxy server is not encrypted. Therefore, any data that flows can be intercepted or snooped by prying eyes. One solution for this is to use a virtual private network (VPN).

A virtual private network is an extension of a private network across the Internet. Individual users, such as those working remotely or those currently traveling on business, oftentimes use a VPN to get access to network resources in the company as if they are logged in to the company's local area network (LAN). Businesses use this all the time, especially if the remote employees do a lot of business using an unknown or untrusted public network, which is always the case when traveling on business. This is because VPN encrypts all communications that pass through the public network, and more importantly, for your purpose, it can mask the real Internet Protocol (IP) and location of the requesting system.

The local system's real IP address is 100 percent hidden when using a virtual private network.

NOTE

A VPN is a good way to secure a computer's Internet session because all the data that is sent and received is encrypted.

To use a VPN, the user must install a VPN client. The client initiates the connection to the VPN servers by making sure that the user has valid credentials to access the VPN servers. Some users see the installation of a client as a hassle, which is why some paid services offer clientless VPN service. All the user needs is a browser.

Like proxies, there are lots of VPN services available for free that are supported by ads on the Internet, while some offer trial versions of their services. Trial versions are good, especially if it is for temporary or experimental purposes. Some of them are listed here:

- ▶ Private Tunnel (https://www.privatetunnel.com)
- ▶ VPNBook (http://www.vpnbook.com)
- ▶ JustFreeVPN (http://www.justfreevpn.com)
- ▶ VPN Account (http://www.vpnaccount.org)
- ▶ L2TP VPN Service (http://www.freel2tpvpn.com)
- ▶ OkayFreedom VPN (https://www.okayfreedom.com)
- ▶ VPN Access (http://freevpnaccess.com)
- ▶ Hotspot Shield Ad Supported (http://www.hotspotshield.com)
- ▶ CyberGhost (http://cyberghostvpn.com)
- ▶ Free UK & US VPN (http://www.ukusvpn.com)
- ▶ Free VPN for UK (http://www.vpnforuk.com)
- ▶ Premium VPN with Public IP (http://www.truvpn.com)
- ▶ Free ProXPN (http://proxpn.com)

TIP

Like with free proxy services, free VPN services carry several privacy risks. Make sure you understand the privacy policy of the free services before using them. Use these services at your own risk.

As mentioned, free services carry with them risks such as those relating to privacy, which is why most researchers, if they have the resources, go for paid services. Although there is no guarantee that these paid services are abuse-free, it is always good to understand the privacy policy, end-user license agreement, or terms of service of your VPN provider.

Online Anonymizers

In cases wherein the online research is done only occasionally by the researcher or analyst, an online anonymizer or web browsing anonymizer is enough to satisfy what is needed. Online anonymizers are services offered, mostly for free, that let the user hide her real IP address and other information from the website being surfed. In short, the webmasters or the owners of the website being surfed will not have the user's real IP address.

LINGO

Online anonymizers are also known as **web proxies.**

An online anonymizer is browser based. This means the user just needs to go to the online anonymizer website and input the URL or website she wants to surf, and anonymous surfing commences. Figure 7-12 displays the main page of Anonymouse.org that shows a typical online anonymizer interface.

There are lots of free online anonymizers on the Internet. Some of them are listed here:

► Anonymouse (http://anonymouse.org/anonwww.html)

► Free Web Proxy (http://www.vpnbook.com/webproxy)

► Online Anonymizer (http://online-anonymizer.com)

► Hide My Ass! Web Proxy (http://hidemyass.com/proxy/)

► KProxy (https://www.kproxy.com)

► Megaproxy (http://www.megaproxy.com/freesurf/)

Using online anonymizers, also known as *web proxies,* is a good way to quickly browse anonymously when the need arises. But then again, be wary of the risks involved when using free services.

Figure 7-12   *Anonymouse.org.*

Tor

Tor, also known as the *onion router,* is another popular way of anonymizing
online activities. It is free and open source. It supports multiple platforms such
as Windows, Mac, and Linux. It also supports Android. Tor, as described in its
main page, is a network of virtual tunnels allowing people and groups to improve
their privacy and security on the Internet. It also enables software developers to
create new communication tools with built-in privacy features. Tor provides the
foundation for a range of applications that allow organizations and individuals to
share information over public networks without compromising their privacy.

Tor is well documented and can be found at https://www.torproject.org/docs/
documentation.html.en.

Isolate the Lab

When it comes to the static analysis lab, it is always good practice to isolate it from any home or production networks. Although it is used for analyzing static malware, there is always a risk for outbreak, especially if the malware is not handled properly and gets executed by accident.

A good rule of thumb for isolating a static analysis lab is to have it connect to the Internet only when needed. The times it will need connection is when doing the following:

▶ Downloading and updating tools

▶ Updating the OS

▶ Updating the software installed on the system

▶ Downloading malware samples

▶ Doing online threat research

And when an Internet connection is needed, make sure that it is done using its own Internet connection and not your home or office Internet connection.

> **TIP**
>
> *MiFi is a good way to connect to the Internet when you need to isolate the static lab. MiFi is a personal hotspot that is offered by different cellular providers.*

The Virtualized Static Analysis Lab

As previously mentioned, static analysis labs can be set up either in a bare-metal environment or in a virtualized environment. It does not really make a difference. Since this is the case, virtualization can be more advantageous, especially when it comes to backing up and restoring a damaged or corrupted static analysis lab.

To create a virtualized static analysis lab, virtualization software is needed. There are lots of virtualization software available. Whichever is chosen always comes down to individual preference. For the purpose of this book, I will focus on the two most used virtualization software products. They are as follows:

▶ VMware

▶ VirtualBox

The most popular VMware products used for virtualization are VMware Desktop and VMware Fusion for Mac. But if your budget is scarce, VMware has a free version called VMware Player. VMware Player can be downloaded from https://my.vmware.com/web/vmware/free#desktop_end_user_computing/vmware_player/4_0.

VirtualBox by Oracle, on the other hand, is freely available as open source software under the terms of the GNU General Public License (GPL) version 2. It can be downloaded from https://www.virtualbox.org/wiki/Downloads.

Both VMware and VirtualBox support Windows, Linux, and Mac as its host OS. Depending on which host OS the researcher or analyst prefers, there is a flavor of VMware and VirtualBox available for the desired platform.

Once a virtualized OS has been installed, the next steps as discussed earlier must still be followed to make the virtualized system an effective static analysis lab.

The following are the two common setups for a virtualized static analysis lab:

▶ Host OS: Windows; guest OS: Windows and Ubuntu
▶ Host OS: Ubuntu; guest OS: Windows and Ubuntu

Whichever setup you choose boils down to preference.

LAB 7-6: *Creating a Virtualized Ubuntu Desktop Using VMware Player*

In this lab, you will create a virtualized Ubuntu desktop that is hosted on a Windows box using VMware Player.

What You Need:

▶ Windows host OS
▶ VMware Player
▶ Ubuntu LTS ISO

Steps:

1. Download the latest LTS version of Ubuntu from http://www.ubuntu.com/download/desktop.
2. Download VMware Player from http://www.vmware.com/go/downloadplayer.
3. Install VMware Player.
4. Open VMware Player and click Create A New Virtual Machine, as shown in Figure 7-13.

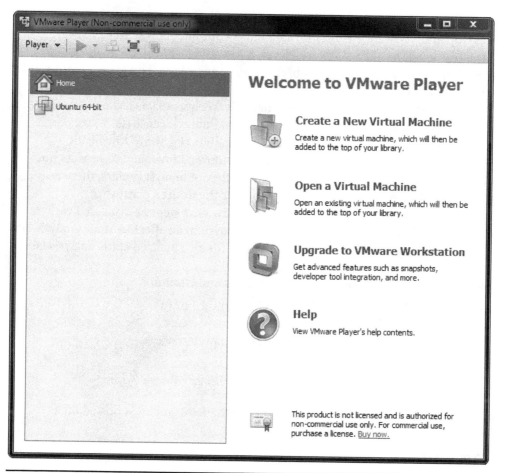

Figure 7-13 *VMware Player.*

5. Choose Installer Disc Image File (ISO): and browse to the location of the Ubuntu ISO file.
6. Click Next and supply the needed information such as username and password for the Ubuntu user. The succeeding windows will ask for the virtual machine name, disk capacity, and other needed information to create the virtual machine.
7. After supplying the needed information, click Finish to create the virtual machine.

8. Wait while VMware Player boots up using the ISO image as its boot disk, simulating an Ubuntu startup disk installation.
9. Proceed with the Ubuntu installation by following what is presented on the Ubuntu installation screen.

LAB 7-7: *Creating a Virtualized Ubuntu Desktop Using VirtualBox*

In this lab, you will create a virtualized Ubuntu desktop that is hosted on a Windows box using VirtualBox.

What You Need:

▶ Windows host OS

▶ VirtualBox

▶ Ubuntu LTS ISO

Steps:

1. Download the latest LTS version of Ubuntu from http://www.ubuntu.com/ download/desktop.
2. Download VirtualBox from https://www.virtualbox.org/wiki/Downloads.
3. Install VirtualBox.
4. Open VirtualBox and click New, as shown in Figure 7-14, to start the creation of a virtual machine.
5. In the next window, provide the preferred name of the virtual machine. Choose Linux in the Type drop-down menu and choose Ubuntu (32 bit) or Ubuntu (64 bit) in the Version drop-down menu. Then click Next.

> **TIP**
>
> *Typing **Ubuntu** in the Name field will automatically change the type to Linux and the version to Ubuntu (64 bit).*

6. On the succeeding window, provide the desired memory size and hard drive settings.
7. Once everything is done, you can start the virtual machine by clicking the Start button represented by an arrow sign pointing to the right.
8. The first time the virtual machine starts, it will ask for a startup disk. Browse to the location of the Ubuntu LTS ISO.
9. Proceed with the Ubuntu installation by following what is presented on the Ubuntu installation screen.

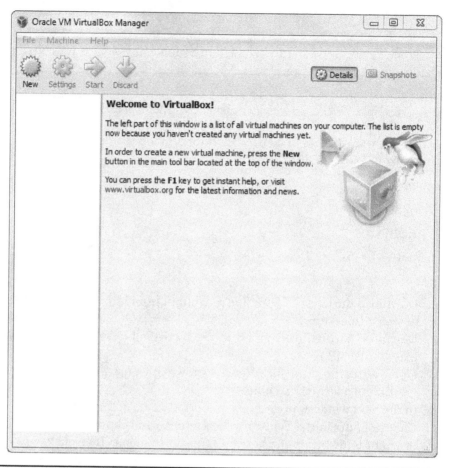

Figure 7-14   *VirtualBox.*

Backing Up and Restoring

It takes time to set up a static analysis lab. Like with any other computer system that has a purpose, it is important to have it available when needed. Therefore, it is always wise to have a backup and a streamlined process of how to restore the system in case it fails. This saves time and gets the system running quickly, especially if time is of the essence.

TIP

For the purpose of portability and easy restoration in case of failure, I always opt for a virtual environment–based static analysis lab.

Most researchers, such as myself, always opt for a virtual environment when it comes to static analysis labs. It makes it portable and easy to restore from failure. Plus, the capability of having multiple image snapshots makes it convenient to have different setup configurations. The good thing about static analysis labs is that they do not have the inherent problems of dynamic analysis labs that run in virtualized environments. The malware is at rest during analysis, so even if the malware has a virtualized environment detection capability, it has no effect on the static analysis process being conducted.

But if the researcher chooses to set up her static analysis lab in a bare-metal environment, there are lots of tools that can be used to back up and restore the bare-metal system in case of failure. My favorite is Clonezilla, which can be downloaded from http://clonezilla.org/downloads.php. It is free and easy to use. I'll delve into Clonezilla further when I start discussing the dynamic analysis lab.

Recap

In this chapter, I discussed the static analysis lab. I identified what makes an effective and well-configured lab. The parameters are as follows:

▶ Can host different file inspection tools regardless of the OS the tools are written for

▶ Can mitigate possible infection through hardening the system

▶ Can mitigate the possibility of the lab becoming a staging point by malware and attackers by isolating the lab from any production network

▶ Can go to different online resources anonymously

I then identified the basic steps in setting up a static analysis lab, which are as follows:

▶ Choose the hardware.

▶ Install the operating system.

▶ Harden the lab.

▶ Anonymize the lab.

▶ Isolate the lab.

▶ Back up and restore.

I tackled how to solve Windows installation problems, especially if the hardware of choice is a laptop with a disc drive but no device driver available or does not come with a disc drive.

I discussed how to harden the lab by following the most common steps, which are as follows:

▶ Update and patch.

▶ Protect the web browser.

▶ Restrict access.

I also discussed how to anonymize the lab using common solutions such as the following:

▶ Proxy servers

▶ Virtual private networks

▶ Online anonymizers

▶ Tor

I also stressed the importance of isolating the lab as a precaution just in case something happens such as the mishandling of malware.

I then touched on setting up a virtualized static analysis lab using VMware Player and VirtualBox.

Last but definitely not the least, I discussed the importance of backup and restoration in case the lab fails. With a process like this in place, there will be minimal downtime in case of failure.

Tools

In this chapter, I discussed and made use of the following tools:

▶ **Windows 7 USB/DVD Download Tool**   http://images2.store.microsoft.com/ prod/clustera/framework/w7udt/1.0/en-us/Windows7-USB-DVD-tool.exe

► **Secunia Online Software Inspector** http://secunia.com/vulnerability_
scanning/online/

► Firefox add-ons and plug-ins

  ► NoScript

  ► Better Privacy

  ► RequestPolicy

  ► Web of Trust (WOT)

  ► Adblock Plus

► Proxy servers

  ► **Hide My Ass!** http://hidemyass.com/proxy/

  ► **Proxy 4 Free** http://www.proxy4free.com

  ► **Samair.RU** http://www.samair.ru/proxy/

  ► **Public proxy servers** http://www.publicproxyservers.com/proxy/
  list1.html

► Virtual private network services

  ► **Private Tunnel** https://www.privatetunnel.com

  ► **VPNBook** http://www.vpnbook.com

  ► **JustFreeVPN** http://www.justfreevpn.com

  ► **VPN Account** http://www.VPN Account.org

  ► **L2TP VPN Service** http://www.freel2tpvpn.com

  ► **OkayFreedom VPN** https://www.okayfreedom.com

  ► **VPN Access** http://freevpnaccess.com

  ► **Hotspot Shield Ad Supported** http://www.hotspotshield.com

  ► **CyberGhost** http://cyberghostvpn.com

  ► **Free UK & US VPN** http://www.ukusvpn.com

  ► **Free VPN for UK** http://www.vpnforuk.com

  ► **Premium VPN with Public IP** http://www.truvpn.com

  ► **Free ProXPN** http://proxpn.com

► Online anonymizers

  ► **Anonymouse** http://anonymouse.org/anonwww.html

  ► **Free Web Proxy** http://www.vpnbook.com/webproxy

  ► **Online Anonymizer** http://online-anonymizer.com

▶ **Hide My Ass! Web Proxy** http://hidemyass.com/proxy/

▶ **KProxy** https://www.kproxy.com

▶ **Megaproxy** http://www.megaproxy.com/freesurf/

▶ **Tor, the onion router** https://www.torproject.org/docs/documentation.html.en

▶ **VMware Player** http://www.vmware.com/go/downloadplayer

▶ **VirtualBox** https://www.virtualbox.org/wiki/Downloads

▶ **Clonezilla** http://clonezilla.org/downloads.php

Dynamic Analysis Lab

S etting up the static analysis lab gave you a good foundation that you can build on when setting up a dynamic analysis lab. Dealing with Windows errors during installation and anonymizing and isolating the lab are among the topics that will help you to set up a dynamic analysis lab.

Using a static analysis lab offers you a glimpse of the nature of malware from the data gathered with the malware at rest. Although the data might not be enough to come up with any definite information to fully determine a malware's behavior or directive, static analysis is still a useful first step in the malware analysis process. The next step that builds upon static analysis is dynamic analysis. With dynamic analysis, you are able to observe malware in its natural environment. You are able to monitor the malware's behavior while it is running in an environment that mimics the system the malware is designed to target. It is analogous to an organism being studied in a small, contained area that mimics its natural habitat. The only difference is that it is a controlled and simulated environment. The controlled environment where dynamic analysis is being conducted that is designed to mimic a malware's target environment is known as the *dynamic analysis lab*. This is where malware behavior can be observed, monitored, and recorded.

In this chapter, I will discuss how to build an effective dynamic analysis lab by making it as close to the desired environment as possible for malware to thrive. I will also discuss how to make sure that the dynamic analysis lab is backed up and restored in case of failure so there will be minimal downtime.

Setting Up the Lab

Similar to a static analysis lab, the dynamic analysis lab can be set up in either a virtual or bare-metal environment. But unlike the static analysis lab, where there is no difference whether the environment is virtual or bare-metal, a dynamic analysis lab environment can make or break an analysis session, especially if the malware is virtual-aware. This is why it is important to take into consideration whether a virtualized environment or a bare-metal one will be used in setting up a dynamic analysis lab.

LINGO

A **virtual-aware** malware is malware that has the ability to detect whether it is running in a virtualized environment.

The ideal setup is to have both because both environments offer several advantages that complement each other. The virtualized environment is easy to manage, replicate, back up, and restore. But then again, virtual-aware malware can render a virtual dynamic analysis lab useless. The bare-metal system, on the other hand, solves the problem of virtual-aware malware from evading dynamic analysis. But it is not as easy to manage, replicate, back up, and restore as a virtualized environment.

Although there are lots of virtual-aware malware out there, a big chunk of malware that is seen every day in the wild does not possess this evasion technique. Therefore, a virtualized environment is still useful. But since there is no initial knowledge of whether the malware being subjected to the virtualized dynamic analysis lab is virtual-aware or not, a good rule of thumb is to have all binary samples processed in a virtualized environment, and then those that do not produce any results will be processed using a bare-metal dynamic analysis lab.

> **TIP**
>
> *Process all samples in a virtualized dynamic analysis lab environment first and use a bare-metal dynamic analysis lab only if the virtualized environment does not yield any results.*

Regardless of the environment, the steps needed to set up a dynamic analysis lab are basically the same. The only difference is how to execute each step.

To set up a dynamic analysis lab, you will be performing the following steps:

1. Choose the hardware.
2. Install the operating system.
3. Make the lab malware friendly.
4. Anonymize the lab.
5. Isolate the lab.

Choose the Hardware

Like with a static analysis lab, a researcher building a dynamic analysis lab has several choices when it comes to hardware. They are as follows:

- ▶ Desktop
- ▶ Laptop

Both of these choices have several advantages, as discussed in Chapter 7. It boils down to the analyst's needs. If the need is more for mobility, a laptop is the best choice. But if the need is more for power, that is, you are hosting a handful of virtualized dynamic analysis lab with different flavors, then the best choice is a powerful desktop or a server. The most important thing when it comes to hardware choice is that it has enough space, memory, and computing power to support the dynamic analysis lab or several dynamic analysis lab images.

LINGO

A *dynamic analysis lab image* is another term for virtualized dynamic analysis lab environment.

Install the Operating System

In the previous chapter when discussing how to set up a static analysis lab, I did not limit the topic to Windows. I also discussed how to set up an Ubuntu system. This is because there are Linux-based file inspection tools that prove valuable in static analysis. But since dynamic analysis is the process of analyzing malware while it is in motion, you do not need any Linux-based dynamic analysis lab because it is not the malware's target OS. Instead, I will concentrate on showing how to set up a Windows system where malware can execute and run as it is intended to run. The focus is on Windows since the scope of the discussion revolves around Windows-based files.

When it comes to a Windows dynamic analysis lab, you must have different flavors of Windows available. The following are the most commonly used in dynamic analysis labs today:

- ▶ Windows XP Service Pack 3 32-bit
- ▶ Windows 7 32-bit
- ▶ Windows 7 Service Pack 1 32-bit
- ▶ Windows 7 64-bit
- ▶ Windows 7 Service Pack 1 64-bit
- ▶ Windows 8

It is always good to have different flavors of Windows available. This makes analysis much more effective and gives the researcher a chance to see how a malware behaves in different Windows flavors. For example, if a malware successfully runs in Windows 7 but not in Windows 7 Service Pack 1, this can already be a good indicator that the malware probably is utilizing some vulnerability in Windows 7 that has been solved by Service Pack 1. This information is already useful. A researcher can simply advise affected users to install Service Pack 1 to stop the malware from spreading while more analysis and a better solution is still being worked on.

> **TIP**
>
> *A Microsoft Developer Network (MSDN) subscription is a good way to have access to different flavors of Windows. Get one if you or the company you work for has the budget for this. If there is no budget for an MSDN subscription, buying separate Windows installers might be the cheaper alternative.*

Since it is always good to have both a virtualized dynamic analysis lab and a bare-metal dynamic analysis lab, you need to familiarize yourself with the basics of installing Windows in these environments.

Installing in a Virtualized Environment

Lots of virtualized environments can be used when creating a dynamic analysis lab. The most common are the following:

- ▶ VMware
- ▶ VirtualBox by Oracle
- ▶ Virtual PC by Microsoft

The most popular VMware virtualization software is VMware Workstation for Windows and Fusion for Mac. These require licenses. The free version of VMware is VMware Player. It is useful for building virtualized environments, but it does not offer as many features as those offered by the paid versions. VirtualBox and Virtual PC, on the other hand, are all free. For these purposes, I will be concentrating more on VMware Player and VirtualBox. Feel free to experiment with using Virtual PC by Microsoft.

Installing the operating system (OS) in a virtualized environment is easy. All that is needed is the ISO image of the OS installer. It is ideal if you have an MSDN subscription because the OS installers are distributed as ISO images.

Another important aspect of creating a virtualized dynamic analysis lab is the choice of the host OS. Some researchers prefer a Linux-based OS such as Ubuntu or even Mac, while others prefer Windows. This is up to you and your needs.

For me, I always prefer Ubuntu as the host OS and simply install a virtualized Windows environment. To do this, I use either VMware Player or VirtualBox. I prefer this setup as a precaution just in case malware has the capability to compromise the host OS because of a hole or vulnerability in the virtualization software. Having a host OS that the malware is not designed to execute in minimizes the risk of malware infection. By taking away the OS dependency of malware, the risk of malware infection is mitigated.

LINGO

The **host OS** is where the virtualization software is installed. The **guest OS** is the OS that is virtualized by the virtualization software.

The following labs will show you how to install and uninstall both VMware Player and VirtualBox in Ubuntu.

LAB 8-1: *Installing VMware Player in Ubuntu*

In this lab, you will be installing VMware Player in Ubuntu. For this purpose, you will be using the 64-bit version of Ubuntu and VMware Player for Linux.

What You Need:

▶ System running Ubuntu 14.04.01 LTS or later

▶ VMware Player for Linux installer

Steps:

1. Register for a VMware account at https://my.vmware.com/web/vmware/login.

2. Download VMware Player for Linux at http://www.vmware.com/go/downloadplayer. For the purpose of this lab, you will be using VMware Player for Linux 64-bit. As of this writing, the latest version is 6.0.3.

3. Open a terminal window and change to the directory where VMware Player was downloaded.

4. Install the required dependencies first.

    ```
    $ sudo apte-get install build-essential linux-headers-$(uname -r)
    ```

5. Install VMware Player. Take note that the VMware Player version may vary.
    Enter the filename you have downloaded and simply follow this pattern:

    ```
    $ chmod +x VMware-Player-6.0.3-1895310.x86_64.bundle
    $ sudo ./VMware-Player-6.0.3-1895310.x86_64.bundle
    ```

6. Follow the prompts in the VMware Player installation window, as shown in
    Figure 8-1, to finish installation.

7. After successful installation, execute VMware. Figure 8-2 shows the VMware
    Player main window.

> ### TIP
> *Using the Ubuntu unity panel located on the upper left, type* **VMware** *to find where VMware is
> and double-click the icon.*

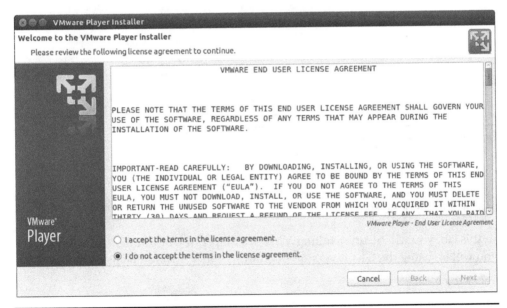

Figure 8-1   *VMware Player installer.*

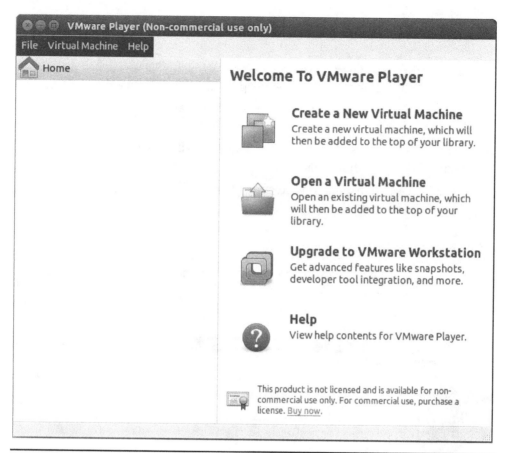

Figure 8-2 *VMware Player main window.*

LAB 8-2: *Uninstalling VMware Player in Ubuntu*

In this lab, you will be uninstalling VMware Player in Ubuntu. For this purpose, you will be using the 64-bit version of Ubuntu and VMware Player for Linux.

What You Need:

▶ System running Ubuntu 14.04.01 LTS or later

▶ VMware Player for Linux installed

Steps:

1. Open a terminal window.

2. Execute the following command line to invoke the VMware Player window:

    ```
    $ sudo vmware-installer -u vmware-player
    ```

3. Follow the instructions in the VMware Player installer window to uninstall VMware Player.

LAB 8-3: *Installing VirtualBox in Ubuntu*

In this lab, you will be installing VirtualBox in Ubuntu. For this purpose, you will be using the 64-bit version of Ubuntu and VirtualBox for Linux.

What You Need:

▶   System running Ubuntu 14.04.01 LTS or later

▶   VirtualBox for Linux installer

Steps:

1. Download VirtualBox Linux from https://www.virtualbox.org/wiki/Linux_Downloads.

2. Choose the flavor that is for Ubuntu 14.04 and download the 64-bit version.

3. Open a terminal window and change to the directory where VirtualBox was downloaded.

4. Install the VirtualBox dependencies.

    ```
    $ sudo apt-get install libsdl1.2debian
    ```

    Just to avoid confusion, take note of the *L* and the number 1 character in *libsdl1*, that is, libsd(L)(1).

5. Install VirtualBox for Linux. Take note that the filename will vary depending on the current version that is available.

    ```
    $ sudo dpkg -i virtualbox-4.3_4.3.16-95972-Ubuntu~raring_adm64.deb
    ```

6. After successful installation, execute VirtualBox. Figure 8-3 shows the main page. You can do this by clicking the Ubuntu unity panel located at the top left and typing **VirtualBox**.

LINGO

The Ubuntu **unity-panel** is also known as **home**, **Big Freaking Button**, **BFB**, and simply **panel**.

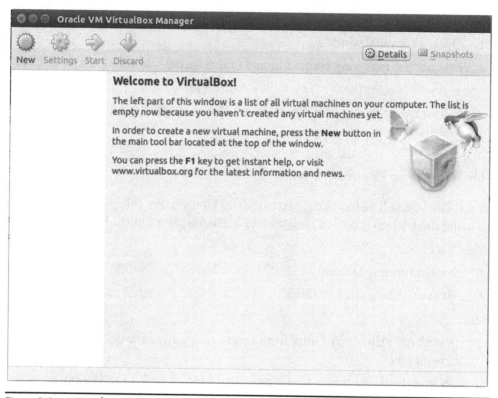

Figure 8-3 *VirtualBox main page.*

LAB 8-4: *Uninstalling VirtualBox in Ubuntu*

In this lab, you will be uninstalling VirtualBox in Ubuntu. For this purpose, you will be using the 64-bit version of Ubuntu and VirtualBox for Linux.

What You Need:

▶ System running Ubuntu 14.04.01 LTS or later

▶ VirtualBox for Linux installed

Steps:

1. Open a terminal window.

2. Execute the following command to uninstall VirtualBox for Linux:

```
$  sudo dpkg -r virtualbox-4.3
```

If you forgot the name of the exact package, you can get a list of packages installed by issuing the following command:

```
$ dpkg –get-selections | grep –v deinstall
```

This will display the packages in alphabetical order. Simply look for virtualbox, and you will know exactly what the package name is. In this specific lab, it is virtualbox-4.3.

> **TIP**
>
> *You can save the output from a command line to a file just by typing* **> filename** *at the end of the command line.*

Installing in a Bare-Metal System

Installing Windows in a bare-metal system has already been well documented. You have been installing Windows in bare-metal systems since the OS was first released, so there is no need to spend too much time on it in this book. But with new hardware today that comes with no disc drive, you have to be familiar with how to install Windows in these devices, especially if you will not be utilizing the hardware manufacturer's OS restore functionality.

> **TIP**
>
> *To be on the safe side, do not rely on a PC manufacturer's OS restore functionality even if the backup OS is found on a separate partition of the local hard disk because there is always a risk of it being compromised by previously executed (accidentally or on purpose) malware. It is always good to have a separate OS installer or image backup that is separated from the dynamic analysis lab to ensure that the image or the installer is not compromised.*

A good way to install the OS is by using a universal serial bus (USB) stick. In the previous chapter, I discussed how to create a bootable USB Windows installer. Follow the instructions in Chapter 7, and you will be all set.

If the hardware comes with a disc drive but the device driver is not available anymore, you will see an error message stating that a required CD/DVD device driver was not found during installation. If this happens, simply follow the steps outlined in Chapter 7.

Plus, I have already discussed how to solve issues commonly faced by users when installing Windows without the required disc device driver and installing it in systems that do not come with a disc drive. You can learn how to solve these issues in Chapter 7.

Make the Lab Malware Friendly

In a static analysis lab, one of the steps you took was to harden the lab so if the malware is accidentally executed, it will be denied the things that it needs to function or at least be impeded in executing its directive. This is to ensure that the effects of malware infection are minimized. But in a dynamic analysis lab, your main goal is the opposite. You want the malware to execute. You want to provide it with everything it needs to execute properly. Because if it executes as it is intended to do, you will have the chance to capture its behavior and understand its main directive. Therefore, you must have a dynamic analysis lab that is malware friendly.

To make a dynamic analysis lab malware friendly, you need to do the following:

1. Make the OS malware friendly.
2. Make the Internet browser malware friendly.
3. Install commonly exploited software.
4. Create enticing files.
5. Create and utilize dummy social media accounts.

Make the OS Malware Friendly

Making the OS malware friendly means having it possess the following characteristics:

▶ The default user must have administrative privileges.

▶ Automatic updates must be disabled.

▶ User Account Control (UAC) must be disabled.

> **NOTE**
>
> Most computer systems sold to consumers that have the OS installed already have default users with admin privileges. Attackers tend to exploit this, especially if the user does not know how to set up a new user account with nonadmin privileges.

LAB 8-5: *Disabling Automatic Updates in Windows 7*

In this lab, you disable Automatic Updates in Windows 7.

What You Need:

▶ System running Windows 7

Steps:

1. Choose Start | Control Panel | Windows Update.

2. In the upper-left corner, click Change Settings.

3. Under Important Updates, choose Never Check For Updates (Not Recommended).

4. Under Recommended Updates, uncheck Give Me Recommended Updates The Same Way I Receive Important Updates.

5. Under Who Can Install Updates, uncheck Allow All Users To Install Updates On This Computer.

   The setting should look like Figure 8-4.

6. Click OK and exit the Windows Update window.

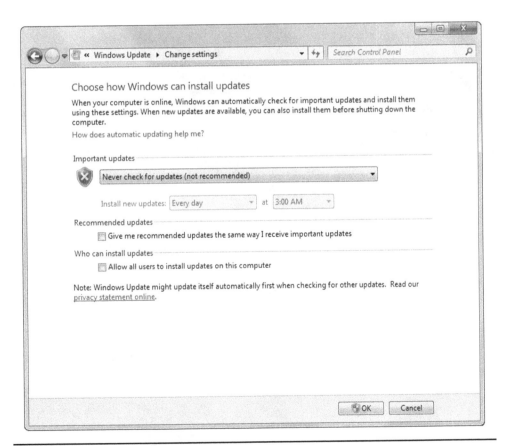

Figure 8-4   *Windows Update settings.*

LAB 8-6: *Disabling User Account Control in Windows 7*

In this lab, you disable User Account Control in Windows 7.

What You Need:

► System running Windows 7

Steps:

1. Choose Start | Control Panel | Action Center.
2. In the upper-left corner, click Change User Account Control Settings.
3. Slide the indicator down to Never Notify, as shown in Figure 8-5.
4. Click OK.
5. After clicking OK, User Account Control will ask whether you want to allow User Account Control Settings to make changes to the computer. Click Yes.
6. Exit the Action Center window.

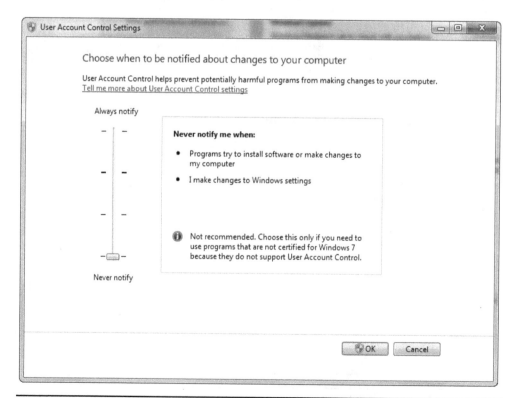

Figure 8-5 *User Account Control settings.*

> **NOTE**
>
> *In some instances, UAC needs to be enabled, especially if analyzing malware that claims to have the ability to disable UAC.*

Make the Internet Browser Malware Friendly

The following are the most common browsers found on a Windows system:

► Internet Explorer

► Mozilla Firefox

► Google Chrome

A dynamic analysis lab must have all of them, and these browsers must have the lowest security setting; therefore, it will be easy for a malware to take advantage of and abuse these browsers. All security features that each of these browsers have must be disabled to make them malware friendly.

LAB 8-7: *Making Internet Explorer Malware Friendly*

In this lab, you will configure Internet Explorer to be malware friendly. You will use Internet Explorer 11 for the purpose of this lab.

What You Need:

► System running Windows 7

► Internet Explorer 11 installed

Steps:

1. Open Internet Explorer 11.

2. Click the cog icon in the upper-right corner of the Internet Explorer window. This will show a drop-down menu.

> **NOTE**
>
> *A cog icon usually symbolizes settings or options in a software menu.*

3. Choose About Internet Explorer. Figure 8-6 shows the About Internet Explorer window.

4. Uncheck the option Install New Versions Automatically. This will ensure that you control what version of Internet Explorer is installed. Doing this will invoke User Account Control. Just click Yes.

Figure 8-6   *About Internet Explorer window.*

5. Once you're back to the About Internet Explorer window, click Close.

6. Click the cog icon again and choose Internet Options.

7. Click the Security tab. Figure 8-7 shows the available settings on the Security tab.

8. Uncheck Enable Protected Mode.

> **NOTE**
>
> *Internet Explorer protected mode is a security feature that makes it more difficult for malware to be installed on the system. Aside from malware installation protection, protected mode allows the installation of approved or wanted ActiveX controls and add-ons when logged in as an administrator. It is turned on by default.*

9. You will notice from Figure 8-7 that there are four available zones.

    ▶ Internet

    ▶ Local intranet

    ▶ Trusted sites

    ▶ Restricted sites

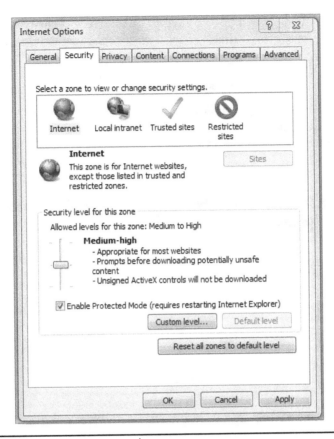

Figure 8-7   *Internet Options Security tab.*

10. Highlight each zone and change the security level to the lowest available one. The following are the zones and the security level allowed for each.

   ▶ **Internet**   Medium to High

   ▶ **Local intranet**   Low to High

   ▶ **Trusted sites**   Low to High

   ▶ **Restricted sites**   High

   NOTE

   In most cases, once you uncheck Enable Protected Mode in one zone, the rest of the zones follow suit. But just in case, double-check whether it is unchecked as you adjust the security level for each zone.

11. Click Apply.

12. A warning message will pop up saying "The current security settings will put your computer at risk." This is exactly what you want, so just click OK.

13. Go to the Privacy tab.

14. Change Settings to the lowest possible, which is Accept All Cookies.

15. Uncheck Turn On Pop-Up Blocker. Leave the InPrivate setting checked. This will be useful if in the future there is a need to experiment on malware that claims to bypass InPrivate browsing.

> **NOTE**
>
> *InPrivate browsing is a feature in Internet Explorer that prevents browsing history, temporary Internet files, form data, cookies, and usernames and passwords from being retained by the browser.*

16. Figure 8-8 shows the Privacy tab settings you want.

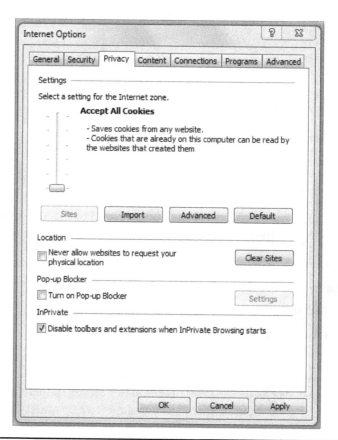

Figure 8-8   *Internet Options Privacy tab.*

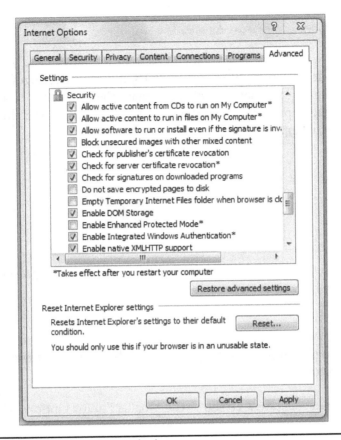

Figure 8-9   *Internet Options Advanced tab.*

17. Click Apply.

18. Go to the Advanced tab.

19. Look for Security under Settings.

20. Select the following:

    ▶ Allow Active Content From CDs To Run On My Computer

    ▶ Allow Active Content To Run In Files On My Computer

    ▶ Allow Software To Run Or Install Even If The Signature Is Invalid

21. Figure 8-9 shows the Advanced security settings you want.

22. Click OK.

23. Restart the system to make sure that the changes made on the Advanced tab take effect.

LAB 8-8: *Making Mozilla Firefox Malware Friendly*

In this lab, you will configure Mozilla Firefox to be malware friendly. As of this writing, the updated version of Firefox is 32.0.3. If there are changes in future versions regarding the settings you will manipulate, there shouldn't be any problems. The changes in manipulating the settings are usually minimal, and the same principles will still apply.

What You Need:

- ▶ System running Windows 7
- ▶ Mozilla Firefox installed

Steps:

1. Open Mozilla Firefox.
2. Go to the upper-right corner and click the menu button represented by three parallel horizontal lines.

> **NOTE**
>
> *Three parallel horizontal lines usually represent menu buttons in graphic-friendly user interface (UI) designs.*

3. Click Options. Figure 8-10 shows the Mozilla Firefox Options window.
4. Go to the Content tab.
5. Uncheck Block Pop-Up Windows.
6. Go to the Applications tab and look for Windows Installer Package.
7. Change Action from Always Ask to Save File.
8. Go to the Security tab.
9. Uncheck the following:
   - ▶ Warn Me When Sites Try To Install Add-Ons
   - ▶ Block Reported Attack Sites
   - ▶ Block Reported Web Forgeries
10. Click OK.

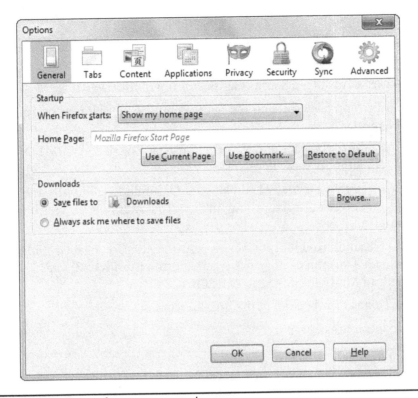

Figure 8-10 *Mozilla Firefox Options window.*

LAB 8-9: *Making Google Chrome Malware Friendly*

In this lab, you will configure Google Chrome to be malware friendly. As of this writing, the version of Google Chrome is 37.0.2062.124. If there are changes in future versions regarding the settings you will manipulate, there shouldn't be any problems. The changes in manipulating the settings are usually minimal, and the same principles will still apply.

What You Need:

▶ System running Windows 7

▶ Google Chrome installed

Steps:

1. Open Google Chrome.

2. Go to the upper-right corner and click the menu button represented by three parallel horizontal lines.

3. Click Settings.

4. Another way to go to Settings is by typing the following in the address bar: **chrome://settings**.

5. Click Show Advanced Settings at the bottom of the page.

6. Under Privacy, click the Content Settings button. A window pop-up will then appear.

7. Navigate down the page and look for Pop-Ups. Toggle the radio button to Allow All Sites To Show Pop-Ups.

8. Navigate further downward and look for Unsandboxed Plug-In Access. Toggle the radio button to Allow All Sites To Use A Plug-In To Access Your Computer.

9. Below Unsandboxed Plug-In Access is Automatic Downloads. Under Automatic Downloads, toggle the radio button to Allow All Sites To Download Multiple Files Automatically.

10. Click Done at the bottom of the pop-up window.

11. Close the Settings page.

Although you want Internet browsers to be malware friendly, there will be instances when you want them to be secure as possible, especially if you are analyzing a malware that has the ability to bypass Internet browser security and privacy features.

Install Commonly Exploited Software

Typically the most popular software is often the most abused because it gives the malware the potential to have greater target coverage. Attackers spend hours finding vulnerabilities in this type of software that they can exploit. Now, there are lots of software that falls into this category, but for the purpose of brevity, I will concentrate on three often abused by attackers, listed here:

▶ Microsoft Office

▶ Adobe Flash Player

▶ Adobe Reader

Microsoft Office is included not only because of its macro capabilities but also because it is widely used in homes, schools, and businesses. Although there is not that much macro malware around, it is still good to have Office installed, especially if you are going to create enticing Office files. Having enticing files in Microsoft Office format but no Office installed might make attackers suspicious. A malware can always have a built-in functionality to detect programs installed in a system. A malware may refuse to steal any documents if the appropriate program for it does not exist in the system, especially if it is targeting a user or non-server system. This is one precaution malware writers take to beat honeypots with enticing files.

> **TIP**
>
> *If you are going to use bait files for information stealers, make sure that the appropriate program for those files are installed. For example, Excel worksheets and Word documents must have Office Windows installed on the system.*

Adobe Flash Player and Adobe Reader are also widely used and are free, making them good targets for attackers to exploit. Adobe Reader's ability to run JavaScript makes it a good platform for attackers. Adobe Flash Player, on the other hand, is exploited through malformed Flash files that the browser loads.

> **TIP**
>
> *The safest places to download Adobe Reader and Adobe Flash Player from are http://get.adobe.com/reader and http://get.adobe.com/flashplayer, respectively.*

LAB 8-10: *Making Microsoft Office Malware Friendly*

In this lab, you will configure Microsoft Office to be malware friendly. The version of Microsoft Office being used is Microsoft Office 2010. Even if you have a different version of Office installed, the same menu options and principles of making the software malware friendly still apply. If there are changes in how a menu is presented, they will be minimal.

What You Need:

▶ System running Windows 7

▶ Microsoft Office installed

Steps:

1. Open Microsoft Word.

2. Click the File tab under Help click Options. The Word Options window will pop up, as shown in Figure 8-11.

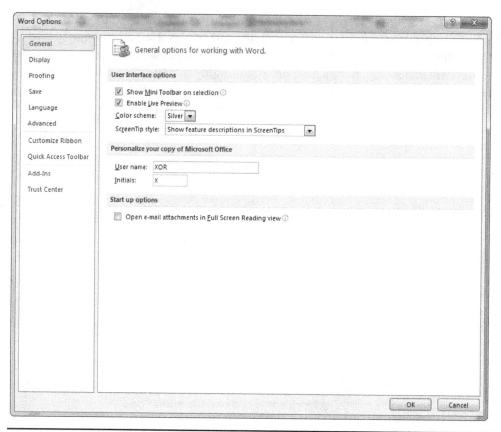

Figure 8-11   *Word Options window.*

3. Click Trust Center at the bottom-left side and then click Trust Center Settings at the lower-right side of the page.

4. In the Trust Center window, click Trusted Locations.

5. Click Add New Location. The Microsoft Office Trusted Location window will pop up.

6. Add the location where you will put suspicious malicious Word documents for opening and then check Subfolders Of This Location Are Also Trusted. Click OK.

> **NOTE**
>
> *A Microsoft trusted location is treated as a trusted source for opening files. Microsoft Office assumes that these file locations are safe; therefore, content, code, and add-ins are allowed to load with a minimal amount of security.*

7. Go to ActiveX Settings. Toggle the radio button Enable All Controls Without Restrictions And Without Prompting (Not Recommended; Potentially Dangerous Controls Can Run).

8. Uncheck Safe Mod (Helps Limit the Control's Access To Your Computer).

9. Go to Macro Settings. Toggle the radio button Enable All Macros (Not Recommended; Potentially Dangerous Code Can Run).

10. Click OK until all pop-up windows are closed and then close Word.

> ### TIP
> *Look at the different options in Trust Center and experiment with how they influence Word documents that have macros. You can always click Restore Defaults after experimenting and reconfigure as stated in the lab or as you see fit.*

11. Open Excel and follow the same procedure.

12. Open PowerPoint and follow the same procedure.

13. Open Access and follow the same procedure.

> ### NOTE
> *Some options that appear in Word will not appear in Excel, PowerPoint, and Access. This is fine. Simply skip those steps.*

14. Open Publisher and follow the same procedure.

15. In Publisher there are two options: Macro Settings and DEP Settings.

16. In Macro Settings, follow the usual procedure.

17. In DEP Settings, uncheck Enable Data Execution Protection Mode.

> ### LINGO
> ***Data Execution Prevention (DEP)*** *is a security feature that can help prevent damage to your computer from malware and other security threats. It can help protect your computer by monitoring programs to make sure they use system memory safely. If a program tries running code from memory in an incorrect way, DEP closes the program.*[1]

18. Click OK until all pop-up windows are closed and then close all Microsoft Office applications.

---

[1] Microsoft Technet: http://technet.microsoft.com/en-US/.

LAB 8-11: *Making Adobe Reader Malware Friendly*

In this lab, you will configure Adobe Reader to be malware friendly. The version of Adobe Reader I'm using is 11.0.09. Don't worry if your available version is different; the same principles and configuration concepts remain the same. There might be minimal changes in the menu, but they can easily be identified.

What You Need:

▶ System running Windows 7

▶ Adobe Reader installer

Steps:

1. Download Adobe Reader from http://get.adobe.com/reader.

2. Choose the appropriate version and make sure that the option to install McAfee Antivirus is unchecked.

3. Install Adobe Reader.

4. Open Adobe Reader.

5. Choose Edit | Preferences.

6. Click JavaScript under Categories on the left side of the window.

7. Make sure Enable Acrobat JavaScript is checked and that Enable Global Object Security Policy is unchecked.

8. Click Security (Enhanced) on the left side of the window.

9. Make sure Enable Protected Mode at startup is unchecked. Once you do this, a message will pop up saying that the application needs to be restarted.

10. Make sure Enable Enhanced Security is unchecked.

11. Click Trust Manager on the left side of the window.

12. Under Internet Access From PDF Files Outside The Web Browser, click the Change Settings button.

13. Toggle the radio button Allow Pdf Files to Access All Websites and click OK.

14. Click Updater on the left side of the window.

15. Toggle the radio button Do Not Download Or Install Updates Automatically and click OK. A message will pop up asking whether you want to make changes to enhance security preferences. Click OK.

16. User Account Control will appear (if it is still enabled) asking whether you would allow Adobe Reader and Acrobat Manager to make changes to the computer. Click Yes.

17. Restart the Adobe Reader application.

Create Enticing Files

Most attacks are all about information stealing. Malware programs are designed to look for files that might contain company secrets or any confidential information that attackers can use to their advantage.

Creating a set of enticing files is easy. Simply get a letterhead of a bogus company or even a legitimate one and then put it in the dynamic analysis lab's Documents folder or any folder renamed to sound like it contains company confidential files. The following are good folder names:

▶ Salaries

▶ Bonuses

▶ MarketingResearch

▶ DesignProposals

These are just suggestions; you are free to use your imagination. Then make sure that the enticing files have enticing names as well, such as EmployeesSalary.XLS. The more enticing it is, the more the attackers or the running malware will be convinced that it is a file worth stealing.

> **TIP**
> *Make sure the enticing files are not empty. Creating enticing files with 0 bytes defeats the whole purpose of having enticing files. Remember that a malware can have checking mechanisms to know whether a file is valid.*

Create and Utilize Dummy Social Media Accounts

Some malware has special needs such as having a Facebook or Twitter account in the compromised machine for it to function. Therefore, it is always good to have personas in your dynamic analysis lab. Having these dummy accounts ready is always helpful, so if you are faced with a malware that requires this, you can simply open a browser and log in to the social network of choice and then let the malware execute.

> ### TIP
>
> *Configure the browsers to remember your social media account so you don't need to input the password over and over again. This is also advantageous if the dynamic analysis lab will be part of an automated malware analysis infrastructure.*

Anonymize the Lab

A dynamic analysis lab is an active computer environment. Depending on the malware running on the lab, the dynamic analysis lab may need to have an Internet connection to facilitate the malware communicating to its command and control, or C2.

> ### LINGO
>
> *C2, C&C, and CnC are all abbreviations of a botnet's command and control.*

Therefore, it is important to anonymize the dynamic analysis lab. This protects the dynamic analysis lab from being tagged by the cybercriminals as research labs so the dynamic analysis systems won't get blocked or attacked.

To anonymize the dynamic analysis lab, you will be using the following:

▶ Proxy servers

▶ Virtual private network

▶ Tor

It is one less than the anonymization technologies I discussed in the previous chapter. The one I took out is the online anonymizer. You do not need this since you will not be actively surfing the Internet, and the other three should take care of the anonymization you need in case the malware needs to utilize the browser.

Chapter 7 discusses all these technologies.

Isolate the Lab

Dynamic analysis labs need to be isolated even more than static analysis labs do. Malware is executed in a dynamic analysis lab; therefore, there is real risk that the malware can and will infect systems connected to it. This is why it is of paramount importance to isolate the dynamic analysis lab from any network.

A good rule of thumb for isolating a dynamic analysis lab is to have it totally isolated from any form of production network. It cannot be part of any network, and it cannot share any Internet connection with any device.

Restoring to a Clean State

Every time a malware is processed, the dynamic analysis lab has to be restored to its original clean state after the analysis process. This ensures that the result of the next dynamic malware analysis is not adulterated by the previous one.

Restoration time is an important characteristic of a dynamic analysis lab. The faster the restoration time, the more malware that can be analyzed dynamically. Restoration time becomes a big factor, especially if the dynamic analysis lab is part of an automated malware analysis system. Obviously, a virtualized dynamic analysis lab environment has faster restoration time compared to a bare-metal system.

Virtualized Environment Clean State Restoration

In a virtualized environment, a researcher can have different image snapshots. Image snapshots capture the current state of a virtual machine when the snapshot was taken. With virtual image snapshots, the researcher and analyst can always revert to an image that she wants to work on. This is great for malware analysis. But if the desire is automated dynamic malware analysis, setting an image to be non-persistent is the best option because it does not involve any manual step. The moment the virtual image is restarted, it automatically reverts to its clean state.

LINGO

A non-persistent image is an image that reverts to its original clean state after a reboot. A persistent image is the opposite.

LAB 8-12: *Setting a Non-persistent Image in VirtualBox*

In this lab, you set up a non-persistent image in VirtualBox.

What You Need:

▶ VirtualBox installed

▶ A working VirtualBox image

Steps:

1. Open VirtualBox.

2. Choose File | Virtual Media Manager.

3. On the Hard Drives tab, click the hard drive you want to make non-persistent.

4. Click Modify under Actions or right-click the selected hard drive and choose Modify. The Modify Medium Attributes window will open.

5. Under Choose Mode, toggle the Writethrough radio button. In VirtualBox, this is the term used for non-persistent disk.

6. Click OK and close the Virtual Media Manager window.

7. Test the image for non-persistency.

> **TIP**
>
> *You can find more information about VirtualBox special image write modes at https://www.virtualbox.org/manual/ch05.html#hdimagewrites.*

LAB 8-13: *Setting a Non-persistent Image in VirtualBox Using the Command Line*

In this lab, you set up a non-persistent image in VirtualBox using the command line in Windows.

What You Need:

▶ System running Windows

▶ VirtualBox installed

▶ A working VirtualBox image

Steps:

1. Open a Windows command line.

2. Go to the VirtualBox folder. Its default location is C:\Program Files\Oracle\VirtualBox.

3. Type and execute the following command line:

    ```
    vboxmanage modifyhd /path/of/vdi/file/harddisk.vdi -type=writethrough
    ```

4. Execute VirtualBox and check the image for non-persistency.

Bare-Metal Environment Clean State Restoration

In the old days of bare-metal system malware analysis, there is no such thing as a non-persistent image. To go back to a clean state, the bare-metal system had to restored. Restoration had to be done all the time from a backup or clean image. This takes a lot of time, usually between 5 to 15 minutes depending on how fast the input/output (I/O) of the system is. Plus, everything is done manually. The most popular tool for a restoring bare-metal system during those days was Norton Ghost. Today, Clonezilla is the most popular and easy-to-use bare-metal system backup and restoration tool. I will discuss Clonezilla in greater detail later in this chapter.

Fortunately, there is a tool that enables non-persistency in a bare-metal system. This means that every time the bare-metal system is restarted or rebooted, it reverts to a clean state without the need for restoration from a backup image. This significantly lessens the time of the dynamic analysis lab's readiness to tackle another malware. The tool is called Deep Freeze by Faronics. This is not a free tool, but in my humble opinion it is worth the money. You can find more information about this tool at http://www.faronics.com/products/deep-freeze/. As of this writing, the cost of this tool, specifically Deep Freeze Standard, is $35. With Deep Freeze, researchers and analysts have the capability to have a non-persistent bare-metal system.

> **TIP**
>
> *Deep Freeze Standard is available for a 30-day trial, so you can test it before making a decision to buy.*

LAB 8-14: *Creating a Non-persistent Bare-Metal System Using Deep Freeze Standard*

In this lab, you see how to use Deep Freeze Standard to create a non-persistent bare-metal system.

What You Need:

▶ System running Windows

▶ Deep Freeze Standard installed

Steps:

1. Download and install Deep Freeze Standard from http://www.faronics.com/products/deep-freeze/standard/. A 30-day trial version is available.

2. Once installed, launch Deep Freeze Standard by pressing the Shift key and double-clicking the Deep Freeze Standard icon, represented by a polar bear, found in the notification area of the Windows taskbar.

3. Enter the password to unlock Deep Freeze Standard. This is the password you set during installation.

4. On the Status tab, choose Boot Frozen. This sets the bare-metal system to not record any changes. After every bootup, the bare-metal system goes back to its clean state.

> **TIP**
>
> *Make sure you have done what needs to be done to the bare-metal dynamic analysis system before freezing it. If you forget to do something or need to update a setting or program, simply reboot to a clean state, set the status to Boot Thawed or Boot Thawed On Next, and make the necessary changes to the bare-metal system. Once done, set the status back to Boot Frozen.*

5. Click OK.

6. You can also click Apply and Reboot for the changes to take effect and reboot the machine.

Backing Up and Restoring

After investing time and effort in creating a dynamic analysis lab, the next step is to back everything up. Nobody wants to go through the process of building the lab again from scratch if things go haywire. Plus, it is always important to back up critical part of your research systems, which includes the dynamic analysis lab. If it ever fails or behaves abnormally because of a new malware, you can easily restore it and be up and running in no time using its backup.

When it comes to backing up the dynamic analysis lab, the following items are important:

▶ The golden image
▶ Host OS
▶ Other systems supporting the lab

The Golden Image

The golden image is the clean image on which all dynamic analysis labs are based. This image is the one that is used by the system to restore the dynamic analysis lab to its clean state.

In a virtualized environment, this is the snapshot or main image of the virtualized dynamic analysis lab. This is easy to back up because a copy of the virtual machine can just be kept offline and serve as the backup.

> **TIP**
>
> *When setting up a virtual machine image, specifically in VMware, choose to have the image files divided into 2GB chunks. This makes it easy to copy and back up.*

In a bare-metal environment, backing it up as an image is easy too. The tool I use is Clonezilla, which can be downloaded from http://clonezilla.org/downloads.php. As mentioned in the previous chapter, it is free and easy to use.

The number of golden images you have depends on the Windows flavor you have plus the different configurations and settings you have for each flavor. For example, if you have the different flavors covered here, then you will have at least six golden images:

- ▶ Windows XP Service Pack 3 32-bit
- ▶ Windows 7 32-bit
- ▶ Windows 7 Service Pack 1 32-bit
- ▶ Windows 7 64-bit
- ▶ Windows 7 Service Pack 1 64-bit
- ▶ Windows 8

If for each of the images you have different variations, such as one image has Adobe installed while the other one does not, then that's an additional six golden images, making your total twelve. It is important to take into consideration the number of golden images you have and their sizes so you can plan your storage and backup space accordingly.

Host OS

Aside from backing up the golden images of a virtualized dynamic analysis lab, it is also important to back up the host OS. This ensures that if the host OS fails, there is no need to restore it from scratch and reconfigure it again to support the virtualized dynamic analysis lab. Sometimes the process of backing up the host

OS is the most effective way to back up the whole dynamic analysis infrastructure because the backup also contains the golden images already. As a result, the system can resume its normal function after restoration, and there is no need to restore the golden images from their separate backups. The only thing that needs to be considered here is the space that will be taken up by backing up the host OS with the golden images.

Other Systems Supporting the Lab

Some dynamic analysis labs have other systems supporting them. For example, an interconnected multiple dynamic analysis lab might have a Dynamic Host Control Protocol (DHCP) server, its own private DNS server, a spoofed Internet box, and so on. These systems will also need backing up so they can easily be up and running in case of failure.

My tool of choice when it comes to backing up and restoring golden images of bare-metal dynamic analysis labs, the host operating system, and other systems supporting the lab is Clonezilla. It is free and easy to use.

As previously discussed, today Clonezilla is the most popular and easiest-to-use bare-metal system backup and restoration tool. Clonezilla, as described at http://clonezilla.org, is a partition and disk imaging/cloning program. It helps the user do system deployment, bare-metal backup, and recovery. There are two types of Clonezilla available: Clonezilla Live and Clonezilla SE (server edition). For these purposes, you will be using Clonezilla Live. Clonezilla Live is a small bootable GNU/Linux distribution for x86/amd64 (x86-64) computers. Clonezilla Live can be used to image or clone individual computers using a disc or USB flash drive. Since most computer systems nowadays, especially laptops, do not come with disc drives anymore, my concentration will be on using USB flash drives.

LAB 8-15: *Creating a Clonezilla Live in USB Flash Drive*

In this lab, you will be creating a Clonezilla Live in a USB flash drive that can be used to boot up a machine with no disc drive.

What You Need:

▶ USB flash drive with at least 8GB of space

▶ System running Windows

▶ Internet connection

Steps:

1. Format the USB flash drive and choose FAT as the file system. Windows will format it as FAT32, which is the default.

2. Download Tuxboot from http://sourceforge.net/projects/tuxboot/files/. As of this writing, the latest version is Tuxboot 0.6.

3. Execute Tuxboot. Make sure the machine is connected to the Internet. Tuxboot will need to download the latest Clonezilla Live files during this process.

4. Fill in the following options, as shown in Figure 8-12:

   A. On-Line Distribution: clonezilla_live_stable | 2.2.4-12-i486 (latest as of this writing)

   B. Type: USB Drive

   C. Drive: The drive letter of the USB flash drive

TIP

Clicking Update in On-Line Distribution updates the version of Clonezilla Live to the latest one that supports the Windows version where Tuxboot is running.

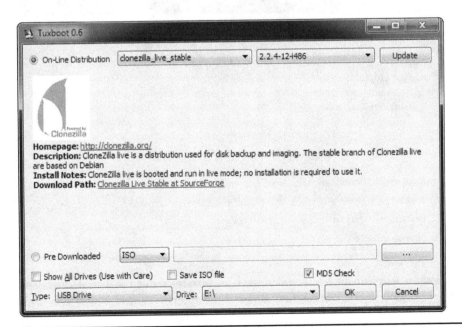

Figure 8-12   *Tuxboot preferred options.*

5. Click OK. Tuxboot will then proceed with the following steps, as shown in Figure 8-13:

   A. **Downloading Files**   The current version of Clonezilla Live is being downloaded by Tuxboot.

   B. **Extracting and Copying Files**   Downloaded files will be loaded to the USB flash drive.

   C. **Installing Bootloader**   This enables the USB flash drive to become bootable.

   D. **Installation Complete, Reboot**   Everything is set, and the USB is ready to be used.

6. Click the Reboot Now button to reboot the system.

7. As displayed in the Tuxboot window, after rebooting, select the USB boot option in the BIOS boot menu.

8. You now have a bootable Clonezilla Live USB installation.

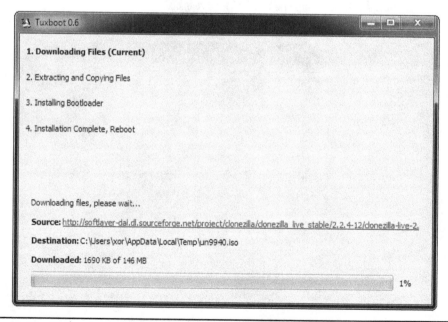

Figure 8-13   *Tuxboot process.*

LAB 8-16: *Backing Up a Partition Using Clonezilla Live*

In this lab, you will use Clonezilla Live to back up a hard disk partition.

What You Need:

▶ Clonezilla Live bootable USB flash drive

▶ System running in Windows

Steps:

1. Make sure the system is shut down and powered off.

2. Insert the bootable Clonezilla Live USB flash drive.

3. Power on the system, go to the BIOS setup, and boot using the USB flash drive. Different systems have different ways of doing this. Please consult your system's manual.

4. After successful reboot using the USB flash drive, the Clonezilla Live splash page is displayed.

5. Click Enter to activate Clonezilla Live. This is the default highlighted option in the Clonezilla Live menu. The system will then initialize.

6. Choose your language. English is the default.

7. Choose a policy for handling keymaps. Don't Touch Keymap is the default. There's no need to change this. Just press Enter.

8. Click Enter again to start Clonezilla.

9. Choose the default setting, which is Device-Image Work With Disks Or Partitions Using Images.

10. The next window will ask where the Clonezilla image will be saved to or read from. For this purpose, you will use the Local_dev option. If you want to use an external hard drive or USB flash drive to save to and read the image from, you can insert it now.

11. Choose the partition where you want to save the image.

12. Choose the directory where you want the image to be saved.

13. Choose the desired wizard mode. For this purpose, I will be using Beginner. Feel free to use Expert and experiment further.

14. The next window asks whether to save the whole disk or parts of the disk. Since you are saving only a partition, choose Saveparts.

15. Input the name for the saved image and press Enter.

16. Choose the source partition, press the spacebar to mark the selection, and click Enter. This is the partition you will back up.

17. Choose whether to check and repair the file system before saving it. If you have time, you can do this, but if you are in a hurry, simply choose Skip. I strongly suggest doing some checking when creating a backup of your system.

18. Follow the prompts to start the backup process. Backup might take a long time, especially if the save location is an external hard drive. A 50GB partition might take at least 30 minutes to back up.

19. After backup is done, you can choose Poweroff mode to shut down the system.

20. Turn on the system again and browse to the location of the saved image to verify it is there. Take note that the saved image is not a single file but rather a collection of different files. The name you assigned during the backup process is the name of the folder where these files are located.

LAB 8-17: *Restoring a Partition Using Clonezilla Live*

In this lab, you will use Clonezilla Live to restore a hard disk partition from an image backup.

What You Need:

▶ Clonezilla Live bootable USB flash drive

▶ System running in Windows

▶ Saved Clonezilla Live image file

Steps:

1. Make sure the system is shut down and powered off.

2. Insert the bootable Clonezilla Live USB flash drive.

3. If applicable, insert the external hard drive or USB flash drive where the Clonezilla Live image is saved. This step can be skipped because Clonezilla Live will let you insert any external media later in the process.

4. Power on the system, go to the BIOS setup, and boot up using the USB flash drive. Different systems have different ways of doing this. Please consult your system's manual.

5. After successful reboot using the USB flash drive, the Clonezilla Live splash page is displayed.

6.   Click Enter to activate Clonezilla Live. This is the default highlighted option in the Clonezilla Live menu. The system will then initialize.

7.   Choose your language. English is the default.

8.   Choose a policy for handling keymaps. Don't Touch Keymap is the default. There's no need to change this. Just press Enter.

9.   Click Enter again to start Clonezilla.

10.   Choose the default setting, which is Device-Image Work With Disks Or Partitions Using Images.

11.   The next window will ask where the Clonezilla image will be saved to or read from. For this purpose, you will use the Local_dev option. If you want to use an external hard drive or USB flash drive to save to and read image from, you can insert it now.

12.   Choose the partition where the saved image is located.

13.   Go to the folder where the saved image is located.

14.   Choose the desired wizard mode. For this purpose, I will be using Beginner. Feel free to use Expert and experiment further.

15.   The next window is asking what Clonezilla Live functionality is needed. Since you are restoring an image to a local partition, choose Restoreparts and click Enter.

16.   Clonezilla Live will ask which image file to restore. Choose the appropriate one and click Enter.

17.   Choose the target partition to be overwritten by the image backup and click Enter.

18.   Follow the prompts to initiate the restoration process. The restoration process may take some time depending on the system's I/O speed. A restoration of 50GB partition can be at least 20 minutes.

19.   After restoration is done, you can choose Poweroff mode to shut down the system.

20.   Remove the Clonezilla Live bootable flash drive and any external hard drives connected to the system.

21.   Reboot the system and check whether the restoration is successful.

Recap

In this chapter, I discussed how to set up a dynamic analysis lab. I identified the basic steps, which are as follows:

1. Choose the hardware.
2. Install the operating system.
3. Make the lab malware friendly.
4. Anonymize the lab.
5. Isolate the lab.

I also discussed the importance of restoration time when it comes to dynamic analysis labs. I explored the different methods and tools that you can use to restore a virtualized dynamic analysis lab and a bare-metal dynamic analysis lab to a clean state.

I stressed the importance of backing up what you have built so if ever a failure or an internal lab malware outbreak occurs, you can restore quickly with minimal downtime. I identified the important things that need to be backed up. They are as follows:

▶ The golden image
▶ Host OS
▶ Other systems supporting the lab

In this chapter, the most important thing is making the dynamic analysis lab malware friendly. It is the key to success that will enable your dynamic analysis lab to successfully execute a malware so monitoring and recording of its behavior is possible.

Tools

▶ Virtualization software
  ▶ **VMware Player**   http://www.vmware.com/go/downloadplayer
  ▶ **VirtualBox**   https://www.virtualbox.org/wiki/Downloads
  ▶ **VirtualPC**   http://www.microsoft.com/en-US/download/details.aspx?id=3702

- ▶ Trusted Adobe download sites
  - ▶ **Adobe Reader**   http://get.adobe.com/reader
  - ▶ **Adobe Flash Player**   http://get.adobe.com/flashplayer
- ▶ **Deep Freeze Standard by Faronics**   http://www.faronics.com/products/deep-freeze/standard/
- ▶ **Clonezilla**   http://clonezilla.org/download.php
- ▶ **Tuxboot**   http://sourceforge.net/projects/tuxboot/files/

Malware Inspection

The Portable Executable File

M alware inspection is where the excitement begins. This is the process where you actually dissect the malware sample and find out what it is capable of doing. But as with any inspection or analysis exercise, a process has to be followed to get the most out of the activity. And in a malware inspection activity (more popularly known as a *malware analysis activity*), there are steps that needed to be followed to effectively analyze malware.

Going back to the malware analysis process discussed in Chapter 1, the malware goes through multiple steps of analysis to get to the bottom of its malicious directive, as shown in Figure 9-1.

But before analysis should begin, an understanding of the file format of the malware is important. Since this book covers Windows files, I will be concentrating on the Windows file format known as Portable Executable (PE).

In this chapter, I will discuss what the PE file format is, how it is structured, and what tools you can use to make sense of the data that you can extract from this format that will aid you in your investigation of malicious activity.

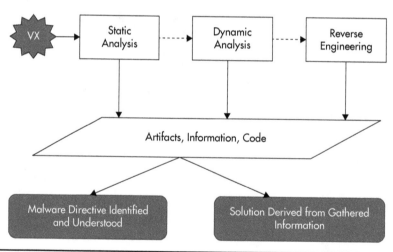

Figure 9-1   *The malware analysis process.*

The Windows Portable Executable File

The Windows PE file is the file type of Windows operating systems starting in Windows NT and Windows 95. It is called Portable Executable because Microsoft's vision was to use the same file format in future flavors of Windows, making the PE file common to all Windows platforms regardless of what central processing unit (CPU) they support. In my humble opinion, this idea has been accomplished because the descendants of Windows NT and Windows 95 still use the same Windows PE file.

The two most common file extensions of PE files are .EXE and .DLL, which I will refer to from now on as EXE and DLL files, respectively. An EXE is an executable file, whereas a DLL is a dynamic link library file. An executable file is pretty self-explanatory. A dynamic link library (DLL) file, as defined by Microsoft, is a library that contains code and data that can be used by more than one program at the same time. The main advantage of using DLLs is to promote code reuse and efficient memory usage. Instead of a program having to load the common functionality it needs on a separate memory space every time as a consequence of that functionality being coded into the program itself, the program can simply use the same functionality that is contained in and imported by the DLL. The program saves on memory usage, and the functionality it needs does not need to be coded into the program itself. Microsoft, as published in its knowledge base, summarizes the advantages offered by a DLL as follows:

▶ **Uses fewer resources**   When multiple programs use the same library of functions, a DLL can reduce the duplication of code that is loaded on the disk and in physical memory. This can greatly influence the performance of not just the program that is running in the foreground but also other programs that are running on the Windows operating system.

▶ **Promotes modular architecture**   A DLL helps promote developing modular programs. This helps you develop large programs that require multiple language versions or a program that requires modular architecture. An example of a modular program is an accounting program that has many modules that can be dynamically loaded at run time.

▶ **Eases deployment and installation**   When a function within a DLL needs an update or a fix, the deployment or installation of DLL does not require the program to be relinked with the DLL. Additionally, if multiple programs use the same DLL, they will all benefit from the update or the fix. This issue may more frequently occur when you use a third-party DLL that is regularly updated or fixed.

TIP

It is important to understand the modular advantage of DLLs because most malware today uses modular architecture, especially malware that updates itself with new functionality in a short period of time.

Even though it seems that there is huge difference in terms of file format between an EXE and a DLL, because of how DLL files are used, when you look closely, the difference is as simple as the difference in their extensions. Dissecting the two files will reveal that the only difference they have is a bit in one field of the PE header that tells Windows whether the file can be treated as an EXE or a DLL. What a PE header is will be discussed in the next section.

This bit is powerful because as long as it is set to characterize the file as a DLL, it will be treated as a DLL regardless of its extension. As a matter of fact, the following file extensions are implemented as DLLs:

▶ **OCX files**   ActiveX control files

▶ **CPL files**   Control Panel files

▶ **DRV files**   Device driver files

In your quest to analyze malware, it is important to know all DLL dependencies the malware needs to function properly. If one of the DLLs that a malware needs is not present in your dynamic analysis lab, the analysis will fail because the malware will not run as intended by the attacker. There will be instances wherein you need to install uncommon DLLs into your dynamic analysis lab to successfully run a malware or a suspected malware file.

A useful tool for this purpose of determining the DLL dependencies of a PE file is Dependency Walker. Dependency Walker is a free utility that scans any 32-bit or 64-bit Windows module (such as EXE, DLL, OCX, or SYS) and builds a hierarchical tree diagram of all the dependent modules. You can download Dependency Walker from http://www.dependencywalker.com.

LAB 9-1: *Using Dependency Walker to Determine a PE File's Dependencies*

In this lab, you will use Dependency Walker to identify the DLL dependencies of PE files.

What You Need:

▶ System running Windows 7

▶ Dependency Walker

Steps:

1. Download Dependency Walker from http://www.dependencywalker.com.

2. Extract Dependency Walker from the downloaded ZIP file.

3. Execute depends.exe.

4. Choose File | Open and choose depends.exe.

5. The window, as shown in Figure 9-2, shows that depends.exe uses nine DLL files. If any of these files are corrupted or missing, Dependency Walker will not work.

6. To export this information to a text file, choose File | Save As.

7. In the next window, choose Text With Import/Export Lists (*.txt) in Save As Type and click Save.

The PE File Format

The Windows PE file format is derived from the Common Object File Format (COFF) that was used in Virtual Address eXtension (VAX) systems running the Virtual Memory System (VMS) operating system produced by Digital Equipment Corporation (DEC), which was acquired by Compaq in 1998 and merged with HP in 2002. Most of the original Windows NT development team came from DEC, and when coming up with the PE format, they used existing code that they were already familiar with.

To get a better feel of the PE format, take a look at a general view of its structure, as shown in Figure 9-3.

The PE file format consists of the following:

► DOS MZ header

► DOS stub

► PE header

► Section table

► Sections

DOS MZ Header

All PE files start with the DOS MZ header. It is located at offset 0 of a PE file. It was put there just in case the program is executed in a system running Disk Operating System (DOS). When the PE format was still being developed, most

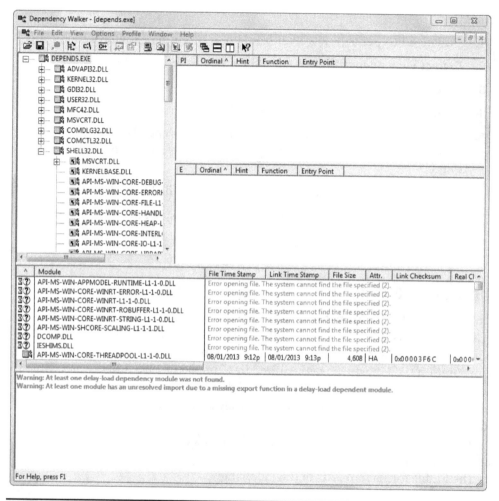

Figure 9-2   *Dependency Walker dependencies.*

systems were still running DOS. So, the developers recognized that there was a possibility that an executable designed to run in the new Windows environment would be executed in a DOS environment. The DOS MZ header was placed there to enable a DOS operating system to recognize the PE file as a valid executable file so it can execute the DOS stub, which is discussed in the next section.

Figure 9-4 shows an example of a DOS MZ header. The hex values 4Dh and 5Ah represent MZ, which is the initial of Mark Zbikowski, who is the one of the original architects of the Microsoft Disk Operating System (MS-DOS).

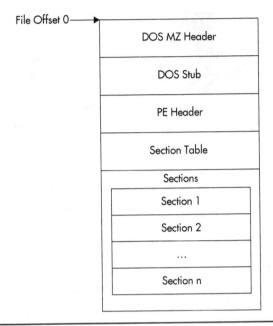

Figure 9-3   *A general view of the PE format.*

DOS Stub

The DOS stub is a valid DOS executable file. As discussed in the previous section, the DOS MZ header enables DOS to recognize the PE file as a valid executable in DOS so the DOS stub can be executed. The main purpose of executing the DOS stub is to tell the user, in case the program was executed under DOS, that the program is for Windows. The stub simply displays a message that the program cannot be run in DOS mode. You can easily see the string in the DOS stub, as shown in Figure 9-5.

PE Header

The PE file header, or simply PE header, is where the fun begins. This structure contains the important fields that the PE loader needs. As discussed previously

```
000000:   4D 5A 90 00-03 00 00 00-04 00 00 00-FF FF 00 00    MZE ▯       ▯
000010:   B8 00 00 00-00 00 00 00-40 00 00 00-00 00 00 00    ╕           @
000020:   00 00 00 00-00 00 00 00-00 00 00 00-00 00 00 00
000030:   00 00 00 00-00 00 00 00-00 00 00 00-F0 00 00 00                ≡
```

Figure 9-4   *DOS MZ Header of Calc.EXE.*

```
000040:  0E 1F BA 0E-00 B4 09 CD-21 B8 01 4C-CD 21 54 68   ▮□¦□ ┤□=!╕ □L=!Th
000050:  69 73 20 70-72 6F 67 72-61 6D 20 63-61 6E 6E 6F   is program canno
000060:  74 20 62 65-20 72 75 6E-20 69 6E 20-44 4F 53 20   t be run in DOS
000070:  6D 6F 64 65-2E 0D 0D 0A-24 00 00 00-00 00 00 00   mode.□□□$
000080:  87 45 16 64-C3 24 78 37-C3 24 78 37-C3 24 78 37   çE□d├$x7├$x7├$x7
000090:  39 07 38 37-C6 24 78 37-19 07 64 37-C8 24 78 37   9□87├$x7□□d7└$x7
0000A0:  C3 24 78 37-C2 24 78 37-C3 24 79 37-44 24 78 37   ├$x7┬$x7├$y7D$x7
0000B0:  39 07 61 37-CE 24 78 37-54 07 3D 37-C2 24 78 37   9□a7╬$x7T□=7┬$x7
0000C0:  19 07 65 37-DF 24 78 37-39 07 45 37-C2 24 78 37   □□e7█$x79□E7┬$x7
0000D0:  52 69 63 68-C3 24 78 37-00 00 00 00-00 00 00 00   Rich├$x7
0000E0:  00 00 00 00-00 00 00 00-00 00 00 00-00 00 00 00
```

Figure 9-5   *DOS stub of Calc.EXE.*

and as shown in Figure 9-3, the PE header is not located at the start of the file. That location is occupied by the DOS MZ header and DOS stub. The location of the PE header can be found in offset 0x3C relative to the start of the file. The 4-byte value starting at address 0x3C represents the address of the PE header relative to the start of the file. So, looking at Figure 9-4, which shows the DOS MZ header of Calc.EXE, you can determine that the address of the PE header is at 0xF0 because the 4 bytes starting from 0x3C are F0h 00h 00h 00h. Take note that x86 processors use little-endian architecture, so data is actually read from right to left. This means that the least significant byte is stored in the smallest address. In the previous example, the least significant byte is F0h, located in address 0x3C. The next significant byte is 00h, 00h, and 00h, located respectively in 0x3D, 0x3E, and 0x3F. So when you write it, the order of the bytes is 00h 00h 00h F0h. 0x3C, being the smallest address, contains the lowest significant byte, which is F0h.

If the 4 bytes seen at the starting address 0x3c are 04h, 03h, 02h, 01h, then the highest significant byte is 01h, and the least significant byte is 04h. It will be written as 01h 02h 03h 04h.

Figure 9-6 shows the start of the PE header at location 0xF0.

The start of the PE header is PE\0\0 or the hex values 50h 45h 00h 00h. This is called the PE signature and, as stated previously, indicates the start of the PE header.

When a PE file is executed, the PE loader goes directly to the PE header. The PE loader bypasses the DOS MZ header and DOS stub and proceeds directly to the

```
0000F0:  50 45 00 00-4C 01 03 00-10 84 7D 3B-00 00 00 00   PE  L□□ □ä};
000100:  00 00 00 00-E0 00 0F 01-0B 01 07 00-00 28 01 00       α □□□□□ (□
000110:  00 9C 00 00-00 00 00 00-75 24 01 00-00 10 00 00   £        u$□  □
000120:  00 40 01 00-00 00 00 00-01-00 10 00 00-02 00 00   @□      □ □   □
000130:  05 00 01 00-05 00 01 00-04 00 00 00-00 00 00 00   □ □ □ □ □
000140:  00 F0 01 00-00 04 00 00-FC D7 01 00-02 00 00 80   ≡□  □   ⁿ╫□ □  ç
000150:  00 00 04 00-00 10 00 00-00 00 10 00-00 10 00 00     □    □   □  □
000160:  00 00 00 00-10 00 00 00-00 00 00 00-00 00 00 00         □
```

Figure 9-6   *PE header of Calc.EXE.*

PE header. As previously discussed, the location of the start of the PE header is found in offset 0x3C of the file. The PE loader reads the address in this offset and goes to that address, which is the start of the PE header.

The PE header contains lots of essential fields utilized by the PE loader. It is actually a general term for the related structure of type IMAGE_NT_HEADERS. The structure is laid out as shown in Figure 9-7.

From the figure, you can see that the structure consists of a DWORD, which represents the PE signature, and two substructures known as the IMAGE_FILE_HEADER and IMAGE_OPTIONAL_HEADER.

> **NOTE**
>
> *In the following discussion, you will encounter a new term, which is the relative virtual address (RVA). I'll discuss what this is in the next section.*

The IMAGE_FILE_HEADER contains basic information about the PE file. According to Microsoft, the structure appears to be unmodified from its original COFF implementations and appears not only as part of the PE header but also at the beginning of the COFF OBJ files produced by Microsoft Win32 compilers. Table 9-1 shows the fields of the IMAGE_FILE_HEADER. Take note that the offsets in the table are relative to the start of the PE header.

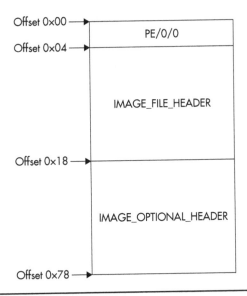

Figure 9-7   *PE header structure.*

Offset	Size	Field Name	Description	Possible Values
0x04	WORD	Machine	The CPU that the file is intended for.	0x14D – Intel i860 0x14C – Intel i386 (same ID used for 486 and 586) 0x162 – MIPS R3000 0x166 – MIPS R4000 0x183 – DEC Alpha AXP
0x06	WORD	NumberOfSections	The number of sections in the file.	
0x08	DWORD	TimeDateStamp	The time that the linker produced the file. The field represents the number of seconds since December 31, 1969, at 4 p.m.	
0x0C	DWORD	PointerToSymbolTable	The file offset of the COFF symbol table. This field is used only in OBJ files and PE files with COFF debug information.	
0x10	DWORD	NumberOfSymbols	The number of symbols in the COFF symbol table.	
0x14	WORD	SizeOfOptionalHeader	This is the size of the IMAGE_OPTIONAL_HEADER.	
0x16	WORD	Characteristics	Flags with information about the file. The following are some important fields: **0x0001** There are no relocations in the file. **0x0002** The file is an executable image. **0x2000** The file is a dynamic link library, not a program.	

Table 9-1 *IMAGE_FILE_HEADER Fields*

A useful tool for parsing the PE header is pefile. It is a multiplatform Python module that enables the user to work with PE files. You can find more information about this tool at https://code.google.com/p/pefile/.

LAB 9-2: *Install pefile in Ubuntu*

In this lab, you will install the pefile module to a system running Ubuntu.

What You Need:

▶   System running Ubuntu 14.04.1

▶   Python 2.7.6

▶   pefile

Steps:

1.   Check whether Python is installed by typing **python** in the command line.

```
$ python
```

2.   If Python is installed, the python command will result in opening the Python command-line environment. If this is the case, simply type **exit()** to exit the environment.

```
>>> exit()
```

3.   If Python is not installed, install it by using apt-get.

```
$ sudo apt-get install python
```

4.   Download pefile from https://code.google.com/p/pefile/downloads/list.

5.   As of this writing, the latest version is pefile 1.2.10-139. Choose and download pefile-1.2.10-139.tar.gz.

6.   Extract the downloaded file.

```
$ tar xzf pefile-1.2.10-139.tar.gz
```

7.   Alternatively, you can download pefile-1.2.10-139.zip and simply decompress the file. The resulting folder is the same.

8.   Go to the resulting folder. In this lab, it will be pefile-1.2.10-139.

9.   Install pefile by issuing the following command line:

```
$ sudo python setup.py install
```

10.   Another way of installing pefile without downloading and extracting it is by simply issuing the following command line:

```
$ sudo apt-get install python-pefile
```

LAB 9-3: *Python Script to Display PE Header Information*

In this lab, you will write a Python script that will display three things about a PE file.

▶ Address of entry point

▶ Image base

▶ Number of sections

What You Need:

▶ System running Ubuntu 14.04.1

▶ Python 2.7.6

▶ pefile

▶ calc.EXE from Windows 7

Steps:

1. Create a Python script file.

2. Write the following code:

```
#!/usr/bin/python
import pefile
pe = pefile.PE('calc.exe')
Address_of_EP = pe.OPTIONAL_HEADER.AddressOfEntryPoint
ImageBase = pe.OPTIONAL_HEADER.ImageBase
NumberOfSections = pe.FILE_HEADER.NumberOfSections
print "Address Of Entrypoint : ", hex(Address_of_EP)
print "Image Base : ", hex(ImageBase)
print "Number of Sections : " hex(NumberOfSections)
exit()
```

3. After creating the Python script, change it to executable mode by issuing the following command:

```
$ chmod +x yourscript.py
```

4. Execute your script. Make sure that calc.EXE is in the same folder as your script.

```
$ ./yourscript.py
```

5. The output should look like the following:

```
Address Of Entrypoint : 0x12475
Image Base : 0x1000000
Number of Sections : 0x3
```

The second substructure is the IMAGE_OPTIONAL_HEADER. Although the name says it's optional, there is nothing optional about this substructure. As stated by Microsoft, this portion of the PE file certainly isn't optional. The COFF format allows individual implementations to define a structure of additional information beyond the standard IMAGE_FILE_HEADER. The fields in the IMAGE_OPTIONAL_HEADER are what the PE designers felt was critical information beyond the basic information in the IMAGE_FILE_HEADER. Table 9-2 shows the fields of the IMAGE_OPTIONAL_HEADER. Take note that the offsets in the table are relative to the start of the PE header.

Offset	Size	Field Name	Description	Possible Values
0x18	WORD	Magic	This value is always set to 0x010B, which can mean that the file is a normal executable image.	0x010B
0x1A	BYTE	MajorLinkerVersion	The version of the linker that produced the file. The numbers are written in decimal instead of hex. This field represents the major version number.	
0x1B	BYTE	MinorLinkerVersion	This is the same as MajorLinkerVersion but represents the minor version number (the number after the dot).	
0x1C	DWORD	SizeOfCode	The combined and rounded-up size of all the code sections. But since most files have only one code section, this field matches the size of the .text section.	
0x20	DWORD	SizeOfInitializedData	This is supposedly the total size of all the sections that are composed of initialized data (excluding code segments). But it does not seem to be consistent with what appears in the file.	
0x24	DWORD	SizeOfUninitializedData	The size of the sections that the loader commits space for in the virtual address space but that don't take up any space in the disk file. These sections don't need to have specific values at program startup, which is why they're called uninitialized data. Uninitialized data usually goes into a section called .bss.	

Table 9-2 *IMAGE_OPTIONAL_HEADER Fields*

Offset	Size	Field Name	Description	Possible Values
0x28	DWORD	AddressOfEntryPoint	The address where the loader will begin execution. This is a relative virtual address usually found in the code (.text) section.	
0x2C	DWORD	BaseOfCode	The RVA where the file's code section begins. The code sections typically come before the data sections and after the PE header in memory.	0x1000
0x30	DWORD	BaseOfData	The RVA where the file's data section begins. The data sections typically come last in memory, after the PE header and the code sections.	
0x34	DWORD	ImageBase	This field contains the address of the specific location in memory where the file will be mapped. The default base address for Win32 files is 0x400000.	0x400000
0x38	DWORD	SectionAlignment	When mapped into memory, each section is guaranteed to start at a virtual address that's a multiple of this value. For paging purposes, the default section alignment is 0x1000.	0x1000
0x3C	DWORD	FileAlignment	In the PE file, the raw data that comprises each section is guaranteed to start at a multiple of this value. The default value is 0x200 bytes, probably to ensure that sections always start at the beginning of a disk sector, which are also 0x200 bytes in length.	0x200
0x40	WORD	MajorOperatingSystemVersion	The minimum version of the operating system required to use this executable. This field defaults to 1.0 in all Win32 executables.	0x100
0x42	WORD	MinorOperatingSystemVersion	Same as MajorOperatingSystemVersion.	
0x44	WORD	MajorImageVersion	A user-definable field, which allows the developer to have different versions of an EXE or DLL. The fields can be set via the linker/VERSION switch.	
0x46	WORD	MinorImageVersion	Same as MajorImageVersion.	

Table 9-2   *IMAGE_OPTIONAL_HEADER Fields* (continued)

Offset	Size	Field Name	Description	Possible Values
0x48	WORD	MajorSubsystemVersion	This field contains the minimum subsystem version required to run the executable. A typical value for this field is 3.10, which means Windows NT 3.1.	
0x4A	WORD	MinorSubsystemVersion	Same as MajorSubsystemVersion.	
0x4C	DWORD	Reserved1	Reserve field and seems to always have 0 as its value.	0x00
0x50	DWORD	SizeOfImage	This is the size of the region starting at the image base up to the end of the last section. The end of the last section is rounded up to the nearest multiple of the section alignment.	
0x54	DWORD	SizeOfHeaders	This is the size of the PE header and the section (object) table. The raw data for the sections starts immediately after all the header components.	
0x58	DWORD	Checksum	CRC checksum of the file. As in other Microsoft executable formats, this field is ignored and set to 0. The one exception to this rule is for trusted services, and these EXEs must have a valid checksum.	
0x5C	WORD	SubSystem	The type of subsystem that this executable uses for its user interface.	1 – NATIVE – Doesn't require a subsystem such as a device driver 2 – WINDOWS_ GUI – Runs in the Windows GUI subsystem 3 – WINDOWS_ CUI – Runs in the Windows character subsystem (a console app) 5 – OS2_CUI – Runs in the OS/2 character subsystem (OS/2 1.x apps only) 7 – POSIX_CUI – Runs in the Posix character subsystem

Table 9-2 *IMAGE_OPTIONAL_HEADER Fields*

Offset	Size	Field Name	Description	Possible Values
0x5E	WORD	DLLCharacteristics	A set of flags indicating under which circumstances a DLL's initialization function (such as DLLmain) will be called. This value appears to be always set to 0, yet the OS still calls the DLL initialization function for all four events.	1 – Call when DLL is first loaded into a process's address space 2 – Call when a thread terminates 4 – Call when a thread starts up 8 – Call when DLL exits
0x60	DWORD	SizeOfStackReserve	The amount of virtual memory to reserve for the initial thread's stack. However, not all of this memory is committed.	
0x64	DWORD	SizeOfStackCommit	The amount of memory initially committed for the initial thread's stack.	
0x68	DWORD	SizeOfHeapReserve	The amount of virtual memory to reserve for the initial process heap. However, not all of this memory is committed.	
0x6C	DWORD	SizeOfHeapCommit	The amount of memory initially committed in the process heap.	
0x70	DWORD	LoaderFlags	These are fields related to debugging support.	1 – Invokes a breakpoint instruction before starting the process 2 – Invokes a debugger on the process after it's been loaded
0x74	DWORD	NumberOfRVAAndSizes	This field represents the number of entries in the DataDirectory array. This value is always set to 16 or 0x10 in hex.	0x10

Table 9-2 *IMAGE_OPTIONAL_HEADER Fields* (continued)

The DataDirectory array discussed in the NumberOfRVAAndSizes field of the IMAGE_OPTIONAL_HEADER substructure is also referred to as the IMAGE_DATA_DIRECTORY. It usually contains 16 entries. The entries are shown in Table 9-3. Take note that the offset is relative to the start of the DataDirectory.

Offset	Size	Field	Description	Possible Values
0x00	DWORD	Export VirtualAddress	Starting RVA of the export table	
0x04	DWORD	Export Size	Size of the export table	
0x08	DWORD	Import VirtualAddress	Starting RVA of the import table	
0x0C	DWORD	Import Size	Size of the import table	
0x10	DWORD	Resource VirtualAddress	Starting RVA of the resource table	
0x14	DWORD	Resource Size	Size of the resource table	
0x18	DWORD	Exception VirtualAddress	Starting RVA of the exception table	
0x1C	DWORD	Exception Size	Size of the exception table	
0x20	DWORD	Certificate VirtualAddress	Starting RVA of the certificate table	
0x24	DWORD	Certificate Size	Size of the certificate table	
0x28	DWORD	BaseRelocation VirtualAddress	Starting RVA of the BaseRelocation table	
0x2C	DWORD	BaseRelocation Size	Size of the BaseRelocation table	
0x30	DWORD	Debug VirtualAddress	Starting RVA of the debug directory	
0x34	DWORD	Debug Size	Size of the debug directory	
0x38	DWORD	Architecture VirtualAddress	Starting RVA of architecture-specific data	
0x3C	DWORD	Architecture Size	Size of the architecture-specific data	
0x40	DWORD	GlobalPtr VirtualAddress	Starting RVA of the GlobalPtr register	
0x44	DWORD	GlobalPtr Size	Size of the GlobalPtr register	
0x48	DWORD	TLS VirtualAddress	Starting RVA of the thread local storage (TLS) table	
0x4C	DWORD	TLS Size	Size of the TLS table	
0x50	DWORD	LoadConfig VirtualAddress	Starting RVA of the load configuration table	

Table 9-3   *IMAGE_DATA_DIRECTORY Entries*

Offset	Size	Field	Description	Possible Values
0x54	DWORD	LoadConfig Size	Size of the load configuration table	
0x58	DWORD	BoundImport VirtualAddress	Starting RVA of the bound import table	
0x5C	DWORD	BoundImport Size	Size of the bound import table	
0x60	DWORD	IAT VirtualAddress	Starting RVA of the import address table (IAT)	
0x64	DWORD	IAT Size	Size of the import address table	
0x68	DWORD	DelayImport VirtualAddress	Starting RVA of the delay load import descriptor	
0x6C	DWORD	DelayImport Size	Size of the delay load import descriptor	
0x70	DWORD	RESERVED		

Table 9-3   *IMAGE_DATA_DIRECTORY Entries* (continued)

The IMAGE_DATA_DIRECTORY array makes it easy for the PE loader to find a particular section of the image without needing to go through each of the image sections and compare section names as it parses the image sections.

> **TIP**
>
> *You can find more information about the IMAGE_DATA_DIRECTORY in WINNT.H.*

Section Table

As shown in Figure 9-3, the section table is located between the PE header and the PE file's sections. The section table contains information about the sections immediately following it in the PE structure. Think of a section table like a phone book. Each entry in the phone book contains information about a person. The more people who are listed, the thicker the phone book is. The number of entries in the section table depends on the number of sections contained in the image file. But unlike a phone book that contains hundreds of thousands of entries, a section table usually has only five. The number of entries (or sections, for that matter) is defined in the NumberOfSections field in the PE header.

The section table is also referred to as the IMAGE_SECTION_HEADER. Table 9-4 contains the fields of this structure. Take note that the offset is relative to the start of each entry.

Offset	Size	Field	Description	Possible Values
0x00	QWORD	Name	The name of the section. It is an 8-byte, null-padded UTF-8 string. There is no terminating null character if the string is exactly 8 characters.	.text .data
0x08	DWORD	Misc	A union of the file's PhysicalAddress and the VirtualSize of the section. The VirtualSize is the total size of the section when loaded into memory, in bytes. If this value is greater than the SizeOfRawData entry, the section is filled with zeroes. This field is used only by executables.	
0x0C	DWORD	VirtualAddress	The address of the first byte of the section when loaded into memory, relative to the image base.	
0x10	DWORD	SizeOfRawData	The size of the initialized data on disk, in bytes. This value must be a multiple of the FileAlignment entry of the IMAGE_OPTIONAL_HEADER structure. If this value is less than the VirtualSize entry, the remainder of the sections is filled with zeroes. If the section contains only uninitialized data, the entry is zero.	

Table 9-4   *IMAGE_SECTION_HEADER Entries*

Offset	Size	Field	Description	Possible Values
0x14	DWORD	PointerToRawData	A file pointer to the first page within the COFF file. This value must be a multiple of the FileAlignment entry of the IMAGE_OPTIONAL_HEADER structure. If the section contains only uninitialized data, the entry is zero.	
0x18	DWORD	PointerToRelocations	A file pointer to the beginning of the relocation entries for the section. If there are no relocations, the value is zero.	
0x1C	DWORD	PointerToLinenumbers	A file pointer to the beginning of the line-number entries for the section. If there are no COFF line numbers, this value is zero.	
0x20	WORD	NumberOfRelocations	The number of relocation entries for the section. This value is zero for executable images.	
0x22	WORD	NumberOfLinenumbers	The number of line-number entries for the section.	
0x24	DWORD	Characteristics	This defines the characteristic of the image. Table 9-5 contains the flags and their meanings.	

Table 9-4 *IMAGE_SECTION_HEADER Entries* (continued)

It is important to note that the section names have only eight characters reserved for them. If an image has more than eight characters for a section name, the name field will contain a forward slash (/) followed by an ASCII representation of a decimal number that is an offset into the string table. An image that has more than eight characters for a section name is anything but an executable file. Executable files only support section names up to eight characters, and they do not use a string table.

The last field in the section table defines the image characteristics. It is aptly called the Characteristics field. Table 9-5 describes the flag values of this field.

Flag	Characteristic Name	Meaning
0x00000008	IMAGE_SCN_TYPE_NO_PAD	The section should not be padded to the next boundary. This flag is obsolete and is replaced by IMAGE_SCN_ALIGN_1BYTES.
0x00000020	IMAGE_SCN_CNT_CODE	The section contains executable code.
0x00000040	IMAGE_SCN_CNT_INITIALIZED_DATA	The section contains initialized data.
0x00000080	IMAGE_SCN_CNT_UNINITIALIZED_DATA	The section contains uninitialized data.
0x00000200	IMAGE_SCN_LNK_INFO	The section contains comments or other information. This is valid only for object files.
0x00000800	IMAGE_SCN_LNK_REMOVE	This section will not become part of the image. This is valid only for object files.
0x00001000	IMAGE_SCN_LNK_COMDAT	The section contains COMDAT data. This is valid only for object files.
0x00004000	IMAGE_SCN_NO_DEFER_SPEC_EXC	Reset speculative exception handling bits in the TLB entries for this section.
0x00008000	IMAGE_SCN_GPREL	The section contains data referenced through the global pointer.
0x00100000	IMAGE_SCN_ALIGN_1BYTES	Align data on a 1-byte boundary. This is valid only for object files.
0x00200000	IMAGE_SCN_ALIGN_2BYTES	Align data on a 2-byte boundary. This is valid only for object files.

Table 9-5 *Characteristics Field Values Defined*

Flag	Characteristic Name	Meaning
0x00300000	IMAGE_SCN_ALIGN_4BYTES	Align data on a 4-byte boundary. This is valid only for object files.
0x00400000	IMAGE_SCN_ALIGN_8BYTES	Align data on a 8-byte boundary. This is valid only for object files.
0x00500000	IMAGE_SCN_ALIGN_16BYTES	Align data on a 16-byte boundary. This is valid only for object files.
0x00600000	IMAGE_SCN_ALIGN_32BYTES	Align data on a 32-byte boundary. This is valid only for object files.
0x00700000	IMAGE_SCN_ALIGN_64BYTES	Align data on a 64-byte boundary. This is valid only for object files.
0x00800000	IMAGE_SCN_ALIGN_128BYTES	Align data on a 128-byte boundary. This is valid only for object files.
0x00900000	IMAGE_SCN_ALIGN_256BYTES	Align data on a 256-byte boundary. This is valid only for object files.
0x00A00000	IMAGE_SCN_ALIGN_512BYTES	Align data on a 512-byte boundary. This is valid only for object files.
0x00B00000	IMAGE_SCN_ALIGN_1024BYTES	Align data on a 1,024-byte boundary. This is valid only for object files.
0x00C00000	IMAGE_SCN_ALIGN_2048BYTES	Align data on a 2,048-byte boundary. This is valid only for object files.
0x00D00000	IMAGE_SCN_ALIGN_4096BYTES	Align data on a 4,096-byte boundary. This is valid only for object files.
0x00E00000	IMAGE_SCN_ALIGN_8192BYTES	Align data on a 8,192-byte boundary. This is valid only for object files.

Table 9-5 *Characteristics Field Values Defined* (continued)

Flag	Characteristic Name	Meaning
0x01000000	IMAGE_SCN_LNK_NRELOC_OVFL	This section contains extended relocations. The count of relocations for the section exceeds the 16 bits reserved for it in the section header. If the NumberOfRelocations field in the section header is 0xFFFF, the actual relocation count is stored in the VirtualAddress field of the first relocation. It is an error if IMAGE_SCN_LNK_NRELOC_OVFL is set and there are fewer than 0xFFFF relocations in the section.
0x02000000	IMAGE_SCN_MEM_DISCARDABLE	The section can be discarded as needed.
0x04000000	IMAGE_SCN_MEM_NOT_CACHED	The section cannot be cached.
0x08000000	IMAGE_SCN_MEM_NOT_PAGED	The section cannot be paged.
0x10000000	IMAGE_SCN_MEM_SHARED	The section can be shared in memory.
0x20000000	IMAGE_SCN_MEM_EXECUTE	The section can be executed as code.
0x40000000	IMAGE_SCN_MEM_READ	The section can be read.
0x80000000	IMAGE_SCN_MEM_WRITE	The section can be written to.

Table 9-5 *Characteristics Field Values Defined*

> **NOTE**
>
> *In the section table, the sections are sorted according to their relative virtual address rather than alphabetically.*

Another useful tool that can be used to dump PE information is pedump. It is a Ruby implementation that can be used in Linux-based systems such as Ubuntu. It supports both 32- and 64-bit PE files. It also supports old file formats such as DOS and Windows NE (New Executable) file format, which is the file format of Windows versions before Windows 95. You can find more information about pedump at https://github.com/zed-0xff/pedump.

pedump can dump the following information:

- ► MZ/NE/PE header
- ► DOS stub
- ► "Rich" header
- ► Data directory
- ► Sections
- ► Resources
- ► Strings
- ► Imports and exports
- ► VS_VERSIONINFO parsing
- ► PE packer/compiler detection

pedump also offers an online service where users can upload PE files for analysis. The website is located at http://pedump.me.

LAB 9-4: *Install and Utilize pedump*

In this lab, you will install pedump and use it to dump information of a PE file.

What You Need:

- ► System running Ubuntu 14.04.1
- ► Ruby
- ► pedump
- ► calc.EXE from Windows 7

Steps:

1. Install Ruby. As of this writing, the recommended version is 2.1.3.

   A. Install Ruby dependencies.

   ```
   $ sudo apt-get update
   $ sudo apt-get install git-core curl zlib1g-dev build-
   essential libssl-dev
   libreadline-dev libyaml-dev libsqlite3-dev sqlite3 libxml2-
   dev libxslt1-dev
   libcurl4-openssl-dev python-software-properties
   ```

   B. Install Ruby.

   ```
   $ sudo apt-get install ruby
   ```

2. Install pedump.

   ```
   $ sudo gem install pedump
   ```

3. Go to the folder where calc.EXE is located and issue the following command line:

   ```
   $ pedump calc.EXE
   ```

4. To save the output to a file, issue the following command line:

   ```
   $ pedump calc.EXE > calcdump.txt
   ```

LAB 9-5: *Python Script to Display PE Section Information*

In this lab, you will write a Python script that will display the section information of a PE file.

What You Need:

► System running Ubuntu 14.04.1

► Python 2.7.6

► pefile

► calc.EXE from Windows 7

Steps:

1. Create a Python script file.

2. Write the following code:

   ```
   #!/usr/bin/python
   import pefile
   ```

```
pe = pefile.PE('calc.exe')
for section in pe.sections:
print (section.Name, hex(section.VirtualAddress), hex(section.
Misc_VirtualSize), section.SizeOfRawData)
exit()
```

3. After creating the Python script, change it to executable mode by issuing the following command:

```
$ chmod +x yourscript.py
```

4. Execute your script. Make sure that calc.EXE is in the same folder as your script.

```
$ ./yourscript.py
```

5. The output should look like the following:

```
('.text\x00\x00\x00', '0x1000', '0x126b0', 75776)
('.data\x00\x00\x00', '0x14000, '0x101c', 2560)
('.rsrc\x00\x00\x00', '0x16000', 0x8960, 35328)
```

Sections

The sections are the meat of the PE file. Together they represent the real content of the PE file. Sections, in general, are simply blocks of data, which can have certain attributes as described in the section table. A section can be code, data, or a combination of both. The main thing they have in common is their attributes.

As discussed previously, each section has a unique name. The name is there to describe what the section is. For example, a section named CODE can represent the code section, while a section named .rdata can represent a read-only data section. As a default setting, Borland linker uses section names such as CODE and DATA, while Microsoft prefixes sections with a period, such as .text and .rdata. It is important to remember that the PE loader and Windows itself does not care what the section is called. The names are there for us humans. A developer is free to name the sections of her programs as she sees fit as long as it does not go over the eight-character limit.

NOTE

The minimum number of sections a PE file can have is two: one for code and the other for data.

As you look at different binaries, you will see different section names. Some make sense and follow the standard naming, while some will have names that are hard to comprehend. To prepare you, it is good to be familiar with common sections. The following is a short list of common sections. Take note that these are section names produced by Microsoft compilers/linkers.

► .text

► .data

► .bss

► .CRT

► .rsrc

► .idata

► .edata

► .reloc

► .tls

► .rdata

► .debug

The default section for code is .text. It is also known as the code section. This section contains all the instructions executed by the program. I'm not sure why Microsoft preferred to use the .text name instead of .code, which is more descriptive. But as previously mentioned, the operating system does not really care what the sections are called.

The .data section, on the other hand, is where all initialized data is stored. This includes global and static variables that are initialized during compile time. Global variables are variables accessible throughout the program, while static variables are variables that have a lifetime that extends from program start to end. The .data section also includes string literals.

For global and static variables that are uninitialized, they are stored in the .bss section. So, it is important to remember that initialized data goes to the .data section, while uninitialized data goes to the .bss section.

The .CRT is a weird one because it contains initialized data as well. It is a mystery why the data contained in the .CRT section is not joined with the data in the .data section.

The .rsrc section contains resource information used by the program. This section begins with a resource directory structure called IMAGE_RESOURCE_DIRECTORY. It contains the following information:

► Characteristics

► TimeDateStamp

- ▶ MajorVersion
- ▶ MinorVersion
- ▶ NumberOfNamedEntries
- ▶ NumberOfIdEntries

> ### TIP
>
> *The application programming interface (API) function EnumResourceTypes can be used to enumerate the types of resources stored in the .rsrc section.*

The .idata section contains function and data information that the program imports from other dynamic link libraries (DLLs). Each function that a program imports is specifically listed in this section.

The .edata section, on the other hand, contains the list of functions and data that the program exports or makes available to other programs or modules. Take note that the .edata section appears only in DLL files because there is rarely a reason for EXE files to import functions to other programs.

The .reloc section contains a table of base relocations. As Microsoft puts it, a base relocation is an adjustment to an instruction or initialized variable value that's needed if the PE loader could not load the file where the linker assumed it would. If the PE loader is able to load the image at the linker's preferred base address, the PE loader completely ignores the relocation information in the .reloc section.

The .tls section contains data that was defined using the compiler directive _ _declspec(thread). The .tls section got its name from TLS, the acronym of thread local storage. When it comes to dealing with the .tls section, Microsoft explains it best: The .tls section is related to the TlsAlloc family of Win32 functions. When dealing with a .tls section, the memory manager sets up the page tables so that whenever a process switches threads, a new set of physical memory pages is mapped to the .tls section's address space. This permits per-thread local variables. In most cases, it is much easier to use this mechanism than to allocate memory on a per-thread basis and store its pointer in a TlsAlloc'ed slot. There's one unfortunate note that must be added about the .tls section and _ _declspec(thread) variables. In Windows NT and Windows 95, this thread local storage mechanism won't work in a DLL if LoadLibrary loads the DLL dynamically. In an EXE or an implicitly loaded DLL, everything works fine. If you can't implicitly link to the DLL but need per-thread data, you'll have to fall back to using TlsAlloc and TlsGetValue with dynamically allocated memory.

The .rdata section contains read-only data such as literal strings, constants, and the debug directory, which can be found only in EXE files. As defined by Microsoft, the debug directory is an array of IMAGE_DEBUG_DIRECTORY structures. These structures hold information about the type, size, and location of the various types of debug information stored in the file.

The .debug section contains all the debug information pointed to by the debug directory in the .rdata section.

NOTE

It is important to remember that TLINK32 EXEs put the debug directory in the .debug section and not the .rdata section. So if you cannot find the debug directory in the .rdata section, look for it in the .debug section.

This concludes the most common sections you will encounter when analyzing PE files.

Relative Virtual Address

You first encountered the relative virtual address while I was discussing the PE header in the previous section. And you will encounter it some more as I discuss the PE file and as you analyze malware.

So, what is a relative virtual address? To understand what it is, you need to know first what a virtual address (VA) space is. As defined by Microsoft, a virtual address space is a set of virtual memory addresses that a process can use. A virtual address does not represent the actual physical location of an object in memory. Instead, the system maintains a page table for each process, which is an internal data structure used to translate virtual address into their corresponding physical addresses. Each time a thread references an address, the system translates the virtual address to a physical address.

NOTE

The virtual address space for 32-bit Windows is 4GB, while for 64-bit Windows, the default is 8TB.

The relative virtual address is simply a distance from a reference point in the virtual address space. A similar concept is a file offset. The file offset describes the location of something relative to the start of the file, while the relative virtual address describes the location of something relative to a point in the virtual address space. To illustrate further, let's take a PE file that usually loads at 0x400000 virtual address, and let's say that the start of the PE file's .text or code section is at 0x401000. From this, the RVA of the code section is 0x1000 because that is where it is relative to the loading location of the file in the virtual address space. The formula for this is simply as follows:

```
RVA = Target Address - Load Address
RVA = 0x401000 - 0x400000
RVA = 0x1000
```

To convert the RVA to the actual address, which is the target address, simply reverse the process by adding the load address to the RVA.

> **NOTE**
>
> *The virtual address is simply an RVA with the HMODULE added in. HMODULE is the same as the load address.*

PE Import Functions

Previously, I discussed that the .idata section contains function and data information that the program imports from other dynamic link libraries. The .idata section is also referred to as the import table of the executable image. This table contains all the information that the PE loader needs to determine the addresses of the functions that the executable image is importing so it can be patched into the executable image. These functions are called import functions because they are the ones being "imported" by the executable. Therefore, import functions are functions that do not reside in the caller's module or program but are called by the caller from another module or program such as a DLL. The caller module only contains information about the functions it is calling from another module, which can be one or more DLLs. The information includes the function names and the names of the dynamic link libraries from which they are imported. This information can be found in the import table.

> **NOTE**
>
> *Import functions reside in DLLs.*

The import table starts with an array of IMAGE_IMPORT_DESCRIPTORs. Each DLL that the executable image or the PE executable file links to will have its own IMAGE_IMPORT_DESCRIPTOR. If the PE file imports from five DLLs, it will have five IMAGE_IMPORT_DESCRIPTORs in its .idata section. Take note that there is no field indicating how many IMAGE_IMPORT_DESCRIPTORs are in an executable image's .idata section. The only way to determine this is to count the number of IMAGE_IMPORT_DESCRIPTORs there are and stopping count only when an IMAGE_IMPORT_DESCRIPTOR with null field values is encountered. This signals the last element of the IMAGE_IMPORT_DESCRIPTOR array. Table 9-6 shows the IMAGE_IMPORT_DESCRIPTOR structure.

IMAGE_THUNK_DATA is a union of DWORD size containing the RVA or pointer to an IMAGE_IMPORT_BY_NAME structure and not the structure itself. The IMAGE_IMPORT_BY_NAME structure, on the other hand, contains information about an import function. Table 9-7 shows the IMAGE_IMPORT_BY_NAME structure.

Size	Name	Description
DWORD	Characteristics	This is an RVA to an array of pointers pointing to an IMAGE_IMPORT_BY_NAME structure.
DWORD	TimeDateStamp	This is the time and date stamp of when the file was built.
DWORD	ForwarderChain	This field contains an index into the FirstThunk array. The function indexed by this field will be forwarded to another DLL. Forwarding, as described by Microsoft, involves one DLL sending on references to one of its functions to another DLL.
DWORD	Imported DLL Name	This is an RVA to a null-terminated ASCII string containing the name of the imported DLL.
	FirstThunk	This is an RVA to an IMAGE_THUNK_DATA union between the OriginalFirstThunk and FirstThunk. The resulting union is a pointer to an IMAGE_IMPORT_BY_NAME structure, which is the same as the Characteristics field. If the field is not one of these pointers, then it is treated as an export ordinal value for the DLL that's being imported.
	Additional IMAGE_IMPORT_DESCRIPTORs	These are additional IMAGE_IMPORT_DESCRIPTORs for other DLLs as necessary.

Table 9-6   *IMAGE_IMPORT_DESCRIPTOR Structure*

Size	Name	Description
WORD	Hint	This field contains the index into the DLL's export table where the function being called resides. Because of this, the PE loader can look up the functions in the DLL's export table quickly.
BYTE	Name	This field contains the name of the import function.

Table 9-7 *IMAGE_IMPORT_BY_NAME Structure*

LAB 9-6: *Python Script to Display PE Import Information*

In this lab, you will write a Python script that will display the import information of a PE file.

What You Need:

- ▶ System running Ubuntu 14.04.1
- ▶ Python 2.7.6
- ▶ pefile
- ▶ calc.EXE from Windows 7

Steps:

1. Create a Python script file.

2. Write the following code:

    ```
    #!/usr/bin/python
    import pefile
    pe = pefile.PE('calc.exe')
    for entry in pe.DIRECTORY_ENTRY_IMPORT:
      print entry.dll
      for imp in entry.imports:
            print '\t', hex(imp.address), imp.name
    exit()
    ```

3. After creating the Python script, change it to executable mode by issuing the following command:

    ```
    $ chmod +x yourscript.py
    ```

4. Execute your script. Make sure that calc.EXE is in the same folder as your script.

    ```
    $ ./yourscript.py
    ```

5. The output should look like the following:

```
SHELL32.dll

    0x100109c    ShellAboutW
msvcrt.dll
    0x10011bc    __CxxFrameHandler
    0x10011c0    _CxxThrowException

...
```

PE Export Functions

Functions that are imported by an image usually come from a DLL file. As far as the image is concerned, it is importing the functions, but as far as the DLL is concerned, it is exporting the function. In short, when an image, usually a dynamic link library file, makes functions and data available for other PE files, it is effectively exporting code or data. And the code and data that is being exported is known as an export function.

The .edata section contains information about functions being exported by a PE file. The .edata section is also known as the export table. An export table usually contains the following:

▶ Tables of function names

▶ Entry point addresses

▶ Export ordinal values

An export table or .edata section starts with an IMAGE_EXPORT_DIRECTORY structure and then is followed by the data pointed to by the fields in this structure. Table 9-8 shows the IMAGE_EXPORT_DIRECTORY structure.

Size	Name	Description
DWORD	Characteristics	For some reason this is always set to zero.
DWORD	TimeDateStamp	This indicates when the file was created.
WORD	MajorVersion	For some reason this is always set to zero.
WORD	MinorVersion	For some reason this is always set to zero.
DWORD	Name	This is the RVA pointing to an ASCIIZ string containing the name of the exporting DLL.

Table 9-8 *IMAGE_EXPORT_DIRECTORY Structure*

Size	Name	Description
DWORD	Base	This is the starting ordinal number for the exported functions. This means that if the file exports functions with ordinal values of 11, 12, and 13, the Base field will contain 11. To get the function's exported ordinal value, add the Base value to the appropriate element of the AddressOfNameOrdinals array.
DWORD	NumberOfFunctions	The number of elements in the AddressOfFunctions array.
DWORD	NumberOfNames	The number of elements in the AddressOfNames array.
PDWORD	*AddressOfFunctions	An RVA that points to an array of function addresses. The function addresses are the RVA entry points for each exported function in this module.
PDWORD	*AddressOfNames	An RVA that points to an array of string pointers. The strings are the names of the exported functions in this module.
PWORD	*AddressOfNameOrdinals	An RVA that points to an array of WORDs. The WORDs are the export ordinals of all the exported functions in this module. However, as stated in the description of the Base field, don't forget to add the starting ordinal number specified in the Base field.

Table 9-8 *IMAGE_EXPORT_DIRECTORY Structure* (continued)

LAB 9-7: *Python Script to Display PE Export Information*

In this lab, you will write a Python script that will display the export information of a PE file.

What You Need:

▶ System running Ubuntu 14.04.1

▶ Python 2.7.6

▶ pefile

▶ comctl32.DLL from Windows 7 or any DLL file you have

Steps:

1. Create a Python script file.

2. Write the following code:

```
#!/usr/bin/python
import pefile
pe = pefile.PE('comctl32.dll')
for exp in pe.DIRECTORY_ENTRY_EXPORT.symbols:
   print hex(pe.OPTIONAL_HEADER.ImageBase + exp.address), exp.
name, exp.ordinal
exit()
```

3. After creating the Python script, change it to executable mode by issuing the following command:

```
$ chmod +x yourscript.py
```

4. Execute your script. Make sure that comctl32.DLL is in the same folder as your script.

```
$ ./yourscript.py
The output should look like the following:
0x7fff7585912c  AddMRUStringW 401
0x7ff75858f94   CreateMRUListW        400
0x7ff75859f9c          CreateMappedBitmap  8
...
```

5. Take note that running this script with a PE file with no exports will display the following message:

```
Traceback (most recent call last):
   File "./yourscript.py", line X, in <module>
          for exp in pe.DIRECTORY_ENTRY_EXPORT.symbols:
AttributeError: PE instance has no attribute 'DIRECTORY_ENTRY_
EXPORT'
```

When it comes to exporting functions, there is one feature that PE files can do, which is *export forwarding*. Export forwarding is a feature of export functions that has the ability to forward and export to another DLL. Let's look at an example published by Microsoft regarding export forwarding.

In Windows NT, Windows 2000, and Windows XP, the KERNEL32 HeapAlloc function is forwarded to the RtlAllocHeap function exported by NTDLL. Forwarding is performed at link time by a special syntax in the EXPORTS section of the .DEF file. Using HeapAlloc as an example, KERNEL32's DEF file would contain the following:

```
EXPORTS
...
HeapAlloc = NTDLL.RtlAllocHeap
```

How can you tell whether a function is forwarded rather than exposed normally? It is somewhat tricky. Normally, the EAT contains the RVA of the exported symbol. However, if the function's RVA is inside the exports section, as given by the VirtualAddress and Size fields in the DataDirectory, the symbol is forwarded.

When a symbol is forwarded, its RVA obviously can't be a code or data address in the current module. Instead, the RVA points to an ASCII string of the DLL and symbol name to which it is forwarded.

LAB 9-8: *Python Script to Display All PE Information*

In this lab, you will write a Python script that will display all available information of a PE file.

What You Need:

▶ System running Ubuntu 14.04.1

▶ Python 2.7.6

▶ pefile

▶ calc.EXE from Windows 7

Steps:

1. Create a Python script file.

2. Write the following code:

```
#!/usr/bin/python
import pefile
pe = pefile.PE('calc.exe')
print pe.dump_info()
exit()
```

3. After creating the Python script, change it to executable mode by issuing the following command:

```
$ chmod +x yourscript.py
```

4. Execute your script. Make sure that calc.EXE is in the same folder as your script.

```
$ ./yourscript.py
```

5. Part of the output should look like the following:

```
...
----------Debug Information---------
[IMAGE_DEBUG_DIRECTORY]
0x640    0x0    Characteristics:        0x0
...
```

64-Bit PE File Format

With the advent of 64-bit Windows operating systems, the PE format, which was originally designed for 32 bits, had to undergo some minor changes. The new format that supports 64-bit Windows is called PE32+. No new fields were added, so structurally the two formats are still the same, with the modifications listed here:

► Fields widened to support 64 bits

► BaseOfData field deleted

► Magic field value changed from 0x10b to 0x20b representing different CPU type

Table 9-9 summarizes the changes that were made to the PE file fields.

That basically wraps up what you need to know about the PE file format. It is knowledge that will come in handy as you analyze malware.

Header Field	Change
Magic	Set to 0x20b from 0x10b
BaseOfData	Deleted
ImageBase	Widened to 64 bits
SizeOfStackReserve	Widened
SizeOfStackCommit	Widened
SizeOfHeapReserve	Widened
SizeOfHeapCommit	Widened

Table 9-9 *PE File Field Changes from 32-Bit to 64-Bit (Source: http://msdn.microsoft.com)*

Recap

In this chapter, I discussed what the PE file format is, how it is structured, and what tools you can use to decipher it. You took a look at the different components of the PE file format, listed here:

► DOS MZ header
► DOS stub
► PE header
► Section table
► Sections

I described each component and how it is structured. I described the different fields and the common entry values each has within each structure. Aside from all of this, you also tackled what a relative virtual address is and how the PE file imports and exports functions.

Tools

► **Dependency Walker** http://www.dependencywalker.com
► **pefile** https://code.google.com/p/pefile/
► **pedump** https://github.com/zed-0xff/pedump
► **pedump online PE file submission** http://pedump.me/

The Proper Way to Handle Files

U nderstanding the Portable Executable (PE) file is a must, as you saw in the previous chapter. You were able to discover the different characteristics of the PE file and what makes it tick. With this newfound basic knowledge of PE files, you are now better equipped to understand Windows malware.

When it comes to malware inspection, you always start with an unknown file. You have no idea, at first, whether the file is malicious. Therefore, it is important to handle the file with great care to avoid any unwanted incidents that might lead to a malware outbreak.

In this chapter, I will discuss how to properly handle unknown files. You will look at the file's analysis life cycle, from transport to storage, and how to handle files in the right way to prevent anything from unauthorized access to compromise of the files. I will also discuss how to properly store files that are found to be malicious or verified to be malware.

File's Analysis Life Cycle

A file for analysis actually undergoes three stages. They are the following:

▶ Transfer

▶ Analysis

▶ Storage

I call this the *file's analysis life cycle*. The file will get transferred or transported from one location to another. When it reaches its destination, it undergoes analysis. It is during this stage that it is determined whether the file is malicious. After the determination has been done, the file is stored for archival and future research purposes.

Throughout the analysis life cycle of the file, it is imperative that it is handled properly to avoid any unwanted incidents.

> **TIP**
>
> *Always handle unknown files for analysis as if they are malicious. It is better to err on the side of caution.*

Transfer

Files that need to be analyzed will usually come from an external source. If this is the case, you need to practice great care when moving the file from the source to the analysis machines. You have to consider the following:

▶ The file must *not* be in an executable state.

▶ The file must *not* be accessible to unauthorized users.

▶ The source of the file must be verifiable.

Non-executable State

When a file is transferred, it is important that it is not in an executable state. For Windows executable files, it is easy to make an executable file not in an executable state or, in short, non-executable. You can simply rename the file's extension. For example, you can rename an .EXE file as .EX_, .EX1, or .EXE.XXX. The main idea here is that you change the original extension to a non-executable extension but won't forget what the original extension was.

Inaccessible to Unauthorized Users

The second thing to consider is access to the file. The file can be transferred via physical means such as a universal serial bus (USB) stick, a hard disk, or any physical storage device. Or it can be transferred automatically via e-mail, direct file transfer, File Transfer Protocol (FTP) server, or download site. These different means of transfer always carry the risk of unauthorized access. Therefore, precautions have to be taken. Unauthorized users must not be able to get hold of the file to be analyzed. Unauthorized access must not occur, especially if the file is of confidential nature. The following are the common practices in the industry when it comes to protecting a file to be analyzed from unauthorized access:

▶ Password-protected compressed file

▶ Public-key cryptography

Password-protected compressed files are the most common way of ensuring a file can be transferred while protecting it from unauthorized users. Only those who know the password can decompress and access the file. But of course, this is not a good way of protecting the file from unauthorized access because there are tools that can decompress password-protected compressed files even without knowledge of the password. In actual practice, password-protected compressed files became popular for the transportation of files because they can bypass e-mail security products. Instead of the file being stripped from the e-mail and deleted, it will simply go through and let the recipient get access to the file. That was the main reason why this method became popular. Because of this popularity, the industry has used common passwords for password-protected compressed files. Some of them are as follows:

- ▶ Infected
- ▶ Virus
- ▶ Novirus (this is for known benign files)

The following are the most common compression tools used for this purpose:

- ▶ **WinZIP**   http://www.winzip.com
- ▶ **WinRAR**   http://www.rarlab.com
- ▶ **7zip**   http://www.7-zip.org/

In Linux systems, the best compression tool in my humble opinion is p7zip. It is 7zip's counterpart in Linux systems. You can find more information about p7zip at http://p7zip.sourceforge.net/.

LAB 10-1: *Installing and Using p7zip*

In this lab, you will install and use p7zip to compress files and decompress an archive file. P7zip is the equivalent of 7zip in Linux systems.

What You Need:

- ▶ System running Ubuntu 14.04.1

Steps:

1. Install p7zip in Ubuntu.

   ```
   $ sudo apt-get install p7zip-full
   ```

2. After successful installation, the system can now support 7zip files or files with the .7Z extension.

3. To compress a file, right-click it and click Compress on the context menu. In this example, I will be using calc.EXE, but please feel free to use any file available.

4. Once the Compress window opens, set the filename extension to .7z and rename the archive file as you want. The default name of the archive file is usually the original filename of the file being compressed. In this example, I will rename the archive to calc-compress.

5. Set the location where you want to save the archive file. The default location is the current directory where the file being compressed is.

6. Click Other Options to set the password. In this section, you will also have the option to encrypt the filenames of the compressed files and to split the archive into volumes.

7. Once the password is set and options chosen, such as encrypting the file list, click Create to create the archive file. Figure 10-1 shows the Compress window with the options chosen.

8. To decompress an archive file, right-click it and choose Extract Here. In this example, you will be decompressing calc-compress.7z. This is the archive you just created.

9. A dialog box asking for a password, as shown in Figure 10-2, will be displayed. Input the password and click OK to extract the file.

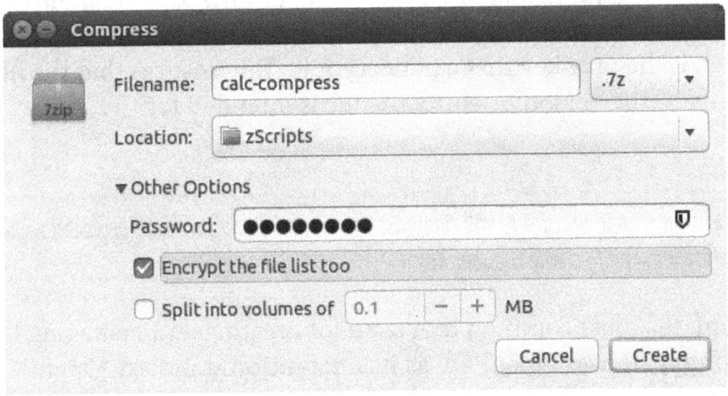

Figure 10-1   *Compress window.*

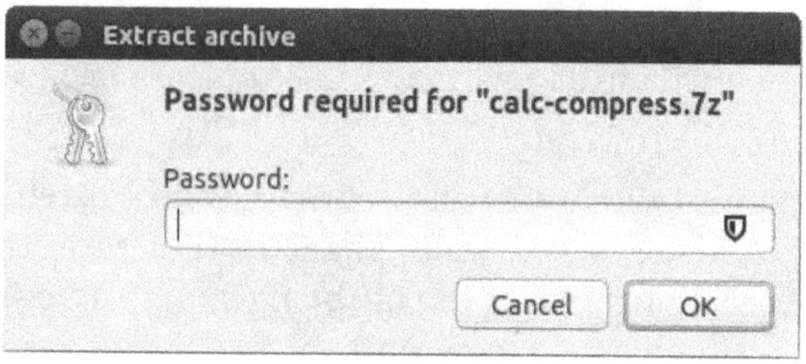

Figure 10-2 *Password dialog box.*

10. Another way to decompress an archive is to simply double-click it.

11. All decompressed files will be in the current folder where the archive file is.

The best way to really protect files from unauthorized access is to use public-key cryptography. Public-key cryptography, also known as *asymmetric cryptography,* requires two unique and separate keys: the private and the public key. Although unique, the two cryptographic keys are related mathematically. As its name suggests, the public key is available publicly. Anyone can have access to it. The private key, on the other hand, is secret and confidential. Only the owner must have access to it.

To keep the file confidential or free from unauthorized access, the public key is used to encrypt the file, and then the private key, which is in the possession of the owner, is the only key that can decrypt it. This ensures that the file can be accessed only by the person or entity the file is intended for.

TIP

It is always good practice to still compress the file to be analyzed and protect it with a password before encrypting it with a public key.

In Ubuntu, the most common tool used for creating and managing key pairs is GnuPG or gpg. It uses OpenPGP as its encryption standard. OpenPGP, as stated in http://www.openpgp.org, is a non-proprietary encryption protocol using public key cryptography. It is based on PGP as originally developed by Phil Zimmermann. The OpenPGP protocol defines standard formats for encrypted messages, signatures, and certificates for exchanging public keys.

LAB 10-2: *Creating a Private and Public Key Pair*

In this lab, you will use gpg (GnuPG) to generate a private and public key pair.

What You Need:

▶ System running Ubuntu 14.04.1

Steps:

1. Open a terminal window in Ubuntu.

2. Install gnupg-agent by issuing the following command:

   ```
   $ sudo apt-get install gnupg-agent
   ```

3. After successful installation, it is time to start the process of generating a key using gpg.

   ```
   $ gpg –gen-key
   ```

4. A screen with selections as listed here will appear. The latest version that came with Ubuntu 14.04.1 as of this writing is 1.4.16.

   ```
   Please select what kind of key you want:
   (1) RSA and RSA (default)
   (2) DSA and Elgamal
   (3) DSA (sign only)
   (4) RSA (sign only)
   Your selection?
   ```

5. Select (1), which is the default, by typing **1** and pressing Enter. This enables encryption and signing.

6. The program will then ask what keysize you want. The default is 2048. To choose this, simply press Enter.

   ```
   What keysize do you want? (2048)
   ```

7. The next step is to set how long the key should be valid. For this experiment, you will set the key to not expire. This is the default. Simply press Enter to choose this option.

   ```
   Please specify how long the key should be valid.
      0       = key does not expire
   <n>        = key expires in n days
   <n>w       = key expires in n weeks
   <n>m       = key expires in n months
   <n>y       = key expires in n years
   Key is valid for? (0)
   ```

TIP

If you choose a key that does not expire, make sure to revoke the key when you no longer need it.

8. Confirm your selection by typing **y** when asked whether the option chosen is correct.

   ```
   Key does not expire at all
   Is this correct? (y/N)
   ```

9. You will then need to input your real name, a comment, and an e-mail address, as shown in Figure 10-3.

10. If everything is good, enter **O** for Okay.

11. A dialog box will pop up asking for a password. Please supply the desired password.

12. GnuPG will then ask you to perform other actions while it is doing its prime generation.

    ```
    Simply follow the instructions displayed in the terminal window.
    We need to generate a lot of random bytes. It is a good idea to perform
    some other action (type on the keyboard, move the mouse, utilize the
    disks) during the prime generation; this gives the random number
    generator a better chance to gain enough entropy.
    ```

13. Perform the actions as instructed. The best way to do this is to do as much activity as you can in your system. Once gpg is satisfied, it will display the screen shown in Figure 10-4.

14. Take note of your key ID. In the example shown in Figure 10-4, it is BB7BCC97.

15. The created keys are located in /home/<user>/.gnupg/.

TIP

Make sure to back up the files in the .gnupg folder, especially secring.gpg, which is your secret keyring.

```
You need a user ID to identify your key; the software constructs the user ID
from the Real Name, Comment and Email Address in this form:
    "Heinrich Heine (Der Dichter) <heinrichh@duesseldorf.de>"

Real name: Christopher Elisan
Email address: christopher.elisan@notmyrealemail.fake
Comment: Lab for Book
You selected this USER-ID:
    "Christopher Elisan (Lab for Book) <christopher.elisan@notmyrealemail.fake>"

Change (N)ame, (C)omment, (E)mail or (O)kay/(Q)uit? O
```

Figure 10-3   *GPG terminal window.*

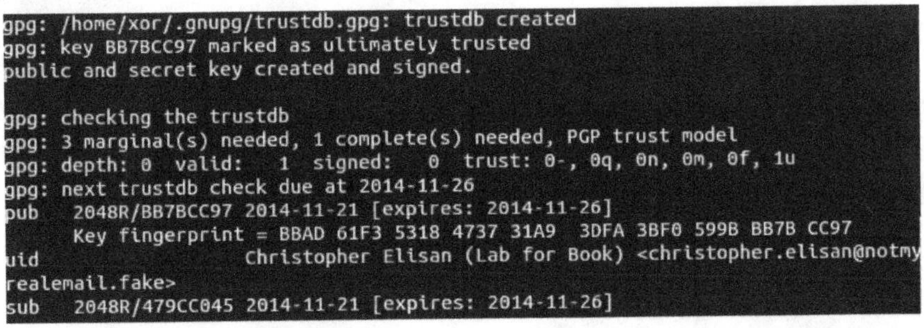

```
gpg: /home/xor/.gnupg/trustdb.gpg: trustdb created
gpg: key BB7BCC97 marked as ultimately trusted
public and secret key created and signed.

gpg: checking the trustdb
gpg: 3 marginal(s) needed, 1 complete(s) needed, PGP trust model
gpg: depth: 0  valid:   1 signed:   0 trust: 0-, 0q, 0n, 0m, 0f, 1u
gpg: next trustdb check due at 2014-11-26
pub   2048R/BB7BCC97 2014-11-21 [expires: 2014-11-26]
      Key fingerprint = BBAD 61F3 5318 4737 31A9  3DFA 3BF0 599B BB7B CC97
uid                  Christopher Elisan (Lab for Book) <christopher.elisan@notmy
realemail.fake>
sub   2048R/479CC045 2014-11-21 [expires: 2014-11-26]
```

Figure 10-4 *Successful key generation.*

LAB 10-3: *Setting the Key as the Default*

In this lab, you will be setting the key you just created as the default in your
.bashrc to allow applications using GPG to automatically use your key.

What You Need:

▶   System running Ubuntu 14.04.1

▶   Generated keys

Steps:

1. Open a terminal window in Ubuntu and enter the following command:

    ```
    $ cd ~
    $ gedit .bashrc
    ```

2. Once the .bashrc file is open, add the following line at the end of the file:

    ```
    $ export GPGKEY=BB7BCC97
    ```

    Take note that your key ID will be different.

3. Save and close .bashrc.

4. In the terminal window, issue the following command to restart gpg-agent
    and source the .bashrc file:

    ```
    $ killall -q gpg-agent
    $ eval $ (gpg-agent -daemon)
    $ source ~/.bashrc
    ```

LAB 10-4: *Uploading Your Key to Ubuntu Keyserver*

In this lab, you will upload your public key to Ubuntu Keyserver so it is available to anyone who needs it to communicate securely with you.

What You Need:

▶ System running Ubuntu

▶ Generated keys

Steps:

1. Determine your public key by displaying your key information. To do this, open a terminal window and enter the following command. In this example, the GPGKEY is BB7BCC97.

   ```
   $ gpg --list-keys
   ```

2. Export the key to http://keyserver.ubuntu.com/ by issuing the following command:

   ```
   $ gpg --send-keys --keyserver keyserver.ubuntu.com BB7BCC97
   ```

3. Another alternative is to go to the Ubuntu Keyserver link using your browser. The page is shown in Figure 10-5.

4. You need to copy your key to the text box on the page and click Submit. But first you need a copy of your ASCII-armored OpenPGP key. To get this, you need to export your key by typing the following command:

   ```
   $ gpg --export -a BB7BCC97 > pubkey.asc
   ```

5. Open pubkey.ask using gedit and copy its contents.

   ```
   $ gedit pubkey.asc
   ```

6. Paste the contents of pubkey.asc into the text box of Ubuntu Keyserver and click Submit.

7. Check the success of your upload by searching your name in the search box.

LAB 10-5: *Backing Up and Restoring Your Key Pair*

In this lab, you will be backing up and restoring both your private and public keys.

What You Need:

▶ System running Ubuntu 14.04.1

▶ Generated keys

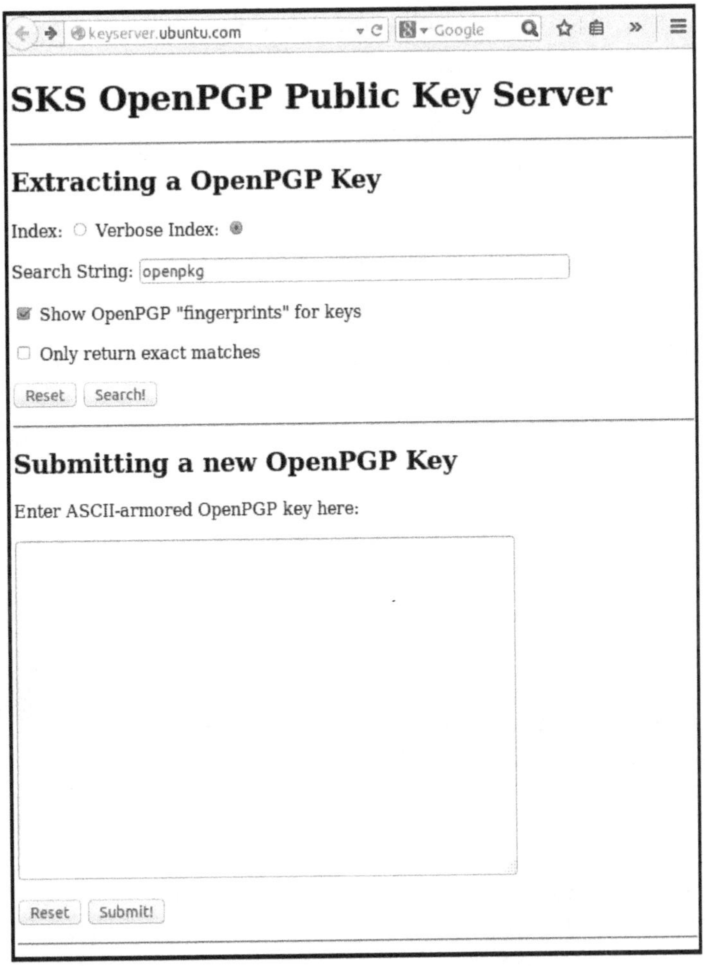

Figure 10-5   *Ubuntu Keyserver.*

Steps:

1. Determine your public key by displaying your key information. To do this, open a terminal window and enter the following command. In this example, the GPGKEY is BB7BCC97.

   ```
   $ gpg --list-keys
   ```

2. Back up your public key by issuing the following command:

   ```
   $ gpg -ao backup-public.key --export BB7BCC97
   ```

3. The resulting file, backup-public.key, is your public key backup. Save it to a secure location.

4. Next is backing up your private key. First, you need to determine your private key information. To do this, issue the following command. In this example, your GPGKEY is BB7BCC97.

   ```
   $ gpg --list-secret-keys
   ```

5. Back up your private key by issuing the following command:

   ```
   $ gpg -ao backup-private.key --export-secret-keys BB7BCC97
   ```

6. The resulting file, backup-private.key, is your private key backup. Save it to a secure location.

7. To restore or import your private key and public key to an existing or new machine, copy the backup files to the machine and enter the following at the command line:

   ```
   $ gpg --import backup-public.key
   $ gpg --import backup-private.key
   ```

8. To verify successful restoration, issue the following:

   ```
   $ gpg --list-keys
   ```

9. If the displayed key information matches the one you are restoring, then restoration is successful.

There will be instances wherein you will not need your keys anymore, probably because it was compromised or you simply want to replace them with a new key pair. In cases like this, the only way to make sure that the key is no longer valid and to tell other users that the key is no longer in use or reliable is to revoke the keys.

The only way to revoke a key pair is with a revocation key; without a revocation key, a key pair cannot be revoked. This is a safety precaution so no unauthorized user can revoke a key easily. It is important to treat the revocation key as you would your private key. Keep it safe and secure.

LAB 10-6: *Revoking a Key Pair*

In this lab, you will create a revocation certificate that you can use to revoke your existing key pair.

What You Need:

▶ System running Ubuntu 14.04.1

▶ Generated keys

Steps:

1. Create a revocation certificate. In this example, you will be revoking GPGKEY BB7BCC97.

   ```
   $ gpg --output revoke.asc --gen-revoke BB7BCC97
   ```

2. gpg will ask whether you really want to create a revocation certificate for your key. Enter **y** and press Enter to proceed.

   ```
   Create a revocation certificate for this key? (y/N)
   ```

3. It will then ask the reason for the revocation. Select the appropriate reason or simply enter **0** for no reason specified and press Enter.

   ```
   Please select the reason for the revocation:
   0 = No reason specified
   1 = Key has been compromised
   2 = Key is superseded
   3 = Key is no longer used
   Q = Cancel
   (Probably you want to select 1 here)
   Your decision?
   ```

4. After deciding which reason is appropriate, gpg will ask you for an optional description. You can skip this by simply pressing Enter.

   ```
   Enter an optional description; end it with an empty line:
   >
   ```

5. Once you have made your choice, it will display the reason and description as a summary and ask whether it is OK. If everything is good, enter **y** and press Enter to proceed.

   ```
   Reason for revocation: Key has been compromised
   (No description given)
   Is this okay? (y/N)
   ```

6. A dialog box will pop up asking for a passphrase to unlock the secret key, as shown in Figure 10-6.

7. Enter your password and click OK.

NOTE

This dialog box will be open for less than a minute. Inactivity will close it, and the program will assume that you have canceled the creation of the revocation certificate. You then have to start again.

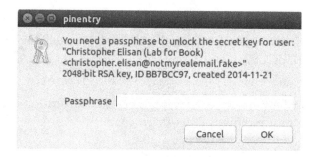

Figure 10-6 *Dialog box to unlock secret key with a passphrase.*

8. The revocation certificate is now created.

    ```
    ASCII armored output forced.
    Revocation certificate created.
    Please more it to a medium which you can hide away; if Mallory gets
    Access to this certificate he can use it to make your key unusable.
    It is smart to print this certificate and store it away, just in case
    your media become unreadable. But have some caution: The print system of
    your machine might store the data and make it available to others!
    ```

9. The revocation key is saved as revoke.asc.

10. Now that you have a revocation certificate, you can revoke your key pair locally by typing the following:

    ```
    $ gpg --import revoke.asc
    ```

11. To check successful revocation, enter the following:

    ```
    $ gpg --list-keys
    ```

12. If revocation was successful, you should see a label saying the key is revoked, as shown here. In this example, the key was created on November 21, 2014, and was revoked on December 5, 2014.

    ```
    pub      2048R/BB7BCC97 2014-11-21 [revoked: 2014-12-05]
    ```

13. To make sure that other users are notified that the key has been revoked, you must upload the revocation certificate to a keyserver. In this example, you used Ubuntu Keyserver.

    ```
    $ gpg --keyserver keyserver.ubuntu.com --send BB7BCC97
    ```

14. When users update their key database, they will see that your key has been revoked.

Revoking a key is not the end of the key pair. There are instances where you realize that your key pair has not been compromised or probably you have revoked it by mistake. If this is a case, there is hope. A revoked key pair can still be unrevoked. Take note that this works only as long as you did not send the revocation certificate to a key server.

LAB 10-7: *Unrevoking a Key Pair*

In this lab, you will unrevoke a revoked key pair.

What You Need:

▶ System running Ubuntu 14.04.1

▶ Revoked key pair

Steps:

1. Export the revoked key. In this example, I am using the revoked key BB7BCC97.

   ```
   $ gpg --export BB7BCC97 > mykey.gpg
   ```

2. Once the revoked key has been exported to mykey.gpg, you need to split it into multiple parts.

   ```
   $ gpgsplit mykey.gpg
   ```

3. Listing the contents of the folder where the terminal is active will reveal files with names starting with 0000. These are the multiple parts of BB7BCC97.

   ```
   000001-006.public_key
   000002-002.sig
   000003-013.user_id
   000004-002.sig
   000005-014.public_subkey
   000006-002.sig
   ```

4. The revocation key is contained in one of these files. It is usually 000002-002. sig.

5. To make sure that 000002-002.sig is the revocation key, you need to verify its sigclass. It must be 0x20. To verify, issue the following command:

   ```
   $ gpg --list-packets 000002-002.sig
   ```

6. The output should be something like this:

   ```
   :signature packet: algo 1, keyed 3BF0599BBB7BCC97
      version 4, created 1417799918, md5len 0, sigclass 0x20
   ...
   ```

7. The second line is where the sigclass is. If it is equal to 0x20, delete the file.

    ```
    $ rm 000002-002.sig
    ```

8. Once you have deleted the revocation key, you can combine the remaining parts minus the 000002-002.sig. This can be done by issuing the following command:

    ```
    $ cat 0000* > restorekey.gpg
    ```

9. Next, you have to delete the revoked BB7BCC97. To do this, issue the following command:

    ```
    $ gpg --expert --delete-key BB7BCC97
    ```

10. Import the restored key, restorekey.gpg.

    ```
    $ gpg --import restorekey.gpg
    ```

11. To check for successful restoration, run the following command:

    ```
    $ gpg --list-keys
    ```

12. If the displayed key does not have the revoked label, then the restoration has been successful.

---

gpg gives the user the ability to edit a generated key pair. Usually when it comes to editing key pairs, the most common information that is edited is the expiration date. Sometimes a user wants to make the keys valid until the end of time or simply just wants the keys to be valid until a certain date. The edit function of gpg gives the user the capability to change the expiration date of a key pair.

LAB 10-8: *Changing the Expiration Date of a Key Pair*

In this lab, you will be changing the expiration date of your key pair.

What You Need:

▶   System running Ubuntu 14.04.1

▶   Generated keys

Steps:

1. Find the GPGKEY or key ID of the key you want to edit by issuing the following command:

    ```
    $ gpg --list-keys
    ```

2. In this example, the key you will edit is BB7BCC97.

   ```
   $ gpg --edit-key BB7BCC97
   ```

3. This will bring you inside the gpg shell. Inside the shell, you can use the list command to list your keys.

   ```
   gpg> list
   ```

4. If you want to work with a subkey, simply invoke the key command followed by the index of the subkey you want to work on. In this example, you will be working on the primary key. The primary key is the default, so there's no need to do anything, but in case you are working with multiple subkeys, issuing the command key 0 sets you up with the primary key.

   ```
   gpg> key 0
   ```

5. To change the key's expiration date, invoke the expire command.

   ```
   gpg> expire
   ```

6. Choose the desired expiration time.

   ```
   Changing expiration time for the primary key.
   Please specify how long the key should be valid.
   0 = key does not expire
   <n>       = key expires in n days
   <n>w      = key expires in n weeks
   <n>m      = key expires in n months
   <n>y      = key expires in n years
   Key is valid for? (0)
   ```

7. Then confirm it by entering **y** and pressing Enter.

   ```
   Is this correct? (y/N)
   ```

8. You will then need to enter your password to unlock the secret key and make the changes to the expiration date active.

9. After successfully changing the expiration date, a summary of the key will be displayed, but this time the expiration is set to never.

10. Exit the gpg shell by entering **quit** and pressing Enter. The system will ask you whether you want to save changes. Enter **y** and press Enter to confirm the changes and exit the gpg shell.

    ```
    gpg> quit
    Save changes? (y/N)
    ```

LAB 10-9: *Encrypting and Decrypting File Using GnuPG*

In this lab, you will use gpg to encrypt and decrypt a file.

What You Need:

▶   System running Ubuntu 14.04.1

Steps:

1.   Open a terminal window.

2.   Choose a file you want to encrypt. In this example, you will be using calc. EXE.

3.   Encrypt the file by issuing the following command:

```
$ gpg -c calc.exe
```

4.   gpg will ask for a password twice.

5.   The resulting encrypted file is calc.exe.gpg.

6.   Another way of doing this is by using a symmetric cipher.

```
$ gpg --output calc.exe.gpg --symmetric calc.exe
```

7.   To decrypt the file, issue the following command:

```
$ gpg calc.exe.gpg
```

8.   Supply the password, and the file will be successfully decrypted.

TIP

Encrypting a file by using gpg before compressing it with password protection using p7zip, or vice versa, will make cracking the file much more difficult.

The best way to lock out unauthorized users from accessing a file being transported is to encrypt it using the public key of the intended recipient.

LAB 10-10: *Encrypting a File with the Public Key of the Intended Recipient*

The purpose of encrypting using a public key of the intended recipient is to make sure that the intended recipient is the only one who can decrypt the file by using the recipient's private key. In this lab, you will be encrypting a file using the public key of the intended recipient.

What You Need:

▶ System running Ubuntu 14.04.1

▶ Intended recipient's public key

Steps:

1. Alice (alice@alicesemail.fake) wants to send Bob (bob@bobsemail.fake) an encrypted file. In this example, I will use calc.EXE. Alice uses Bob's public key to encrypt calc.EXE.

```
alice$ gpg --output calc.exe.gpg --encrypt \
--recipient bob@bobsemail.fake \
calc.exe
```

2. In the previous command line, Alice used Bob's public key associated with his e-mail. This means that Bob is the only one who can decrypt the file using his private key. If Alice wants to decrypt the file, she needs to add her public key.

```
alice$ gpg --output calc.exe.gpg --encrypt \
  --recipient bob@bobsemail.fake \
  --recipient alice@alicesemail.fake \
  calc.exe
```

3. If Alice wants to add more recipient, she can simply follow the same format as shown previously.

4. Once Bob gets the encrypted file, he can decrypt the file using his private key by issuing the following command:

```
bob$ gpg --output calc.exe --decrypt calc.exe.gpg
```

5. Bob will be asked a password to unlock his key. Once the correct password is supplied, the file will be decrypted.

> **NOTE**
>
> *As an added level of security, the file is actually compressed in addition to encrypted.*

> **TIP**
>
> *If you want to send multiple files, it is best to compress and password protect all the files first using a file compressor such as p7zip and then use GPG to encrypt the resulting archive file using the intended recipient's public key.*

Verifiable Source

Another thing to be considered when it comes to transferring a file for analysis is to make sure that it came from the source it was supposed to come from. The receiver must be able to verify the source of the file. When the file came from e-mail, it was easy to verify where it came from. But you know that e-mail (or anything else that can be used to transport or publish a file for download) can be compromised. So if you are paranoid and want to make sure that the file did came from the person it is supposed to, private key signing is the answer.

LINGO

Private key signing means encrypting something using a private key. It can be decrypted using the public key of the signer.

In the previous section, I discussed what private and public keys are and how the public key is used to encrypt the file so that only the private key of the recipient can be used to decrypt the file. In this section, it is more about verifying the source. So, the process is reversed. The sender or source signs or encrypts the file using his private key, and it can be decrypted only using the signer's public key. Private key signing ensures that the file came from the real source it is supposed to come from. This ensures the integrity of the file.

Since the file can be decrypted by the signer's public key, this means anybody who has access to the public key can have access to the file. This is the reason why the process of signing is done on top of encrypting the file using the public key of the receiver. Anybody, including the intended receiver, can verify the source of the file, but only the receiver, using his private key, can decrypt the file after verifying the source. This combination of private key signing and public key encryption ensures file integrity and confidentiality.

LAB 10-11: *Signing a File*

In this lab, you will be signing a file using your private key so the intended recipient can verify that the file indeed came from a trusted source, which is you.

What You Need:

▶ System running Ubuntu 14.04.1
▶ Generated keys

Steps:

1. Open a terminal window and enter the following command. In this example, you will be signing calc.EXE.

   ```
   $ gpg --output calc.exe.sig --sign calc.exe
   ```

2. The system will ask for a passphrase to unlock your secret key. After supplying the password, the file will be signed.

   NOTE

   For added security, the file for signing is compressed and then signed.

3. The signed file is calc.exe.sig.

4. To verify the signature, enter the following command:

   ```
   $ gpg --verify calc.exe.sig
   ```

5. If the signature is good, you will see something like this:

   ```
   gpg: Signature made Mon 08 Dec 2014 02:02:19 PM EST using RSA key
   ID BB7BCC97
   gpg: Good signature from "Christopher Elisan (Lab for Book) <my
   email>"
   Primary key fingerprint: BBAD 61F3…
   ```

6. To decrypt the file, issue the following command:

   ```
   $ gpg --output calc.exe --decrypt calc.exe.sig
   ```

7. During the decryption, gpg will display the key of the signer similar to what was displayed when the private key of the sender was verified.

   ```
   gpg: Signature made Mon 08 Dec 2014 02:02:19 PM EST using RSA key
   ID BB7BCC97
   gpg: Good signature from "Christopher Elisan (Lab for Book) <my
   email>"
   Primary key fingerprint: BBAD 61F3…
   ```

8. The decrypted file is calc.EXE, as supplied in the --output argument.

   NOTE

   Anybody can verify the source of the signed file by using the --verify switch, but only those whose public key is included as the intended recipient can decrypt the file.

> **NOTE**
>
> *The way unknown files are transferred is the same as how known malware files are transferred. As previously mentioned, unknown files must be treated like they are malware. It is better to be safe than sorry.*

Now you have an idea of how to do the following:

▶ Compress and password protect a file

▶ Encrypt using a public key of the intended recipient

▶ Sign using your private key so the source can be verified

It is a good idea to combine these three before transferring or transporting a file.

Analysis

After an unknown file has been transferred from the verified source, the next step is to analyze it. The analysis can be done manually or through an automated system. As I discussed in previous chapters, static analysis requires the file to be static, or at rest. This means you do not need to execute the file to get the information you need when conducting static malware inspection. Since this is the requirement, you do not need to do anything with the file after it is decrypted and decompressed. There is no need to revert the file into an executable state. The only time a file is needed to be in an executable state is during dynamic analysis, which I will discuss in future chapters.

Therefore, when it comes to handling a file during analysis, it stays in its non-executable state. This is the same state the file was in when being transferred from source to destination. The only action needed is to decrypt and decompress it. Any form of analysis, except for dynamic analysis, must always handle the file in a non-executable state.

Storage

Analysis answers the question, "Is the file malicious?" Some research organizations discard the files that are benign and keep only those that are deemed malicious. In this section, I will concentrate more on storing files that are deemed malicious or verified to be malware, including the metadata of the files.

> **NOTE**
>
> *Some research organizations keep the files found to be benign for whitelisting purposes.*

Storing files deemed malicious follows almost the same concept as when a file is being transferred. This means that when a file is stored, it must be in a non-executable state and must be inaccessible to unauthorized users.

To effectively store malicious or malware files, it must in line with the following principles:

▶ Confidentiality

▶ Integrity

▶ Availability

This is also known as the CIA model or triad. CIA is an acronym for confidentiality, integrity, and availability. This is a set of guidelines and policies that help an organization in protecting data and information. Confidentiality restricts or limits the access to data and information to those who are authorized. Integrity ensures that the data and information have not been modified or altered in any way, therefore maintaining its trustworthiness and accuracy. Availability ensures that the data and information are accessible to authorized users when needed without delay.

In your case, you are protecting malware files. Some may comment that this is going overboard, but when it comes to malware, in my humble opinion, there is no going overboard, especially if it has something to do with preventing any sample leaks. You do not want these files or information about these files to fall into the wrong hands (especially the files because they either can be used in their original form or can be modified to be much more resilient in an attack campaign). Also, you do not want any inadvertent execution of malware files that may cause a malware outbreak.

> **NOTE**
>
> *"Wrong hands" includes not only the bad guys but also good guys who do not know how to properly handle malware.*

Confidentiality

You need to make sure that neither malware samples nor information about these samples reaches any unauthorized entities. This is considered sensitive data and information, so preventing unauthorized access is of paramount importance. I touched on this already in the previous section by using password-protected compressed files and public key cryptography. In most cases, and as widely practiced, the state of malware when it is transferred is the same as how it is stored, which means it undergoes compression and encryption. When a file for analysis is received and then proven to be malware after analysis, it undergoes the following:

- ▶ Converted into a non-executable state
- ▶ Compressed and password protected
- ▶ Encrypted

When it comes to compressing with password protection, some malware research group or companies have their own password that is different from the ones commonly used such as infected, virus, and novirus. As an added precaution, the password-protected compressed file is encrypted. It can be encrypted using public key cryptography, and only the private keys of the authorized users or researchers can decrypt it. Or the drive or data storage where the files reside is encrypted, and the only ones who can decrypt the data storage are those who have knowledge of and access to the needed credentials or tokens. In short, encryption when it comes to storage can occur by using the following:

- ▶ Public key cryptography
- ▶ Whole data storage encryption

Also, when it comes to confidentiality, it is important to consider data transmission and the security of the credentials needed to access to data. If for some reason the credentials, such as usernames, passwords, tokens, and private keys, are compromised and the malware samples and information are intercepted during transmission or a location, such as a backup, is breached, then no matter how strong the encryption is, the data and information can be stolen. Therefore, it is important to also secure the assets where the data and information resides and the credentials that grant access to them.

Integrity

As I defined earlier, integrity ensures that the data and information has not been modified or altered in any way, therefore maintaining its trustworthiness and accuracy.

There are lots of causes that can contribute to data integrity violations. Some of them are as follows:

- ▶ System error
- ▶ User error

- ▶ Malware
- ▶ Malicious actor

Data in storage or static data can be corrupted because of system error. Static data can be corrupted if the hardware or storage device starts to malfunction or starts deteriorating, causing bad sectors that can result in some data being lost. Sadly, disks today can be corrupted without being detected. This is because of the complexity of disk technology that has multiple points of failure such as a faulty disk controller that can cause data not to be written where it is supposed to be written on disk causing corrupt data. There are also cases wherein data is hosted in a very old system that is just waiting for a nudge to break down.

System error can also be caused by software. Buggy and poorly designed software can cause data modification without the knowledge of the user or the system.

Data that is transmitted, or dynamic data, is also susceptible to corruption, especially if it is being transmitted through unreliable networks. Unreliable networks usually corrupt data that pass through them because of intermittent connection losses. Without any error checking, the data that is transferred from the source might be different once it reaches the receiver.

User error also plays a role in violating data integrity. Using a tool or software in an incorrect manner while dealing with data can corrupt the data. A user can also inadvertently destroy or delete data without knowing it, especially if the user is not well trained to handle that sort of data.

Aside from system and user error, there is a more sinister cause that can contribute to data integrity violation, which is malicious intent. Malicious intent to destroy or violate the integrity of data must be considered at all times. It can be carried out through the use of malware or unauthorized breach by an attacker or group of attackers. Therefore, it is important to consider the security of where the data is stored and how it is accessed. Regular checks of software that can be exploited through vulnerabilities must be done. This includes but is not limited to the operating system and the different kinds of software used to manage data.

To help ensure data integrity, the following are common techniques used in the industry:

- ▶ Data replication
- ▶ Parity computations
- ▶ Checksum

Data replication is the simplest way of ensuring data integrity. The main idea here is to have multiple copies of the data and then have regular integrity checks comparing the copies. If one copy is different, then that is flagged as corrupt data and corrected by overwriting it with the right copy. Although this is the simplest way and the easiest to implement, it is not scalable. It is inefficient as data grows. The storage needs multiply depending on how many copies there are, and the time needed to do integrity checking between the copies can become very long.

LINGO

*Data replication is also known as **mirroring**.*

Parity computations are used in RAID drive arrays, such RAID-3, RAID-4, and RAID-5, for fault tolerance and validating data written to the RAID array by calculating the data in two drives and storing the resulting calculation on a third one. The Exclusive OR (XOR) logical operator is used to calculate parity across the RAID array. The main idea here is that if one drive fails, it can be replaced, and the data can be rebuilt from the other two drives.

NOTE

RAID drives have a "hot-swappable" drive on standby to replace a failed or corrupted drive.

Getting the checksum of the data (in this case, the malware samples) and storing it in one place is another method of integrity checking. This is a well-known method. It actually reminds me of Microsoft Anti-Virus (MSAV) during the DOS days. The main idea here is to get the checksum of the data and then using it to check whether that data changed. Checksums can be as simple as a hash.

Availability

Availability ensures that the data is accessible or available when needed. The ideal is no downtime. But since we do not live in an ideal world, there will be downtime. The main idea is to have as little downtime as technically possible. This can be achieved by having the system, both hardware and software, working in tip-top shape. A good way to ensure this is periodic and proper maintenance of the systems where the data is hosted. And if something fails, there has to be immediate response in repairing or replacing the failed component.

The most common way to achieve availability is through redundancy. This ensures that if one site is down, the other sites can take over, and the availability of data is not affected in any way. When it comes to availability, there shouldn't be any denial of service.

Recap

In this chapter, I discussed how to properly handle an unknown file during the whole file's analysis life cycle. I discussed each stage of the life cycle, as listed here, and how to properly handle files in each of the stages:

▶ Transfer

▶ Analysis

▶ Storage

I identified three ways to properly handle files during transfer or transport by making sure that the file meets the following conditions:

▶ In a non-executable state

▶ Inaccessible to unauthorized users

▶ Came from a verifiable or trustworthy source

When it comes to the second stage, which is analysis, I stressed the importance of having the file remain in a non-executable state all the time except when it undergoes dynamic analysis.

Last but not least, I discussed how to properly store files. I discussed the CIA triad and how it can be applied to protecting malware files.

Tools

▶ Compression tools

▶ **WinZip**   http://www.winzip.com

▶ **WinRAR**   http://www.rarlab.com

▶ **7zip**   http://www.7-zip.org

▶ **p7zip**   http://p7zip.sourceforge.net/

▶ **GnuPG**   http://www.gnupg.org

Inspecting Static Malware

The previous two chapters gave you an overview of the Portable Executable (PE) file and the proper way of handling unknown files and those that are found to be malicious. They introduced you to concepts that needed to be understood and done before you can begin malware analysis. Now that you have an understanding of these concepts and an increased awareness of the dangers and pitfalls that you might face if you do not follow them, you are now ready to analyze malware.

In this chapter, I will discuss how to inspect static malware, a process also known as *static malware analysis* or simply *static analysis*. I will go through the step-by-step process of analyzing static malware and the tools needed to accomplish your goal of extracting information from static malware.

Static Analysis Techniques

Malware analysis must answer the question of whether a file is malicious. And if it is malicious, what is the malicious file's main directive?

In static analysis, you might not get as far as figuring out the malicious file's main directive, but it is an important first step in malware analysis nonetheless. In static analysis, your main goal is to gather as much data and information as possible to aid you in determining the malware's true nature and, if this is not possible, aid in a more effective and efficient way in dynamic analysis.

Since you are going to find out whether a file is malicious, you always start with the assumption that the file is unknown. You will also assume that any unknown file that is analyzed is malicious until proven benign. It is better to err on the side of caution.

To conduct an effective static analysis, you will be following some basic steps and techniques. And since you are concentrating on Windows malware, the following are more tuned to analyzing Windows files:

▶ ID assignment

▶ File type identification

▶ Antivirus detection

▶ Protective mechanisms identification

▶ PE structure verification

▶ Strings analysis

▶ Static code analysis

NOTE

Malware analysis is an art. The steps or techniques identified are to serve as a guide and not a checklist.

ID Assignment

The first thing you must do is to assign a unique identifier to the file. A common practice in the industry is to use a hash to identify a file uniquely. MD5 and SHA-1 are the most commonly used hashes. SHA-2 is another alternative that makes for minimal hash collision and better resistance from pre-image attack breaks. It includes SHA-224, SHA-256, SHA-384, SHA-512, SHA-512/224, and SHA-512/256.

LINGO

*Hash collisions are when two different inputs produce the same hash. A **pre-image attack**, on the other hand, is finding the original input from its hash value.*

There are lots of available tools to do this, including the following two:

▶ **MD5SUM**   http://www.etree.org/md5com.html
▶ **Microsoft File Checksum Integrity Verifier**   http://www.microsoft.com/en-us/download/details.aspx?id=11533

Besides using these tools, you can create a script using hash libraries included in programming or scripting languages, such as Python. Whichever method is preferred, the main idea is to assign a unique ID to a file.

LAB 11-1: *Using a Python Script to Compute MD5 and SHA-1*

In this lab, you will create a script that computes a file's MD5 and SHA-1 hash.

What You Need:

▶ System running Ubuntu 14.04.1
▶ Python 2.7.6
▶ Calc.EXE from Windows 7

Steps:

1. Create a Python script file.

2. Write the following code:

```
#!/usr/bin/python
import hashlib
f = open('calc.exe', 'rb')
md5sum = hashlib.md5(f.read()).hexdigest()
sha1sum = hashlib.sha1(f.read()).hexdigest()
f.close()
print 'MD5 =', md5sum
print 'SHA1 =', sha1sum
exit()
```

3. After creating the Python script, change it to executable mode by issuing the following command:

```
$ chmod +x yourscript.py
```

4. Execute your script. Make sure that calc.EXE is in the same folder as your script.

```
$ ./yourscript.py
```

5. The output should look like the following. Take note that depending on your calc.EXE, the hash might be different.

```
MD5 = 829e4805b0e12b383ee09abdc9e2dc3c
SHA1 = da39a3ee5e6b4b0d3255bfef95601890afd80709
```

File Type Identification

Once a unique ID has been assigned to the file, the next step is to find out its file type. This helps the analyst weed out file types that are not supported by any analysis systems or those that are not needed to be analyzed.

It is important to take note that different file types require different approaches for analysis, so it is imperative that the file type is known before any analysis takes place. In this book, the concentration is on Windows files, so you will tackle only those that are identified as such.

When it comes to identifying file types, the following are the most common tools:

▶ PEiD

▶ Linux-based file command

PEiD is a file type detector tool. Aside from detecting the file type, it can also detect whether a binary is packed or protected by common packers such as UPX, Armadillo, and so on. PEiD is a classic tool and has not been updated for a long time. The latest version, which is considered the final one, is v0.95. Regardless of its age, this tool is still useful because it has a customizable database commonly known as UserDB.TXT. This is a text file that can be modified or expanded to include new signatures to detect new file types and new packer programs. PEiD and its latest public release of UserDB.TXT can be downloaded from http:// woodmann.com/BobSoft/Pages/Programs/PEiD.

TIP

There are lots of websites publishing PEiD. Take precaution when downloading this tool and make sure that the one you are downloading is legitimate and not carrying any malicious software.

Another common file type detection tool is the one that comes with Linux. It is the file command. To invoke the tool, simply open a terminal window and type **file** and the file in question, as shown here:

```
$ file unknown_file.ex1
```

NOTE

The file command-line tool also displays whether a binary is packed or not as long as the packer is included in its signature database.

LAB 11-2: *Using PEiD*

In this lab, you will get and use PEiD.

What You Need:

▶ System running Windows 7

▶ PEiD and UserDB.TXT

Steps:

1. Download PEiD and UserDB.TXT from http://woodmann.com/BobSoft/ Pages/Programs/PEiD.

2. Extract the files. Make sure to replace the old UserDB.TXT that is included in the PEiD ZIP file with the latest one released in 2007 that comes in the UserDB ZIP file.

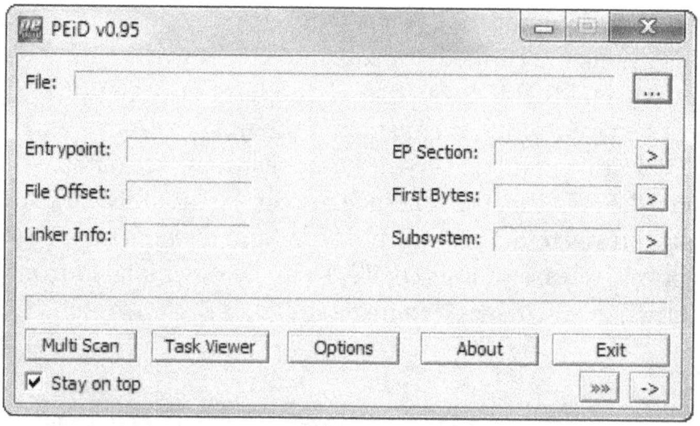

Figure 11-1 *PEiD window.*

3. Go to the folder where PEiD was extracted and double-click PEiD.exe. Figure 11-1 shows the PEiD window.

4. Choose a file you want to play with and try different options of the tool to see what happens. Try playing with packed files also if you have some available.

In some cases, a script is much more desirable when identifying file types. For instances like this, you can use a Python script to identify file types.

LAB 11-3: *Creating a Python Script That Identifies File Type*

In this lab, you will create a script that identifies file type of a given file.

What You Need:

▶ System running Ubuntu 14.04.1

▶ Python 2.7.6

▶ Calc.EXE from Windows 7

Steps:

1. Install python-pip. (You can skip this if pip is already installed.)

    ```
    $ sudo apt-get install python-pip
    ```

2. Install python-magic using pip.

    ```
    $ sudo pip install python-magic
    ```

3. Create a Python script file.

4. Write the following code:

```
#!/usr/bin/python
import magic
filetype = magic.from_file('calc.exe')
print filetype
exit()
```

5. After creating the Python script, change it to executable mode by issuing the following command:

```
$ chmod +x yourscript.py
```

6. Execute your script. Make sure that calc.EXE is in the same folder as your script.

```
$ ./yourscript.py
```

7. The output should look like the following:

```
PE32 executable (GUI) Intel 80386, for MS Windows
```

Antivirus Detection

When it comes to figuring out whether a file is malicious, a good indicator is the result of an antivirus product scan. This process also helps in determining the possible family of the malware. Take note that I am not talking in absolutes here because there is always the possibility of a false positive and misnaming of malware detection. In the analysis process, you use antivirus detection simply as an indicator to help you identify the maliciousness of a file and its possible malware family group.

There are two ways to subject a file to an antivirus scan. They are as follows:

▶ On-premise antivirus scanning
▶ Online antivirus scanning

On-premise antivirus scanning means you have the antivirus product installed in a system you control. It can be a set of different virtualized machines hosting different antivirus products each or an offline tool that utilizes different antivirus product engines to scan a file for possible infection. In an on-premise setup, the management of the system, such as updating scan signatures and ensuring uptime, is your responsibility. So, aside from hardware and software license cost, there is also maintenance cost. One thing that is important to remember is that no matter what the implementation is, the main idea is that you control the system and all the data and information produced by the system.

Online antivirus scanning is a cheaper alternative because there is no hardware and software to manage and maintain. Plus, most online antivirus scanning services are free or can be accurately described as having a *zero dollar cost*. The caveat is that whatever files you submit to them eventually become their property, and they can do whatever they want with those files and the information collected from those files by their systems. In reality, it is not really free. Some online antivirus scanning companies that offer this service for free sell the files and information gathered from those files.

The most popular online antivirus scanning service is Google's VirusTotal, as shown in Figure 11-2. It is the most trusted and widely used in the industry.

> **TIP**
>
> Be mindful of submitting files for analysis, especially if they contain private or confidential information. If possible, such as in documents, remove all private or confidential information. If this is not possible, I suggest not submitting any of these files.

The following are the online antivirus scanning services that are free to use:

▶ **VirusTotal by Google** https://www.virustotal.com

▶ **VirSCAN** http://www.virscan.org

Figure 11-2 *VirusTotal splash page.*

► **Metascan by OPSWAT**   https://www.metascan-online.com

► **Jotti**   http://virusscan.jotti.org

The online services enumerated in the previous list use multiple antivirus engines or scanners. They are a good way not only to check for file infection but also to compare different antivirus detection names. Figure 11-3 shows an example output of a scan session in VirusTotal.

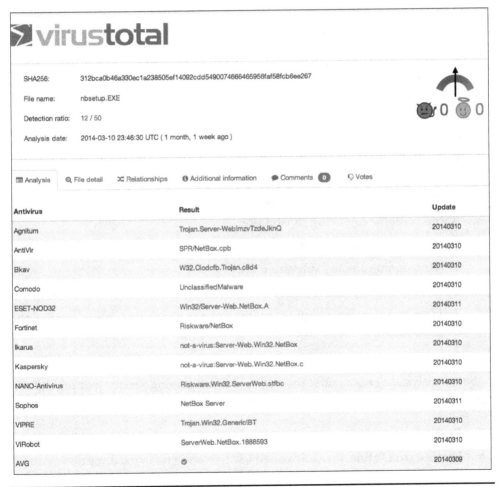

Figure 11-3   *VirusTotal output of a scanning session.*

> **TIP**
>
> *Before using any free online antivirus scanning service, make sure to read their terms of service and privacy policy.*

VirusTotal offers a public application programming interface (API). It is a free service available to anyone as long as the API is not used in commercial products or services. It is useful if you need to write client applications that can interact directly with VirusTotal.

LAB 11-4: *Getting Started with the VirusTotal Public API*

In this lab, you will experiment using VirusTotal Public API. Since VirusTotal already has detailed documentation on how to do this, the lab will refer to the documentation and let you experiment on your own.

What You Need:

▶ VirusTotal Public API

Steps:

1. Request the VirusTotal Public API from VirusTotal.
2. Read and familiarize yourself with the documentation at https://www.virustotal .com/en/documentation/public-api/.
3. Accomplish the following capabilities:
   A. Sending and scanning files
   B. Rescanning already submitted files
   C. Retrieving file scan reports
4. Feel free to experiment with other features and capabilities mentioned in the documentation.

Some antivirus vendors offer their own online scanning service that highlights their antivirus product or scan engine. Some of them are the following:

▶ **Dr. Web**   http://www.drweb-online.com/en/online_check.asp
▶ **Fortiguard Online Virus Scanner**   http://www.fortiguard.com/antivirus/ virus_scanner.html

Alternatively, antivirus vendors offer a way for users to submit samples to them for analysis. Unlike an online scanning service where the result of the scan is posted immediately, the user has to wait for a response from the vendor. The response usually comes via e-mail. This means that when a user submits a sample, the user has to give up some information such as an e-mail address.

The following are some vendors that offer sample submission services to users:

▶ **F-Secure Sample Analysis**   http://www.f-secure.com/en/web/labs_global/submit-samples/sas

▶ **Sophos**   https://secure2.sophos.com/en-us/support/contact-support/sample-submission.aspx

Antivirus vendors offering these services for free not only help the user but also themselves, the antivirus companies. This is because they are able to collect suspicious samples for free. It is crowdsourcing at its best. Also, this helps the different antivirus vendors get a pulse of what's going on in the digital world. If there is a set of samples being submitted (hundreds or even thousands of times in a short period of time), chances are these samples are hot and attention must be given to them.

Aside from on-premise and online virus scanning services, there is another alternative. This alternative relies more on the open source community. This caters to researchers who do not have a budget to create their own on-premise antivirus scanning infrastructure and do not want to submit any samples to an online antivirus scanning service provider. The alternative is using ClamAV.

ClamAV, as described by its publisher, is an open source (General Public License [GPL]) antivirus engine designed for detecting Trojans, viruses, malware, and other malicious threats. It provides a high-performance multi-threaded scanning daemon, command-line utilities for on-demand file scanning, and an intelligent tool for automatic signature updates. The ClamAV virus databases are updated regularly and posted online for download by users. This is a cheaper alternative to the on-premise virus scanning infrastructure and does not carry the privacy concerns of submitting samples to online antivirus scanning service providers.

You can find more information and download links for ClamAV at http://www.clamav.net.

LAB 11-5: *Using ClamAV for File Scanning*

In this lab, you will install and use ClamAV to scan files for possible infection.

What You Need:

▶ System running Ubuntu 14.04.1

Steps:

1. Install ClamAV.

    ```
    $ sudo apt-get install clamav
    ```

2. Update ClamAV virus definitions.

    ```
    $ sudo freshclam
    ```

3. ClamAV virus definition updates are located in http://lurker.clamav.net/list/clamav-virusdb.html.

4. Scan files using ClamAV.

    ```
    $ clamscan OPTIONS <file>
    ```

5. To see what options are available, simply invoke help.

    ```
    $ clamscan –help
    ```

ClamAV also offers a UI version called ClamTK.

LAB 11-6: *Using ClamTK for File Scanning*

In this lab, you will install and use ClamTK to scan files for possible infection.

What You Need:

▶ System running Ubuntu 14.04.1

Steps:

1. Install ClamTK.

    ```
    $ sudo apt-get install clamtk
    ```

2. Open ClamTK by going to Applications and double-clicking ClamTK. Figure 11-4 shows ClamTK window.

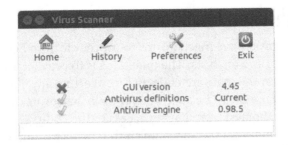

Figure 11-4   *ClamTK.*

3. To scan a file or folder, go to the Scan menu and choose the appropriate scanning option.

4. Familiarize yourself with the different capabilities offered by ClamTK by playing around with the different options.

If you need a new virus definition added to ClamAV and the most updated virus definitions found in http://lurker.clamav.net/list/clamav-virusdb.html does not include it, you can create your own signature and add it to your ClamAV virus definition.

LAB 11-7: *Writing a Signature for ClamAV*

In this lab, you will write a signature for ClamAV.

What You Need:

▶ System running Ubuntu 14.04.1

Steps:

1. Download the "how-to" document from https://github.com/vrtadmin/clamav-devel/raw/master/docs/signatures.pdf.

2. Experiment with the different signature formats discussed in the document.

    A. Hash-based signature

    B. File checksum (SHA-1, SHA256)

    C. PE section based

    D. Body-based signature

    E. Signatures for version information metadata in PE files

    F. Signature based on different metadata

Protective Mechanisms Identification

Most malware has protective mechanisms to prevent it from being analyzed by malware researchers and analysts. The main idea is to prevent anyone or anything from having access to the malware code. Before exerting any effort, it is important to determine whether a file to be analyzed statically has protective mechanisms that will prevent the analyst from having access to the code.

The most common protective mechanism that malware employs when it comes to protecting its code is encryption. The most common tools malware authors employ to accomplish this are crypters and real-time packers. Crypters are tools that encrypt malware code. Real-time packers, on the other hand, not only encrypt but also compress the target malware.

It is important to identify whether a malware has undergone encryption through the use of a crypter or real-time packer before the attackers deployed it so that the appropriate decrypter or unpacker can be used to decrypt and unpack the malware. Unfortunately, an encrypted or packed malware renders static analysis useless. Knowing about a packed malware beforehand helps you conserve analysis energy by not bothering to put that malware into static analysis unless it has been successfully unpacked or decrypted.

LINGO

A **packed malware** is a malware file that has been encrypted and compressed by real-time packers.

Most crypters and real-time packers have a specific decrypter and unpacker. In cases like this, it is easy to decrypt or unpack the malware. The researcher can simply identify the specific crypter or packer used and then subject the malware to the appropriate decrypter or unpacker. The real challenge is when the identified protective mechanism does not have an appropriate decrypter or unpacker. This requires a manual unpacking session, which is a completely different topic.

In this book, I will concentrate more on real-time packers since they are the widely used protective mechanism employed by attackers. The following are the most common packers:

▶ **Armadillo**   http://www.siliconrealms.com/armadillo.php
▶ **ASPack**   http://www.aspack.com/aspack.html

▶ **ASProtect32** http://www.aspack.com/asprotect32.html

▶ **ASProtect64** http://www.aspack.com/asprotect64.html

▶ **PECompact** http://bitsum.com/pecompact/

▶ **UPX** http://upx.sourceforge.net/

It is important to be familiar with all the packers you can get your hands on and how they work. It is also important to know how a binary looks like after it is packed. Having this knowledge is key in identifying packed malware.

NOTE

Real-time packers are not necessarily malicious. They can be software designed to protect a program code. They are also used by legitimate software writers to protect their code from piracy and also to make the program smaller for easy online distribution.

LAB 11-8: *Packing a File Using UPX*

In this lab, you will pack a file using the most common packer of all, UPX.

What You Need:

▶ System running Ubuntu 14.04.1

▶ Calc.EXE from Windows 7

▶ UPX

Steps:

1. Install UPX.

   ```
   $ sudp apt-get install upx
   ```

2. Pack calc.EXE.

   ```
   $ upx calc.exe
   ```

3. Check whether calc.EXE has been successfully packed using the file command-line tool.

   ```
   $ file calc.exe
   ```

4. The output should be as follows:

   ```
   calc.exe: PE32 executable (GUI) Intel 80386, for MS Windows, UPX compressed
   ```

LAB 11-9: *Using a Python Script to Identify Packed Binaries*

In this lab, you will create a script that can detect whether a binary is packed and, if it is, what packer was used to pack it.

What You Need:

▶ System running Ubuntu 14.04.1

▶ Python

▶ UserDB.TXT

▶ Packed binary, preferably from the previous lab, 11-8

Steps:

1. Create a Python script file.

2. Write the following code:

```
#!/usr/bin/python
import peutils
import pefile
packer_signatures = peutils.SignatureDatabase('UserDB.TXT')
pe = pefile.PE('packed_file.exe')
matches = packer_signatures.match(pe, ep_only = True)
print matches
exit()
```

3. After creating the Python script, change it to executable mode by issuing the following command:

```
$ chmod +x yourscript.py
```

4. Execute your script. Make sure that the packed file is in the same folder as your script.

```
$ ./yourscript.py
```

5. The output should look like the following:

```
['UPX 2.90 [LZMA] -> Markus Oberhumer, Laszlo Molnar & John Reiser']
```

NOTE

In the script, ep_only stands for scan entry point only. If it is set to True, the script will scan only the entry point, but if it is set to False, the script will scan the whole body of the file, making the scanning process slower.

TIP

UserDB.TXT can be modified to include new packer signatures.

Identifying whether a file is packed is just half the battle. The challenging part is to unpack it. An unpacked and unencrypted file makes it easier for analysts and researchers to proceed in the static analysis process. There are lots of tools out there that can unpack a protected binary, especially if the packer used is common. For those packers that do not have unpackers, reverse engineering is the key to unpacking the file. The analyst then has to weigh whether the time needed to unpack the binary manually is worth it or just proceed directly to dynamic analysis. In most cases, the latter is chosen.

Most PE tools that are available in the market have the ability to unpack packed binaries. One of my favorites is PE Explorer (http://www.heaventools.com/overview.htm). It supports unpacking of UPX, Upack, and NsPack.

For packed binaries that are not supported by most tools, I usually go to this site to find an unpacker: http://www.woodmann.com/crackz/Packers.htm. Again, do not execute any of the tools published on this site in a production network. Always treat tools such as this with great caution and suspicion. It is always better to use these tools in a controlled environment.

PE Structure Verification

Another indicator of whether a file is malicious is a malformed PE structure. A malformed PE structure often indicates an infection or a sloppy way of hiding malicious code. Having knowledge of the PE structure is critical in this static analysis technique. An abnormal field value, a non-standard section, or anything that appears off is a good candidate for further investigation.

TIP

In Chapter 9, I discussed the PE file structure. It is always good to refer to that chapter as reference when it comes to the different fields and their possible values.

Strings Analysis

A file sample that is unencrypted can reveal a lot by looking at the strings found in its code. Just by extracting strings, you can identify a lot of things from a possible malware sample. The following are the more interesting ones:

▶ Location of malicious dropped files
▶ Name of the dropped files

▶ Domain name of a possible command-and-control (C&C) server

▶ Internet Protocol (IP) address of a possible C&C server

Aside from these, another set of strings might be of interest, especially if it comes to tying the malware samples to their writers or the threat actors that are using them. Some strings might contain the following information:

▶ Dedications

▶ Political statements

▶ Group affiliations and mottos

▶ Incendiary messages

LAB 11-10: *Extracting Strings from Files (Ubuntu)*

In this lab, you will use the command-line strings that come with Ubuntu to extract strings from files.

What You Need:

▶ System running Ubuntu 14.04.1

▶ Unpacked and unencrypted binary

Steps:

1. Open a terminal window.

2. Type the following command. You will use the unpacked version of calc.EXE from Windows 7.

   ```
   $ strings calc.exe
   ```

3. If you want to save the output to a text file, issue the following command:

   ```
   $ strings calc.exe > calc.txt
   ```

4. Examine the output, and you will notice a lot of useful information such as libraries and function calls that the program needs to run.

LAB 11-11: *Extracting Strings from Files (Windows)*

In this lab, you will use strings.EXE from Sysinternals to extract strings from files.

What You Need:

▶ System running Windows

▶ strings.EXE from Sysinternals

Steps:

1. Download strings.EXE from http://technet.microsoft.com/en-us/sysinternals/ bb897439.

2. Open a command prompt and go to the folder where strings.EXE is saved.

3. Issue the following command. You will use the unpacked version of calc.EXE from Windows.

   ```
   > strings calc.exe
   ```

4. If you want to save the output to a text file, issue the following command:

   ```
   > strings calc.exe > calc.txt
   ```

5. Examine the output, and you will notice a lot of useful information such as libraries and function calls that the program needs to run.

Recap

In this chapter, I discussed different static analysis steps and techniques to get as much information as you can from a static file. They are as follows:

- ▶ File type identification
- ▶ Antivirus detection
- ▶ Protective mechanisms identification
- ▶ PE structure verification
- ▶ Strings analysis

I also discussed different tools that are available to you from Windows and Ubuntu. You also created some scripts that will help you in your static analysis process.

Tools

- ▶ **MD5SUM**   http://www.etree.org/md5com.html
- ▶ **Microsoft File Checksum Integrity Verifier**   http://www.microsoft.com/ en-us/download/details.aspx?id=11533
- ▶ **PEiD**   http://woodmann.com/BobSoft/Pages/Programs/PEiD

- ▶ **ClamAV** http://www.clamav.net
- ▶ Sample submission online services
  - ▶ **F-Secure Sample Analysis** http://www.f-secure.com/en/web/labs_global/submit-samples/sas
  - ▶ **Sophos** https://secure2.sophos.com/en-us/support/contact-support/sample-submission.aspx
- ▶ Malware scanning services
  - ▶ **VirusTotal by Google** https://www.virustotal.com
  - ▶ **VirSCAN** http://www.virscan.org
  - ▶ **Metascan by OPSWAT** https://www.metascan-online.com
  - ▶ **Jotti** http://virusscan.jotti.org
  - ▶ **Dr. Web** http://www.drweb-online.com/en/online_check.asp
  - ▶ **Fortiguard Online Virus Scanner** http://www.fortiguard.com/antivirus/virus_scanner.html
- ▶ Packers
  - ▶ **Armadillo** http://www.siliconrealms.com/armadillo.php
  - ▶ **ASPack** http://www.aspack.com/aspack.html
  - ▶ **ASProtect32** http://www.aspack.com/asprotect32.html
  - ▶ **ASProtect64** http://www.aspack.com/asprotect64.html
  - ▶ **PECompact** http://bitsum.com/pecompact/
  - ▶ **UPX** http://upx.sourceforge.net/
- ▶ **PE Explorer** http://www.heaventools.com/overview.htm
- ▶ **Packers and Unpackers** http://www.woodmann.com/crackz/Packers.htm
- ▶ **Sysinternals Strings.EXE** http://technet.microsoft.com/en-us/sysinternals/bb897439

Inspecting Dynamic Malware

The previous chapter discussed how to inspect or analyze static malware, or malware that is not running. I discussed the most common static analysis techniques and how information gathered from each of those techniques can be used to identify whether a file is malicious and, if it is indeed malicious, possibly identify its directive based on data gathered statically.

It is a known fact that static analysis is limited because most of the magic happens when the malware is running. When the malware is running in an environment it was designed to execute in, it reveals most of its functionalities, thus opening it up for observation and experimentation by malware analysts and researchers. This is inspecting dynamic malware, more popularly known as *dynamic malware analysis* or simply *dynamic analysis.*

In this chapter, I will discuss how to inspect and analyze dynamic malware. I will go through the different tools, techniques, and processes of dynamic analysis to accomplish your goal of extracting information from dynamic malware and ultimately get to the bottom of the malware behavior and its main attack directive.

Virtual vs. Bare Metal

When it comes to dynamic analysis, there is always a dilemma about whether to use a virtual environment or a bare-metal machine to host the operating system in which the malware will be executed. In my humble opinion, it is not a matter of *or* but *and.* It is best to have both. The two environments complement each other. Malware that is not virtual-aware can be executed and analyzed in a virtual environment, and malware that is virtual-aware can be executed and analyzed in a bare-metal environment. The researcher, with these two environment implementations on hand, gets the benefits these two setups have to offer as discussed in previous chapters.

It is best to execute malware first in a virtual environment. If execution fails, the next step is to execute it in a bare-metal system. This is to see whether the malware is virtual-aware. If execution fails in a bare-metal system, further investigation is needed to determine *why* the malware failed to execute in these two environments. It probably has something to do with the lab setup.

Chapter 8 discussed how to set up both virtual and bare-metal dynamic analysis labs. The chapter also discussed how to make the dynamic analysis lab malware friendly so malware execution will be successful as much as possible. That is the key in any dynamic analysis lab. A lab that is not malware friendly will have little chance of capturing dynamic malware behavior.

Dynamic Analysis

When it comes to observing malware behavior, it can be divided into two parts.

- ▶ Host behavior
- ▶ Network behavior

In the early years of malware, dynamic analysis was confined to analyzing a malware's host behavior. The early malware did not have any network functionality. A dynamic analysis lab was a single isolated system. But with the advances of malware and its ability to communicate remotely with other malware and with its controller, it is a must to analyze its network behavior as well. Therefore, when it comes to dynamic analysis collecting and analyzing, both the malware host and the network behavior must be studied.

Analyzing Host Behavior

Dynamic analysis is all about monitoring and capturing information from malware in a target or compromised system. To do this, it is important to understand fundamental malware behavior in an infected system; in this case, the dynamic analysis lab.

For malware to accomplish its main directive, it has to do a number of modifications and actions in a target system. This is what you need to determine. Most of the actions the malware does in a compromised host are designed to achieve one or a combination of the following:

- ▶ Malware component installation
- ▶ Malware persistency
- ▶ Malware protective mechanism
- ▶ Malware directive

During infection or system compromise, the malware installs a copy of itself and other components if needed. This means additional files are added to the system without the victim's knowledge. In most cases, the malware is deployed using a dropper, a downloader, or a hybrid of both.

The following are the most common locations where malware installs its components:

- ▶ Windows folder
- ▶ System folder
- ▶ Temporary folders

A dropper is a malware installer that contains all the malware and all its components. It is like a typical software installer. Upon execution, it installs the malware and all its components, collectively also known as the *malware package,* to the appropriate location in the system.[1]

A downloader, on the other hand, does not contain the malware package. Instead, it downloads the package to be installed from the malware-serving domains. A downloader is similar to a download manager used by some software vendors wherein the user downloads a small executable, which upon execution checks the system for compatibility and then downloads and installs the appropriate software package. The same thing is done by a malware downloader, except for the fact that it downloads and installs malware instead of legitimate software.[1] It is important to note that the downloader relies heavily on the compromised machine having an Internet connection. This is why dynamic analysis labs of today have a controlled environment that allows them to connect to the Internet when needed, especially if the malware needs to download its components.

> **TIP**
>
> *When an Internet connection is needed for malware analysis purposes, always make sure that the Internet connection is not used by any system not designed to capture or analyze malware. It is also good practice to read and comply with the terms and agreements of your Internet service provider.*

The attackers understand that some of the systems will have a limited Internet connection. To solve this, a hybrid of a downloader and a dropper is often used to deploy malware. A hybrid malware installer functions as a downloader first to ensure that the updated version of the malware is installed into the system. If there is no Internet connection, the hybrid malware installer functions as a dropper by installing the malware package it is carrying with it.

---

[1] *Malware, Rootkits & Botnets* by Christopher C. Elisan, published by McGraw-Hill.

NOTE

A downloader usually has a significantly smaller size compared to its dropper and hybrid counterpart since it does not have to bear the weight of the malware package. A hybrid and a dropper usually are similar in size.

After installing all the malware components, the malware installer, regardless of whether it is a dropper, downloader, or hybrid, deletes itself and passes control to the newly installed malware components. The malware installer deletes itself to remove of any traces it was there. It is important to remember that the malware installer is a separate technical component of the threat ecosystem, and its value increases for every successful malware deployment it does without a sample of it being captured by researchers. You can find a detailed discussion of this and the threat ecosystem in *Malware, Rootkits & Botnets: A Beginner's Guide*, published by McGraw-Hill.

The malware then proceeds to make sure it survives a shutdown or a reboot. This is where it sets itself up and the other malware components to be persistent. This is achieved by using different autostart techniques in Windows. The following are some of the autostart techniques:

▶ Hijacking the boot sector

▶ Infecting system files

▶ Adding the malware in the StartUp folder

▶ Utilizing Task Scheduler

▶ Utilizing the registry

Utilizing the registry is the most common autostart technique used by malware. With the registry, the malware can start up during the following:

▶ Boot execution

▶ Loading of drivers and services

▶ Upon logon

▶ Loading of Explorer shell extensions

▶ Loading of browser extensions

Aside from making sure the malware is persistent, it also takes the precaution to protect itself and its components in the compromised system. It does this by using some of the following techniques:

▶ Hiding using attributes

▶ Hiding in plain sight

▶ Using rootkit technology

Although this technique is considered rudimentary, most malware today still utilizes file and folder attributes to protect itself. The most common way to do this is to set the attributes of the malware files and the folders they are located in to Hidden or System. This is designed to fool optical inspection by researchers and analysts. Even with the ability to override this using operating system settings and widely available tools today, malware is still using this technique.

Another rudimentary technique is hiding in plain sight. The main idea here is that the malware components are dropped into a folder where there are thousands of files so they can blend in. The most common location utilized by malware is the Windows system folder. It contains lots of files that have names that are not easily recognizable, which is perfect for this kind of protective mechanism. One common way of hiding in plain sight is by using filename obfuscation by replacing the uppercase letter O with the number 0 (zero). Another one is by adding common strings as a prefix such as *win* to a malware filename or by simply adding 32 or 64 to the filename.

The most reliable way of hiding malware, of course, is by using rootkit technology. This is the best way to hide the presence of any malware components. You can learn more about rootkits and hiding in plain sight in *Malware, Rootkits & Botnets: A Beginner's Guide*, published by McGraw-Hill.

The need to install malware components, make malware persistent, and protect the malware components' presence in the system sums up a malware's general initial host behavior. But this is just the tip of the iceberg; what you are really after is the malware directive. Depending on the attack type, a malware's directive can be a simple nuisance, destructive, or data exfiltration, among others.

A malware that simply displays a message or reorient a screen can be viewed as a nuisance. A malware that deletes critical files in a system can be deemed as destructive. A malware that scrapes memory, captures the desktop, or logs keystrokes obviously is an information stealer. Identifying the malware's main directive requires a combination of monitoring and recording what's going on in the system after the malware has installed and protected its components and established its persistency.

To do this, you will monitor and record changes in the following areas of the system:

- ▶ File system
- ▶ Registry
- ▶ Memory

File System

Changes in the file system help you determine how the malware installs and protects itself in the system during the initial stages of infection and upon successful system compromise. It can also offer a view of how malware achieves persistency through malware component placement, especially if it utilizes nonregistry techniques such as utilizing the StartUp folder.

File system changes can also be a good indicator of malware directive, especially if it has something to do with destroying files. It can also offer a glimpse of how it spreads through other systems such as infecting other files or creating bogus files for copying in local and network share folders.

There are three changes to the file system that you need to monitor.

- ▶ Added files
- ▶ Deleted files
- ▶ Modified files

Added Files   As previously mentioned, during the malware installation stage, the malware usually drops a copy of itself and other components it needs to function. Most malware nowadays is deployed or installed using a dropper, downloader, or hybrid of both. If the malware utilizes a dropper or a downloader, the installation of malware components is similar to the installation of legitimate software. The only difference is that the dropper or downloader deletes a copy of itself after control is passed to the malware components.

It is important to record all files that have been added to the system because chances are these are all malware components and getting hold of these files and where they are located is key to understanding how the malware installs itself in the system and how each file functions. In modern malware, each component has a separate function that complements each other. The following are the most common malware components:

- ▶ Main malware file
- ▶ Bot agent

- ▶ Rootkit component
- ▶ Regeneration component
- ▶ Attack component
- ▶ Configuration files

A malware package can contain one or a combination of any of the mentioned components.

The main malware file is the one that utilizes the other components to ensure its success. The bot agent is the one responsible for communicating to the attacker via command and control (C&C) or to any network resource the malware needs. The rootkit component possesses the rootkit technology that enables the malware to hide in the system. The regeneration component is the one responsible for rebuilding malware if one of its components is removed or any entry in the registry has been modified. The attack component defines the malware's main directive. This component contains the functionality the malware needs to conduct the attack. If the malware is designed for a distributed denial-of-service (DDOS) attack, this component will contain DDOS functionality. If the malware is more for data exfiltration, this component will contain information-stealing capabilities. Getting hold of this component is critical in understanding the malware's capability and directive. Last but definitely not the least, the configuration file contains information for other components. It can contain system targets, special instructions, updated network resources, or any information the malware needs to function. Usually, configuration files are used to change the malware's behavior based on the attacker's need.

NOTE

Older malware attacks consist of only a single file; that is, the malware itself and all the component functions are coded into the malware itself, and updating any functionality means updating the whole malware file. Modern malware is modular. Each component is a separate file for easy updates by the attacker.

Getting a copy of all these components enables the researcher or analyst to understand the malware's behavior better.

LINGO

__Modularized malware__ is malware whose functions are assigned to different files and not coded into a single malware code.

It is also important to remember that most malware authors do not want to reinvent the wheel. If the functionalities they need are present in existing tools, they will use those tools as a separate module or simply copy that tool's code into the malware code. For example, if a malware wants to download files via File Transfer Protocol (FTP), it might use known FTP download tools. This is why it became common during the heyday of network worms that malware usually utilized network tools used by network administrators. The advantage of this is that the tools will not be flagged as malware because they are known to be benign tools. It came to the point that malware specifically written to compromise servers already assumes that the tools it needs are already installed there because these are the same tools used by network administrators to manage their servers.

Deleted Files   Not counting droppers and downloaders, in some cases malware will delete files in the system that pose a threat to its existence. The following are the most common files deleted by malware during installation:

- ▶ System restore files
- ▶ Configuration files
- ▶ Security product files

If a malware is designed to be destructive and its main directive is to delete files, knowing what files were deleted will aid in identifying the malware's main file target and what files needed to be restored.

Modified Files   When file infectors ruled the threat landscape, the best way to tell whether a system was infected was by identifying all modified files and flagging them as possibly infected by a virus. This is the main reason why early antivirus solutions relied on cyclic redundancy check (CRC) and checksum. The idea here is that if a file's CRC changes unexpectedly from the previous check, it is infected.

In today's threat landscape, the importance of identifying modified files during compromise is still important. It usually is an indication of system or third-party software files infected by malware or modified for a specific purpose that will aid the malware in its operation. One operation is extortion. Malware such as CryptoLocker and CryptoWall encrypts important document files so that they cannot be accessed or read by the user. A series of modified document files can signal the presence of a ransomware that locks files for ransom.

File modification can also aid malware when it comes to persistency. One example is the modification of a .INI file to get itself started on every bootup. In the DOS days, the most common file that was modified to get malware to start up on every bootup was AUTOEXEC.BAT.

Registry

Modifications to the registry are usually made to achieve persistency. The following are the common registry entries modified by malware to achieve persistency.[1] The registry keys are grouped according to the autostart technique utilized by malware to achieve persistency.

- ▶ Boot execution
  - ▶ HKLM\System\CurrentControlSet\Control\Session Manager
- ▶ Loading of driver and services
  - ▶ HKLM\System\CurrentControlSet\Services
- ▶ Upon logon
  - ▶ HKLM\Software\Microsoft\Windows\CurrentVersion\Run
  - ▶ HKLM\Software\Microsoft\Windows\CurrentVersion\ RunOnce
  - ▶ HKLM\Software\Microsoft\Active Setup\Installed Components
- ▶ Loading of Explorer shell extensions
  - ▶ HKLM\Software\Classes*\ShellEx\ContextMenuHandlers
  - ▶ HKLM\Software\Classes\Directory\ShellEx\ContextMenuHandlers
  - ▶ HKLM\Software\Classes\Directory\ShellEx\DragDropHandlers
  - ▶ HKLM\Software\Classes\Folder\ShellEx\ContextMenuHandlers
  - ▶ HKLM\Software\Classes\Folder\ShellEx\DragDropHandlers
- ▶ Loading of browser extensions
  - ▶ HKLM\Software\Microsoft\Windows\CurrentVersion\Explorer\ Browser Helper Objects
  - ▶ HKLM\Software\Microsoft\Internet Explorer\Extensions

Please take note that this also applies to other registry hives such as HKEY_ CURRENT_USER and specific user profile hives. A user profile hive, as defined by Microsoft, contains specific registry information pertaining to the user's application settings, desktop, environment, network connection, and printers. User profile hives are located under the HKEY_USERS key.

Upon infection, some malware disables REGEDIT to prevent any user from viewing the registry. One disadvantage of this protective mechanism is that it raises suspicion that the system is compromised.

> **NOTE**
>
> Similar to the file system, a malware can add, modify, or delete a registry key depending on the malware's purpose.

LAB 12-1: Detecting System Changes Using InstallRite

In this lab, you will use installation/uninstallation tools to determine system changes made by malware. These tools are designed to create uninstallers to effectively remove any software that is installed, but they are also useful in tracking changes made by malware. The tool you will use in this experiment is a classic tool called InstallRite.

This lab works well if you have in your possession a malware sample. If you do not have one, please review previous chapters on how to collect malware samples.

What You Need:

► System running Windows

► Malware sample

Steps:

1. Download and install InstallRite from http://www.softpedia.com/get/System/System-Info/InstallRite.shtml.

2. Start InstallRite. Figure 12-1 shows the InstallRite main window.

3. Click Install New Software And Create An InstallKit and follow the prompts, as shown in Figures 12-2 to 12-4.

4. The window in Figure 12-2 enables you to configure the tool. In this lab, there is no need to configure anything, but feel free to play around with the tool. Notice that the default configuration is that the entire registry should be monitored and all directories in all hard drives should be monitored as well.

5. The window in Figure 12-3 informs the user that a snapshot will be created. Clicking Next will initiate the snapshot creation. This becomes the base snapshot, and the tool will report any deviation or changes in the snapshot after the binary is installed/executed.

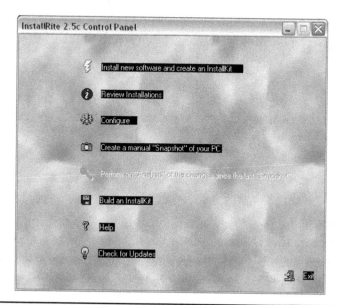

Figure 12-1   *InstallRite main window.*

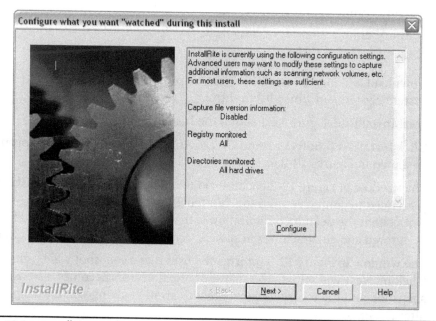

Figure 12-2   *InstallRite configuration window.*

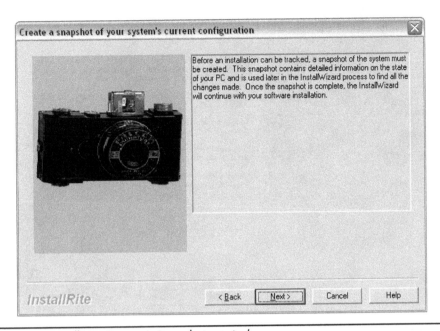

Before an installation can be tracked, a snapshot of the system must be created. This snapshot contains detailed information on the state of your PC and is used later in the InstallWizard process to find all the changes made. Once the snapshot is complete, the InstallWizard will continue with your software installation.

Figure 12-3   *InstallRite Create A Snapshot... window.*

6. Once the snapshot is done, it is time to choose the program to run, as shown in Figure 12-4. You can type the file location in the space provided under Installation Program To Run or simply click the button on the right side to browse for the malware file you want to monitor.

7. In the succeeding illustrations, you will be using VOHO malware. If you do not have access to VOHO malware, any malware that you have collected following the steps outlined in previous chapters will do.

8. Figure 12-5 shows the file changes recorded by InstallRite after running the VOHO malware.

9. Figure 12-6 shows the registry changes recorded by InstallRite after running the VOHO malware.

10. To save the output, simply right-click each branch and choose the format you want the output to be saved as.

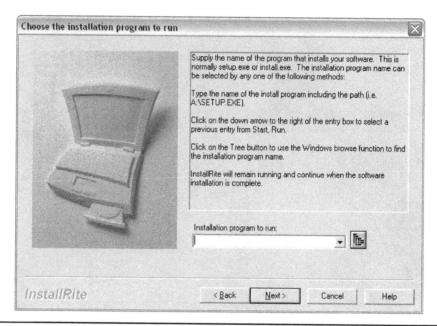

Figure 12-4 *InstallRite window to choose which program to run.*

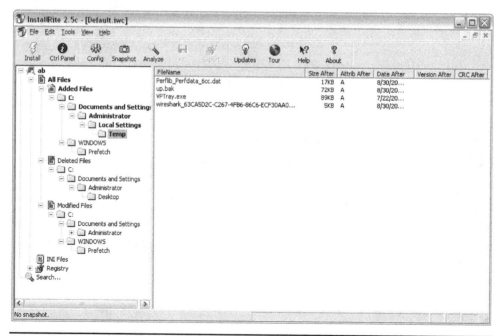

Figure 12-5 *VOHO malware file changes.*

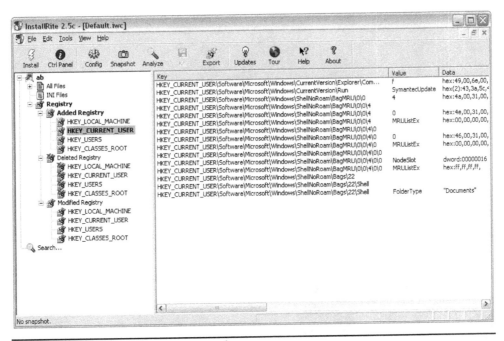

Figure 12-6 *VOHO malware registry changes.*

LAB 12-2: *Detecting System Changes Using Uninstall Tool*

In this lab, you will use installation/uninstallation tools to determine system changes made by malware. These tools are designed to create uninstallers to effectively remove any software that is installed, but they are also useful in tracking changes made by malware. The tool you will use in this experiment is Uninstall Tool by CrystalIdea Software.

This lab works well if you have in your possession a malware sample. If you do not have one, please review the previous chapters on how to collect malware samples.

What You Need:

▶ System running Windows

▶ Malware sample

Steps:

1. Download and install Uninstall Tool from http://www.crystalidea.com/uninstall-tool.

2. Take note that this is not free software, but it can be used as a trial for 30 days.

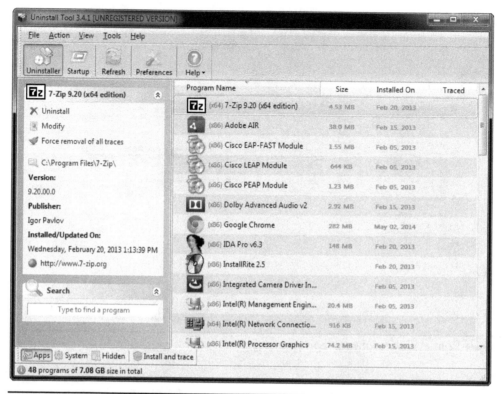

Figure 12-7 *Uninstall Tool main window.*

3. Start Uninstall Tool. Figure 12-7 shows the main window. As you can see, the Uninstaller tab displays all installed software.

4. At the bottom of the main window, click Install And Trace.

5. The Install And Trace A Program window opens, as shown in Figure 12-8.

6. From here, you can choose the file you want to install and trace.

7. In this experiment, I will be using VOHO malware. For your own experiment, please use the malware you have in your possession. Figure 12-9 shows the chosen malware.

8. Once the malware is chosen, click Install And Trace.

9. Once the installation process is finished, you will see a window, as shown in Figure 12-10, enumerating the changes that were traced by Uninstaller Tool.

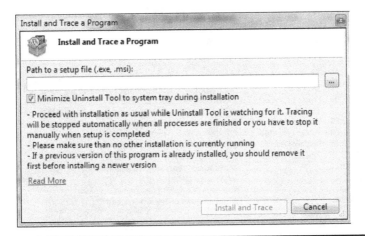

Figure 12-8 *Install And Trace A Program window.*

10. Click Save Log and save the log as a text file. I will come back to this later.

11. To keep better track of the installed and traced malware, you can create a custom item name so it will show on the list in the main window. Clicking Save opens the window shown in Figure 12-11, which will enable you to create a name for the installed malware so you can see it in the list.

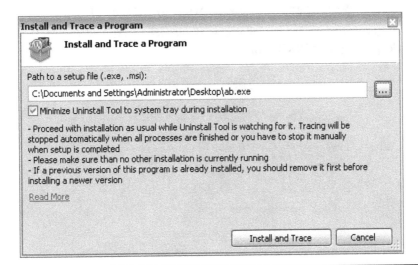

Figure 12-9 *Installing and tracing VOHO malware.*

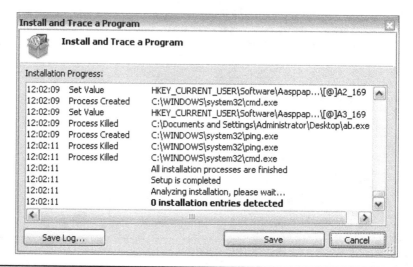

Figure 12-10 *Install And Trace A Program output.*

12. After you assign a name, you will be able to see it on the main page, as shown in Figure 12-12. In the example, I have used "ab."

13. From here, you can right-click the newly installed malware and choose Traced Data, as shown in Figure 12-13.

14. Choosing Traced Data will show the window in Figure 12-14.

15. From here, you can see the changes it has made to the system in Extensible Markup Language (XML) format.

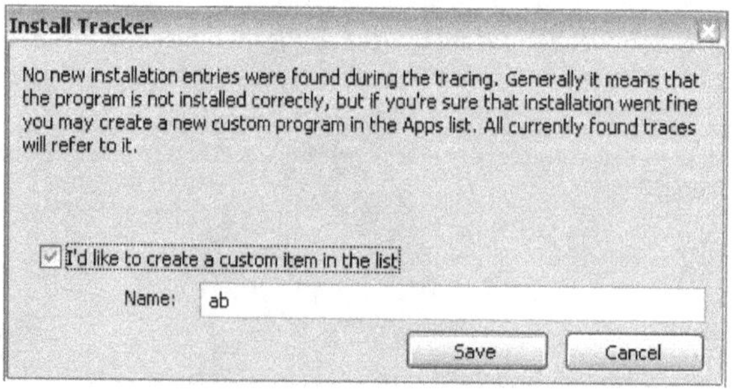

Install Tracker

No new installation entries were found during the tracing. Generally it means that the program is not installed correctly, but if you're sure that installation went fine you may create a new custom program in the Apps list. All currently found traces will refer to it.

☑ I'd like to create a custom item in the list

Name: ab

Save Cancel

Figure 12-11 *Install Tracker custom item name.*

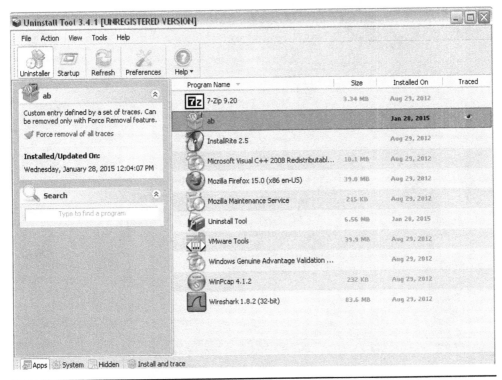

Figure 12-12   *Uninstaller Tool main window showing the chosen name.*

16. In the previous step, you saved the log to a text file. Open this text file and see what it contains. What you will see is similar to Figure 12-15.

17. The significance of this log is that it shows not only the changes done by the malware but also the chronological order of what was done.

Memory

The system's memory is where the action takes place. Code and data are decrypted in memory. Having the ability to monitor and capture unencrypted code and data from memory is one of the best ways to understand a malware's behavior.

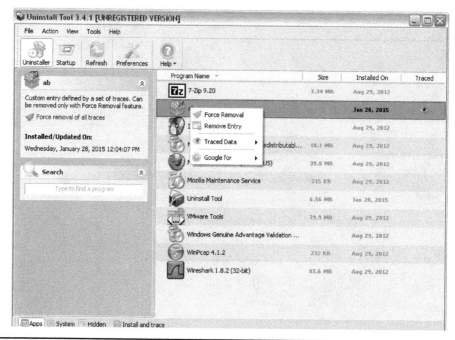

Figure 12-13 *Right-click context menu for installed programs.*

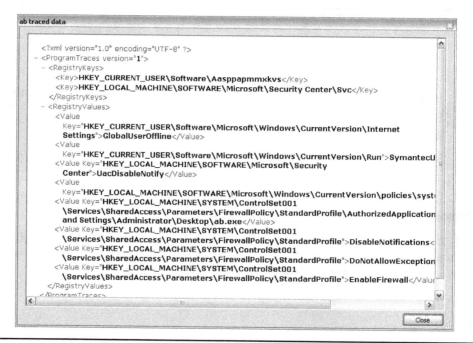

Figure 12-14 *Traced data output.*

```
12:02:04                        Starting Install Tracker service...
12:02:04                        Service version is: 0x103
12:02:04                        Starting ab.exe...
12:02:04                        Installation monitor is started
12:02:04     Set Value         HKEY_LOCAL_MACHINE\SOFTWARE\Microsoft\Security Center\[@]UacDisableNotify
12:02:04     Create Key        HKEY_LOCAL_MACHINE\SOFTWARE\Microsoft\Security Center\Svc
12:02:04     Set Value         HKEY_LOCAL_MACHINE\SOFTWARE\Microsoft\Security Center\Svc\[@]AntiVirusOverride
12:02:04     Set Value         HKEY_LOCAL_MACHINE\SOFTWARE\Microsoft\Security Center\Svc\
[@]AntiVirusDisableNotify
12:02:04     Set Value         HKEY_LOCAL_MACHINE\SOFTWARE\Microsoft\Security Center\Svc\
[@]FirewallDisableNotify
12:02:05     Set Value         HKEY_LOCAL_MACHINE\SOFTWARE\Microsoft\Security Center\Svc\[@]FirewallOverride
12:02:05     Set Value         HKEY_LOCAL_MACHINE\SOFTWARE\Microsoft\Security Center\Svc\[@]UpdatesDisableNotify
12:02:05     Set Value         HKEY_LOCAL_MACHINE\SOFTWARE\Microsoft\Security Center\Svc\[@]UacDisableNotify
12:02:05     Create File       C:\Documents and Settings\Administrator\Local Settings\Temp\VPTray.exe
12:02:05     Set Value         HKEY_CURRENT_USER\SOFTWARE\Microsoft\Windows\CurrentVersion\Internet Settings\
[@]GlobalUserOffline
12:02:05     Set Value         HKEY_LOCAL_MACHINE\SOFTWARE\Microsoft\Windows\CurrentVersion\policies\system\
[@]EnableLUA
12:02:05     Set Value         HKEY_LOCAL_MACHINE\SYSTEM\ControlSet001\Services\SharedAccess\Parameters
\FirewallPolicy\StandardProfile\AuthorizedApplications\List\[@]C:\Documents and Settings\Administrator\Desktop
\ab.exe
12:02:05     Set Value         HKEY_LOCAL_MACHINE\SYSTEM\ControlSet001\Services\SharedAccess\Parameters
\FirewallPolicy\StandardProfile\[@]EnableFirewall
12:02:05     Set Value         HKEY_LOCAL_MACHINE\SYSTEM\ControlSet001\Services\SharedAccess\Parameters
\FirewallPolicy\StandardProfile\[@]DoNotAllowExceptions
12:02:05     Set Value         HKEY_LOCAL_MACHINE\SYSTEM\ControlSet001\Services\SharedAccess\Parameters
\FirewallPolicy\StandardProfile\[@]DisableNotifications
12:02:05     Create Key        HKEY_CURRENT_USER\Software\Aasppapmmxkvs
12:02:05     Create Key        HKEY_CURRENT_USER\Software\Aasppapmmxkvs\-993627007
12:02:05     Set Value         HKEY_CURRENT_USER\Software\Aasppapmmxkvs\-993627007\[@]1768776769
12:02:05     Set Value         HKEY_CURRENT_USER\Software\Aasppapmmxkvs\-993627007\[@]-757413758
12:02:05     Set Value         HKEY_CURRENT_USER\Software\Aasppapmmxkvs\-993627007\[@]1011363011
12:02:05     Set Value         HKEY_CURRENT_USER\Software\Aasppapmmxkvs\-993627007\[@]-1514827516
12:02:05     Set Value         HKEY_CURRENT_USER\Software\Aasppapmmxkvs\-993627007\[@]253949253
12:02:05     Set Value         HKEY_CURRENT_USER\Software\Aasppapmmxkvs\-993627007\[@]2022726022
12:02:05     Set Value         HKEY_CURRENT_USER\Software\Aasppapmmxkvs\-993627007\[@]-503464505
12:02:05     Set Value         HKEY_CURRENT_USER\Software\Microsoft\Windows\CurrentVersion\Run\[@]SymantecUpdate
12:02:05     Set Value         HKEY_CURRENT_USER\Software\Aasppapmmxkvs\[@]A1_0
12:02:05     Set Value         HKEY_CURRENT_USER\Software\Aasppapmmxkvs\[@]A2_0
12:02:05     Set Value         HKEY_CURRENT_USER\Software\Aasppapmmxkvs\[@]A3_0
12:02:05     Set Value         HKEY_CURRENT_USER\Software\Aasppapmmxkvs\[@]A4_0
12:02:05     Set Value         HKEY_CURRENT_USER\Software\Aasppapmmxkvs\[@]A1_1
12:02:05     Set Value         HKEY_CURRENT_USER\Software\Aasppapmmxkvs\[@]A2_1
12:02:05     Set Value         HKEY_CURRENT_USER\Software\Aasppapmmxkvs\[@]A3_1
12:02:05     Set Value         HKEY_CURRENT_USER\Software\Aasppapmmxkvs\[@]A4_1
12:02:05     Set Value         HKEY_CURRENT_USER\Software\Aasppapmmxkvs\[@]A1_2
12:02:05     Set Value         HKEY_CURRENT_USER\Software\Aasppapmmxkvs\[@]A2_2
12:02:05     Set Value         HKEY_CURRENT_USER\Software\Aasppapmmxkvs\[@]A3_2
12:02:05     Set Value         HKEY_CURRENT_USER\Software\Aasppapmmxkvs\[@]A4_2
12:02:05     Set Value         HKEY_CURRENT_USER\Software\Aasppapmmxkvs\[@]A1_3
12:02:05     Set Value         HKEY_CURRENT_USER\Software\Aasppapmmxkvs\[@]A2_3
12:02:05     Set Value         HKEY_CURRENT_USER\Software\Aasppapmmxkvs\[@]A3_3
12:02:05     Set Value         HKEY_CURRENT_USER\Software\Aasppapmmxkvs\[@]A4_3
12:02:05     Set Value         HKEY_CURRENT_USER\Software\Aasppapmmxkvs\[@]A1_4
12:02:05     Set Value         HKEY_CURRENT_USER\Software\Aasppapmmxkvs\[@]A2_4
12:02:05     Set Value         HKEY_CURRENT_USER\Software\Aasppapmmxkvs\[@]A3_4
12:02:05     Set Value         HKEY_CURRENT_USER\Software\Aasppapmmxkvs\[@]A4_4
12:02:05     Set Value         HKEY_CURRENT_USER\Software\Aasppapmmxkvs\[@]A1_5
12:02:05     Set Value         HKEY_CURRENT_USER\Software\Aasppapmmxkvs\[@]A2_5
12:02:05     Set Value         HKEY_CURRENT_USER\Software\Aasppapmmxkvs\[@]A3_5
12:02:05     Set Value         HKEY_CURRENT_USER\Software\Aasppapmmxkvs\[@]A4_5
```

Figure 12-15   *Uninstall Tool saved log.*

LAB 12-3: *Analyzing Running Processes in Memory Using Process Explorer*

In this lab, you will use Process Explorer to analyze a malware's running process.

What You Need:

► Infected Windows system

► Sysinternals Suite

Steps:

1. Download and install Sysinternals Suite from https://technet.microsoft.com/en-us/sysinternals/bb842062.aspx.

2. Extract the downloaded ZIP file to your desired folder.

3. Go to that folder, look for Process Explorer (procexp.exe), and open it.

4. If you do not want to download the whole Sysinternals Suite and want only Process Explorer, you can download it from https://technet.microsoft.com/en-us/sysinternals/bb896653.

5. In this experiment, you will be using the infected Windows system you used in previous experiments where you ran the infected malware. For this specific lab, I will use the system infected with the VOHO malware.

6. Figure 12-16 shows Process Explorer running in a system infected by VOHO malware.

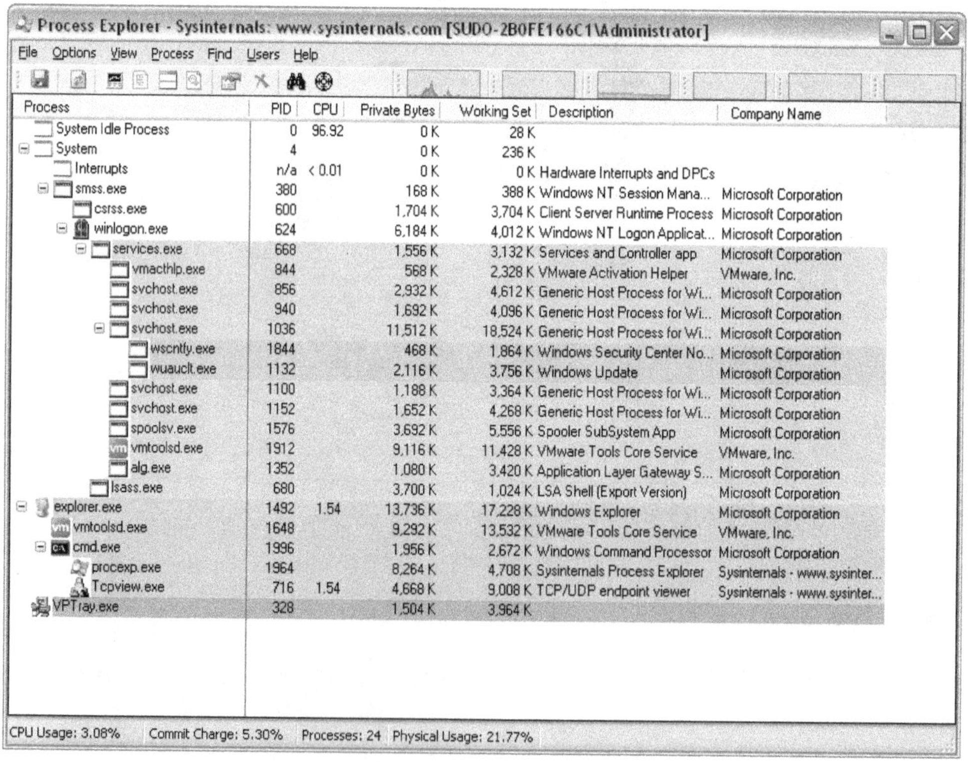

Figure 12-16 *Process Explorer running in an infected system.*

7. You know from the monitoring tools you used that VPTray.exe is one of the files installed by the VOHO malware. It can easily be spotted in the Process Explorer window.

8. Hovering the mouse pointer over the VPTray.exe process will reveal its location on disk. Figure 12-17 shows this.

NOTE

This capability of revealing the path of a running process is useful, especially if you want to map a process to a file when doing system forensics and you have no idea which of the processes are malicious.

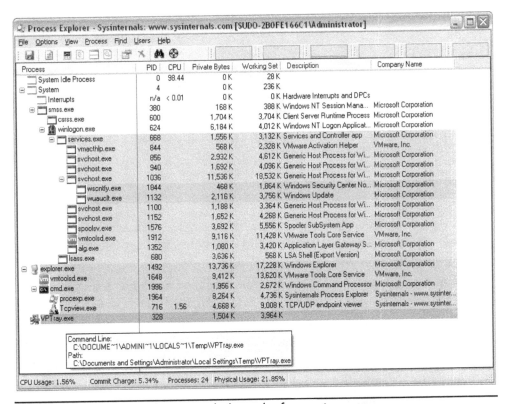

Figure 12-17 *Process Explorer reveals the path of a running process.*

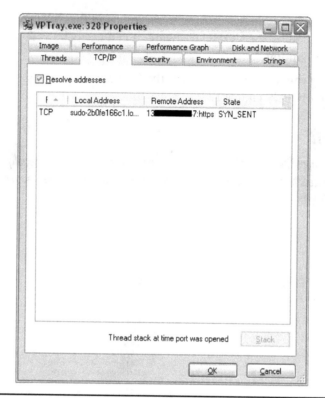

Figure 12-18 *Running process properties TCP/IP tab.*

9. Double-clicking the process will reveal its properties, as shown in Figure 12-18. Another way of revealing its properties is by right-clicking the running process and clicking Properties.

10. From here, you can look at the different tabs to reveal information about the running process. The TCP/IP tab shown in Figure 12-18 reveals its network capability.

11. One interesting tab is the Threads tab, as shown in Figure 12-19.

12. Clicking the Stack button reveals the stack for that specific process thread. Figure 12-20 shows the stack for this specific malware.

13. Another interesting tab is the Strings tab, as shown in Figure 12-21. This reveals the strings as shown on the file image and in memory.

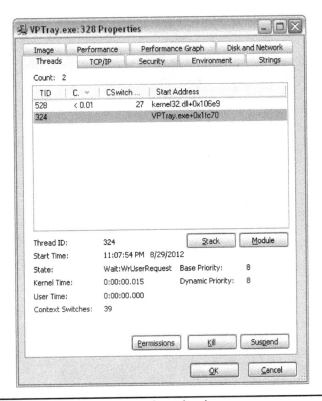

Figure 12-19   *Running process properties Threads tab.*

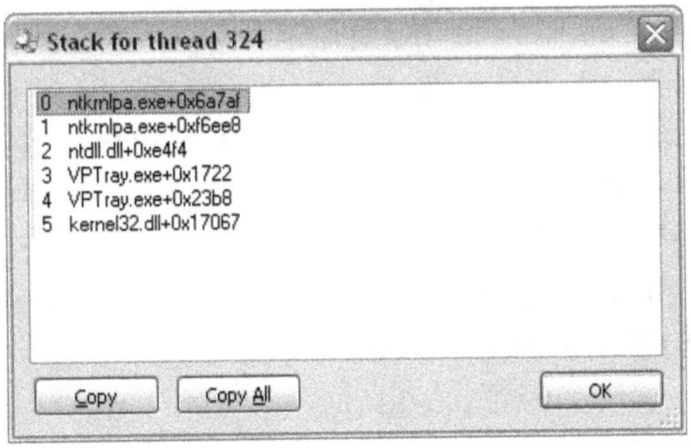

Figure 12-20   *Stack of a chosen thread in Process Explorer.*

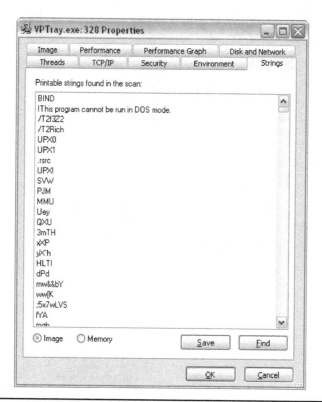

Figure 12-21 *Running process properties Strings tab.*

14. The default display on the Strings tab is the set of strings found on the file's image. If the file is encrypted, the strings here will be encrypted as well. Notice that the fourth and fifth strings show UPX0 and UPX1, respectively. These are section names that tell you that the file is probably packed with UPX. I say probably because it can be faked. But upon inspection using static scanning, you are able to determine that the file is indeed packed by UPX.

15. Clicking Save will save these strings to a file. There is also a Find functionality if you want to find specific strings within the file's image.

16. To see how the strings look like in memory, click the Memory radio button, as shown in Figure 12-22. Notice the difference between the strings in the file image (encrypted) and the strings as they are in memory.

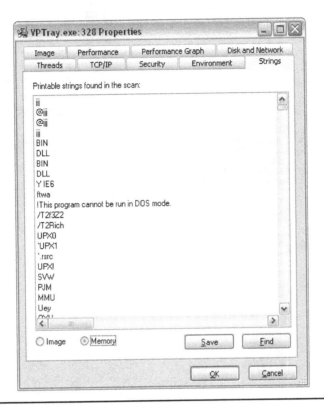

Figure 12-22 *Strings in memory.*

17. Remember that data in memory has to be decrypted so it can be processed. This means that the strings you see are decrypted. If you scroll down, you can see some useful strings. In this example, you can see the malware dropped file (VPTray.exe and up.bak), its fake name (pretending to be SymantecUpdate), and a command line it uses for one of its functionalities. Figure 12-23 shows these useful strings.

18. You can save the strings found in memory for future reference.

19. Feel free to experiment some more with the other capabilities of Process Explorer.

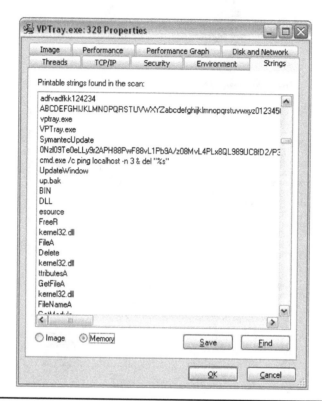

Figure 12-23 *Strings in memory revealing useful information.*

LAB 12-4: *Quickly Inspecting Whether a Process Is Persistent*

In this lab, you will determine whether the malware process you identified and analyzed using Process Explorer is persistent or has the capability to start up after every shutdown or reboot. For this specific purpose, you will be using Sysinternals Autoruns.

What You Need:

▶ Infected Windows system

▶ Sysinternals Suite

Steps:

1. Download and install Sysinternals Suite from https://technet.microsoft.com/en-us/sysinternals/bb842062.aspx.

2. Extract the downloaded ZIP file to your desired folder.

3. Go to that folder, look for Autoruns (autoruns.exe), and open it.

4. If you do not want to download the whole Sysinternals Suite and want only Autoruns, you can download it from https://technet.microsoft.com/en-us/sysinternals/bb963902.aspx.

5. In this experiment, you will be using the infected Windows system you used in previous experiments where you ran the infected malware. For this specific lab, I will use the system infected with the VOHO malware.

6. Figure 12-24 shows Autoruns running in a system infected with VOHO malware.

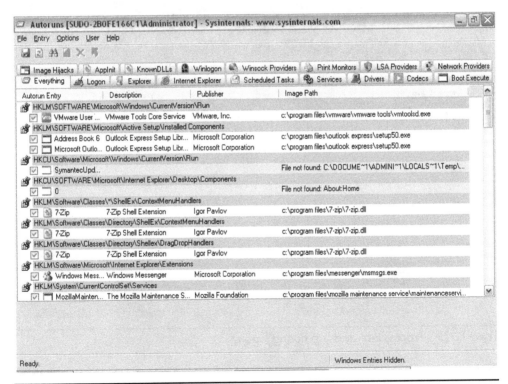

Figure 12-24 *Autoruns running in a system infected with VOHO malware.*

7. From Figure 12-24, you can see that SymantecUpdate is among the startup
    processes. Since you were able to determine that this is the process name
    used by VOHO in your previous laboratories and you know that your
    malware research lab does not have Symantec installed on it, you know
    already that this is the malware.

8. You can see that there are lots of tabs in the tool. Each tab represents the
    way a process starts up. Since you can see that the malicious process is being
    started up from the registry, you already know that the file starts during
    logon. To simplify the view and to target only those items that start up
    during logon, simply click the Logon tab. Figure 12-25 shows the resulting
    window.

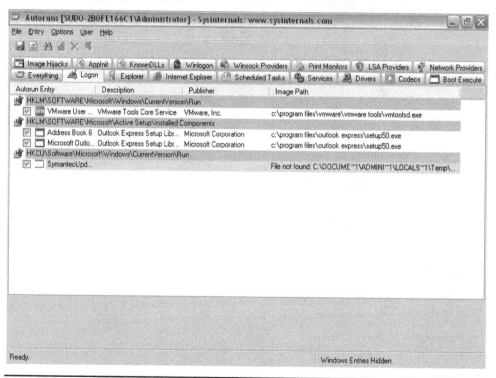

Figure 12-25   *Process that starts up during logon.*

9. To go to the registry entry or to the folder of the file that initiated the process, right-click the process and choose either Jump To Entry if you want to go to the registry entry or Jump To Folder if you want to go to the folder where the file is located. Figure 12-26 shows this.

10. Notice also in Figure 12-26 that highlighting the process reveals the path and filename of the file that started it.

11. Feel free to experiment with the other capabilities of Autoruns.

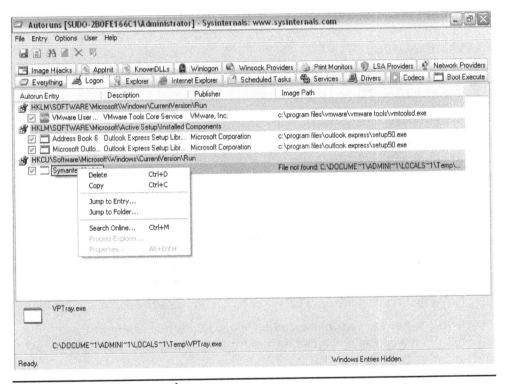

Figure 12-26 *Context menu of startup process.*

Analyzing Network Behavior

As previously mentioned, modern malware has the capability to use different network resources for its malicious purpose. Malware can use network resources as a drop zone for stolen information, as a server for malware component updates, and as a command and control server where malware can interface with the attackers. In analyzing malware, it is important to understand its network behavior as well.

When it comes to network behavior, it is important to identify the network resources the malware is connecting to. Identifying the domains or Internet Protocol (IP) addresses that the malware connects to aids greatly in identifying the malware's main purpose and also helps in attribution if there is enough information available.

LAB 12-5: *Analyzing Network Behavior Using TCPView*

In this lab, you will analyze network behavior of a malware using TCPView.

What You Need:

▶ Infected Windows system

▶ Sysinternals Suite

Steps:

1. Download and install Sysinternals Suite from https://technet.microsoft.com/en-us/sysinternals/bb842062.aspx.

2. Extract the downloaded ZIP file to your desired folder.

3. Go to that folder, look for TCPView (tcpview.exe), and open it.

4. If you do not want to download the whole Sysinternals Suite and want only TCPView, you can download it from https://technet.microsoft.com/en-us/sysinternals/bb897437.aspx.

5. In this experiment, you will be using the infected Windows system you used in previous experiments where you ran the infected malware. For this specific lab, I will use the system infected with the VOHO malware.

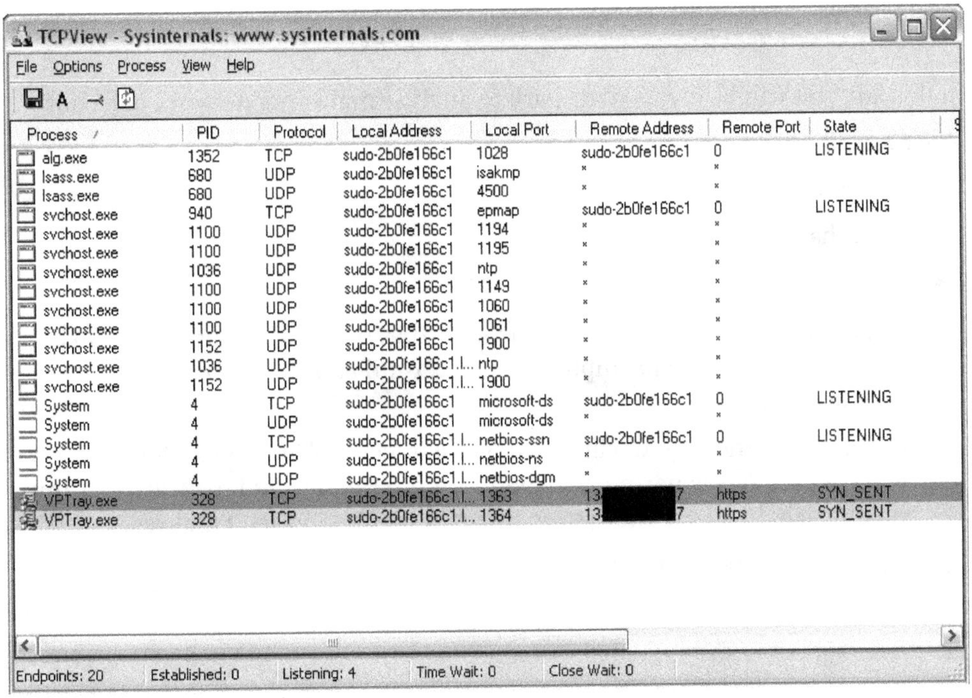

Figure 12-27 *TCPView running in a system infected by VOHO malware.*

6. Figure 12-27 shows TCPView running in a system infected with VOHO malware.

7. TCPView helps you determine where the malware connects. This information is contained under Remote Address. It can be either an IP address or a domain name. Be mindful also of the state of the connection. If the state does not change to LISTENING, chances are the network resource that the malware is attempting to connect to is already dead.

8. Feel free to explore and experiment with the other capabilities of TCPView.

LAB 12-6: *Analyzing Network Behavior Using Wireshark*

In this lab, you will be using Wireshark to analyze malware's network behavior.

What You Need:

▶ Infected Windows system

▶ Wireshark

Steps:

1. Download and install Wireshark from https://www.wireshark.org/. Take note that you will be prompted to install WinPcap if you do not have it on your system.

2. In this experiment, you will be using the infected Windows system you used in previous experiments where you ran the infected malware. For this specific lab, I will use the system infected with the VOHO malware.

3. Figure 12-28 shows the Wireshark main window.

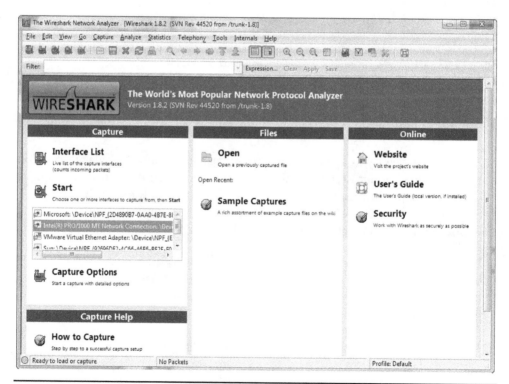

Figure 12-28 *Wireshark main window.*

4. To start the capture session, select an interface to monitor on the left-side menu under the Start button and then click the Start button. Take note that Wireshark needs to run under administrator mode.

5. Once the capture session starts, you can see the TCP connection to the destination address that has been shown in the TCPView session in your previous lab. Figure 12-29 shows this.

6. Once the connection session has been identified, it can be further analyzed by expanding the data shown in the second window below the capture session. Figure 12-30 shows the expanded view of the session.

7. From here you can view a lot of information about the packet.

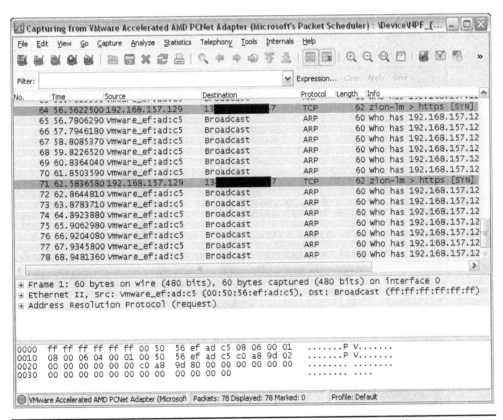

Figure 12-29 *Capture session showing malware connection to its network resource.*

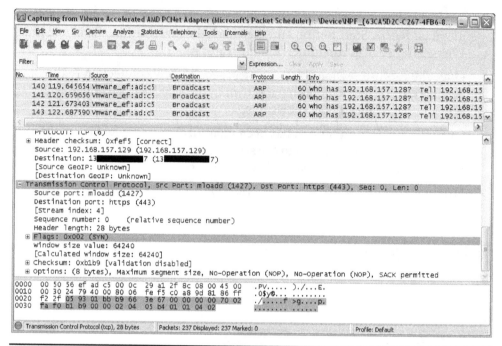

Figure 12-30 *Expanded view of a session in Wireshark.*

Dynamic Analysis Limitations

Dynamic analysis has its limitations. Malware will reveal information only as it executes. It is possible that not all of its functions or capabilities will be revealed because they may require certain conditions that you are not aware of. It is therefore an accepted limitation of dynamic analysis that certain functionalities of the malware cannot be monitored and captured. This is the reason why dynamic analysis is a feedback system. Malware that produces little or nothing at all in the target environment is further analyzed to determine the reason why. In most cases, malware reversing is conducted to find out why. Any new findings or any new conditions identified to make the system malware friendly is then added to the dynamic analysis lab so that other malware that relies on the same conditions will execute as intended by the attacker, which will result in the monitoring and capturing of the functions or capabilities that rely on those conditions.

Recap

In this chapter, I discussed how to analyze dynamic malware. I touched on how virtual and bare-metal environments can complement each other instead of making a hard choice of just using one and not the other. I discussed the two areas of dynamic analysis that is important in getting to the bottom of modern malware's behavior. They are as follows:

- Analyzing host behavior
- Analyzing network behavior

In analyzing host behavior, I broke it down into monitoring and collecting data from the following areas of the dynamic analysis lab or target system:

- File system
- Registry
- Memory

I discussed different tools and techniques in your lab to accomplish your goal of monitoring and recording data gathered from malware as it behaves on the host system and as it leaves traces while communicating through the network.

I also discussed the limitations of dynamic analysis to end the chapter so that there is clear understanding of the advantages you can get from conducting dynamic analysis while also recognizing that not all information can be gathered because it is dependent on the malware's ability to execute within the environment.

Tools

- **Sysinternals Suite**   https://technet.microsoft.com/en-us/sysinternals/bb842062.aspx
- System monitoring tools
  - **InstallRite**   http://www.softpedia.com/get/System/System-Info/InstallRite.shtml
  - **Uninstall Tool**   http://www.crystalidea.com/uninstall-tool

- ► Memory analysis tools

  - ► **Process Explorer**   https://technet.microsoft.com/en-us/sysinternals/bb896653

  - ► **Autoruns**   https://technet.microsoft.com/en-us/sysinternals/bb963902.aspx

- ► Network analysis tools

  - ► **TCPView**   https://technet.microsoft.com/en-us/sysinternals/bb897437.aspx

  - ► **Wireshark**   https://www.wireshark.org/

I n malware analysis, it is important to have the right tools. Familiarity with these tools and how to use them properly is the difference between success and failure in malware analysis. The use of tools to perform malware analysis has been discussed throughout this book. In previous chapters, I discussed how to use certain tools to perform static and dynamic malware analysis.

The right tools together with the right skills are a powerful combination when faced with a difficult malware to analyze.

In this chapter, you will take a look at more tools that are important when it comes to malware analysis. I consider them tools of the trade.

Malware Analysis Use Cases

When it comes to tool selection, it is important to understand first what you want to do and then choose the appropriate tool for the job. For example, if you want to know the file type of a suspicious file, you know that you can use PEiD or the Linux file command line. But if one of the things you want to do is to have the ability to add signatures so the tool can detect new file types or characterize a file based on your need, the best tool for the job is PEiD.

The choice of the tool, therefore, must be dictated by what you want to accomplish. What you want to accomplish is also known as a *malware analysis use case*. You must choose your tool or a set of tools based on satisfying your malware analysis use cases.

The following are some examples of malware analysis use cases:

▶ Ability to determine whether a file is packed

▶ Ability to unpack a packed binary

▶ Ability to determine file system changes done by malware

▶ Ability to determine registry changes done by malware

▶ Ability to dump memory contents of an infected system

▶ Ability to determine a malware's network connections

▶ Ability to determine what data is being exfiltrated by malware

In one way or another, you were able to satisfy these use cases in previous chapters.

Malware Analyst Toolbox

As a malware analyst, having a toolbox is important. What makes up this toolbox is dependent upon your malware analysis use cases. If you are a security professional, your use cases are dictated by your research tasks or operational tasks. If you are a hobbyist, your use cases are dictated by what you want to learn or do when it comes to malware analysis. Regardless of your use cases, there are some tools that are indispensable. I call these tools the tools of the trade.

Tools of the Trade

The following are some of the tools I consider to be important when it comes to malware analysis:

▶ Sysinternals Suite

▶ Yara

▶ Cygwin

▶ Debuggers

▶ Disassemblers

▶ Memory dumpers

▶ PE viewers

▶ PE reconstructors

▶ Malcode Analyst Pack

▶ Rootkit tools

▶ Network capturing tools

▶ Automated sandboxes

▶ Free online automated sandbox services

Sysinternals Suite

As discussed in previous chapters, Sysinternals is an indispensible tool. It comes as a suite containing all the tools, or you can download each tool separately if you do not want to get the whole package.

```
rule silent_banker : banker
{
    meta:
        description = "This is just an example"
        thread_level = 3
        in_the_wild = true

    strings:
        $a = {6A 40 68 00 30 00 00 6A 14 8D 91}
        $b = {8D 4D B0 2B C1 83 C0 27 99 6A 4E 59 F7 F9}
        $c = "UVODFRYSIHLNWPEJXQZAKCBGMT"

    condition:
        $a or $b or $c
}
```

Figure 13-1   *Example Yara rule.*

You can download the suite from https://technet.microsoft.com/en-us/ sysinternals/bb842062.aspx, and if you want to download just a specific tool from the suite, simply click the name of the tool you want from the page pointed to by the link, and you will be all set.

Yara

Yara is a versatile pattern-matching tool. As claimed on its website, it is indeed the pattern-matching Swiss Army knife for malware researchers and everyone else. Yara is a tool aimed at, but not limited to, helping malware researchers to identify and classify malware samples. With Yara, you can create descriptions of malware families or whatever you want to describe based on textual or binary patterns.[1]

A description is also known as a Yara *rule*. Each rule consists of a set of strings and a Boolean expression, which determines its logic. The strings, which comprise the textual or binary patterns, are then used as signatures to detect a possible match based on the logic written in the rule.

Figure 13-1 is an example of a Yara rule taken from https://github.com/plusvic/ yara.

The first line contains the keyword rule, which means that what follows is a Yara rule. The string after it, which is silent_banker, is the name of the rule. If a

---

[1] Yara: https://plusvic.github.io/yara/.

binary or file that is scanned matches this specific rule, that file will be labeled as silent_banker. The string after the colon is a grouping. This means that the rule named silent_banker is part of the group banker. The grouping name is not displayed when a match is found.

The meta section includes a description of the rule. This is merely an aid for Yara rule creators. Think of it as a comment section.

The strings section contains the strings that serve as the signature. It can be in hexadecimal or text.

The condition section contains the logic of the rule. It contains a Boolean expression telling how the rule will be satisfied. In the example in Figure 13-1, if any of the strings are found in the file, the rule is satisfied, and the file is considered a match for silent_banker.

Think of a Yara rule as the signature and Yara as the engine. It works similar to a traditional file scanner or antivirus program.

To get started with Yara, read the full documentation at http://yara.readthedocs .org/en/v3.3.0/, or you can simply go to https://plusvic.github.io/yara/ and click Read The Documentation on the right side of the page. From this link you can also download the latest release, send bug reports, and ask for help from Yara's group.

LAB 13-1: *Installing Yara*

In this lab, you will install Yara on a system running in Ubuntu.

What You Need:

► System running Ubuntu 14.04.1

► Yara

Steps:

1. Download Yara from https://github.com/plusvic/yara/releases/tag/v3.3.0 or go to https://plusvic.github.io/yara/ and click Download Latest Release on the right side of the page. As of this writing, the latest version is Yara 3.3.0. Since you are using Ubuntu, download the source code (tar.gz) under the Downloads section. This is the source tarball.

2. The file that will be downloaded is yara-3.3.0.tar.gz.

3. Open a terminal window and go to the folder where yara-3.3.0.tar.gz was downloaded.

4. Compile Yara.

```
$ tar -zxf yara-3.3.0.tar.gz
$ cd yara-3.3.0
$ ./bootstrap.sh
```

5. If the command ./bootstrap.sh spews out any kind of error regarding autoreconf, issue the following command line to install autoconf and libtool:

```
$ sudo apt-get install autoconf
$ sudo apt-get install libtool
```

6. Run bootstrap.sh again.

```
$ ./bootstrap.sh
```

7. After a successful run of bootstrap.sh, issue the following commands:

```
$ ./configure
$ make
$ sudo make install
```

8. Another way of installing Yara is by issuing the following command line:

```
$ sudo apt-get install yara
```

9. Type the following command line to check whether Yara was installed successfully:

```
$ yara --help
```

10. If the help section of Yara is displayed, you now have Yara successfully installed on your system.

LAB 13-2: *Creating a Yara Rule*

In this lab, you will create your first Yara rule.

What You Need:

▶ System running Ubuntu 14.04.1

▶ Yara

▶ Calc.EXE from Windows

Steps:

1. Create a new text file and type the following:

```
rule calc_match
{
  meta:
```

```
          description = "This is a sample rule to detect calc.exe."
     strings:
          $a = "ADB880A6-D8FF-11CF-9377-00AA003B7A11"
condition:
          $a
}
```

2. The previous strings make up the file's CLSID found in file offset 0x9A7. It might be different from the CLSID that your Calc.EXE has. To check, run the following command line, browse to the mentioned offset, and adjust the rule appropriately. It is also possible that the CLSID is found in a different offset.

```
$ hexedit calc.exe
```

3. Save the text file as yara_rule.txt.

4. Issue the following command:

```
$ yara yara_rule.txt calc.exe
```

The first argument is the rule file, and the second argument is the file to be scanned.

5. If the strings match what is in the file, the following output is displayed:

```
calc_match calc.exe
```

calc_match is the name of the rule, and calc.exe is the file that matches it.

6. Open the yara_rule.txt file and add another string from file offset 0x6F0. But instead of using its text equivalent, use hex values representing the string. Change the condition to $b, which means that the rule will use only $b as the matching string. Comment out the $a string using /* and */ and then save the file.

```
rule calc_match
{
meta:
          description = "This is a sample rule to detect calc.exe."
strings:
          /* $a = "ADB880A6-D8FF-11CF-9377-00AA003B7A11" */
          $b = {43 00 61 00 6C 00 63 00 4D 00 73 00}
condition:
          $b
}
```

7. Run Yara to check for a match. If the strings are written correctly, there will be a positive match.

8. Open the yara_rule.txt file, uncomment the $a string, and modify the condition to $a or $b. This means that if any of the strings are present in the file, it will be a positive match. The final rule will look like this:

```
rule calc_match
{
meta:
        description = "This is a sample rule to detect calc.exe."
strings:
        $a = "ADB880A6-D8FF-11CF-9377-00AA003B7A11"
        $b = {43 00 61 00 6C 00 63 00 4D 00 73 00}
condition:
        $a or $b
}
```

9. For more about Yara writing rules, visit http://yara.readthedocs.org/en/v3.3.0/writingrules.html.

LAB 13-3: *Installing Yara Support for Python*

In this lab, you will install Yara support for Python so you can utilize it in a Python script.

What You Need:

▶ System running Ubuntu 14.04.1

▶ Yara

▶ Python

Steps:

1. Install python-dev using the command line in a terminal window.

```
$ sudo apt-get install python-dev
```

2. Build and install the yara-python extension. From the terminal window, go to the folder where Yara was extracted. From Lab 13-1, the folder is yara-3.3.0. The folder name changes based on the version of Yara you downloaded. As of this writing, the latest is 3.3.0. From inside the yara-3.3.0 folder, issue the following commands:

```
$ cd yara-python
$ sudo python setup.py build
$ sudo python setup.py install
```

3. To avoid an ImportError in Ubuntu, add the path /usr/local/lib to the loader configuration file by issuing the following command line:

```
$ sudo echo "/usr/local/lib" >> /etc/ld.so.conf
$ sudo ldconfig
```

4. If the command line is not letting you make the necessary changes to /etc/ld.so.conf, you can use gedit as an alternative. From a terminal window, issue the following commands:

```
$ cd /
$ cd etc
$ sudo gedit ld.so.conf
```

5. Add the line /usr/local/lib without the quotes at the end of the file.

6. Save and close the file.

7. In the terminal window, run the command to load the config file.

```
$ sudo ldconfig
```

8. To check for successful installation, run the Python development environment by issuing the following command line:

```
$ python
```

9. In the development environment, issue the following command:

```
>>> import yara
```

10. If there are no errors, this means that the installation is successful. Type **exit()** to exit the development environment.

```
>>> exit()
```

LAB 13-4: *Using a Python Script That Utilizes Yara Rules*

In this lab, you will create a Python script that utilizes Yara rules to classify files.

What You Need:

▶ System running Ubuntu 14.04.1

▶ Yara

▶ Python

▶ Calc.EXE from Windows

Steps:

1. Create a Python script file and write the following code:

```
#!/usr/bin/python
import yara
yara_rule = 'yara_rule.txt'
file = 'calc.exe'
rules = yara.compile(yara_rule)
matches = rules.match(file)
print matches, file
exit()
```

2. After creating the Python script, change it to executable mode by issuing the following command:

```
$ chmod +x yourscript.py
```

3. Execute your script. Make sure that yara_rule.txt and calc.EXE are in the same folder as your script.

```
$ ./yourscript.py
```

4. The output will look like the following:

```
[calc_match] calc.exe
```

5. You can find more about using Yara with Python at http://yara.readthedocs .org/en/v3.3.0/yarapython.html.

Cygwin

Cygwin is a tool that gives you that Linux feeling in Windows. Cygwin is a large collection of GNU and open source tools that provide functionality similar to a Linux distribution in Windows. But it is not a way to run native Linux apps on Windows nor is it a way to magically make Windows programs aware of Unix functionalities. Instead, Cygwin is a DLL that provides substantial POSIX application programming interface (API) functionality.[2] The Cygwin DLL is cygwin1.dll.

---

[2] Cygwin: https://www.cygwin.com/.

Cygwin provides a quick and easy way for analysts to have access to some GNU command lines from Windows without switching operating systems.

LAB 13-5: *Installing Cygwin*

In this lab, you will install Cygwin in a Windows box, specifically Window 7.

What You Need:

▶ System running Windows 7

▶ Cygwin

Steps:

1. Download Cygwin from https://www.cygwin.com. For this purpose, you will be downloading the 64-bit version. The downloaded file is setup-x86_64.exe.

2. Install Cygwin and follow the prompts. Figure 13-2 shows the installation window of Cygwin. Click Next.

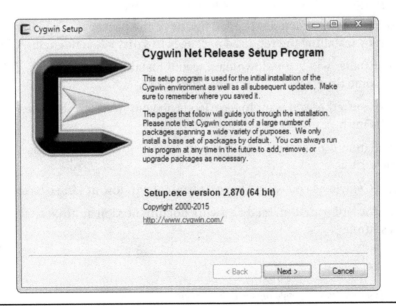

Figure 13-2 *Cygwin installation window.*

3. In the next window, choose Install From Internet. This is the default. Click Next.

4. Choose the root directory of Cygwin. For this purpose, you will stick with the default, which is C:\cygwin64. You will also install for All Users, which is the default. Click Next.

5. Choose where to put the local package. This stores all the installation files for future use. Click Next.

6. Select the appropriate Internet connection for download. A direct connection is the default connection. Click Next.

7. Choose a download site. If you have your own user uniform resource locator (URL) such as from your university or work that hosts Cygwin, it is advisable to use that one. Click Next.

8. The installer will parse the mirror for packages. If the speed is slow, you can always cancel the installation, restart it, and choose a different download site.

9. Once parsing is complete and available packages have been identified, you will be asked to choose the packages you want to install. Installing all packages is the default. Simply remove the packages you don't want. But for the purpose of this lab, you will install all packages. Click Next.

10. If there are dependencies needed by any of the packages, Cygwin will resolve them by installing the required packages to satisfy dependencies. Click Next.

11. The installer will begin downloading and installing the packages. This may take some time. Once this is done, click Next.

12. Choose whether you want to have icons on your desktop, Start menu, or both. Click Finish.

13. Installation is now complete. You now have Cygwin Terminal, as shown in Figure 13-3.

14. Treat Cygwin as you would have a terminal window in Linux-based systems.

15. For more information, read Cygwin's documentation at https://cygwin.com/docs.html.

TIP

To update Cygwin, simply run the installer again.

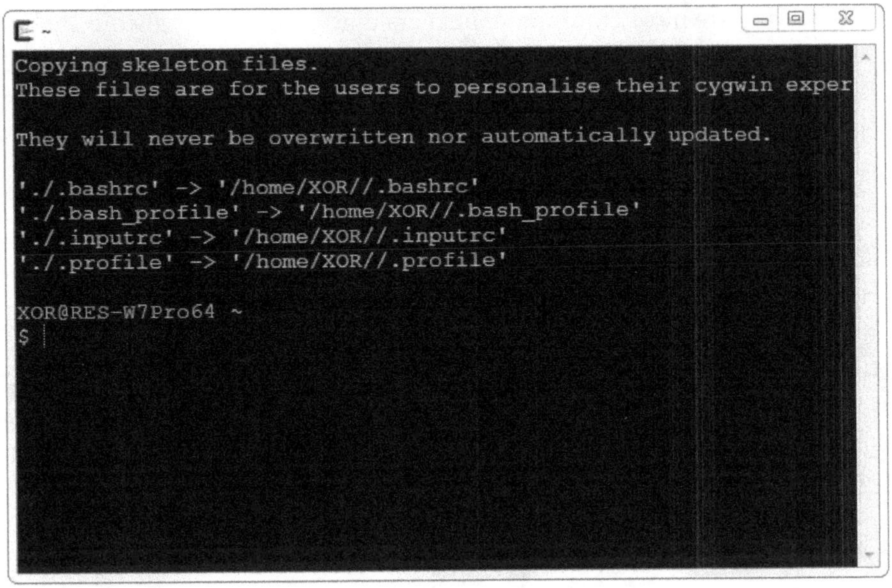

```
Copying skeleton files.
These files are for the users to personalise their cygwin exper

They will never be overwritten nor automatically updated.

'./.bashrc' -> '/home/XOR//.bashrc'
'./.bash_profile' -> '/home/XOR//.bash_profile'
'./.inputrc' -> '/home/XOR//.inputrc'
'./.profile' -> '/home/XOR//.profile'

XOR@RES-W7Pro64 ~
$
```

Figure 13-3   *Cygwin Terminal window.*

Debuggers

In computer science, debugging is the process of finding errors or bugs in a program or a device. The tools that are used for debugging are called *debuggers*. In DOS, a reliable tool for this is Debug.COM, but the world of debuggers has come a long way after that.

In malware analysis, debugging is the process of tracing code to find out what it does. It is a step-by-step tracing of malware code to determine its true intention. This is why debugging is a critical ingredient of reverse engineering.

For the purpose of this book, debugging is a helpful process to determine whether a binary is encrypted, packed, or neither. Learning this skill is needed, especially if the packer or cryptor is new and no PEiD or Yara signature exists yet to detect it. Remember, any file that is encrypted or packed usually renders static analysis useless. But if a malware is unpacked or decrypted through the use of tools, it will be easy to get information from it using static analysis; thus, you have more data to help you classify whether a file is malicious and even cluster it with its group or malware family for better identification.

The following are most common debuggers that are used in malware analysis:

► OllyDbg
► Immunity Debugger
► Windows Debuggers

OllyDbg

OllyDbg is a classic tool that is still popular with malware analysts today. You can download it from http://www.ollydbg.de/. One great thing about OllyDbg, called Olly for short, is that there is a wealth of plug-ins available for download all over the Internet to make debugging easier. A search for OllyDbg plug-ins will yield lots of resources when it comes to useful plug-ins. But as with other things available freely on the Web, exercise caution when downloading and using them.

Immunity Debugger

Immunity Debugger is a debugger that boasts of features that are deemed friendly for security experts. You can download it from http://debugger.immunityinc.com/. On its main page, it is described as a powerful new way to write exploits, analyze malware, and reverse engineer binary files. It can also be extended by using a large and well-supported Python API.

Windows Debuggers

The most common Windows debuggers are WinDbg, KD, and NTKD. The one that encompasses all, at least in my humble opinion, is WinDbg. WinDbg is Microsoft's own Windows debugger. It is part of the Windows Driver Kit, but it can also be downloaded as a stand-alone tool from https://msdn.microsoft.com/en-us/windows/hardware/hh852365.aspx.

WinDbg is thought to have an "inside" advantage compared to other debuggers because it is written specifically for Windows. It has the following features:

► Kernel mode debugging
► User mode debugging
► Managed debugging
► Unmanaged debugging

- ▶ Remote debugging
- ▶ Ability to attach to a process
- ▶ Ability to detach from a process

It basically covers all the bases of other Windows debuggers such as KD and NTKD. You can find more information about KD and NTKD from https://msdn.microsoft.com/en-us/library/windows/hardware/hh406279%28v=vs.85%29.aspx.

Disassemblers

A *disassembler* is a tool that breaks down a binary into assembly code. A disassembler is often used in tandem with a debugger. A debugger follows the assembly code in memory, and the output of the disassembler serves as a map or a good indicator whether the code being traced in memory is still in line with the disassembled code. Sometimes there will be differences, which means that either the debugging session is going to a dead end or the disassembled code is not as reliable probably because the malware has an anti-disassemble capability.

The most popular disassembler is IDA. It is also considered a debugger. IDA is a little pricey, but the good thing about it is that there is always a free version available that is for non-commercial use. You can download it from https://www.hex-rays.com/products/ida/support/download.shtml.

IDA is a powerful tool. I suggest downloading a free copy of it and playing around with it. There are lots of resources from its website that will help you get started. The more you use it, the better you will become at using IDA.

Memory Dumpers

Memory dumpers are tools that dump a running process from memory. There are a handful of process dumpers available such as Microsoft's ProcDump, but the most useful tools, in my humble opinion, when it comes to malware analysis are LordPE and Volatility.

LordPE

LordPE is a tool that can dump a process from memory and has the ability to edit basic PE header information. You can download the tool from http://www.woodmann.com/collaborative/tools/index.php/LordPE.

Volatility Framework

Volatility is a free, useful memory dump analyzer. It is a single, cohesive framework that supports 32-bit and 64-bit Windows, Linux, Mac, and Android systems. It is a Python-based framework that allows users to analyze an OS environment from a static dump file. Being Python-based makes Volatility versatile. It can be programmed to do almost anything a memory dump analyzer can do. To get started on Volatility, visit https://code.google.com/p/volatility/wiki/VolatilityIntroduction.

PE Viewers

PE viewers are tools that provide a glimpse of a PE file. There are lots of PE viewers available depending on your needs. The following are some of them:

► Hiew

► Heaventools PE Explorer

► PEview

► Dependency Walker

► Resource Hacker

Hiew

Hiew is a classic PE viewer. It has the ability to not only view and edit files of any length in text and hex but also disassemble a PE file. Some of the features are as follows:

► x86-64 disassembler and assembler

► View and edit physical and logical drive

► Pattern search in disassembler

► Built-in simple 64-bit decrypt/crypt system

► Block operations: read, write, fill, copy, move, insert, delete, crypt

► Multifile search and replace

► Unicode support

You can find more information about the tool at http://www.hiew.ru/.

Heaventools PE Explorer

PE Explorer has all the capabilities of a typical PE viewer. The following are the extra features it offers:

- ▶ API function syntax lookup
- ▶ Dependency scanner
- ▶ Section editor
- ▶ Unpacker support for UPX, Upack, and NsPack

PE Explorer is not free, but it offers a 30-day trial version. You can download it from http://www.heaventools.com/overview.htm.

PEview

PEview, as stated on its website, provides a quick and easy way to view the structure and content of PE and COFF files. It displays header, section, directory, import table, export table, and resource information within EXE, DLL, OBJ, LIB, DBG, and other file types. You can download it from http://wjradburn.com/software/.

Dependency Walker

Dependency Walker, as discussed in previous chapters, is a free utility that scans any 32-bit or 64-bit Windows module and builds a hierarchical tree diagram of all dependent modules.

You can download Dependency Walker from http://www.dependencywalker.com/.

Resource Hacker

Resource Hacker is a freeware utility to view, modify, rename, add, delete, and extract resources in 32-bit and 64-bit Windows executables and resource files. It incorporates an internal resource script compiler and decompiler and works on all Windows operating systems, at least up to Windows 7.

You can download Resource Hacker from http://www.angusj.com/resourcehacker/.

PE Reconstructors

PE reconstructors are tools that have the ability to reconstruct a portable executable file from memory or from a dump file given that these tools have all the information they need such as the entry point, relative virtual address, and size. The most common PE reconstructor used in malware analysis is ImpREC by MackT. It has the ability to rebuild the import address table (IAT) from a memory dump. You can download the tool from http://www.woodmann.com/collaborative/tools/index.php/ImpREC.

The tools discussed so far are stand-alone, and each has their own purpose. Combining their use to solve a malware analysis problem or use case is not a foreign idea. For example, manually unpacking a malware is one problem that all malware analysts and researchers have faced throughout the years. The right combination of tools can help a malware analyst and researcher break a packed or encrypted malware.

LAB 13-6: *Manually Unpacking a Packed Malware*

In this lab, you will use the different tools discussed so far to manually unpack a packed malware. The malware that you will use specifically for this lab has the following characteristics:

- ▶ **MD5**   c0c9c7ea235e4992a67caa1520421941
- ▶ **SHA1**   da39a3ee5e6b4b0d3255bfef95601890afd80709
- ▶ **SHA256**   e3b0c44298fc1c149afbf4c8996fb92427ae41e4649b-934ca495991b7852b855

What You Need:
- ▶ Debuggers
- ▶ Disassemblers
- ▶ Static analysis tools
- ▶ Dynamic analysis tools
- ▶ System running Windows
- ▶ Packed malware

Steps:
1. The first thing to do is to use PEiD to determine whether it is packed.
2. Figure 13-4 shows the output of PEiD. As you can see, PEiD did not detect anything. Even its Entropy shows that the file is not packed.

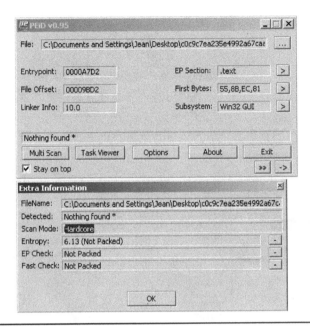

Figure 13-4   *PEiD output.*

3. Let's try PEView. Figure 13-5 shows the output. You can see in the IAT that there are many imports, which oftentimes depict that the file is unpacked and everything looks normal.

4. Let's try IDA. Figure 13-6 shows the output. From here, you can see that there is only one function, the start function. Close to the end of the start function there is a CALL instruction to a value stored in the stack. The value is the return value of the function InverRect that was called before, and its return value plus 27C8Ah was stored on the stack. With this information, you come into the conclusion that this file is packed after all, even if PEiD and PEView say otherwise.

5. At this point, you need to drop the file into a debugger, look at the assembly instructions, and attempt to unpack the file.

6. In this lab, you will be using Immunity Debugger. Figure 13-7 shows the debugging session of the packed file in Immunity Debugger.

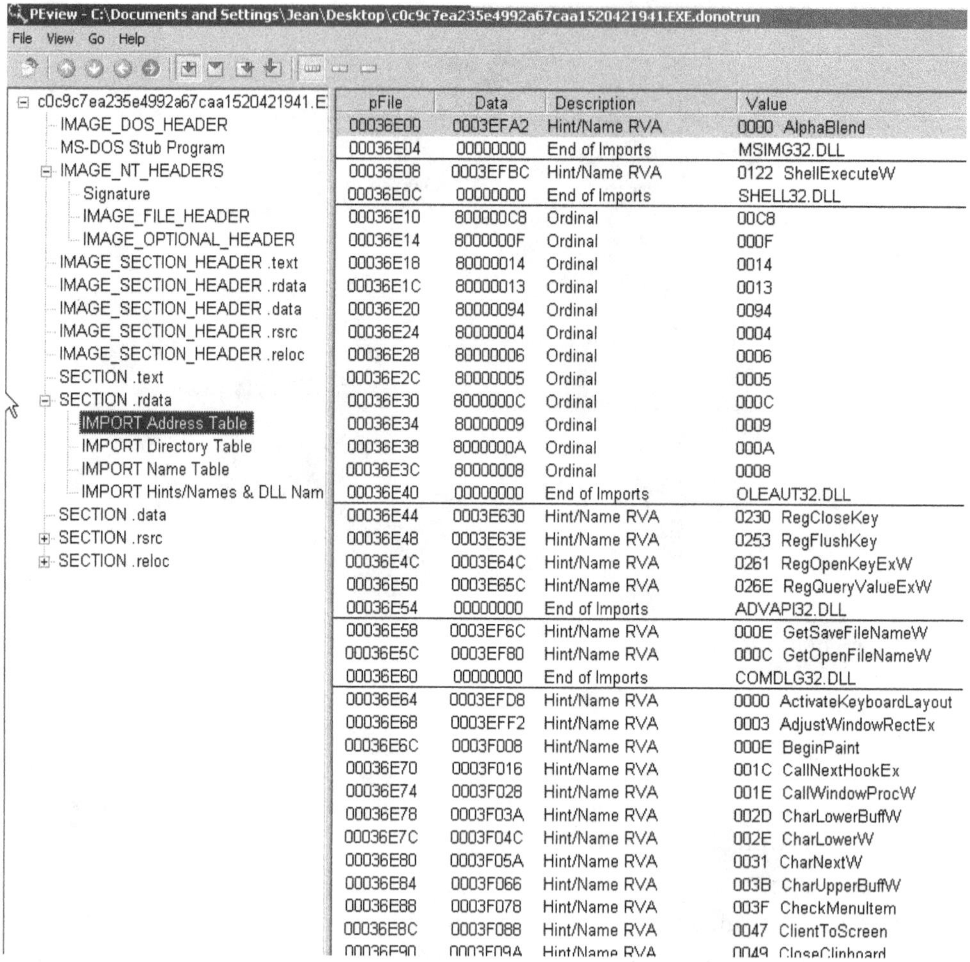

Figure 13-5 *PEView output.*

TIP

The general approach with unpacking is to step over calls and not step into function calls unless you have a good reason to do it. Also, make a lot of snapshots every time you are stepping over a call you are not sure about. This will allow you to revert to your last position in an instant when needed.

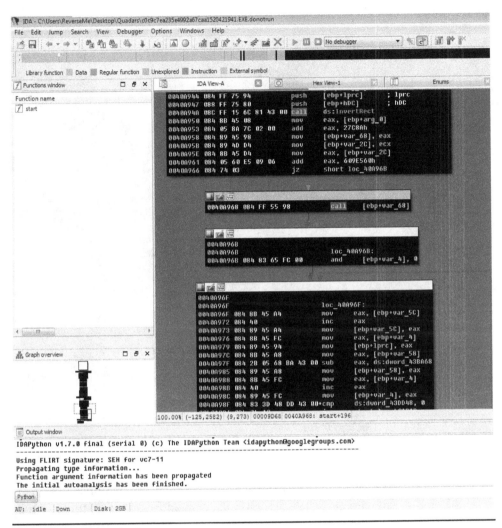

Figure 13-6   *IDA output.*

7. In Immunity Debugger, you start off at the entry point. Scrolling down a bit reveals some calls to legitimate functions such as GetConsoleOutputCP, GetDriveTypeW, InvertRec, and GlobalAddAtomW.

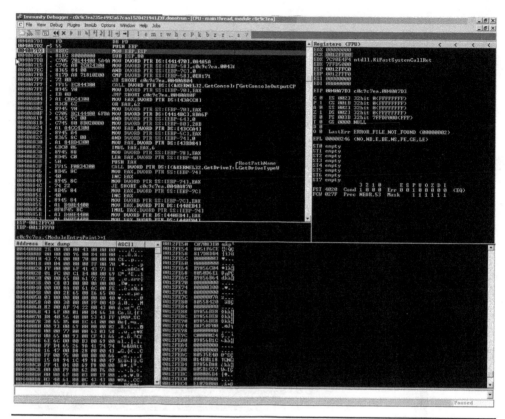

Figure 13-7   *Immunity Debugger session.*

8. Step over the instructions by pressing F8 until you get a CALL instruction at <ModuleEntryPoint> + 196, which calls to an address that is stored in the local variable EBP-68 in the stack. Figure 13-8 shows this session.

9. In this specific case, the address points to 0x00427C8A, but this is not necessarily the same address every time the binary is loaded. This is where you left your sample in IDA. Step into this CALL by pressing F7. Figure 13-9 shows the resulting session.

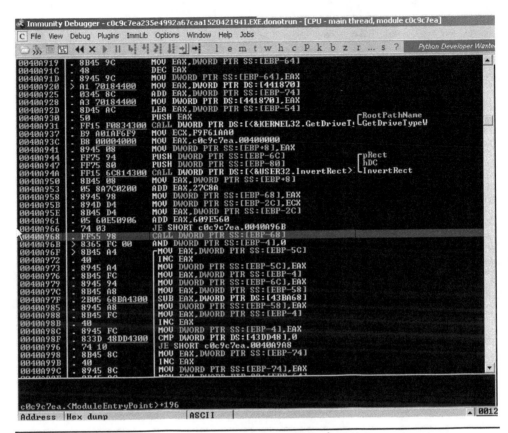

Figure 13-8   *Immunity Debugger session reaching desired CALL instruction.*

10. After stepping in, what you see (Figure 13-9) looks like obfuscated or scrambled code, which is common with packed files.

11. Following the jump brings you to the session shown in Figure 13-10.

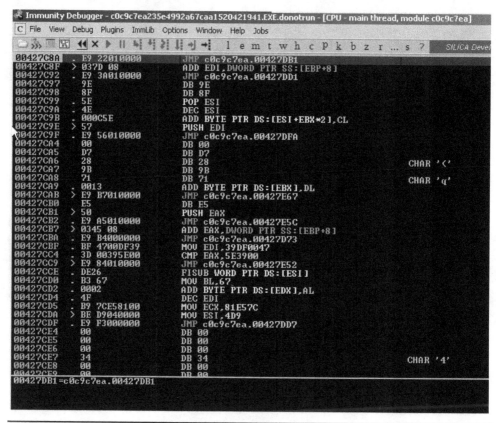

Figure 13-9 *Immunity Debugger session in address 0x427C8A.*

12. After stepping over JMP and PUSH instructions, you will reach a CALL
EAX instruction, as shown in Figure 13-11. The instructions are generally
suspicious, and in some cases you will want to step in, but in this case,
this is actually a dynamic call to VirtualProtect, which is used to conceal
its true purpose. The permissions of the sections in the addresses
0x00400000–0x00442000 (PE Headers + .text section) is changed to RWE
(Read Write Execute) so that the binary will be able to change its own code
by writing a new "unpacked" version of itself to the .text section.

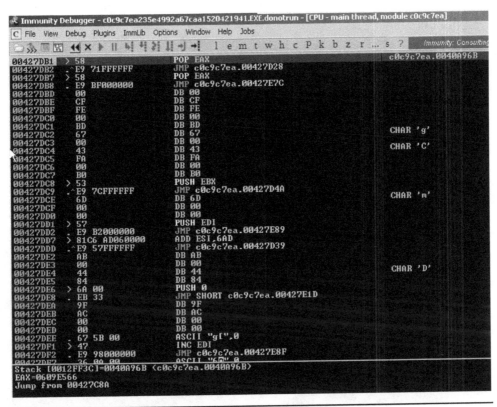

Figure 13-10   *Immunity Debugger session following the JMP instruction.*

13. The memory map shown in Figure 13-12 displays the current permissions of each section in memory.

14. Continue stepping over more JMP instructions. You can also use the animate over (CTRL+F8) feature for this purpose but not before making a snapshot.

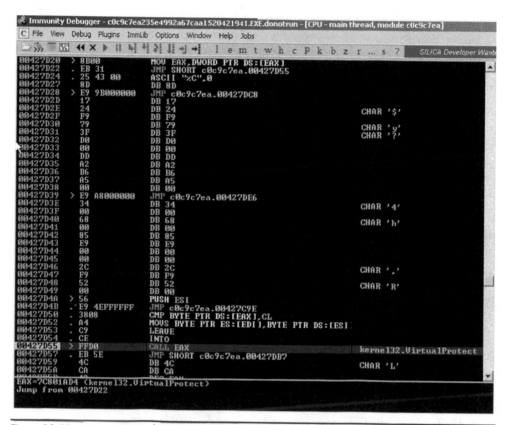

Figure 13-11 *Immunity Debugger session reaching CALL EAX instruction.*

15. After trying to animate over, you will notice the JMPs make it too difficult to follow, and thus a new approach is needed. You may have noticed that you stumbled upon the same CMP ECX, ESI instruction quite a few times while stepping over, so it seems that this is obfuscated code that might repeat itself in a loop 2,950 times. The number 2,950 comes from the hex value B86, which is the value of ESI, as shown in Figure 13-13.

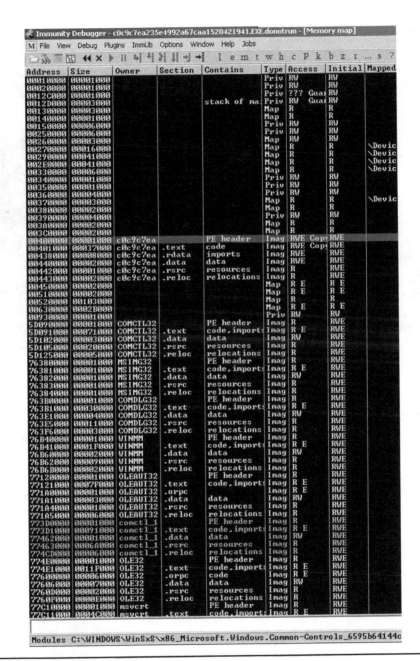

Figure 13-12 *Memory map.*

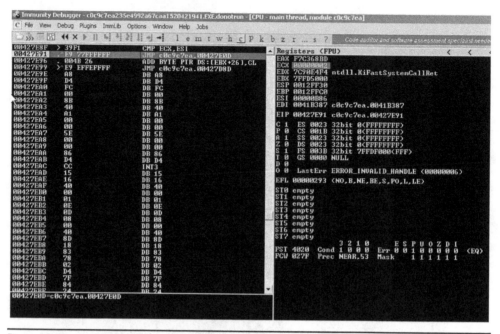

Figure 13-13   *Immunity Debugger session showing ESI value.*

16. To skip doing the stepping over 2,950 times, you will be setting a conditional breakpoint (CTRL+T) and use a trace over (CTRL+F12), as shown in Figure 13-14. You set the value of ECX to B86.

17. Once ECX reaches the value of B86, the resulting session is as shown in Figure 13-15.

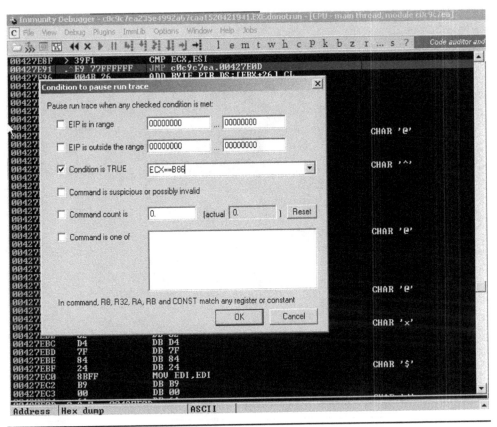

Figure 13-14 *Conditional breakpoint and trace over.*

18. Take the JMP instruction to reach a new section in the code, as shown in Figure 13-16.

19. Keep stepping over the instructions until you reach a JMP EAX instruction, as shown in Figure 13-17.

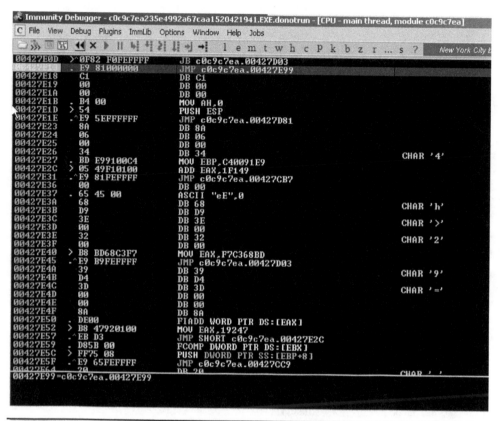

Figure 13-15 *Immunity Debugger session after the breakpoint.*

20. There is an alternative strategy to reaching this JMP EAX instruction. Assuming that the packer is trying to hide any JMP to the deobfuscated code, a good bet is that it will call a function using a CALL EAX/JMP EAX instruction. With that logic in mind, you can search (CTRL+F) for a CALL EAX/JMP EAX instruction and set a breakpoint (F2) on that instruction. Before pressing F9 to run, make sure you create a snapshot.

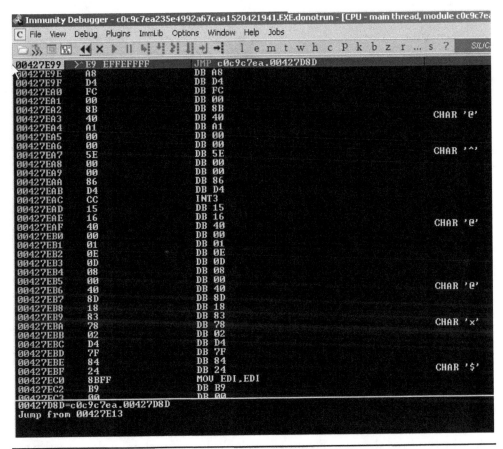

Figure 13-16 *Immunity Debugger session after taking the JMP instruction.*

21. The JMP EAX takes you to 0x0041B385, as shown in Figure 13-18.

22. At this point, you click the current instruction and then choose Analysis |
     Analyse Code (CTRL+A), as shown in Figure 13-19.

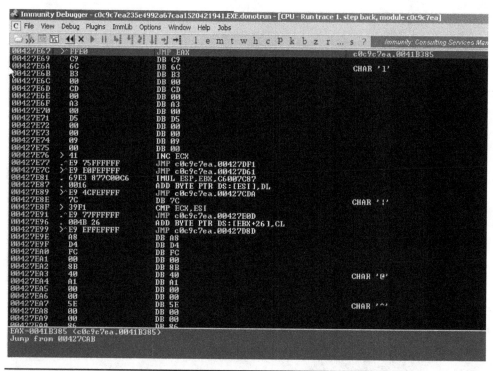

Figure 13-17   *Immunity Debugger session reaching JMP EAX.*

23. The result, as shown in Figure 13-20, looks like a function prologue setting
     up the stack frame. The code looks readable. Could this be the original
     entrypoint (OEP) of the original packed binary?

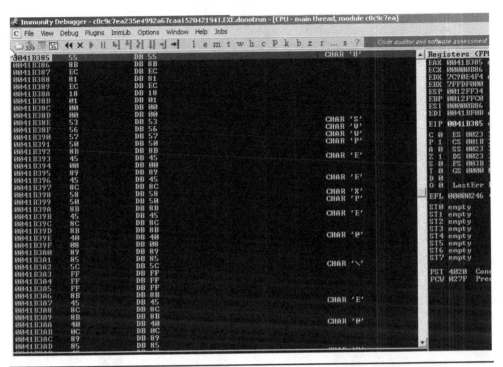

Figure 13-18   *Immunity Debugger session reaching address 0x0041B385.*

24. Keep stepping over to find out. Whenever you hit a loop, set a breakpoint (F2) right after it, press F9 (Run) until the breakpoint (BP), take the BP off, and keep stepping over instructions. Figure 13-21 shows this session.

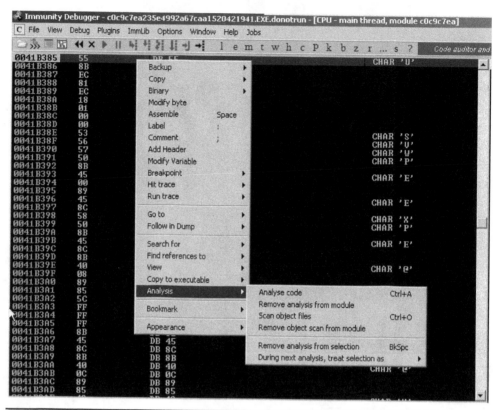

Figure 13-19   *Immunity Debugger Analyse Code menu option.*

25. When you scroll down, you will see function names as strings in the code, as shown in Figure 13-22.

26. At this point, you come to the conclusion that this is still the packer code. Or is it the unpacker code? It looks like the packer is a string pointer to function names in the KERNEL32.DLL library by using GetProcAddress. This is done by the packer so it won't have to call these functions explicitly and there will be no trace of these functions in the IAT.

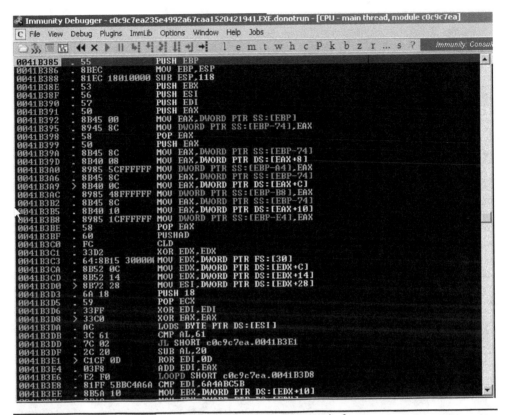

Figure 13-20 *Immunity Debugger result from Analyse Code function.*

Specifically, the following instructions get string pointers to the function names embedded in the code:

```
003B042F CALL    0041B468
003B0434         POP     EAX
003B0435 JMP     003B0447
003B0437 [String Data]
003B0447 ADD     EAX, 3
```

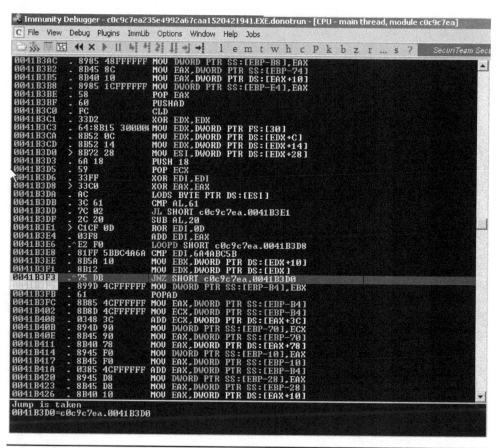

Figure 13-21 *Immunity Debugger session hitting a loop.*

In this snippet, the CALL instruction pushes the next instruction's address, which is found in the EIP to the stack, and jumps to the function's address, which in this case is the address of the next instruction, POP EAX. After executing the next instruction POP EAX, EAX will contain the address of the POP EAX instruction, which is just 3 bytes before the string that contains a function name. The next instruction is an unconditional jump instruction (JMP) that jumps over the string. The next instruction that will be executed is ADD EAX, 3. After the execution of this instruction, EAX will be pointing to a null-terminated string containing the function name.

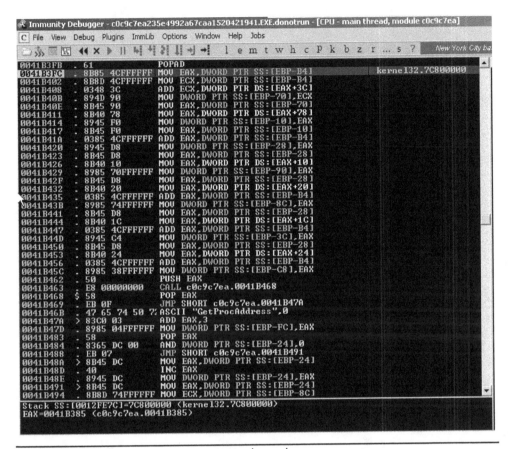

Figure 13-22 *Function names as strings in the code.*

This technique is repeated in a loop for many functions that are actually used by the malware but were hidden by the packer such as GetModuleHandleA, GetOutputDebugString, and so on. The function names are saved in local variables so they can be accessed later when the IAT is reconstructed in memory.

Figure 13-23 shows this whole thing in the session.

27. Continue stepping over the instructions until you hit JMP EAX, as shown in Figure 13-24.

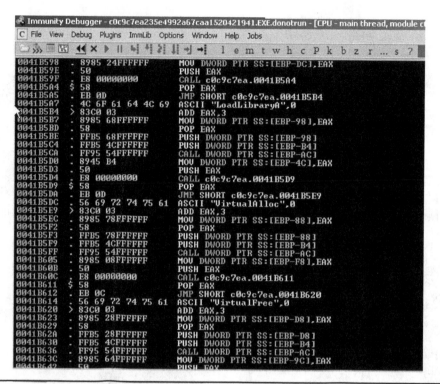

Figure 13-23 *Immunity Debugger session showing string pointer technique.*

28. After the JMP, you come across the same technique once again, but this time the string containing the function name is hidden better. Also, notice that the JMP instruction is jumping to an unaligned address. This means that the code will get a different meaning after the jump. Figure 13-25 shows this session.

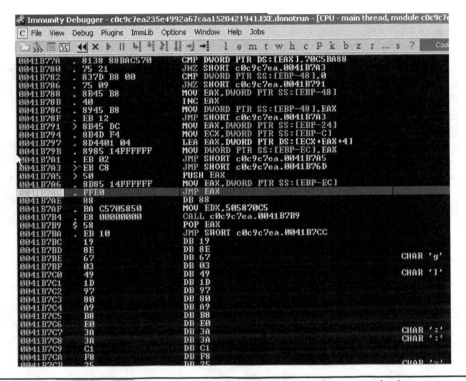

Figure 13-24   *Immunity Debugger session showing JMP EAX being reached.*

29. Keep going until instruction ADD EAX, 3 is revealed, as shown in Figure 13-26.

30. Keep stepping over until you reach the infamous technique's set of instructions again.

```
CALL    003B0994
POP EAX
JMP 003B099A
```

The session in Figure 13-27 shows the sets of instructions.

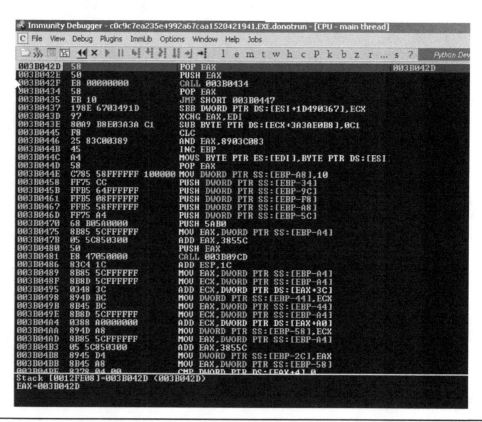

Figure 13-25 *Immunity Debugger session showing the same technique but in an unaligned address.*

31. After the jump, you should see the instruction ADD EAX, 3; also, the "magic jump" JMP EAX should be revealed. Figure 13-28 shows this session.

32. But just before you reach the magic jump, you might have one last obstacle, a CALL to OutputDebugStringA, as shown in Figure 13-29. OutputDebugStringA is sometimes used as an anti-debugging technique.

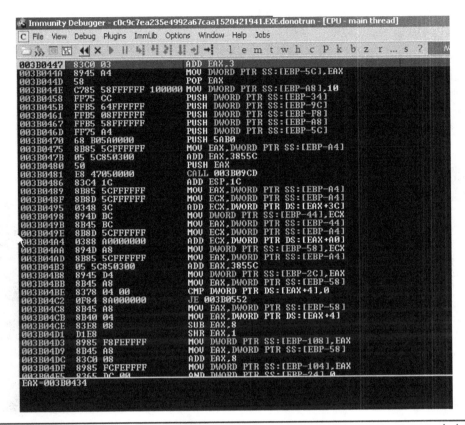

Figure 13-26 *Immunity Debugger session after the ADD EAX, 3 instruction is revealed.*

33. The actual function is typically used to output a string value to the debugging data stream, which will then display the debugger. OutputDebugString() acts differently based on the existence of a debugger on the running process. If a debugger is attached to the process, the function will execute normally, and no error state will be registered. However, if there is no debugger attached,

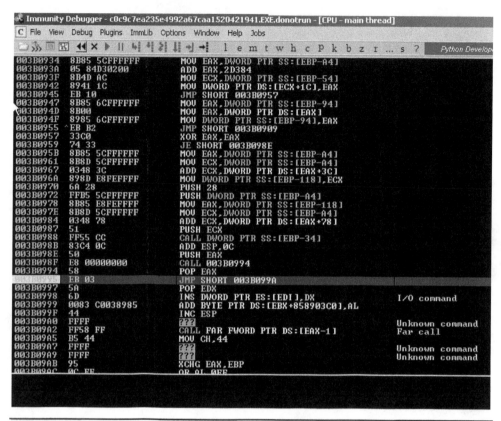

Figure 13-27   *Immunity Debugger session showing the infamous technique.*

LastError will be set by the process, letting you know that you are debugger free. Malware authors can use this to change the execution flow of the malware if a debugger is detected. For the malware author to do this, she would typically use the following implementation:

```
Prototype:
void WINAPI OutputDebugString(__in_opt  LPCTSTR lpOutputString);
Example:
DWORD Val = 123;
SetLastError(Val);
OutputDebugString("whatever");
if (GetLastError() == Val)
```

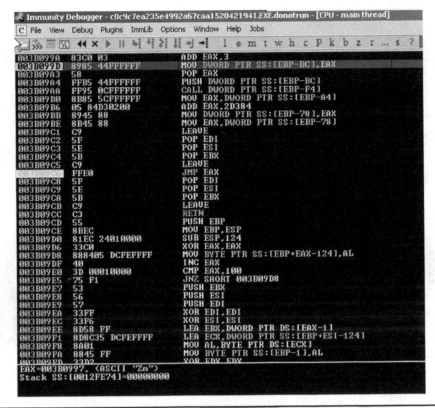

Figure 13-28   *Immunity Debugger session showing ADD EAX, 3 and JMP EAX.*

```
        {
                //Debugger Detected - Do Something Here
        }
        else
        {
                //No Debugger Detected - Continue
        }
```

Luckily for you, it was not implemented correctly as an anti-debugging mechanism, and there is no distinction between the two cases, debugger attached or not.

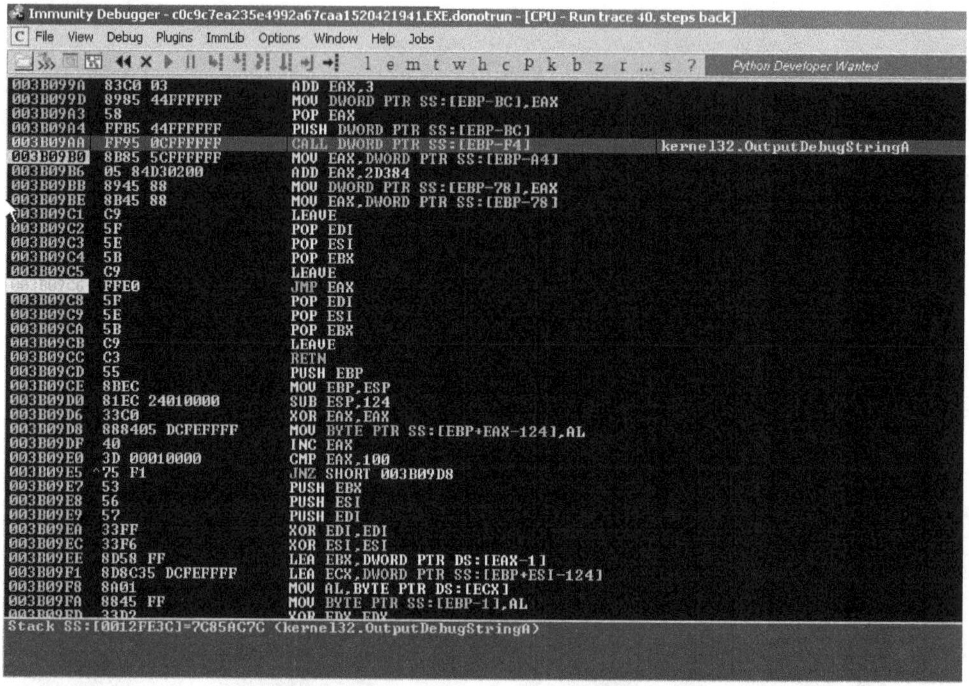

Figure 13-29   *Immunity Debugger session showing CALL to OutputDebugStringA.*

34. You take the jump and get to a new section, as shown in Figure 13-30.

35. Analyze the code, as shown in Figure 13-31.

36. The OEP is found, as shown in Figure 13-32.

37. At this point, you need to dump the memory so you can get the unpacked image of the binary. For this purpose, you will use LordPE. For LordPE to be able to attach to a process, it must be run in administrator mode, and then you pick the process that you would like to dump.

38. Once you find the process that you would like to dump, right-click it, choose Dump Full, and choose a location where to save it. See Figure 13-33 showing this process.

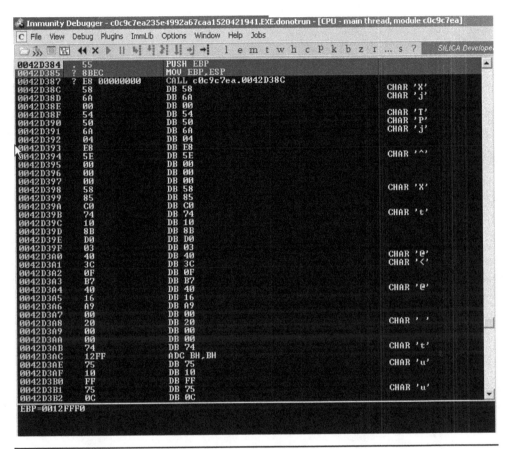

Figure 13-30 *Immunity Debugger session after taking the jump.*

39. After dumping the process, you can use LordPE's PE Editor to overwrite the entry point and other PE headers depending on the sample. The button to invoke PE Editor is in the upper-right corner of LordPE. PE Editor will need you to choose a valid PE file to work on. Choose the file you saved while dumping the process from memory. Figure 13-34 shows the result when the file is loaded using LordPE's PE Editor.

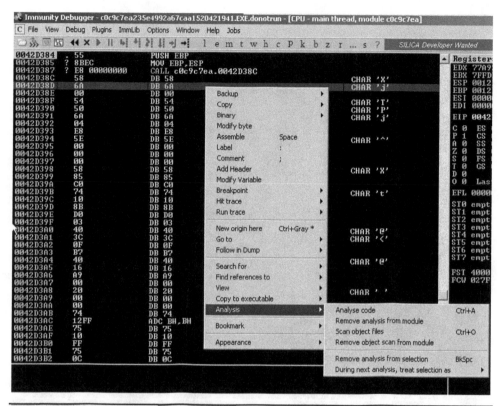

Figure 13-31 *Analyze the code in Immunity Debugger.*

40. Once the file is loaded successfully, overwrite the EntryPoint value, as shown in Figure 13-35, with the RVA of the OEP you found. The RVA of the OEP is 42D384 – 400000 = 2D384.

41. Check the sections were not corrupted by checking that their Virtual Offset (VOffset) and Virtual Size (VSize) values match their Relative Offset (ROffset) and Relative Size (RSize) values. As you can see in Figure 13-36, all the values match for each one of the sections.

42. At this point, you will use ImpREC to rebuild the IAT. Execute ImpREC and attach the malware process, as shown in Figure 13-37.

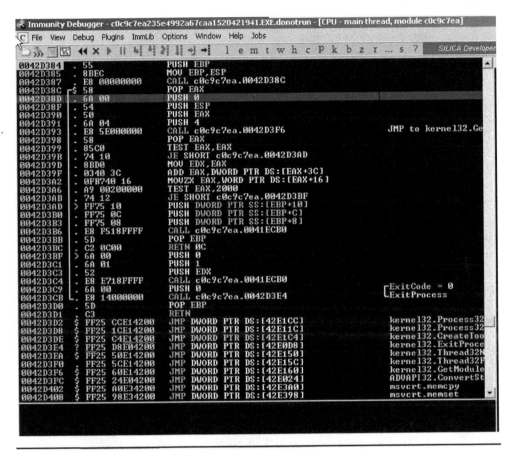

Figure 13-32 *OEP found in Immunity Debugger.*

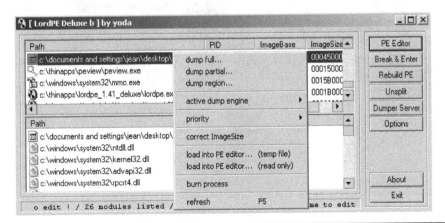

Figure 13-33 *LordPE dumping a desired process.*

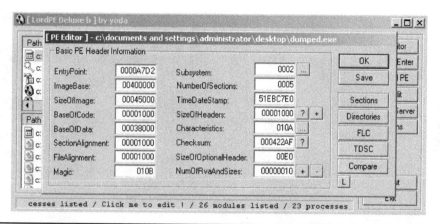

Figure 13-34 *Dumped process loaded into LordPE's PE Editor.*

43. Change the OEP to the RVA of the OEP you found and click IAT AutoSearch. After this process, ImpREC tells you that it found the OEP, as shown in Figure 13-38.

44. Click Get Imports. This will fill up the Imported Functions Found list. See whether there are invalid thunks by clicking Show Invalid. Figure 13-39 shows the output. From what is shown so far, everything looks good.

45. Once everything looks good and is completed, click Fix Dump and choose the file you dumped with LordPE. ImpREC will create a new file ending with .EXE. This is now your new unpacked binary.

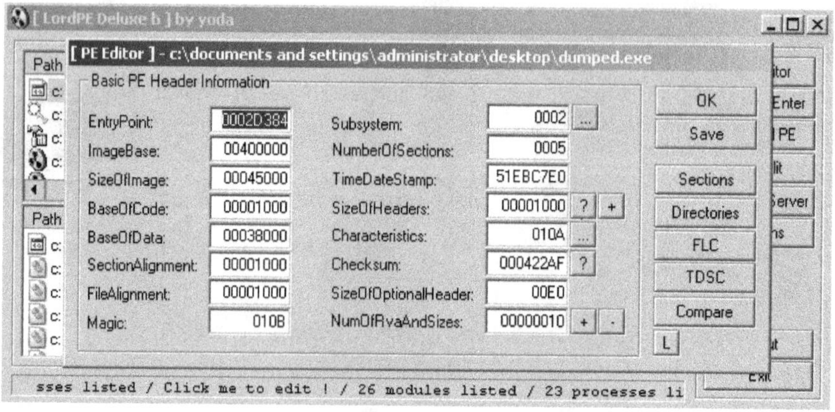

Figure 13-35 *EntryPoint value modified to reflect RVA of OEP.*

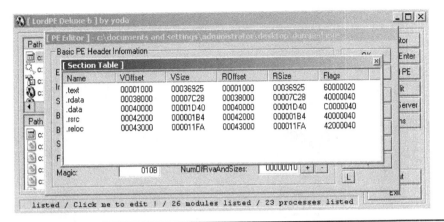

Figure 13-36   *Section table of the dumped process.*

46. Static analysis can now be done in this unpacked binary. You can now also disassemble and analyze it statically using IDA. Figure 13-40 shows the result in IDA.

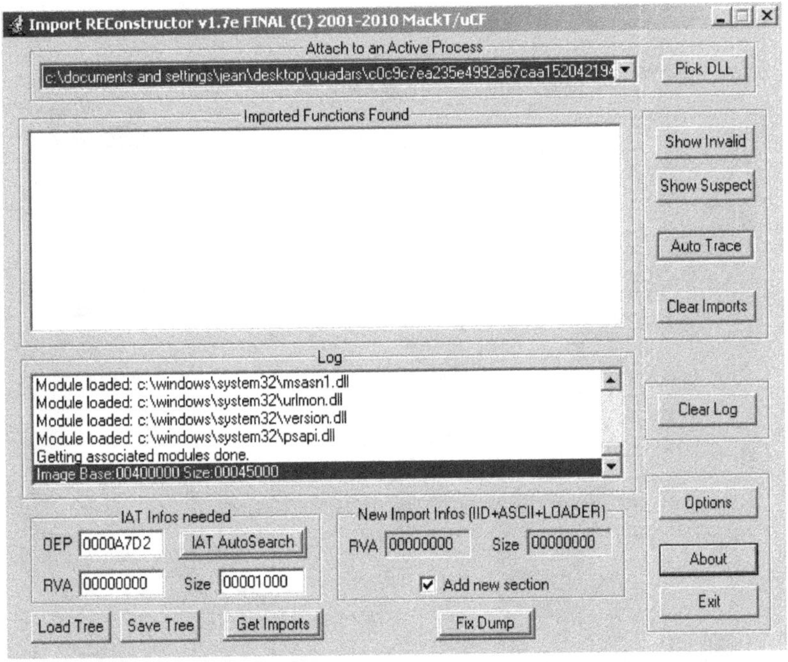

Figure 13-37   *Malware process attached to ImpREC.*

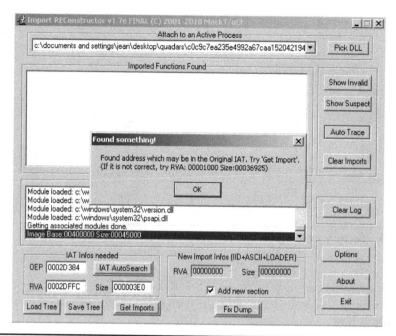

Figure 13-38 *ImpREC found the OEP.*

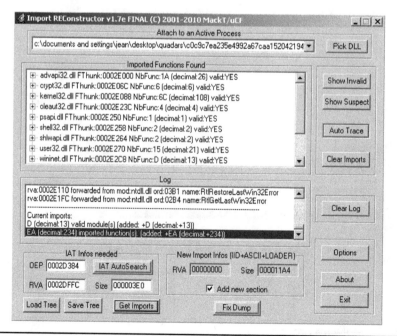

Figure 13-39 *Imports found by ImpREC.*

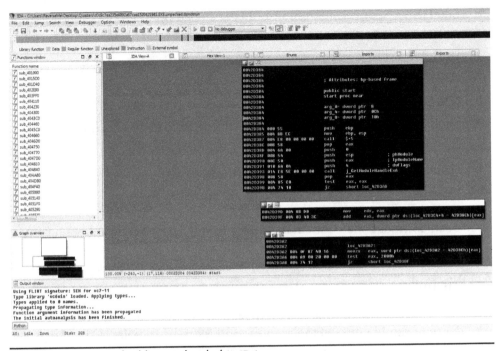

Figure 13-40 *Unpacked binary loaded in IDA.*

Malcode Analyst Pack

Malcode Analyst Pack by David Zimmer is a package of utilities that helps in performing rapid malware code analysis. The package includes the following tools:

- ▶ Shell extensions, including the following:
  - ▶ MD5 hash
  - ▶ Strings
  - ▶ Query VirusTotal
  - ▶ Submit to VirusTotal
- ▶ **socketTool**   Manual TCP client for probing functionality
- ▶ **MailPot**   Mail server capture pot

▶ **fakeDNS** Spoofs DNS responses to controlled Internet Protocol (IP) addresses

▶ **sniff_hit** HTTP, IRC, and DNS sniffer

▶ **sclog** Shellcode research and analysis application

▶ **IDCDumpFix** Aids in quick RE of packed applications

▶ **Shellcode2Exe** Embeds multiple shellcode formats in EXE husk

▶ **GdiProcs** Detect hidden processes

▶ **Finddll** Scan processes for loaded DLL by name

▶ **Virustotal** Virus reports for single and bulk hash lookups

You can download Malcode Analysis Pack from http://www.woodmann.com/collaborative/tools/index.php/Malcode_Analysis_Pack.

Rootkit Tools

Finding a rootkit is tricky. It takes a lot of patience to uncover one. Couple that with the right combination of tools, and a rootkit can be revealed. One of my favorite tools that helps in analyzing malware with rootkit capabilities is Rootkit Unhooker. It's a classic tool, but it is still useful.

Some of its capabilities include the following:

▶ SSDT hooks detection and restoration

▶ Shadow SSDT hooks detection and restoration

▶ Hidden processes detection, termination, and dumping

▶ Hidden drivers detection and dumping

▶ Hidden files detection, copying, and deletion

▶ Code hooks detection and restoration

You can download Rootkit Unhooker from http://www.antirootkit.com/software/RootKit-Unhooker.htm.

Rootkit Revealer is another classic rootkit tool. Unfortunately, Microsoft has discontinued it, but it can still be downloaded from different file hosting sites. Just be careful when downloading this file from non-Microsoft sources; it might come with some extra "bonus content." But if you are adventurous, one site you can download this from is http://download.cnet.com/RootkitRevealer/3000-2248_4-10543918.html.

Network Capturing Tools

A malware's network communication can reveal a lot about malware, the most important of which is what data is being exfiltrated out. It also reveals the malware's network resources, such as its command and control if it is part of a botnet, its domain or IP drop zone if it is an information stealer, and its malware-serving domain or IP address if it has the capability to update itself on a regular basis. It is therefore important to capture any network communication a malware makes while it is executing in a controlled environment.

The following are the three most common network capturing tools used in malware analysis:

▶ Wireshark
▶ TCPDump
▶ TCPView

Wireshark

Wireshark is a popular, versatile, and easy-to-use tool when it comes to capturing network traffic, as demonstrated in Lab 12-6 in the previous chapter.

You can download Wireshark from https://www.wireshark.org/.

TCPDump

TCPDump is a command-line packet analyzer tool. It is an open source tool commonly used for monitoring or sniffing network traffic. It captures and displays packet headers and everything that you need to know to understand a target file's network communication.

You can download TCPDump from http://www.tcpdump.org/.

TCPView

TCPView is part of Sysinternals Suite. It is a tool that shows detailed listings of all Transmission Control Protocol (TCP) and User Datagram Protocol (UDP) endpoints on your system, including the local and remote addresses and the state of TCP connections.[3]

---

[3] Microsoft Technet: http://technet.microsoft.com/en-US/.

Lab 12-5 in the previous chapter shows how to use TCPView.

You can download TCPView from https://technet.microsoft.com/en-us/sysinternals/bb897437.aspx.

As previously stated, combining the use of different tools to solve a malware analysis problem or use case is not a foreign idea. In the previous lab, you manually unpacked a packed malware. This is a problem every malware analyst and researcher has faced, but there is one more that proves to be equally or even more of a headache than packed malware. It's a malware with rootkit capabilities. The right combination of tools can help a malware analyst and researcher reveal the presence of a rootkit in an infected system. This is made possible if you know what to look for and how to correctly analyze a rootkit.

LAB 13-7: *Analyzing a User Mode Rootkit*

In this lab, you will perform a complete analysis of a user-mode rootkit using the tools discussed in this book. You will look at the different indicators of a rootkit and how to find them.

The malware that you will use specifically for this lab has the following characteristics:

▶ **MD5** b4024172375dca3ab186648db191173a

▶ **SHA1** da39a3ee5e6b4b0d3255bfef95601890afd80709

▶ **SHA256** e3b0c44298fc1c149afbf4c8996fb92427ae41e4649b-934ca495991b7852b855

What You Need:

▶ Static analysis tools

▶ Dynamic analysis tools

▶ Sysinternals Suite

▶ PE viewers

▶ Network capturing tools

▶ System running Windows

▶ Rootkit malware

Steps:

1. You will perform basic static analysis on the file before you do anything else.

2. You start by calculating the file's hashes. Hashes are often used as unique identifiers of files. The following are the resulting hashes:

   ▶ **MD5**   b4024172375dca3ab186648db191173a

   ▶ **SHA1**   da39a3ee5e6b4b0d3255bfef95601890afd80709

   ▶ **SHA256**   e3b0c44298fc1c149afbf4c8996fb92427ae41e4649b-934ca495991b7852b855

   ▶ **SHA512**   cf83e1357eefb8bdf1542850d66d8007d620e4050b5715dc-83f4a921d36ce9ce47d0d13c5d85f2b

      ▶ 0ff8318d2877eec2f63b931bd47417a81a538327af927da3e

   ▶ **SSDeep**   12288:tcJkcAWoVBMRLuDHt9pH4jZ/6v5hLl4sk8rEvCV1MK SK:gTr+OpuDH8N4Xw8AKfnSK

   ▶ **ImpHash**   ef471c0edf1877cd5a881a6a8bf647b9

   MD5 has been an industry standard for a long time, but because of MD5 collisions, it is always better to get more hashes. ImpHash is a relatively new hash that was created from the import table rather than the raw data of the file. ImpHash is only for PE files.

3. Aside from hashes serving as unique identifiers, it will also allow you to look for this sample in publicly available malware databases such as VirusTotal and even look at publicly available sandboxes to see whether it has been analyzed already. Remember that all the information you get helps you in analyzing malware, especially if you are struggling.

4. Check the file type. Usually, when you get a sample, it is always assumed that it is a PE file, but this is not always the case. Also, using the different file type checkers in your arsenal such as PEiD and a Python script powered with Yara will help you identify not only the file type but also whether the file is packed, encrypted, or neither.

5. For this file, you will use the easiest way to determine the file type. You will use GNU file command.

```
$ file sample.bin
sample.bin: PE32 executable (GUI) Intel 80386, for MS Windows,
UPX compressed
```

The output tells you that this file is UPX compressed. You will find out later if it is indeed UPX compressed.

6. Get the strings present in the file. You can do this by using the GNU command strings or SysInternals strings.exe in Windows. Here is a partial list of the strings found in the file:

```
0000004D   !This program cannot be run in DOS mode.
000000F0   Rich
00000200   UPX0
00000228   UPX1
00000250   .rsrc
000003DB   3.08
000003E0   UPX!
00000518   _^1[5xi
00000568   $322
000005EF   |$L;
00000629   +&)V
00000692   u,Iw
000006D8   VN $hqgd(,4A4<
00000773   NZ#YW(;
000007C2   -3lh'
00000885   (l$.p,t
0004E3A3   AutoIt
```

7. From the strings output, notice the following strings: UPX0, UPX1, UPX!, and AutoIt. The first three are indicators that the file is packed by UPX, and the fourth string indicates that there might be an AutoIt script embedded in the file, which might be a second packer.

8. Investigate the file's PE characteristics. You can do this using PEView. Figure 13-41 shows the file's compile time. The compile time is found inside the PE structure as a member called TimeDateStamp in the NT headers. The compile time value should be taken into limited consideration because this value can be faked easily.

9. Figure 13-42 shows the file's machine value. The machine value is a member in the NT headers structure, and it can have one of two values: 0x014C, which indicates a 32-bit Windows PE file, or 0x8664, which indicates a 64-bit Windows PE file.

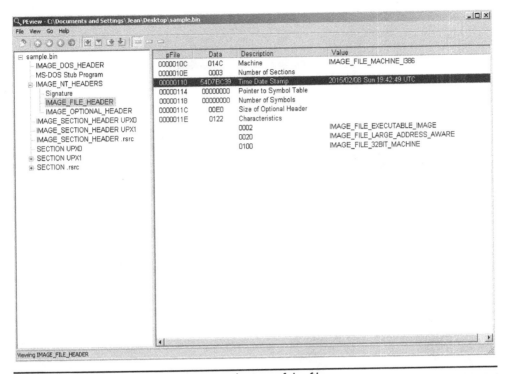

Figure 13-41 *PEView showing the compile time of the file.*

10. Looking at the PEView windows, it is easy to notice one section name. Sometimes the PE section name can give you some information about the file. In this example, the PE section names that can be seen are UPX0, UPX1, and .rsrc, as shown in Figure 13-43. UPX0 and UPX1 indicate that the file has been packed with UPX. PEView is the third tool that confirms the file is packed with UPX. The first two are the GNU file and strings command line.

11. The section named .rsrc suggests that the file contains a resource section. This is a good place to extract some useful information. For this purpose, you will use Resource Hacker, which allows you to look at the resources

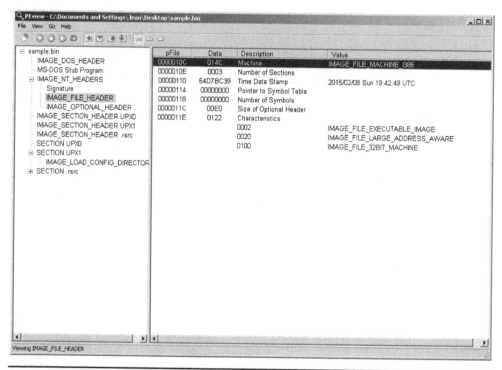

Figure 13-42 *PEView showing the file's machine value.*

embedded into the binary, as shown in Figure 13-44. Notice the suspicious little resource SCRIPT that is under RCDATA. This may be the AutoIt script in an encrypted format.

12. Get Imports/Exports information. A great tool for this specific purpose is Dependency Walker. This tool shows all the libraries imported by the binary and which functions are imported from each library (green) as well as all the exported functions of each library and the binary, if any. Figure 13-45 shows this.

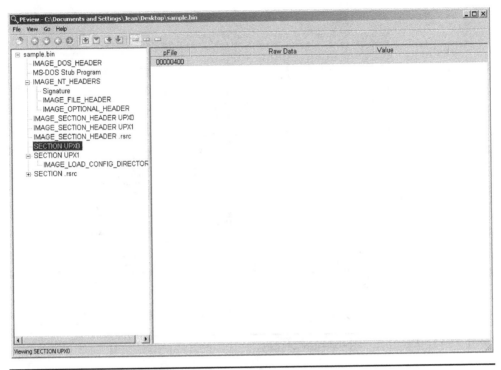

Figure 13-43 *PEView showing UPX section.*

13. Some of the information including the MD5 hash, strings, size, and compile time can be collected using Malcode Analyst Pack. This also enables you to submit the file to VirusTotal or simply run a query to check whether security products already detect the file.

14. You can now proceed to dynamic analysis. You will be using a clean malware analysis system that you built from previous labs. For this example, you will be using a virtual machine.

15. Run Process Explorer, Process Monitor, and TCPView in the malware analysis system (guest OS) or sandbox. Doing this will start their monitoring functionality.

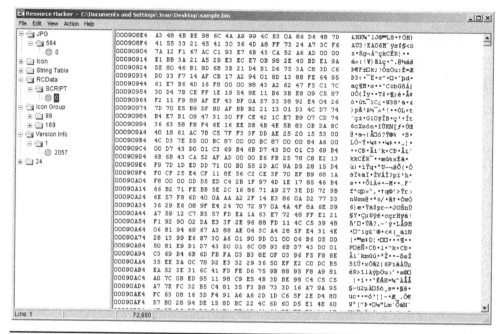

Figure 13-44   *Resource Hacker view of .rsrc.*

> ### TIP
>
> *Having these tools run in clean systems makes you familiar with the output of these tools in a clean system, which is good for baselining. Doing this will give you experience spotting something out of the ordinary in case you are using these tools to determine a possible infection and not for analyzing a specific malware sample.*

16. Run Wireshark in promiscuous mode on the host OS. Make sure you are capturing communication traffic on the network adapter that the VM is connected to. In this lab, the name of the interface is vmnet8.

17. Once everything is set, run the malware sample.

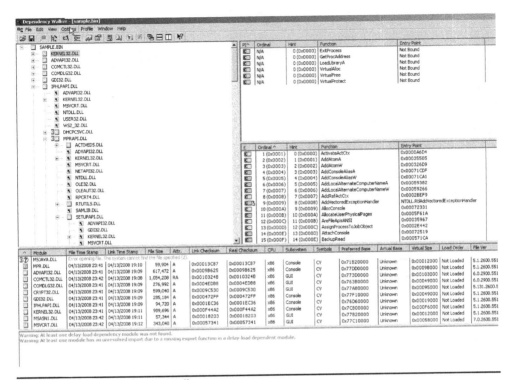

Figure 13-45   *Dependency Walker.*

18. Watch closely and take notes on both TCPView's and Process Explorer's
     windows. In Process Explorer, look for any new processes/children exiting
     and dying. New sessions/processes are green, and those that are killed are
     red. In TCPView, look for any network sessions being created and dropped.
     See Figures 13-46, 13-47, and 13-48.

19. Take notes of all these traces. It will give you some insight later during
     analysis.

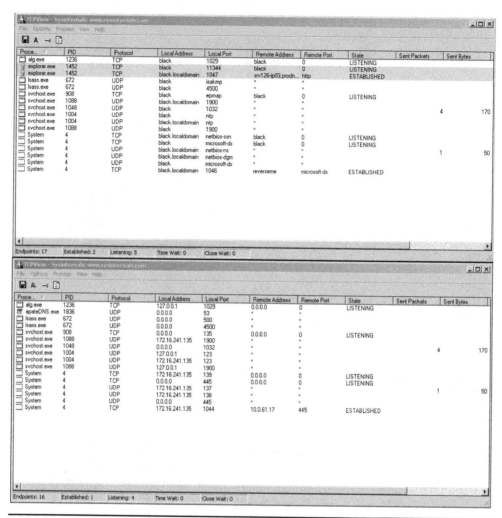

Figure 13-46 *Two instances of TCPView output.*

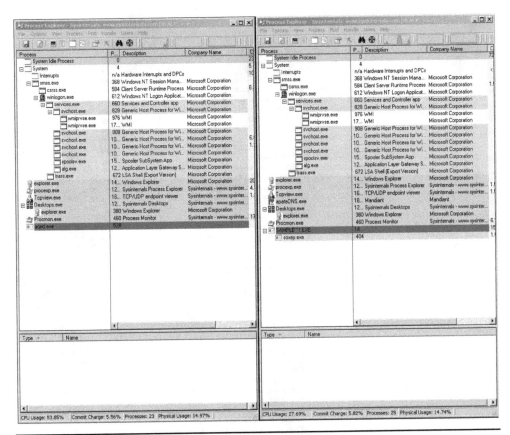

Figure 13-47 *Two instances of Process Explorer output.*

20. Check out the output of Wireshark running in the host OS. Figure 13-49 shows this.

21. Let the sample run for a few minutes.

22. After letting the sample run for a few minutes, stop the captures on both Process Monitor and Wireshark. Save the capture log from Process Monitor and save the pcap capture from Wireshark.

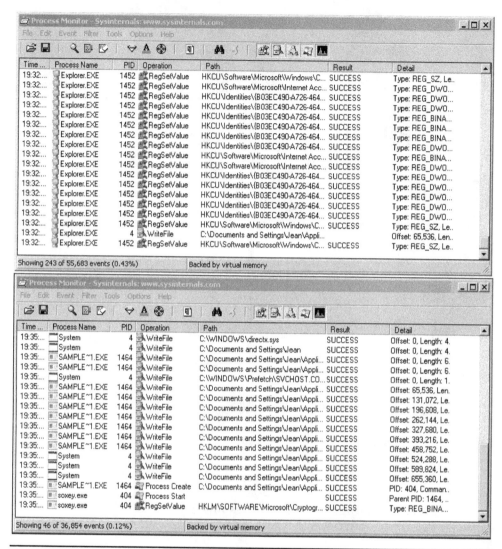

Figure 13-48 *Two instances of Process Monitor output.*

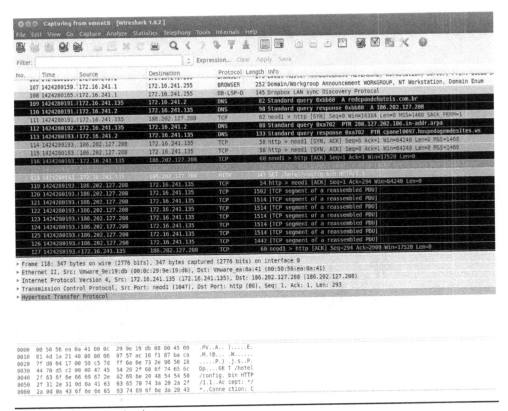

Figure 13-49   *Wireshark output.*

23. Pause the VM.

24. Let's analyze the pcap capture from Wireshark. You should be able to see a few Domain Name System (DNS) queries followed by an HTTP GET request downloading a file called config.bin, as shown in Figure 13-50. Take note of the filter.

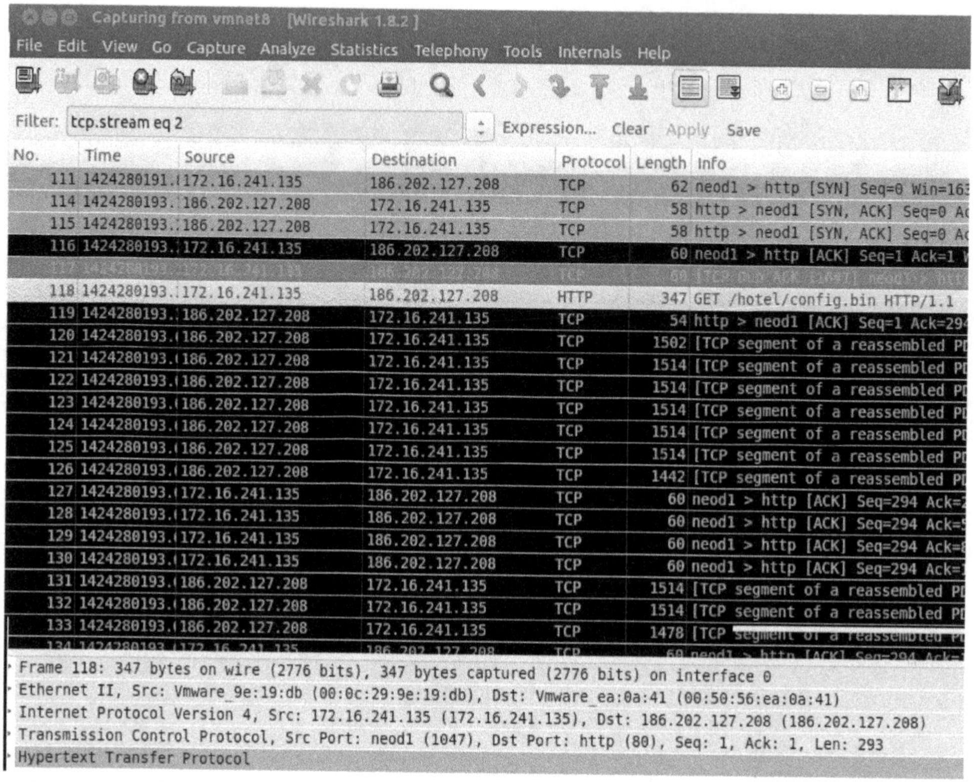

Figure 13-50 *HTTP GET request in Wireshark.*

25. Follow the TCP stream of the HTTP GET request. Figure 13-51 shows the result. Take note of the address redepandehoteis.com.br/hotel/config.bin. You got redepandehoteis.com from the Host section and /hotel/config.bin from the GET request.

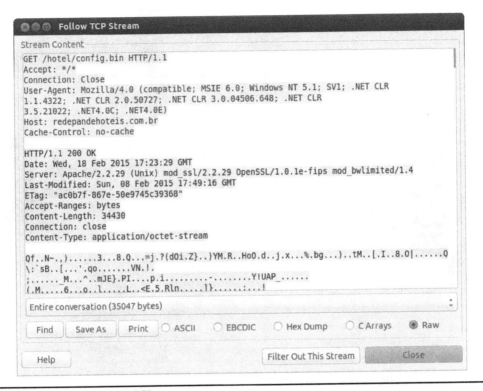

Figure 13-51 *HTTP GET TCP stream.*

26. Next you see a few HTTP POST requests to the same server, as shown in Figure 13-52. Take note of the address redepandehoteis.com.br/hotel/gate .php.

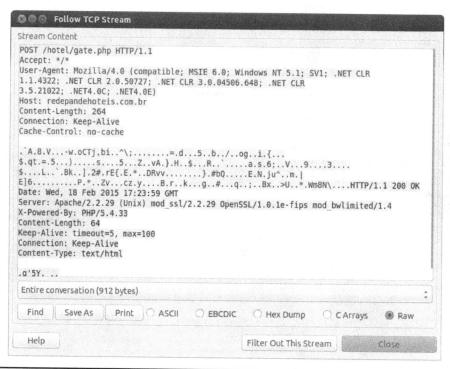

Figure 13-52 *HTTP POST TCP stream.*

27. Let's go to the capture log from Process Monitor. Process Monitor captures the file's activity in the following: processes, the registry, and files. For the purpose of this lab, you will group the file activities by deployment process, persistency mechanism, browser settings, and malicious activity. This means you will identify which of the malware activities in the processes, the registry, and files have contributed to the deployment process, persistency mechanism, browser settings, and malicious activity.

The following are the tables for the deployment process.

Here is the table for processes:

Explorer.EXE	1452	Process Create	C:\WINDOWS\svchost.com	SUCCESS	PID: 1772	Command line: "C:\WINDOWS\svchost.com" "C:\DOCUME~1\xxx\Desktop\SAMPLE~1.EXE"
svchost.com	1772	Process Start		SUCCESS	Parent PID: 1452	Command line: "C:\WINDOWS\svchost.com" "C:\DOCUME~1\xxx\Desktop\SAMPLE~1.EXE"
svchost.com	1772	Process Create	C:\DOCUME~1\xxx\Desktop\SAMPLE~1.EXE	SUCCESS	PID: 1408	Command line: C:\DOCUME~1\xxx\Desktop\SAMPLE~1.EXE
SAMPLE~1.EXE	1408	Process Start		SUCCESS	Parent PID: 1772	Command line: C:\DOCUME~1\xxx\Desktop\SAMPLE~1.EXE
svchost.com	1772	Process Exit		SUCCESS	Exit Status: 0	
SAMPLE~1.EXE	1408	Process Create	C:\DOCUME~1\xxx\Desktop\SAMPLE~1.EXE	SUCCESS	PID: 984	Command line: C:\DOCUME~1\xxx\Desktop\SAMPLE~1.EXE
SAMPLE~1.EXE	984	Process Start		SUCCESS	Parent PID: 1408	Command line: C:\DOCUME~1\xxx\Desktop\SAMPLE~1.EXE
SAMPLE~1.EXE	1408	Process Exit		SUCCESS	Exit Status: 0	
SAMPLE~1.EXE	984	Process Create	C:\Documents and Settings\xxx\Application Data\Ulkua\soul.exe	SUCCESS	PID: 1732	Command line: "C:\Documents and Settings\xxx\Application Data\Ulkua\soul.exe"
soul.exe	1732	Process Start		SUCCESS	Parent PID: 984	Command line: "C:\Documents and Settings\xxx\Application Data\Ulkua\soul.exe"
soul.exe	1732	Process Create	C:\Documents and Settings\xxx\Application Data\Ulkua\soul.exe	SUCCESS	PID: 1516	Command line: "C:\Documents and Settings\xxx\Application Data\Ulkua\soul.exe"
soul.exe	1516	Process Start		SUCCESS	Parent PID: 1732	Command line: "C:\Documents and Settings\xxx\Application Data\Ulkua\soul.exe"
soul.exe	1732	Process Exit		SUCCESS	Exit Status: 0	
SAMPLE~1.EXE	984	Process Create	C:\WINDOWS\system32\cmd.exe	SUCCESS	PID: 488	Command line: "C:\WINDOWS\system32\cmd.exe" /c "C:\DOCUME~1\xxx\LOCALS~1\Temp\tmp80419312.bat"
cmd.exe	488	Process Start		SUCCESS	Parent PID: 984	Command line: "C:\WINDOWS\system32\cmd.exe" /c "C:\DOCUME~1\xxx\LOCALS~1\Temp\tmp80419312.bat"
SAMPLE~1.EXE	984	Process Exit		SUCCESS	Exit Status: 0	
cmd.exe	488	Process Exit		SUCCESS	Exit Status: 1	
soul.exe	1516	Process Exit		SUCCESS	Exit Status: 0	

Here is the table for files:

svchost.exe	1004	WriteFile	C:\WINDOWS\Prefetch\SAMPLE~1.EXE-12C79E79.pf	SUCCESS	Offset: 0	Length: 18
cmd.exe	488	SetDispositionInformationFile	C:\Documents and Settings\xxx\Desktop\sample.bin.exe	SUCCESS	Delete: True	
cmd.exe	488	SetDispositionInformationFile	C:\Documents and Settings\xxx\Local Settings\Temp\tmp80419312.bat	SUCCESS	Delete: True	
svchost.exe	1004	WriteFile	C:\WINDOWS\Prefetch\CMD.EXE-087B4001.pf	SUCCESS	Offset: 0	Length: 11

The following tables relate to the persistency mechanism.

Here is the table for the registry:

Explorer.EXE	1452	RegSetValue	HKCU\Software\Microsoft\Windows\CurrentVersion\Run\{9EBEC959-DCC9-EA18-5427-D5C9258D0AD8}	SUCCESS	Type: REG_SZ	Length: 130	Data: "C:\Documents and Settings\xxx\Application Data\Ulkua\soul.exe"
Explorer.EXE	1452	RegSetValue	HKCU\Software\Microsoft\Windows\CurrentVersion\Run\{9EBEC959-DCC9-EA18-5427-D5C9258D0AD8}	SUCCESS	Type: REG_SZ	Length: 130	Data: "C:\Documents and Settings\xxx\Application Data\Ulkua\soul.exe"
Explorer.EXE	1452	RegSetValue	HKCU\Software\Microsoft\Windows\CurrentVersion\Run\{9EBEC959-DCC9-EA18-5427-D5C9258D0AD8}	SUCCESS	Type: REG_SZ	Length: 130	Data: "C:\Documents and Settings\xxx\Application Data\Ulkua\soul.exe"
Explorer.EXE	1452	RegSetValue	HKCU\Software\Microsoft\Windows\CurrentVersion\Run\{9EBEC959-DCC9-EA18-5427-D5C9258D0AD8}	SUCCESS	Type: REG_SZ	Length: 130	Data: "C:\Documents and Settings\xxx\Application Data\Ulkua\soul.exe"
Explorer.EXE	1452	RegSetValue	HKCU\Software\Microsoft\Rupe\Katifa	SUCCESS	Type: REG_BINARY	Length: 116	Data: 72 9A 1D 2D 6A 6B EF DC 7F EF F4 FD 07 EB F3 07
Explorer.EXE	1452	RegSetValue	HKCU\Software\Microsoft\Rupe\Katifa	SUCCESS	Type: REG_BINARY	Length: 116	Data: 72 9A 1D 2D 6A 6B EF DC 7F EF F4 FD 07 EB F3 07
apateDNS.exe	1836	RegSetValue	HKCU\Software\Microsoft\Rupe\Katifa	SUCCESS	Type: REG_BINARY	Length: 116	Data: 72 9A 1D 2D 6A 6B EF DC 7F EF F4 FD 07 EB F3 07
Desktops.exe	1292	RegSetValue	HKCU\Software\Microsoft\Rupe\Katifa	SUCCESS	Type: REG_BINARY	Length: 116	Data: 72 9A 1D 2D 6A 6B EF DC 7F EF F4 FD 07 EB F3 07
Explorer.exe	380	RegSetValue	HKCU\Software\Microsoft\Rupe\Katifa	SUCCESS	Type: REG_BINARY	Length: 116	Data: 72 9A 1D 2D 6A 6B EF DC 7F EF F4 FD 07 EB F3 07

Here is the table for the files:

SAMPLE~1.EXE	984	WriteFile	C:\Documents and Settings\xxx\Application Data\Ulkua\soul.exe	SUCCESS	Offset: 0	Length: 668

The following tables relate to browser settings.

Here is the table for the registry:

Explorer.E XE	1452	RegSetValue	HKCU\Software\Microsoft\Internet Explorer\Privacy\CleanCookies	SUCCESS	Type: REG_DWORD	Length: 4	Data: 0
Explorer.E XE	1452	RegSetValue	HKCU\Software\Microsoft\Windows\CurrentVersion\Internet Settings\Zones\0\1609	SUCCESS	Type: REG_DWORD	Length: 4	Data: 0
Explorer.E XE	1452	RegSetValue	HKCU\Software\Microsoft\Windows\CurrentVersion\Internet Settings\Zones\1\1406	SUCCESS	Type: REG_DWORD	Length: 4	Data: 0
Explorer.E XE	1452	RegSetValue	HKCU\Software\Microsoft\Windows\CurrentVersion\Internet Settings\Zones\1\1609	SUCCESS	Type: REG_DWORD	Length: 4	Data: 0
Explorer.E XE	1452	RegSetValue	HKCU\Software\Microsoft\Windows\CurrentVersion\Internet Settings\Zones\2\1609	SUCCESS	Type: REG_DWORD	Length: 4	Data: 0
Explorer.E XE	1452	RegSetValue	HKCU\Software\Microsoft\Windows\CurrentVersion\Internet Settings\Zones\3\1406	SUCCESS	Type: REG_DWORD	Length: 4	Data: 0
Explorer.E XE	1452	RegSetValue	HKCU\Software\Microsoft\Windows\CurrentVersion\Internet Settings\Zones\3\1609	SUCCESS	Type: REG_DWORD	Length: 4	Data: 0
Explorer.E XE	1452	RegSetValue	HKCU\Software\Microsoft\Windows\CurrentVersion\Internet Settings\Zones\4\1406	SUCCESS	Type: REG_DWORD	Length: 4	Data: 0
Explorer.E XE	1452	RegSetValue	HKCU\Software\Microsoft\Windows\CurrentVersion\Internet Settings\Zones\4\1609	SUCCESS	Type: REG_DWORD	Length: 4	Data: 0
Explorer.E XE	1452	RegSetValue	HKCU\Software\Microsoft\Windows\CurrentVersion\Run\{9EBEC959-DCC9-EA18-5427-D5C9258D0AD8}	SUCCESS	Type: REG_SZ	Length: 130	Data: "C:\Documents and Settings\xxx\Application Data\Ulkua\soul.exe"
Explorer.E XE	1452	RegSetValue	HKCU\Software\Microsoft\Windows\CurrentVersion\Internet Settings\MigrateProxy	SUCCESS	Type: REG_DWORD	Length: 4	Data: 1
Explorer.E XE	1452	RegSetValue	HKCU\Software\Microsoft\Windows\CurrentVersion\Internet Settings\ProxyEnable	SUCCESS	Type: REG_DWORD	Length: 4	Data: 0
Explorer.E XE	1452	RegDeleteValue	HKCU\Software\Microsoft\Windows\CurrentVersion\Internet Settings\ProxyServer	NAME NOT FOUND			
Explorer.E XE	1452	RegDeleteValue	HKCU\Software\Microsoft\Windows\CurrentVersion\Internet Settings\ProxyOverride	NAME NOT FOUND			
Explorer.E XE	1452	RegDeleteValue	HKCU\Software\Microsoft\Windows\CurrentVersion\Internet Settings\AutoConfigURL	NAME NOT FOUND			
Explorer.E XE	1452	RegSetValue	HKLM\System\CurrentControlSet\Hardware Profiles\0001\Software\Microsoft\windows\CurrentVersion\Internet Settings\ProxyEnable	SUCCESS	Type: REG_DWORD	Length: 4	Data: 0
Explorer.E XE	1452	RegSetValue	HKCU\Software\Microsoft\Windows\CurrentVersion\Internet Settings\Connections\SavedLegacySettings	SUCCESS	Type: REG_BINARY	Length: 56	Data: 3C 00 00 00 1A 00 00 00 01 00 00 00 00 00 00 00 00
Explorer.E XE	1452	RegSetValue	HKCU\Software\Microsoft\Internet Account Manager\Accounts\Active Directory GC\LDAP Server ID	SUCCESS	Type: REG_DWORD	Length: 4	Data: 0
Explorer.E XE	1452	RegSetValue	HKCU\Software\Microsoft\Internet Account Manager\Accounts\Bigfoot\LDAP Server ID	SUCCESS	Type: REG_DWORD	Length: 4	Data: 1
Explorer.E XE	1452	RegSetValue	HKCU\Software\Microsoft\Internet Account Manager\Accounts\VeriSign\LDAP Server ID	SUCCESS	Type: REG_DWORD	Length: 4	Data: 2
Explorer.E XE	1452	RegSetValue	HKCU\Software\Microsoft\Internet Account Manager\Accounts\WhoWhere\LDAP Server ID	SUCCESS	Type: REG_DWORD	Length: 4	Data: 3
Explorer.E XE	1452	RegSetValue	HKCU\Software\Microsoft\Internet Account Manager\Server ID	SUCCESS	Type: REG_DWORD	Length: 4	Data: 4
Explorer.E XE	1452	RegSetValue	HKCU\Software\Microsoft\Internet Account Manager\Accounts\PreConfigVer	SUCCESS	Type: REG_DWORD	Length: 4	Data: 4

Explorer.E XE	1452	RegSetValue	HKCU\Software\Microsoft\Internet Account Manager\Accounts\PreConfigVerNTDS	SUCCESS	Type: REG_DWORD	Length: 4	Data: 1
Explorer.E XE	1452	RegSetValue	HKCU\Software\Microsoft\Internet Account Manager\Accounts\Active Directory GC\Account Name	SUCCESS	Type: REG_SZ	Length: 34	Data: Active Directory
Explorer.E XE	1452	RegSetValue	HKCU\Software\Microsoft\Internet Account Manager\Accounts\Active Directory GC\LDAP Server	SUCCESS	Type: REG_SZ	Length: 10	Data: NULL
Explorer.E XE	1452	RegSetValue	HKCU\Software\Microsoft\Internet Account Manager\Accounts\Active Directory GC\LDAP Search Return	SUCCESS	Type: REG_DWORD	Length: 4	Data: 100
Explorer.E XE	1452	RegSetValue	HKCU\Software\Microsoft\Internet Account Manager\Accounts\Active Directory GC\LDAP Timeout	SUCCESS	Type: REG_DWORD	Length: 4	Data: 60
Explorer.E XE	1452	RegSetValue	HKCU\Software\Microsoft\Internet Account Manager\Accounts\Active Directory GC\LDAP Authentication	SUCCESS	Type: REG_DWORD	Length: 4	Data: 2
Explorer.E XE	1452	RegSetValue	HKCU\Software\Microsoft\Internet Account Manager\Accounts\Active Directory GC\LDAP Simple Search	SUCCESS	Type: REG_DWORD	Length: 4	Data: 0
Explorer.E XE	1452	RegSetValue	HKCU\Software\Microsoft\Internet Account Manager\Accounts\Active Directory GC\LDAP Bind DN	SUCCESS	Type: REG_DWORD	Length: 4	Data: 0
Explorer.E XE	1452	RegSetValue	HKCU\Software\Microsoft\Internet Account Manager\Accounts\Active Directory GC\LDAP Port	SUCCESS	Type: REG_DWORD	Length: 4	Data: 3268
Explorer.E XE	1452	RegSetValue	HKCU\Software\Microsoft\Internet Account Manager\Accounts\Active Directory GC\LDAP Resolve Flag	SUCCESS	Type: REG_DWORD	Length: 4	Data: 1
Explorer.E XE	1452	RegSetValue	HKCU\Software\Microsoft\Internet Account Manager\Accounts\Active Directory GC\LDAP Secure Connection	SUCCESS	Type: REG_DWORD	Length: 4	Data: 0
Explorer.E XE	1452	RegSetValue	HKCU\Software\Microsoft\Internet Account Manager\Accounts\Active Directory GC\LDAP User Name	SUCCESS	Type: REG_SZ	Length: 10	Data: NULL
Explorer.E XE	1452	RegSetValue	HKCU\Software\Microsoft\Internet Account Manager\Accounts\Active Directory GC\LDAP Search Base	SUCCESS	Type: REG_SZ	Length: 10	Data: NULL
Explorer.E XE	1452	RegSetValue	HKCU\Software\Microsoft\Internet Account Manager\Accounts\Bigfoot\Account Name	SUCCESS	Type: REG_SZ	Length: 70	Data: Bigfoot Internet Directory Service
Explorer.E XE	1452	RegSetValue	HKCU\Software\Microsoft\Internet Account Manager\Accounts\Bigfoot\LDAP Server	SUCCESS	Type: REG_SZ	Length: 34	Data: ldap.bigfoot.com
Explorer.E XE	1452	RegSetValue	HKCU\Software\Microsoft\Internet Account Manager\Accounts\Bigfoot\LDAP URL	SUCCESS	Type: REG_SZ	Length: 46	Data: http://www.bigfoot.com
Explorer.E XE	1452	RegSetValue	HKCU\Software\Microsoft\Internet Account Manager\Accounts\Bigfoot\LDAP Search Return	SUCCESS	Type: REG_DWORD	Length: 4	Data: 100
Explorer.E XE	1452	RegSetValue	HKCU\Software\Microsoft\Internet Account Manager\Accounts\Bigfoot\LDAP Timeout	SUCCESS	Type: REG_DWORD	Length: 4	Data: 60
Explorer.E XE	1452	RegSetValue	HKCU\Software\Microsoft\Internet Account Manager\Accounts\Bigfoot\LDAP Authentication	SUCCESS	Type: REG_DWORD	Length: 4	Data: 0
Explorer.E XE	1452	RegSetValue	HKCU\Software\Microsoft\Internet Account Manager\Accounts\Bigfoot\LDAP Simple Search	SUCCESS	Type: REG_DWORD	Length: 4	Data: 1
Explorer.E XE	1452	RegSetValue	HKCU\Software\Microsoft\Internet Account Manager\Accounts\Bigfoot\LDAP Logo	SUCCESS	Type: REG_EXPAND_SZ	Length: 98	Data: %ProgramFiles%\Common Files\Services\bigfoot.bmp
Explorer.E XE	1452	RegSetValue	HKCU\Software\Microsoft\Internet Account Manager\Accounts\VeriSign\Account Name	SUCCESS	Type: REG_SZ	Length: 72	Data: VeriSign Internet Directory Service
Explorer.E XE	1452	RegSetValue	HKCU\Software\Microsoft\Internet Account Manager\Accounts\VeriSign\LDAP Server	SUCCESS	Type: REG_SZ	Length: 46	Data: directory.verisign.com
Explorer.E XE	1452	RegSetValue	HKCU\Software\Microsoft\Internet Account Manager\Accounts\VeriSign\LDAP URL	SUCCESS	Type: REG_SZ	Length: 48	Data: http://www.verisign.com

Process	PID	Operation	Path	Result	Type	Length	Data
Explorer.EXE	1452	RegSetValue	HKCU\Software\Microsoft\Internet Account Manager\Accounts\VeriSign\LDAP Search Return	SUCCESS	Type: REG_DWORD	Length: 4	Data: 100
Explorer.EXE	1452	RegSetValue	HKCU\Software\Microsoft\Internet Account Manager\Accounts\VeriSign\LDAP Timeout	SUCCESS	Type: REG_DWORD	Length: 4	Data: 60
Explorer.EXE	1452	RegSetValue	HKCU\Software\Microsoft\Internet Account Manager\Accounts\VeriSign\LDAP Authentication	SUCCESS	Type: REG_DWORD	Length: 4	Data: 0
Explorer.EXE	1452	RegSetValue	HKCU\Software\Microsoft\Internet Account Manager\Accounts\VeriSign\LDAP Search Base	SUCCESS	Type: REG_SZ	Length: 10	Data: NULL
Explorer.EXE	1452	RegSetValue	HKCU\Software\Microsoft\Internet Account Manager\Accounts\VeriSign\LDAP Simple Search	SUCCESS	Type: REG_DWORD	Length: 4	Data: 1
Explorer.EXE	1452	RegSetValue	HKCU\Software\Microsoft\Internet Account Manager\Accounts\VeriSign\LDAP Logo	SUCCESS	Type: REG_EXPAND_SZ	Length: 100	Data: %ProgramFiles%\Common Files\Services\verisign.bmp
Explorer.EXE	1452	RegSetValue	HKCU\Software\Microsoft\Internet Account Manager\Accounts\WhoWhere\Account Name	SUCCESS	Type: REG_SZ	Length: 72	Data: WhoWhere Internet Directory Service
Explorer.EXE	1452	RegSetValue	HKCU\Software\Microsoft\Internet Account Manager\Accounts\WhoWhere\LDAP Server	SUCCESS	Type: REG_SZ	Length: 36	Data: ldap.whowhere.com
Explorer.EXE	1452	RegSetValue	HKCU\Software\Microsoft\Internet Account Manager\Accounts\WhoWhere\LDAP URL	SUCCESS	Type: REG_SZ	Length: 48	Data: http://www.whowhere.com
Explorer.EXE	1452	RegSetValue	HKCU\Software\Microsoft\Internet Account Manager\Accounts\WhoWhere\LDAP Search Return	SUCCESS	Type: REG_DWORD	Length: 4	Data: 100
Explorer.EXE	1452	RegSetValue	HKCU\Software\Microsoft\Internet Account Manager\Accounts\WhoWhere\LDAP Timeout	SUCCESS	Type: REG_DWORD	Length: 4	Data: 60
Explorer.EXE	1452	RegSetValue	HKCU\Software\Microsoft\Internet Account Manager\Accounts\WhoWhere\LDAP Authentication	SUCCESS	Type: REG_DWORD	Length: 4	Data: 0
Explorer.EXE	1452	RegSetValue	HKCU\Software\Microsoft\Internet Account Manager\Accounts\WhoWhere\LDAP Simple Search	SUCCESS	Type: REG_DWORD	Length: 4	Data: 1
Explorer.EXE	1452	RegSetValue	HKCU\Software\Microsoft\Internet Account Manager\Accounts\WhoWhere\LDAP Logo	SUCCESS	Type: REG_EXPAND_SZ	Length: 100	Data: %ProgramFiles%\Common Files\Services\whowhere.bmp
Explorer.EXE	1452	RegSetValue	HKCU\Software\Microsoft\Internet Account Manager\Accounts\PreConfigVer	SUCCESS	Type: REG_DWORD	Length: 4	Data: 4
Explorer.EXE	1452	RegSetValue	HKCU\Software\Microsoft\Internet Account Manager\Default LDAP Account	SUCCESS	Type: REG_SZ	Length: 40	Data: Active Directory GC
Explorer.EXE	1452	RegSetValue	HKCU\Software\Microsoft\Internet Account Manager\Server ID	SUCCESS	Type: REG_DWORD	Length: 4	Data: 4
Explorer.EXE	1452	RegSetValue	HKCU\Software\Microsoft\Windows\CurrentVersion\Explorer\Shell Folders\AppData	SUCCESS	Type: REG_SZ	Length: 96	Data: C:\Documents and Settings\xxx\Application Data
Explorer.EXE	1452	RegSetValue	HKCU\Software\Microsoft\Windows\CurrentVersion\Internet Settings\MigrateProxy	SUCCESS	Type: REG_DWORD	Length: 4	Data: 1
Explorer.EXE	1452	RegSetValue	HKCU\Software\Microsoft\Windows\CurrentVersion\Internet Settings\ProxyEnable	SUCCESS	Type: REG_DWORD	Length: 4	Data: 0
Explorer.EXE	1452	RegDeleteValue	HKCU\Software\Microsoft\Windows\CurrentVersion\Internet Settings\ProxyServer	NAME NOT FOUND			
Explorer.EXE	1452	RegDeleteValue	HKCU\Software\Microsoft\Windows\CurrentVersion\Internet Settings\ProxyOverride	NAME NOT FOUND			
Explorer.EXE	1452	RegDeleteValue	HKCU\Software\Microsoft\Windows\CurrentVersion\Internet Settings\AutoConfigURL	NAME NOT FOUND			
Explorer.EXE	1452	RegSetValue	HKLM\System\CurrentControlSet\Hardware Profiles\0001\Software\Microsoft\windows\CurrentVersion\Internet Settings\ProxyEnable	SUCCESS	Type: REG_DWORD	Length: 4	Data: 0
Explorer.EXE	1452	RegSetValue	HKCU\Software\Microsoft\Windows\CurrentVersion\Internet Settings\Connections\SavedLegacySettings	SUCCESS	Type: REG_BINARY	Length: 56	Data: 3C 00 00 00 1B 00 00 00 01 00 00 00 00 00 00 00

Here is the table for the files:

Explorer.EXE	1452	SetDispositionInformationFile	C:\Documents and Settings\xxx\Cookies\xxx@ads.yahoo[1].txt	SUCCESS	Delete: True	
Explorer.EXE	1452	SetDispositionInformationFile	C:\Documents and Settings\xxx\Cookies\xxx@atdmt[2].txt	SUCCESS	Delete: True	
Explorer.EXE	1452	SetDispositionInformationFile	C:\Documents and Settings\xxx\Cookies\xxx@auto.search.msn[1].txt	SUCCESS	Delete: True	
Explorer.EXE	1452	SetDispositionInformationFile	C:\Documents and Settings\xxx\Cookies\xxx@bing[1].txt	SUCCESS	Delete: True	
Explorer.EXE	1452	SetDispositionInformationFile	C:\Documents and Settings\xxx\Cookies\xxx@browser[1].txt	SUCCESS	Delete: True	
Explorer.EXE	1452	SetDispositionInformationFile	C:\Documents and Settings\xxx\Cookies\xxx@c.atdmt[2].txt	SUCCESS	Delete: True	
Explorer.EXE	1452	SetDispositionInformationFile	C:\Documents and Settings\xxx\Cookies\xxx@c.bing[2].txt	SUCCESS	Delete: True	
Explorer.EXE	1452	SetDispositionInformationFile	C:\Documents and Settings\xxx\Cookies\xxx@c.il.msn[2].txt	SUCCESS	Delete: True	
Explorer.EXE	1452	SetDispositionInformationFile	C:\Documents and Settings\xxx\Cookies\xxx@google[1].txt	SUCCESS	Delete: True	
Explorer.EXE	1452	SetDispositionInformationFile	C:\Documents and Settings\xxx\Cookies\xxx@hit.gemius[2].txt	SUCCESS	Delete: True	
Explorer.EXE	1452	SetDispositionInformationFile	C:\Documents and Settings\xxx\Cookies\xxx@il.msn[2].txt	SUCCESS	Delete: True	
Explorer.EXE	1452	SetDispositionInformationFile	C:\Documents and Settings\xxx\Cookies\xxx@invitemedia[1].txt	SUCCESS	Delete: True	
Explorer.EXE	1452	SetDispositionInformationFile	C:\Documents and Settings\xxx\Cookies\xxx@microsoft[1].txt	SUCCESS	Delete: True	
Explorer.EXE	1452	SetDispositionInformationFile	C:\Documents and Settings\xxx\Cookies\xxx@msn[1].txt	SUCCESS	Delete: True	
Explorer.EXE	1452	SetDispositionInformationFile	C:\Documents and Settings\xxx\Cookies\xxx@privacy[2].txt	SUCCESS	Delete: True	
Explorer.EXE	1452	SetDispositionInformationFile	C:\Documents and Settings\xxx\Cookies\xxx@scorecardresearch[2].txt	SUCCESS	Delete: True	
Explorer.EXE	1452	SetDispositionInformationFile	C:\Documents and Settings\xxx\Cookies\xxx@ssl.bing[2].txt	SUCCESS	Delete: True	
Explorer.EXE	1452	SetDispositionInformationFile	C:\Documents and Settings\xxx\Cookies\xxx@wireshark[1].txt	SUCCESS	Delete: True	
Explorer.EXE	1452	SetDispositionInformationFile	C:\Documents and Settings\xxx\Cookies\xxx@www.bing[2].txt	SUCCESS	Delete: True	
Explorer.EXE	1452	SetDispositionInformationFile	C:\Documents and Settings\xxx\Cookies\xxx@www.msn[1].txt	SUCCESS	Delete: True	
Explorer.EXE	1452	SetDispositionInformationFile	C:\Documents and Settings\xxx\Cookies\xxx@yahoo[2].txt	SUCCESS	Delete: True	

Here is the malicious activity for files:

svchos t.com	1772	WriteFile	C:\WINDOWS\directx.sys	SUCCESS	Offset: 0	Length: 137

28. Regarding browser settings, from the logs you can see that the malware is overwriting a lot of the system's browser settings as well as deleting cookies and proxy settings. The reason for this is that the malware does not want any interference with its operation and is eliminating potential interferences by doing that. Another reason for cookie deletion and emptying different caches is that the malware wants the user to log in to websites so the credentials can be stolen.

29. Regarding deployment, the logs reveal that the malware copies itself to the C:\Documents and Settings folder and eventually runs a batch file that creates and runs qyecy.EXE.

30. Regarding the persistency mechanism, the malware creates a registry key under HKCU\Software\Microsoft\Windows\CurrentVersion\Run, which is a known registry location to execute files during startup. The key name is {9EBEC959-DCC9-EA18-5427-D5C9258D0AD8}, and it contains the path to the malware's file location, which is C:\Documents and Settings\xxx\ Application Data\Ulkua\soul.exe.

31. Also notice that the following registry event repeats itself every few seconds. This will re-create the malware's persistency in case someone intentionally deletes it. The malware also saves some encrypted configuration data at HKCU\Software\Microsoft\Rupe\Katifa.

Explorer.E XE	1452	RegSetValue	HKCU\Software\Microsoft\Windows\CurrentV ersion\Run\{9EBEC959-DCC9-EA18-5427-D5C9258D0AD8}	SUCCESS	Type: REG_SZ	Length: 130	Data: "C:\Documents and Settings\xxx\Application Data\Ulkua\soul.exe"

32. Regarding malicious activity, at first glance it might seem that the file C:\ Windows\directx.sys dropped by the malware is a driver and that the malware has kernel mode capabilities, but this is not the case. The filename was carefully picked in order for it to blend in with the rest of the files in that folder. If you look at the contents of the file, you will see clear text separated by newline characters.

```
C:\ThinApps\SYSINT~1\Desktops.exe
C:\ThinApps\SYSINT~1\procexp.exe
C:\ThinApps\SYSINT~1\Procmon.exe
C:\ThinApps\SYSINT~1\Tcpview.exe
C:\ThinApps\RKU373~1\RKU373~1.EXE
C:\ThinApps\SYSINT~1\ROOTKI~1.EXE
```

This file is where the malware keeps a list of currently running processes.

33. You may have noticed that most suspicious registry events were initiated by a process named Explorer.EXE, which was running even before you ran the malware on the machine and is actually a legitimate Windows process that is responsible for Windows' graphical user interface (GUI) environment. Also, you may have noticed that some suspicious events happened more than once and were sometimes initiated by a few different processes that are also legitimate and were running before you infected the machine. The simple explanation for this is that this malware is creating a thread that runs the malware inside all processes that are already running on the machine. This process is called *code injection* or *thread injection*. When malware is injecting itself into a process, it is doing it to hide its process from showing when process listing occurs. This technique is usually utilized by a *user mode rootkit*.

34. Aside from code injection, another technique that is commonly used by user mode rootkits is *hooking*. User mode hooks are implemented in many creative ways; the most common techniques are IAT modification and inline patching.

    In IAT modification, the malware changes the IAT of each binary that is loaded by the OS in memory and changes the imported libraries and functions to their own malicious version of the same library containing the same functions with "extra functionality."

    With inline patching, the malware will patch the code of the library in memory in a way that prior to the execution of the function, it will jump to the malware's code, and after executing the malicious code, it will jump back to the original function and continue with the original function's execution flow.

    Both methods will not be detected by checking whether any of the operating system's file integrity was compromised because the malware is doing all its work in memory. As a result, no traces will be found in the original files in the file system.

> **NOTE**
>
> *Hooking techniques such as IAT modification and inline patching are also used by legitimate applications/programs; therefore, the existence of hooks does not necessarily mean that the machine is infected with malware.*

35. To check for hooks, you will scan the machine using Rootkit Unhooker. At this point, you should resume the VM and run Rootkit Unhooker. To scan for user mode hooks, go to the Code Hooks tab and click the Scan button. If there are code hooks on the infected system, it should look like Figure 13-53.

36. Save the output by going to the Report tab and clicking the Scan button. Uncheck all boxes except Code Hooks and click OK. Once the report is done, copy the text and save it to a file.

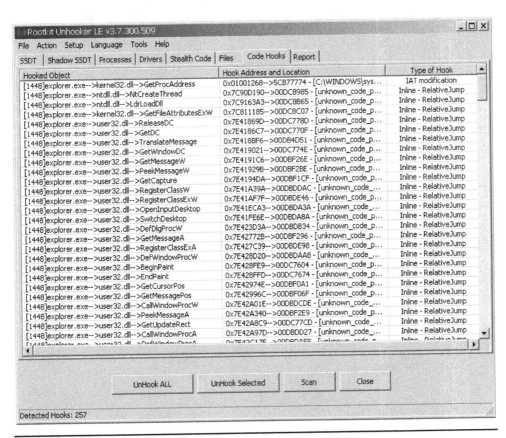

Figure 13-53 *Rootkit Unhooker output.*

37. The complete output with the result is shown here:

```
ntkrnlpa.exe+0x0006AA5A, Type: Inline - RelativeJump at address
0x80541A5A hook handler located in [ntkrnlpa.exe]
[1448]explorer.exe-->kernel32.dll-->GetFileAttributesExW, Type:
Inline - RelativeJump at address 0x7C811185 hook handler located
in [unknown_code_page]
[1448]explorer.exe-->kernel32.dll-->GetProcAddress, Type: IAT
modification at address 0x01001268 hook handler located in
[shimeng.dll]
[1448]explorer.exe-->ntdll.dll-->LdrLoadDll, Type: Inline -
RelativeJump at address 0x7C9163A3 hook handler located in
[unknown_code_page]
[1448]explorer.exe-->ntdll.dll-->NtCreateThread, Type: Inline
- RelativeJump at address 0x7C90D190 hook handler located in
[unknown_code_page]
[1448]explorer.exe-->user32.dll-->BeginPaint, Type: Inline
- RelativeJump at address 0x7E428FE9 hook handler located in
[unknown_code_page]
[1448]explorer.exe-->user32.dll-->CallWindowProcA, Type: Inline
- RelativeJump at address 0x7E42A97D hook handler located in
[unknown_code_page]
[1448]explorer.exe-->user32.dll-->CallWindowProcW, Type: Inline
- RelativeJump at address 0x7E42A01E hook handler located in
[unknown_code_page]
[1448]explorer.exe-->user32.dll-->DefDlgProcA, Type: Inline
- RelativeJump at address 0x7E43E577 hook handler located in
[unknown_code_page]
[1448]explorer.exe-->user32.dll-->DefDlgProcW, Type: Inline
- RelativeJump at address 0x7E423D3A hook handler located in
[unknown_code_page]
[1448]explorer.exe-->user32.dll-->DefFrameProcA, Type: Inline
- RelativeJump at address 0x7E44F965 hook handler located in
[unknown_code_page]
[1448]explorer.exe-->user32.dll-->DefFrameProcW, Type: Inline
- RelativeJump at address 0x7E430833 hook handler located in
[unknown_code_page]
[1448]explorer.exe-->user32.dll-->DefMDIChildProcA, Type: Inline
- RelativeJump at address 0x7E44F9B4 hook handler located in
[unknown_code_page]
[1448]explorer.exe-->user32.dll-->DefMDIChildProcW, Type: Inline
- RelativeJump at address 0x7E430A47 hook handler located in
[unknown_code_page]
```

```
[1448]explorer.exe-->user32.dll-->DefWindowProcA, Type: Inline
- RelativeJump at address 0x7E42C17E hook handler located in
[unknown_code_page]
[1448]explorer.exe-->user32.dll-->DefWindowProcW, Type: Inline
- RelativeJump at address 0x7E428D20 hook handler located in
[unknown_code_page]
[1448]explorer.exe-->user32.dll-->EndPaint, Type: Inline -
RelativeJump at address 0x7E428FFD hook handler located in
[unknown_code_page]
[1448]explorer.exe-->user32.dll-->GetCapture, Type: Inline
- RelativeJump at address 0x7E4194DA hook handler located in
[unknown_code_page]
[1448]explorer.exe-->user32.dll-->GetClipboardData, Type: Inline
- RelativeJump at address 0x7E430DBA hook handler located in
[unknown_code_page]
[1448]explorer.exe-->user32.dll-->GetCursorPos, Type: Inline
- RelativeJump at address 0x7E42974E hook handler located in
[unknown_code_page]
[1448]explorer.exe-->user32.dll-->GetDC, Type: Inline -
RelativeJump at address 0x7E4186C7 hook handler located in
[unknown_code_page]
[1448]explorer.exe-->user32.dll-->GetDCEx, Type: Inline -
RelativeJump at address 0x7E42C595 hook handler located in
[unknown_code_page]
[1448]explorer.exe-->user32.dll-->GetMessageA, Type: Inline
- RelativeJump at address 0x7E42772B hook handler located in
[unknown_code_page]
[1448]explorer.exe-->user32.dll-->GetMessagePos, Type: Inline
- RelativeJump at address 0x7E42996C hook handler located in
[unknown_code_page]
[1448]explorer.exe-->user32.dll-->GetMessageW, Type: Inline
- RelativeJump at address 0x7E4191C6 hook handler located in
[unknown_code_page]
[1448]explorer.exe-->user32.dll-->GetUpdateRect, Type: Inline
- RelativeJump at address 0x7E42A8C9 hook handler located in
[unknown_code_page]
[1448]explorer.exe-->user32.dll-->GetUpdateRgn, Type: Inline
- RelativeJump at address 0x7E42F5EC hook handler located in
[unknown_code_page]
[1448]explorer.exe-->user32.dll-->GetWindowDC, Type: Inline
- RelativeJump at address 0x7E419021 hook handler located in
[unknown_code_page]
```

[1448]explorer.exe-->user32.dll-->OpenInputDesktop, Type: Inline
- RelativeJump at address 0x7E41ECA3 hook handler located in
[unknown_code_page]
[1448]explorer.exe-->user32.dll-->PeekMessageA, Type: Inline
- RelativeJump at address 0x7E42A340 hook handler located in
[unknown_code_page]
[1448]explorer.exe-->user32.dll-->PeekMessageW, Type: Inline
- RelativeJump at address 0x7E41929B hook handler located in
[unknown_code_page]
[1448]explorer.exe-->user32.dll-->RegisterClassA, Type: Inline
- RelativeJump at address 0x7E42EA5E hook handler located in
[unknown_code_page]
[1448]explorer.exe-->user32.dll-->RegisterClassExA, Type: Inline
- RelativeJump at address 0x7E427C39 hook handler located in
[unknown_code_page]
[1448]explorer.exe-->user32.dll-->RegisterClassExW, Type: Inline
- RelativeJump at address 0x7E41AF7F hook handler located in
[unknown_code_page]
[1448]explorer.exe-->user32.dll-->RegisterClassW, Type: Inline
- RelativeJump at address 0x7E41A39A hook handler located in
[unknown_code_page]
[1448]explorer.exe-->user32.dll-->ReleaseCapture, Type: Inline
- RelativeJump at address 0x7E42C37A hook handler located in
[unknown_code_page]
[1448]explorer.exe-->user32.dll-->ReleaseDC, Type: Inline -
RelativeJump at address 0x7E41869D hook handler located in
[unknown_code_page]
[1448]explorer.exe-->user32.dll-->SetCapture, Type: Inline
- RelativeJump at address 0x7E42C35E hook handler located in
[unknown_code_page]
[1448]explorer.exe-->user32.dll-->SetCursorPos, Type: Inline
- RelativeJump at address 0x7E4561B3 hook handler located in
[unknown_code_page]
[1448]explorer.exe-->user32.dll-->SwitchDesktop, Type: Inline
- RelativeJump at address 0x7E41FE6E hook handler located in
[unknown_code_page]
[1448]explorer.exe-->user32.dll-->TranslateMessage, Type: Inline
- RelativeJump at address 0x7E418BF6 hook handler located in
[unknown_code_page]
[1448]explorer.exe-->wininet.dll-->HttpQueryInfoA, Type: Inline
- RelativeJump at address 0x771C79C2 hook handler located in
[unknown_code_page]

```
[1448]explorer.exe-->wininet.dll-->HttpSendRequestA, Type: Inline
- RelativeJump at address 0x771C60A1 hook handler located in
[unknown_code_page]
[1448]explorer.exe-->wininet.dll-->HttpSendRequestExA, Type:
Inline - RelativeJump at address 0x77212FC1 hook handler located
in [unknown_code_page]
[1448]explorer.exe-->wininet.dll-->HttpSendRequestExW, Type:
Inline - RelativeJump at address 0x771CE9C1 hook handler located
in [unknown_code_page]
[1448]explorer.exe-->wininet.dll-->HttpSendRequestW, Type: Inline
- RelativeJump at address 0x77212EBC hook handler located in
[unknown_code_page]
[1448]explorer.exe-->wininet.dll-->InternetCloseHandle, Type:
Inline - RelativeJump at address 0x771C4D8C hook handler located
in [unknown_code_page]
[1448]explorer.exe-->wininet.dll-->InternetQueryDataAvailable,
Type: Inline - RelativeJump at address 0x771D89F7 hook handler
located in [unknown_code_page]
[1448]explorer.exe-->wininet.dll-->InternetReadFile, Type: Inline
- RelativeJump at address 0x771C82EA hook handler located in
[unknown_code_page]
[1448]explorer.exe-->wininet.dll-->InternetReadFileExA, Type:
Inline - RelativeJump at address 0x771F9100 hook handler located
in [unknown_code_page]
[1448]explorer.exe-->ws2_32.dll-->closesocket, Type: Inline
- RelativeJump at address 0x71AB3E2B hook handler located in
[unknown_code_page]
[1448]explorer.exe-->ws2_32.dll-->send, Type: Inline -
RelativeJump at address 0x71AB4C27 hook handler located in
[unknown_code_page]
[1448]explorer.exe-->ws2_32.dll-->WSASend, Type: Inline -
RelativeJump at address 0x71AB68FA hook handler located in
[unknown_code_page]
!!POSSIBLE ROOTKIT ACTIVITY DETECTED!! =)
```

38. From this output, you can definitely say that you are dealing with a user
     mode rootkit. Also based on this output, this malware hooks functions in
     wininet.DLL and ws2_32.dll, which are libraries that deal with network
     communications and Hypertext Transfer Protocol (HTTP). By hooking
     functions in these libraries, the malware may be able to tamper with network
     traffic and set up a man-in-the-middle attack.

39. Next is dump analysis. This is done by taking a memory dump of the malicious process. In this case, the malware injected itself into each one of the running processes, with Explorer.EXE being the most significant. You will therefore pick Explorer.EXE as your memory dump's target. You can use either Process Explorer or Rootkit Unhooker to take a memory dump.

40. Dump a process with Process Explorer. Right-click the target process, which is Explorer.EXE, and go to Create Dump | Create Full Dump; then save the dump file. You can name the file MEMORY.DMP. See Figure 13-54.

41. Dump a process with Rootkit Unhooker. Go to the Processes tab. Right-click the target process, which is Explorer.EXE. Click Dump All Process Memory and save to a file. You can name the file MEMORY.DMP. See Figure 13-55.

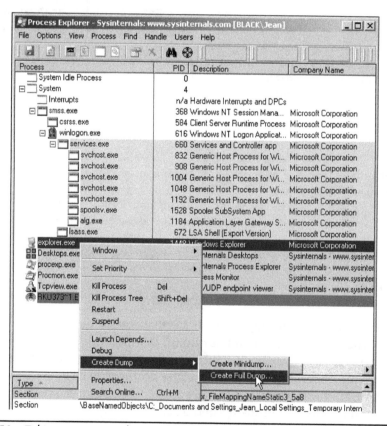

Figure 13-54   *Taking a memory dump using Process Explorer.*

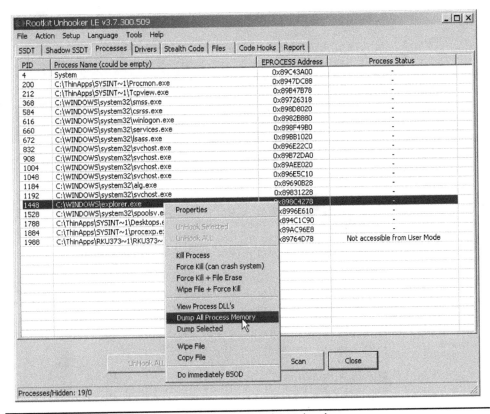

Figure 13-55 *Taking a memory dump using Rootkit Unhooker.*

42. Once you have the memory dump, you can proceed to analyze it using the different tools you have in your disposal. A basic analysis can start with the strings GNU command line or Sysinternals Strings.EXE.

43. In this lab, you will use the GNU strings command line and save the file to a text file named memory_dmp_strings.txt.

```
$ strings MEMORY.DMP > memory_dmp_strings.txt
```

> *TIP*
>
> *The output of strings is really huge; it's always a good idea to redirect the output to a file and review it with a text editor.*

44. The following is the output from strings:

```
-DTabD
pskill.exe
www.google.co.il
/C:\
ThinApps
pslist.exe
Desktop
Zeus
config.bin
r.ln
PsInfo.exe
www.google.com
RAMMap.exe
BlOgg
readme.txt
psping.exe
sync.exe
etwo
whois.exe
www.google.com
/jT"4
Microsoft Windows Network
Microsoft Network
[=#_
Vmmap.chm
Sign
ZoomIt.exe
/C:\
ThinApps
pskill.exe
www.google.com
O2Kp
www.google.co.il
Winobj.exe
'IK
WINOBJ.HLP
PsExec.exe
livekd.exe
PsInfo.exe
redepandehoteis.com.br
psfile.exe
```

```
Microsoft Windows Network
Microsoft Network
Eula.txt
redepandehoteis.com.br
DMON.SYS
Ay*$Lu
handle.exe
```

45. Grep for specific patterns such as *http*. You can do this together with strings by using a pipe.

```
$ strings MEMORY.DMP | grep http > memory_dmp_strings_http.txt
```

46. The following is the output:

```
$http://www.trustcenter.de/guidelines0
#http://www.entrust.net/CRL/net1.crl0+
&http://www.certplus.com/CRL/class3.crl0
5http://www.digsigtrust.com/DST_TRUST_CPS_v990701.html0
$http://crl.verisign.com/pca2.1.1.crl0G
http://pki.google.com/GIAG2.crt0+
http://clients1.google.com/ocsp0
http://pki.google.com/GIAG2.crl0
http://pki.google.com/GIAG2.crt0+
http://clients1.google.com/ocsp0
http://pki.google.com/GIAG2.crl0
http://redepandehoteis.com.br/hotel/bot.exe
http://redepandehoteis.com.br/hotel/bot.exe#N
http://redepandehoteis.com.br/hotel/gate.php
```

47. Notice the last three from the output; these strings are part of the config file that was downloaded at the beginning of the malware's execution.

48. What you have done is a basic dump analysis. There is a more advanced way of doing this. For this purpose, you will use the Volatility framework. As previously discussed, Volatility is a Python-based framework that allows a user to analyze the OS environment from a static dump file. It has many plug-ins that are useful when it comes to memory analysis. You can find a list of its basic plug-ins in Appendix C.

    Volatility analyzes .VMEM files created by VMware. Volatility also supports other virtualization products such as VirtualBox.

    To get started, you need to suspend the VM prior to analyzing the .VMEM.

49. Once the VM is suspended, copy the .VMEM file to your working folder. Let's assume your .VMEM file is Sandbox.VMEM.

50. Find API hooks (user mode hooks) using Volatility. For this purpose, you will use the apihooks plug-in.

```
$ vol.py apihooks -f Sandbox.vmem
```

51. The following is the output:

```
**********************************************************************
Hook mode: Usermode
Hook type: Inline/Trampoline
Process: 1448 (explorer.exe)
Victim module: ntdll.dll (0x7c900000 - 0x7c9af000)
Function: ntdll.dll!LdrLoadDll at 0x7c9163a3
Hook address: 0xdc8b65
Hooking module: <unknown>

Disassembly(0):
0x7c9163a3 e9bd274b84      JMP 0xdc8b65
0x7c9163a8 68f864917c      PUSH DWORD 0x7c9164f8
0x7c9163ad e8f984ffff      CALL 0x7c90e8ab
0x7c9163b2 a1c8b0977c      MOV EAX, [0x7c97b0c8]
0x7c9163b7 8945e4          MOV [EBP-0x1c], EAX
0x7c9163ba 8b              DB 0x8b

Disassembly(1):
0xdc8b65 55                PUSH EBP
0xdc8b66 8bec              MOV EBP, ESP
0xdc8b68 e8373f0000        CALL 0xdccaa4
0xdc8b6d 84c0              TEST AL, AL
0xdc8b6f 7507              JNZ 0xdc8b78
0xdc8b71 5d                POP EBP
0xdc8b72 ff25e039dd00      JMP DWORD [0xdd39e0]
0xdc8b78 53                PUSH EBX
0xdc8b79 56                PUSH ESI
0xdc8b7a 8b7514            MOV ESI, [EBP+0x14]


**********************************************************************
Hook mode: Usermode
Hook type: Inline/Trampoline
Process: 1448 (explorer.exe)
Victim module: ntdll.dll (0x7c900000 - 0x7c9af000)
Function: ntdll.dll!NtCreateThread at 0x7c90d190
Hook address: 0xdc8985
Hooking module: <unknown>
```

```
Disassembly(0):
0x7c90d190 e9f0b74b84      JMP 0xdc8985
0x7c90d195 ba0003fe7f      MOV EDX, 0x7ffe0300
0x7c90d19a ff12            CALL DWORD [EDX]
0x7c90d19c c22000          RET 0x20
0x7c90d19f 90              NOP
0x7c90d1a0 b836000000      MOV EAX, 0x36
0x7c90d1a5 ba              DB 0xba
0x7c90d1a6 0003            ADD [EBX], AL

Disassembly(1):
0xdc8985 55                PUSH EBP
0xdc8986 8bec              MOV EBP, ESP
0xdc8988 83e4f8            AND ESP, -0x8
0xdc898b 83ec20            SUB ESP, 0x20
0xdc898e 53                PUSH EBX
0xdc898f 57                PUSH EDI
0xdc8990 e80f410000        CALL 0xdccaa4
0xdc8995 8b7d14            MOV EDI, [EBP+0x14]
0xdc8998 84c0              TEST AL, AL
0xdc899a 747c              JZ 0xdc8a18
0xdc899c 8d                DB 0x8d
```

****

52. As shown in the output, the plug-in shows you each function that is hooked, what type of hook is used, and the original code versus the tampered code.

53. Find arbitrary malicious pieces of code. To do this, you will use the malfind plug-in, which allows you to find where exactly in a process memory the malware's injected code is.

    ```
    $ vol.py malfind -f Sandbox.vmem
    ```

54. The following is the output:

    ```
    Process: explorer.exe Pid: 1448 Address: 0xdb0000
    Vad Tag: VadS Protection: PAGE_EXECUTE_READWRITE
    Flags: CommitCharge: 39, MemCommit: 1, PrivateMemory: 1,
    Protection: 6

    0x00db0000  4d 5a 00 00 00 00 00 00 00 00 00 00 00 00 00 00
    MZ..............
    0x00db0010  00 00 00 00 00 00 00 00 00 00 00 00 00 00 00 00
    ................
    ```

```
0x00db0020   00 00 00 00 00 00 00 00 00 00 00 00 00 00 00 00
. . . . . . . . . . . . . . . .
0x00db0030   00 00 00 00 00 00 00 00 00 00 00 00 d8 00 00 00
. . . . . . . . . . . . . . .

0xdb0000 4d               DEC EBP
0xdb0001 5a               POP EDX
0xdb0002 0000             ADD [EAX], AL
0xdb0004 0000             ADD [EAX], AL
0xdb0006 0000             ADD [EAX], AL
0xdb0008 0000             ADD [EAX], AL
0xdb000a 0000             ADD [EAX], AL
0xdb000c 0000             ADD [EAX], AL
0xdb000e 0000             ADD [EAX], AL
0xdb0010 0000             ADD [EAX], AL
0xdb0012 0000             ADD [EAX], AL
0xdb0014 0000             ADD [EAX], AL
0xdb0016 0000             ADD [EAX], AL
0xdb0018 0000             ADD [EAX], AL
0xdb001a 0000             ADD [EAX], AL
0xdb001c 0000             ADD [EAX], AL
0xdb001e 0000             ADD [EAX], AL
0xdb0020 0000             ADD [EAX], AL
0xdb0022 0000             ADD [EAX], AL
0xdb0024 0000             ADD [EAX], AL
0xdb0026 0000             ADD [EAX], AL
0xdb0028 0000             ADD [EAX], AL
0xdb002a 0000             ADD [EAX], AL
0xdb002c 0000             ADD [EAX], AL
0xdb002e 0000             ADD [EAX], AL
0xdb0030 0000             ADD [EAX], AL
0xdb0032 0000             ADD [EAX], AL
0xdb0034 0000             ADD [EAX], AL
0xdb0036 0000             ADD [EAX], AL
0xdb0038 0000             ADD [EAX], AL
0xdb003a 0000             ADD [EAX], AL
0xdb003c d800             FADD DWORD [EAX]
0xdb003e 0000             ADD [EAX], AL
```

55. As shown in the output, the plug-in shows you the injected malware in the process Explorer.EXE.

56. Feel free to experiment some more on the different plug-ins offered by Volatility to see whether you can gather more information from the .VMEM file that will help you paint a clearer picture of the malware.

57. Once you have all the information you need from the tools discussed in this lab, you can write a detailed report about the rootkit capability of this malware.

LAB 13-8: *Analyzing a Kernel Mode Rootkit*

In this lab, you will perform a complete analysis of a kernel mode rootkit using the tools discussed in this book. The sample used for this lab is Hacker Defender version 1.00.

What You Need:

▶   Static analysis tools

▶   Dynamic analysis tools

▶   Sysinternals Suite

▶   PE viewers

▶   Network capturing tools

▶   OSR driver loader

▶   System running Windows

▶   Rootkit malware

Steps:

1. You begin with basic dynamic analysis of the sample by running it in a virtual environment malware analysis system and monitoring all processes, the registry, and the file system by using the techniques discussed in Lab 13-7. Take note that the username of the analysis system is Jean, so you will see this in the output of the tools and some screenshots in this lab.

2. After infecting the VM, you monitor the following events in Process Monitor.

Here is the ProcMon output:

Explorer.EXE	1480	Process Create	C:\WINDOWS\svchost.com	SUCCESS	PID: 1832, Command line: "C:\WINDOWS\svchost.com" "C:\DOCUME~1\Jean\Desktop\hxdef100\hxdef100.exe"
svchost.com	1832	Process Start		SUCCESS	Parent PID: 1480, Command line: "C:\WINDOWS\svchost.com" "C:\DOCUME~1\Jean\Desktop\hxdef100\hxdef100.exe"
svchost.com	1832	WriteFile	C:\WINDOWS\directx.sys	SUCCESS	Offset: 0, Length: 34
svchost.com	1832	WriteFile	C:\WINDOWS\directx.sys	SUCCESS	Offset: 0, Length: 82
svchost.com	1832	WriteFile	C:\Documents and Settings\Jean\Desktop\hxdef100\hxdef100.exe	SUCCESS	Offset: 0, Length: 41,472
svchost.com	1832	WriteFile	C:\WINDOWS\directx.sys	SUCCESS	Offset: 0, Length: 82
System	4	WriteFile	C:\Documents and Settings\Jean\Desktop\hxdef100\hxdef100.exe	SUCCESS	Offset: 0, Length: 45,056
System	4	WriteFile	C:\WINDOWS\directx.sys	SUCCESS	Offset: 0, Length: 4,096
System	4	WriteFile	C:\Documents and Settings\Jean\Desktop\hxdef100\hxdef100.exe	SUCCESS	Offset: 69,632, Length: 4,096
svchost.com	1832	Process Create	C:\DOCUME~1\Jean\Desktop\hxdef100\hxdef100.exe	SUCCESS	PID: 1844, Command line: C:\DOCUME~1\Jean\Desktop\hxdef100\hxdef100.exe
hxdef100.exe	1844	Process Start		SUCCESS	Parent PID: 1832, Command line: C:\DOCUME~1\Jean\Desktop\hxdef100\hxdef100.exe
hxdef100.exe	1844	RegSetValue	HKLM\System\CurrentControlSet\Control\SafeBoot\Minimal\HackerDefender100\(Default)	SUCCESS	Type: REG_SZ, Length: 16, Data: Service
hxdef100.exe	1844	RegSetValue	HKLM\System\CurrentControlSet\Control\SafeBoot\Network\HackerDefender100\(Default)	SUCCESS	Type: REG_SZ, Length: 16, Data: Service
services.exe	656	RegSetValue	HKLM\System\CurrentControlSet\Services\HackerDefender100\Type	SUCCESS	Type: REG_DWORD, Length: 4, Data: 16
services.exe	656	RegSetValue	HKLM\System\CurrentControlSet\Services\HackerDefender100\Start	SUCCESS	Type: REG_DWORD, Length: 4, Data: 2
services.exe	656	RegSetValue	HKLM\System\CurrentControlSet\Services\HackerDefender100\ErrorControl	SUCCESS	Type: REG_DWORD, Length: 4, Data: 0
services.exe	656	RegSetValue	HKLM\System\CurrentControlSet\Services\HackerDefender100\ImagePath	SUCCESS	Type: REG_EXPAND_SZ, Length: 94, Data: C:\DOCUME~1\Jean\Desktop\hxdef100\hxdef100.exe
services.exe	656	RegSetValue	HKLM\System\CurrentControlSet\Services\HackerDefender100\DisplayName	SUCCESS	Type: REG_SZ, Length: 32, Data: HXD Service 100
services.exe	656	RegSetValue	HKLM\System\CurrentControlSet\Services\HackerDefender100\Security\Security	SUCCESS	Type: REG_BINARY, Length: 168, Data: 01 00 14 80 90 00 00 00 9C 00 00 00 14 00 00 00
services.exe	656	RegSetValue	HKLM\System\CurrentControlSet\Services\HackerDefender100\ObjectName	SUCCESS	Type: REG_SZ, Length: 24, Data: LocalSystem
services.exe	656	RegSetValue	HKLM\System\CurrentControlSet\Services\HackerDefender100\Description	SUCCESS	Type: REG_SZ, Length: 40, Data: powerful NT rootkit
services.exe	656	RegSetValue	HKLM\System\CurrentControlSet\Enum\Root\LEGACY_HACKERDEFENDER100\NextInstance	SUCCESS	Type: REG_DWORD, Length: 4, Data: 1

service s.exe	656	RegSetValue	HKLM\System\CurrentControlSet\Enum\Root\LEGACY_HACK ERDEFENDER100\0000\Control*NewlyCreated*	SUCCESS	Type: REG_DWORD, Length: 4, Data: 0
service s.exe	656	RegSetValue	HKLM\System\CurrentControlSet\Enum\Root\LEGACY_HACK ERDEFENDER100\0000\Service	SUCCESS	Type: REG_SZ, Length: 36, Data: HackerDefender100
service s.exe	656	RegSetValue	HKLM\System\CurrentControlSet\Enum\Root\LEGACY_HACK ERDEFENDER100\0000\Legacy	SUCCESS	Type: REG_DWORD, Length: 4, Data: 1
service s.exe	656	RegSetValue	HKLM\System\CurrentControlSet\Enum\Root\LEGACY_HACK ERDEFENDER100\0000\ConfigFlags	SUCCESS	Type: REG_DWORD, Length: 4, Data: 0
service s.exe	656	RegSetValue	HKLM\System\CurrentControlSet\Enum\Root\LEGACY_HACK ERDEFENDER100\0000\Class	SUCCESS	Type: REG_SZ, Length: 26, Data: LegacyDriver
service s.exe	656	RegSetValue	HKLM\System\CurrentControlSet\Enum\Root\LEGACY_HACK ERDEFENDER100\0000\ClassGUID	SUCCESS	Type: REG_SZ, Length: 78, Data: {8ECC055D-047F-11D1-A537-0000F8753ED1}
service s.exe	656	RegSetValue	HKLM\System\CurrentControlSet\Enum\Root\LEGACY_HACK ERDEFENDER100\0000\DeviceDesc	SUCCESS	Type: REG_SZ, Length: 32, Data: HXD Service 100
service s.exe	656	RegSetValue	HKLM\System\CurrentControlSet\Services\HackerDefender1 00\Enum\0	SUCCESS	Type: REG_SZ, Length: 70, Data: Root\LEGACY_HACKERDEFENDER100\0000
service s.exe	656	RegSetValue	HKLM\System\CurrentControlSet\Services\HackerDefender1 00\Enum\Count	SUCCESS	Type: REG_DWORD, Length: 4, Data: 1
service s.exe	656	RegSetValue	HKLM\System\CurrentControlSet\Services\HackerDefender1 00\Enum\NextInstance	SUCCESS	Type: REG_DWORD, Length: 4, Data: 1
service s.exe	656	Process Create	C:\DOCUME~1\Jean\Desktop\hxdef100\hxdef100.exe	SUCCESS	PID: 468, Command line: C:\DOCUME~1\Jean\Desktop\hxdef100\hxdef100.exe
hxdef1 00.exe	468	Process Start		SUCCESS	Parent PID: 656, Command line: C:\DOCUME~1\Jean\Desktop\hxdef100\hxdef100.exe
service s.exe	656	RegSetValue	HKLM\System\CurrentControlSet\Control\ServiceCurrent\(De fault)	SUCCESS	Type: REG_DWORD, Length: 4, Data: 11
service s.exe	656	RegSetValue	HKLM\System\CurrentControlSet\Enum\Root\LEGACY_HACK ERDEFENDER100\0000\Control\ActiveService	SUCCESS	Type: REG_SZ, Length: 36, Data: HackerDefender100
hxdef1 00.exe	1844	Process Exit		SUCCESS	Exit Status: 0
svchos t.com	1832	Process Exit		SUCCESS	Exit Status: 0
hxdef1 00.exe	468	WriteFile	C:\Documents and Settings\Jean\Desktop\hxdef100\hxdefdrv.sys	SUCCESS	Offset: 0, Length: 3,342
hxdef1 00.exe	468	SetDispositio nInformation File	C:\Documents and Settings\Jean\Desktop\hxdef100\hxdefdrv.sys	SUCCESS	Delete: True
hxdef1 00.exe	468	WriteFile	C:\Documents and Settings\Jean\Desktop\hxdef100\hxdefdrv.sys	SUCCESS	Offset: 0, Length: 3,342
hxdef1 00.exe	468	RegSetValue	HKLM\System\CurrentControlSet\Services\HackerDefenderD rv100\ErrorControl	SUCCESS	Type: REG_DWORD, Length: 4, Data: 0
hxdef1 00.exe	468	RegSetValue	HKLM\System\CurrentControlSet\Services\HackerDefenderD rv100\ImagePath	SUCCESS	Type: REG_EXPAND_SZ, Length: 102, Data: \??\C:\DOCUME~1\Jean\Desktop\hxdef100\hxdefdrv.sys
hxdef1 00.exe	468	RegSetValue	HKLM\System\CurrentControlSet\Services\HackerDefenderD rv100\Start	SUCCESS	Type: REG_DWORD, Length: 4, Data: 3

hxdef1 00.exe	468	RegSetValue	HKLM\System\CurrentControlSet\Services\HackerDefenderD rv100\Type	SUCCESS	Type: REG_DWORD, Length: 4, Data: 1
Syste m	4	WriteFile	C:\Documents and Settings\Jean\Desktop\hxdef100\hxdefdrv.sys	SUCCESS	Offset: 0, Length: 4,096
Syste m	4	RegSetValue	HKLM\System\CurrentControlSet\Enum\Root\LEGACY_HACK ERDEFENDERDRV100\NextInstance	SUCCESS	Type: REG_DWORD, Length: 4, Data: 1
Syste m	4	RegSetValue	HKLM\System\CurrentControlSet\Enum\Root\LEGACY_HACK ERDEFENDERDRV100\0000\Control*NewlyCreated*	SUCCESS	Type: REG_DWORD, Length: 4, Data: 0
Syste m	4	RegSetValue	HKLM\System\CurrentControlSet\Enum\Root\LEGACY_HACK ERDEFENDERDRV100\0000\Service	SUCCESS	Type: REG_SZ, Length: 42, Data: HackerDefenderDrv100
Syste m	4	RegSetValue	HKLM\System\CurrentControlSet\Enum\Root\LEGACY_HACK ERDEFENDERDRV100\0000\Legacy	SUCCESS	Type: REG_DWORD, Length: 4, Data: 1
Syste m	4	RegSetValue	HKLM\System\CurrentControlSet\Enum\Root\LEGACY_HACK ERDEFENDERDRV100\0000\ConfigFlags	SUCCESS	Type: REG_DWORD, Length: 4, Data: 0
Syste m	4	RegSetValue	HKLM\System\CurrentControlSet\Enum\Root\LEGACY_HACK ERDEFENDERDRV100\0000\Class	SUCCESS	Type: REG_SZ, Length: 26, Data: LegacyDriver
Syste m	4	RegSetValue	HKLM\System\CurrentControlSet\Enum\Root\LEGACY_HACK ERDEFENDERDRV100\0000\ClassGUID	SUCCESS	Type: REG_SZ, Length: 78, Data: {8ECC055D-047F-11D1-A537-0000F8753ED1}
Syste m	4	RegSetValue	HKLM\System\CurrentControlSet\Enum\Root\LEGACY_HACK ERDEFENDERDRV100\0000\DeviceDesc	SUCCESS	Type: REG_SZ, Length: 42, Data: HackerDefenderDrv100
Syste m	4	RegSetValue	HKLM\System\CurrentControlSet\Services\HackerDefenderD rv100\Enum\0	SUCCESS	Type: REG_SZ, Length: 76, Data: Root\LEGACY_HACKERDEFENDERDRV100\0000
Syste m	4	RegSetValue	HKLM\System\CurrentControlSet\Services\HackerDefenderD rv100\Enum\Count	SUCCESS	Type: REG_DWORD, Length: 4, Data: 1
Syste m	4	RegSetValue	HKLM\System\CurrentControlSet\Services\HackerDefenderD rv100\Enum\NextInstance	SUCCESS	Type: REG_DWORD, Length: 4, Data: 1
Syste m	4	RegSetValue	HKLM\System\CurrentControlSet\Enum\Root\LEGACY_HACK ERDEFENDERDRV100\0000\Control\ActiveService	SUCCESS	Type: REG_SZ, Length: 42, Data: HackerDefenderDrv100
Syste m	4	RegSetValue	HKLM\System\CurrentControlSet\Services\HackerDefenderD rv100\Enum\Count	SUCCESS	Type: REG_DWORD, Length: 4, Data: 1
Syste m	4	RegSetValue	HKLM\System\CurrentControlSet\Services\HackerDefenderD rv100\Enum\NextInstance	SUCCESS	Type: REG_DWORD, Length: 4, Data: 1
Explor er.EXE	1480	RegSetValue	HKCU\Software\Microsoft\Windows\ShellNoRoam\Bags\67\ Shell\FolderType	SUCCESS	Type: REG_SZ, Length: 20, Data: Documents
Syste m	4	WriteFile	C:\Documents and Settings\Jean\Local Settings\Temp\MICROSOFT .NET FRAMEWORK 4 SETUP_4.0.30319	SUCCESS	Offset: 0, Length: 8,192
svchos t.com	936	WriteFile	C:\Documents and Settings\Jean\Local Settings\Temp\tmp5023.tmp	SUCCESS	Offset: 0, Length: 8
svchos t.com	936	Process Exit		SUCCESS	Exit Status: 0

3. The following are some things that are noticeable in the dynamic analysis session:

   ▶ A file named hexdefdrv.sys was written in C:\Documents and Settings\<User>\Desktop\hxdef100\.

   ▶ A service named HackerDefender100 was created by writing values to the registry.

     This tells you that the malware is possibly installed as a kernel mode driver on the system, which is used to gain kernel rootkit capabilities.

4. Notice that all the files related to the malware have vanished. In Figure 13-56, you can see that the listed directory in the File Explorer doesn't actually exist on the desktop.

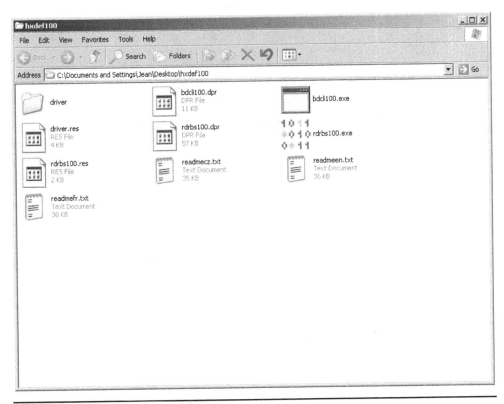

Figure 13-56 *File listing of hxdef100.*

5. When you try to find the newly installed service in the Services snap-in by going to Run, typing **services.msc**, and clicking Enter, you will not be able to find it in the listing, as shown in Figure 13-57.

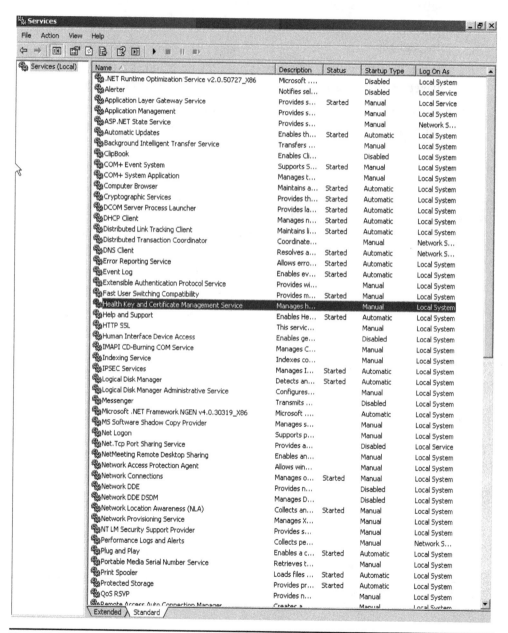

Figure 13-57 *Running services in the local machine.*

6. Another way to check the service status and parameters is through the command line by running the following command:

```
> sc query <servicename>
```

7. In this case, you want to check about a service named HackerDefender100. You know this through the output of Process Monitor.

```
> sc query HackerDefender100
```

8. The following output reveals that the service exists, but it is hidden from any user mode application that tries to list the system's services:

```
SERVICE_NAME: HackerDefender100
    TYPE               : 10    WIN32_OWN_PROCESS
    STATE              : 4     RUNNING
                               (STOPPABLE,NOT_PAUSABLE,ACCEPTS_
                               SHUTDOWN)
    WIN32_EXIT_CODE    : 0     (0x0)
    SERVICE_EXIT_CODE  : 0     (0x0)
    CHECKPOINT         : 0x0
    WAIT_HINT          : 0x0
```

9. A scan with Rootkit Revealer should confirm these suspicions.

10. Here is the rootkit revealer output:

```
>Processes
!!!!!!!!!!!Hidden process: C:\DOCUME~1\Jean\Desktop\hxdef100\
hxdef100.exe
Process Id: 1384
EPROCESS Address: 0x898E2978

>Drivers
>Stealth
>Files
Suspect File: C:\Documents and Settings\Jean\Desktop\hxdef100\
bdcli100.dpr Status: Hidden
Suspect File: C:\Documents and Settings\Jean\Desktop\hxdef100\
bdcli100.exe Status: Hidden
Suspect File: C:\Documents and Settings\Jean\Desktop\hxdef100\
driver.res Status: Hidden
Suspect File: C:\Documents and Settings\Jean\Desktop\hxdef100\
driver\driver.c Status: Hidden
Suspect File: C:\Documents and Settings\Jean\Desktop\hxdef100\
driver\driver.h Status: Hidden
```

```
Suspect File: C:\Documents and Settings\Jean\Desktop\hxdef100\
driver\driver.sys Status: Hidden
Suspect File: C:\Documents and Settings\Jean\Desktop\hxdef100\
driver\makefile Status: Hidden
Suspect File: C:\Documents and Settings\Jean\Desktop\hxdef100\
driver\sources Status: Hidden
Suspect File: C:\Documents and Settings\Jean\Desktop\hxdef100\
hxdef100.2.ini Status: Hidden
Suspect File: C:\Documents and Settings\Jean\Desktop\hxdef100\
hxdef100.dpr Status: Hidden
Suspect File: C:\Documents and Settings\Jean\Desktop\hxdef100\
hxdef100.exe Status: Hidden
Suspect File: C:\Documents and Settings\Jean\Desktop\hxdef100\
hxdef100.ini Status: Hidden
Suspect File: C:\Documents and Settings\Jean\Desktop\hxdef100\
hxdefdrv.sys Status: Hidden
Suspect File: C:\Documents and Settings\Jean\Desktop\hxdef100\
rdrbs100.dpr Status: Hidden
Suspect File: C:\Documents and Settings\Jean\Desktop\hxdef100\
rdrbs100.exe Status: Hidden
Suspect File: C:\Documents and Settings\Jean\Desktop\hxdef100\
rdrbs100.res Status: Hidden
Suspect File: C:\Documents and Settings\Jean\Desktop\hxdef100\
readmecz.txt Status: Hidden
Suspect File: C:\Documents and Settings\Jean\Desktop\hxdef100\
readmeen.txt Status: Hidden
Suspect File: C:\Documents and Settings\Jean\Desktop\hxdef100\
readmefr.txt Status: Hidden
Suspect File: C:\Documents and Settings\Jean\Desktop\hxdef100\
staticAnalyzer.py Status: Hidden
Suspect File: C:\Documents and Settings\Jean\Desktop\hxdef100\
userdb.txt Status: Hidden
Suspect File: C:\WINDOWS\Prefetch\HXDEF100.EXE-13D28C3E.pf
Status: Hidden
>Hooks
ntkrnlpa.exe+0x0006AA5A, Type: Inline - RelativeJump at address
0x80541A5A hook handler located in [ntkrnlpa.exe]
[1028]svchost.exe-->advapi32.dll-->EnumServiceGroupW, Type:
Inline - RelativeJump at address 0x77E36A61 hook handler located
in [unknown_code_page]
[1028]svchost.exe-->advapi32.dll-->EnumServicesStatusA, Type:
Inline - RelativeJump at address 0x77DF6B17 hook handler located
in [unknown_code_page]
```

```
[1028]svchost.exe-->advapi32.dll-->EnumServicesStatusExA, Type:
Inline - RelativeJump at address 0x77E36C07 hook handler located
in [unknown_code_page]
[1028]svchost.exe-->advapi32.dll-->EnumServicesStatusExW, Type:
Inline - RelativeJump at address 0x77E36990 hook handler located
in [unknown_code_page]
[1028]svchost.exe-->kernel32.dll-->ReadFile, Type: Inline -
RelativeJump at address 0x7C801812 hook handler located in
[unknown_code_page]
[1028]svchost.exe-->ntdll.dll-->LdrLoadDll, Type: Inline -
RelativeJump at address 0x7C9163A3 hook handler located in
[unknown_code_page]
[1028]svchost.exe-->ntdll.dll-->NtCreateFile, Type: Inline
- RelativeJump at address 0x7C90D090 hook handler located in
[unknown_code_page]
[1028]svchost.exe-->ntdll.dll-->NtDeviceIoControlFile, Type:
Inline - RelativeJump at address 0x7C90D260 hook handler located
in [unknown_code_page]
[1028]svchost.exe-->ntdll.dll-->NtEnumerateKey, Type: Inline
- RelativeJump at address 0x7C90D2B0 hook handler located in
[unknown_code_page]
[1028]svchost.exe-->ntdll.dll-->NtEnumerateValueKey, Type: Inline
- RelativeJump at address 0x7C90D2D0 hook handler located in
[unknown_code_page]
[1028]svchost.exe-->ntdll.dll-->NtOpenProcess, Type: Inline
- RelativeJump at address 0x7C90D5E0 hook handler located in
[unknown_code_page]
[1028]svchost.exe-->ntdll.dll-->NtQueryDirectoryFile, Type:
Inline - RelativeJump at address 0x7C90D750 hook handler located
in [unknown_code_page]
[1028]svchost.exe-->ntdll.dll-->NtQuerySystemInformation, Type:
Inline - RelativeJump at address 0x7C90D910 hook handler located
in [unknown_code_page]
[1028]svchost.exe-->ntdll.dll-->NtQueryVolumeInformationFile,
Type: Inline - RelativeJump at address 0x7C90D970 hook handler
located in [unknown_code_page]
[1028]svchost.exe-->ntdll.dll-->NtReadVirtualMemory, Type: Inline
- RelativeJump at address 0x7C90D9E0 hook handler located in
[unknown_code_page]
[1028]svchost.exe-->ntdll.dll-->NtResumeThread, Type: Inline
- RelativeJump at address 0x7C90DB20 hook handler located in
[unknown_code_page]
```

```
[1028]svchost.exe-->ntdll.dll-->NtVdmControl, Type: Inline
- RelativeJump at address 0x7C90DF00 hook handler located in
[unknown_code_page]
[1028]svchost.exe-->ws2_32.dll-->recv, Type: Inline -
RelativeJump at address 0x71AB676F hook handler located in
[unknown_code_page]
[1028]svchost.exe-->ws2_32.dll-->WSARecv, Type: Inline -
RelativeJump at address 0x71AB4CB5 hook handler located in
[unknown_code_page]
[1144]svchost.exe-->advapi32.dll-->EnumServiceGroupW, Type:
Inline - RelativeJump at address 0x77E36A61 hook handler located
in [unknown_code_page]
[1144]svchost.exe-->advapi32.dll-->EnumServicesStatusA, Type:
Inline - RelativeJump at address 0x77DF6B17 hook handler located
in [unknown_code_page]
[1144]svchost.exe-->advapi32.dll-->EnumServicesStatusExA, Type:
Inline - RelativeJump at address 0x77E36C07 hook handler located
in [unknown_code_page]
[1144]svchost.exe-->advapi32.dll-->EnumServicesStatusExW, Type:
Inline - RelativeJump at address 0x77E36990 hook handler located
in [unknown_code_page]
[1144]svchost.exe-->kernel32.dll-->ReadFile, Type: Inline -
RelativeJump at address 0x7C801812 hook handler located in
[unknown_code_page]
[1144]svchost.exe-->ntdll.dll-->LdrLoadDll, Type: Inline -
RelativeJump at address 0x7C9163A3 hook handler located in
[unknown_code_page]
[1144]svchost.exe-->ntdll.dll-->NtCreateFile, Type: Inline
- RelativeJump at address 0x7C90D090 hook handler located in
[unknown_code_page]
[1144]svchost.exe-->ntdll.dll-->NtDeviceIoControlFile, Type:
Inline - RelativeJump at address 0x7C90D260 hook handler located
in [unknown_code_page]
[1144]svchost.exe-->ntdll.dll-->NtEnumerateKey, Type: Inline
- RelativeJump at address 0x7C90D2B0 hook handler located in
[unknown_code_page]
[1144]svchost.exe-->ntdll.dll-->NtEnumerateValueKey, Type: Inline
- RelativeJump at address 0x7C90D2D0 hook handler located in
[unknown_code_page]
[1144]svchost.exe-->ntdll.dll-->NtOpenProcess, Type: Inline
- RelativeJump at address 0x7C90D5E0 hook handler located in
[unknown_code_page]
```

```
[1144]svchost.exe-->ntdll.dll-->NtQueryDirectoryFile, Type:
Inline - RelativeJump at address 0x7C90D750 hook handler located
in [unknown_code_page]
[1144]svchost.exe-->ntdll.dll-->NtQuerySystemInformation, Type:
Inline - RelativeJump at address 0x7C90D910 hook handler located
in [unknown_code_page]
[1144]svchost.exe-->ntdll.dll-->NtQueryVolumeInformationFile,
Type: Inline - RelativeJump at address 0x7C90D970 hook handler
located in [unknown_code_page]
[1144]svchost.exe-->ntdll.dll-->NtReadVirtualMemory, Type: Inline
- RelativeJump at address 0x7C90D9E0 hook handler located in
[unknown_code_page]
[1144]svchost.exe-->ntdll.dll-->NtResumeThread, Type: Inline
- RelativeJump at address 0x7C90DB20 hook handler located in
[unknown_code_page]
[1144]svchost.exe-->ntdll.dll-->NtVdmControl, Type: Inline
- RelativeJump at address 0x7C90DF00 hook handler located in
[unknown_code_page]
[1144]svchost.exe-->ws2_32.dll-->recv, Type: Inline -
RelativeJump at address 0x71AB676F hook handler located in
[unknown_code_page]
[1144]svchost.exe-->ws2_32.dll-->WSARecv, Type: Inline -
RelativeJump at address 0x71AB4CB5 hook handler located in
[unknown_code_page]
```

11. After your initial analysis, you should have a picture of what kind of malware you are dealing with. You know that it installs a driver and that it hides certain files. You should now try to analyze the driver itself.

12. At this point, you should revert the machine to its original state before the infection so you can use a kernel debugger to see what the driver is actually doing and to extract the driver's files.

> **TIP**
>
> *It is always wise to save a snapshot of your dynamic analysis session so you can come back to it when needed without going through the whole process of infection again.*

13. Let's set up your debugger and debuggee machine. The debugger machine is where WinDbg will be, and the debuggee machine is where the malware will run. This can be the VM you just reverted to its original state. Both these machines are virtual environments. You will set up the environment using VMware hosted on a Linux machine.

14. The first VM, which is the debuggee or debugged machine, is running Windows XP SP3. As mentioned, this is where you will run the malware. The second VM, which is the debugger machine, is running Windows 7 (XP can also be used). As mentioned, this machine will run WinDbg attached to the other VM via the serial port (COM port).

15. The first thing you have to do is add a serial port to both VMs. This is the medium to form a link between the debugger running on the debugger machine to the debuggee or debugged machine. The next steps of adding a serial port must be done for both VMs.

16. To add a serial port, turn off the virtual machine; then go to Virtual Machine Settings, as shown in Figure 13-58.

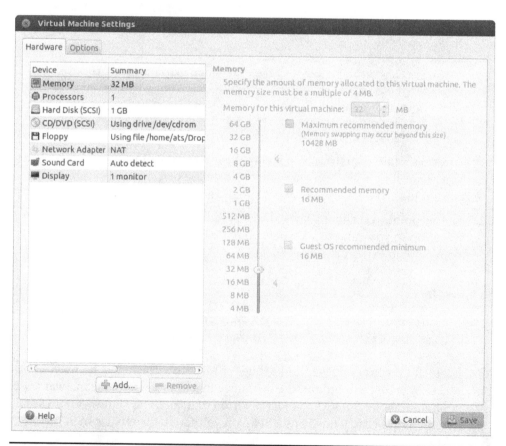

Figure 13-58 *VMWare Virtual Machine Settings.*

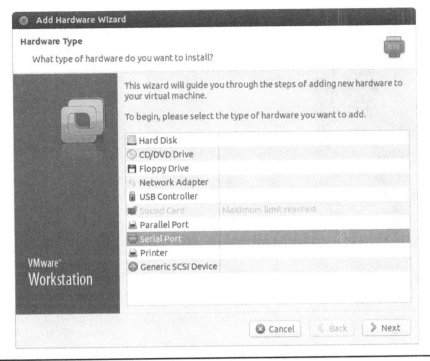

Figure 13-59 *VMWare Add Hardware Wizard.*

17. Click + Add, choose Serial Port, and click Next, as shown in Figure 13-59.

18. Choose Output To Socket and then click Next, as shown in Figure 13-60.

19. Since you are using a Linux host, the following applies. On both machines, enter the socket name **/tmp/<socket>**. <socket> should be replaced with a short string (for instance, debugport0) and should be the same on both virtual machines.

20. On the debugged VM or debuggee, set From to Server and set To to A Virtual Machine, as shown in Figure 13-61.

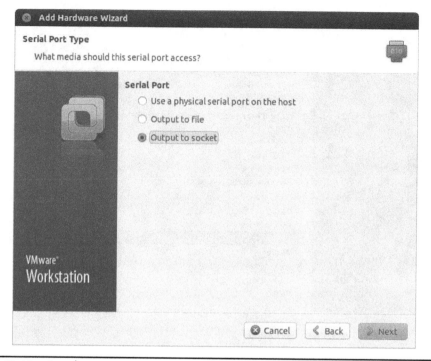

Figure 13-60 *Serial Port Type.*

21. On the debugger VM, set From to Client and set To to A Virtual Machine, as shown in Figure 13-62.

22. Just in case you want to use a Windows machine to host the two virtual machines, the process is the same except for the Socket (Named Pipe) path. It should follow the Windows path and should look like this: \\.\pipe\<namedpipe>.

23. After creating the serial ports on both machines, the next step is to boot into Windows in Debug mode on the debuggee.

24. To boot Windows in Debug mode, edit the Boot.INI file located in C:\. This is usually the case unless your boot partition is in another drive.

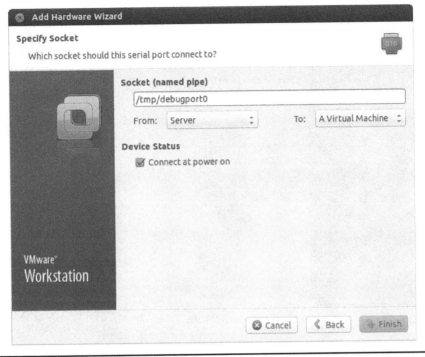

Figure 13-61 *From server to a virtual machine.*

25. Start the debuggee and open Boot.INI using a text editor.

26. Assuming you have only one OS installed on your VM, the default should look like the following:

```
[boot loader]
timeout=30
default=multi(0)disk(0)rdisk(0)partition(1)\WINDOWS
[operating systems]
multi(0)disk(0)rdisk(0)partition(1)\WINDOWS="Microsoft Windows XP
Professional" /noexecute=optin /fastdetect
```

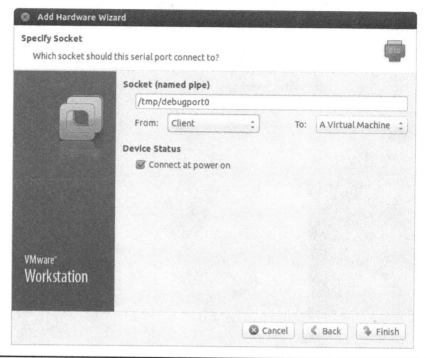

Figure 13-62 *From client to a virtual machine.*

27. Add a second line under [operating systems]. The second line is the same as the first line plus the parameters for debugging. The resulting Boot.INI file should look like the following:

```
[boot loader]
timeout=30
default=multi(0)disk(0)rdisk(0)partition(1)\WINDOWS
[operating systems]
multi(0)disk(0)rdisk(0)partition(1)\WINDOWS="Microsoft Windows XP
Professional" /noexecute=optin /fastdetect
multi(0)disk(0)rdisk(0)partition(1)\WINDOWS="Microsoft Windows XP
Professional with Kernel Debugging" /noexecute=optin /fastdetect
/debug /debugport=COM2 /baudrate=115200
```

28. Pay attention to the /debugport=COM? and replace it with the right COM port number for the serial port you added earlier to the debugged machine. In the setup used to create this lab, it is COM2.

29. Reboot the debugee and use the second option in the BootLoader: Microsoft Windows XP Professional With Kernel Debugging.

30. Once this is done, you can run WinDbg on the debugger machine. But before you attach to the debugee, you need to configure the symbols in WinDbg.

31. Choose File | Symbol File Path or simply press CTRL+S. Set the search path to SRV*<your_symbol_path>*http://msdl.microsoft.com/download/symbols. The <your_symbol_path> should be replaced in your VM with the path to your symbols. In the VM you used to make this lab, it is C:\WebSymbols.

32. Attach to the debuggee. Choose File | Kernel Debug or simply press CTRL+K.

33. Set the baud rate to 115200 and set the COM port to the same port number as configured for the debugger machine, as shown in Figure 13-63. Then click OK. You are now ready to do some kernel debugging.

34. After clicking the OK button, you should get the screen shown in Figure 13-64.

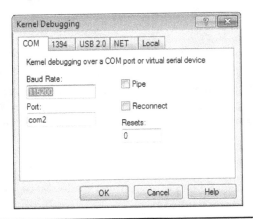

Figure 13-63 *Kernel Debugging COM tab.*

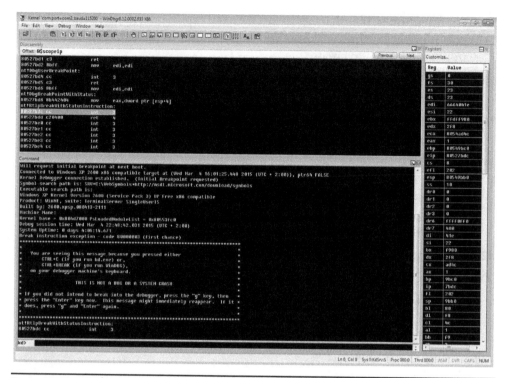

Figure 13-64   *Debugging window.*

35. In case your screen keeps saying "Debuggee not connected" at the bottom left, you can try to remedy this by choosing Debug | Kernel Connection | Resynchronize or by pressing CTRL+ALT+B and waiting for a few seconds. If this does not help, check the machine configurations and check whether you got all the COM port numbers right.

36. Once a connection is established successfully, you can proceed.

37. At this point, you established the connection to the debuggee and broke into a random address in the OS code. This is irrelevant for your analysis. This is a side effect of you breaking into the debugged machine. There is unresponsiveness to any input/output (I/O) operation until you continue the execution of the OS code.

38. Before you continue the execution of the OS and infect the machine, choose
    Debug | Event Filters and then set the Load module to enabled and handled,
    as shown in Figure 13-65.

39. Since you need some interaction with the debugged machine in order to
    infect the machine prior to your analysis, you will continue the execution
    by pressing F5 or typing **g** (an abbreviation for go) and pressing Enter at the
    WinDbg command prompt.

    ```
    kd> g
    ```

40. After continuing the execution, WinDbg should show "Debuggee is running..."
    on the console line.

41. At this point, you should infect the debugged machine by running the
    malware. This time you will break once the driver module is loaded.
    Figure 13-66 shows what the WinDbg window should look like once you
    break into DriverEntry.

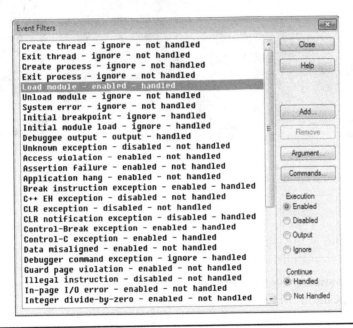

Figure 13-65   *Event filters.*

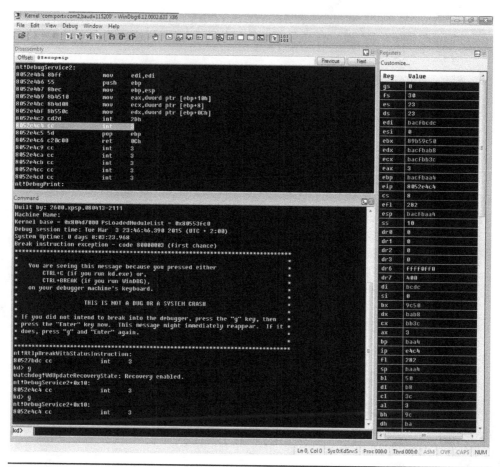

Figure 13-66 *Breaking into DriverEntry.*

42. Typing **lmf** at the command prompt reveals that the driver module was loaded successfully, as shown in Figure 13-67.

43. Type **dd $iment(hxdefdrv)** to check the driver's entry point and then put a breakpoint in that address by typing **bp <entry_point_address>**. In the current setup when this lab was being created, the address is 0xBAFA3718.

44. Continue the execution by pressing F5 or typing **g** in the console until you hit the driver's entry point. Figure 13-68 shows the whole session.

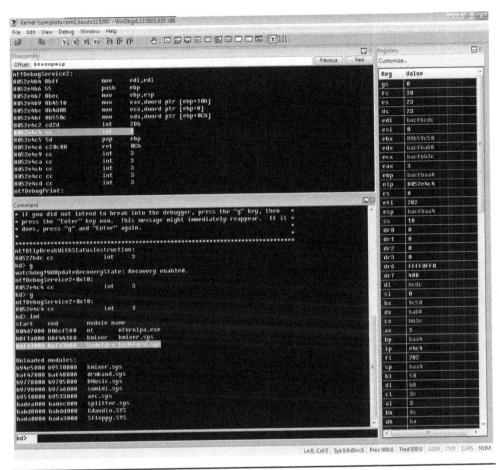

Figure 13-67 *Rootkit driver loaded.*

45. Once you hit the driver's entry point, you can start debugging it to see how it works by using the Step Over (F10) and Step Into (F11) functions. But it would be easier to dump the driver's module and analyze it with IDA first.

46. To do this, you create a snapshot of the debugged machine so you can continue debugging later with WinDbg, and then you pause the virtual machine.

47. Use Volatility to see some of the kernel structures and dump the driver file. Refer to the previous Lab 13-7 for more information on using Volatility for this purpose.

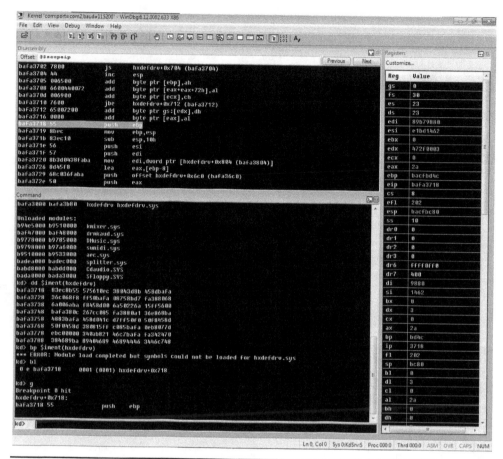

Figure 13-68   *Revealing the driver's entry point.*

48. You'll start with checking the loaded modules, which includes drivers, by running the following command:

```
vol.py modules -f <.vmem_path>
```

49. Among the list of modules produced, you can see your suspicious hxdefdrv. sys module, which is loaded in the address 0xBAFA300. Take note that this address might be different in your own experiment.

```
0x89b59c50 hxdefdrv.sys 0xbafa3000  0x1000 \??\C:\...\hxdef100\
hxdefdrv.sys
```

50. Now you can dump all of the loaded modules along with your malicious driver by running the following command, as shown in Figure 13-69:

```
vol.py moddump -f <.vmem_path> --dump-dir <dump_path>
```

51. You should now have a directory full of .sys files in this format: driver.<address>.sys.

```
r@ReverseMe:~$ vol.py moddump -f /opt/VMs/WinXP_Black/Black-42315c2d.vmem --dump-dir ./modules
Volatility Foundation Volatility Framework 2.4
Module Base Module Name           Result
---------- ---------------------  ------
0x0804d7000 ntoskrnl.exe          OK: driver.804d7000.sys
0x0806d0000 hal.dll               OK: driver.806d0000.sys
0x0ba559000 ks.sys                OK: driver.ba559000.sys
0x0babf0000 Npfs.SYS              OK: driver.babf0000.sys
0x0ba57c000 parport.sys           OK: driver.ba57c000.sys
0x0ba8b8000 MountMgr.sys          OK: driver.ba8b8000.sys
0x0badbe000 USBD.SYS              OK: driver.badbe000.sys
0x0baae8000 HIDCLASS.SYS          OK: driver.baae8000.sys
0x0bac00000 usbccgp.sys           OK: driver.bac00000.sys
0x0ba600000 Mup.sys               OK: driver.ba600000.sys
0x0badc2000 Beep.SYS              OK: driver.badc2000.sys
0x0ba723000 dmio.sys              OK: driver.ba723000.sys
0x0b9884000 ndisuio.sys           OK: driver.b9884000.sys
0x0ba9b8000 cdrom.sys             OK: driver.ba9b8000.sys
0x0badc6000 RDPCDD.sys            OK: driver.badc6000.sys
0x0babe8000 Msfs.SYS              OK: driver.babe8000.sys
0x0ba5a7000 hidusb.sys            OK: driver.ba5a7000.sys
0x0ba988000 i8042prt.sys          OK: driver.ba988000.sys
0x0ba4e9000 psched.sys            OK: driver.ba4e9000.sys
0x0ba8c8000 VolSnap.sys           OK: driver.ba8c8000.sys
0x0baab8000 wanarp.sys            OK: driver.baab8000.sys
0x0babd0000 flpydisk.sys          OK: driver.babd0000.sys
0x0b92f8000 mrxdav.sys            OK: driver.b92f8000.sys
0x0bab90000 kbdclass.sys          OK: driver.bab90000.sys
0x0ba3f1000 rdpdr.sys             OK: driver.ba3f1000.sys
0x0baa18000 rasl2tp.sys           OK: driver.baa18000.sys
0x0b9533000 wdmaud.sys            OK: driver.b9533000.sys
0x0babb8000 TDI.SYS               OK: driver.babb8000.sys
0x0ba256000 rdbss.sys             OK: driver.ba256000.sys
0x0baa08000 intelppm.sys          OK: driver.baa08000.sys
0x0bab98000 mouclass.sys          OK: driver.bab98000.sys
0x0ba779000 ACPI.sys              OK: driver.ba779000.sys
0x0bae42000 ParVdm.SYS            OK: driver.bae42000.sys
0x0bad9c000 gameenum.sys          OK: driver.bad9c000.sys
0x0ba8d8000 disk.sys              OK: driver.ba8d8000.sys
0x0baba0000 fdc.sys               OK: driver.baba0000.sys
0x0ba281000 afd.sys               OK: driver.ba281000.sys
0x0bf9c3000 dxg.sys               OK: driver.bf9c3000.sys
0x0bada4000 rasacd.sys            OK: driver.bada4000.sys
0x0ba1e6000 mrxsmb.sys            OK: driver.ba1e6000.sys
0x0ba647000 Ntfs.sys              OK: driver.ba647000.sys
0x0bac08000 HIDPARSE.SYS          OK: driver.bac08000.sys
0x0bab28000 PCIIDEX.SYS           OK: driver.bab28000.sys
0x0bff50000 framebuf.dll          OK: driver.bff50000.sys
```

Figure 13-69 *Volatility moddump results.*

52. Since your driver was loaded in 0xBAFA3000, you should look for driver. bafa3000.sys.

> **NOTE**
>
> *Another thing that can be interesting is checking for any SSDT hooks by running vol.py ssdt –f <.vmem_path>. You did not do it for this lab because this specific malware is not using SSDT hooking.*

53. Now you can take the dumped file and feed it in IDA for analysis.

54. Once it is loaded in IDA, you should land on DriverEntry, as shown in Figure 13-70.

55. After analyzing the code, you should also find the DriverUnload function, as shown in Figure 13-71.

56. Eventually, you will arrive at the function that contains the main functionality of the malware, as shown in Figure 13-72.

Figure 13-70   *Dumped file loaded in IDA.*

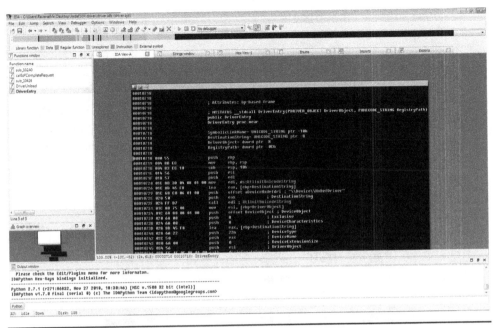

Figure 13-71   *DriverUnload function revealed.*

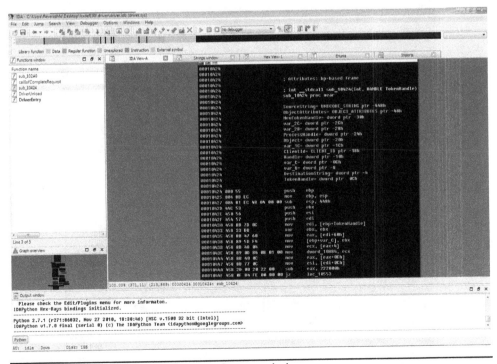

Figure 13-72   *Main malicious functionality revealed.*

57. Analysis of kernel mode rootkits requires familiarity with the kernel mode API. If you are not familiar with kernel mode API calls, please consult Microsoft TechNet and see the available documentation. Google is also your friend. The basic idea is that every Win32 API function encapsulates a kernel mode function and basically switches to kernel mode and calls the appropriate kernel mode function with the correct parameters.

58. After you are done with the dynamic analysis of the driver's sys file, you can go back to the infected machine and keep debugging it by resuming the VM. Once the VM is running again, you can see the installed driver by continuing execution in WinDbg (F5 or typing **g**) and breaking again (CTRL+BREAK) after about 10 seconds and then pausing the machine again.

59. Now you can use Volatility again to analyze the VM's kernel for Interrupt Request Procedure (IRP) drivers by running the following command. Figure 13-73 shows the result.

```
vol.py driverirp -f <.vmem_path>
```

```
---------------------------------------------------
DriverName: HackerDefenderDrv100
DriverStart: 0xbafa3000
DriverSize: 0xb80
DriverStartIo: 0x0
   0 IRP_MJ_CREATE                          0xbafa340a hxdefdrv.sys
   1 IRP_MJ_CREATE_NAMED_PIPE               0x804f354a ntoskrnl.exe
   2 IRP_MJ_CLOSE                           0xbafa340a hxdefdrv.sys
   3 IRP_MJ_READ                            0xbafa340a hxdefdrv.sys
   4 IRP_MJ_WRITE                           0xbafa340a hxdefdrv.sys
   5 IRP_MJ_QUERY_INFORMATION               0x804f354a ntoskrnl.exe
   6 IRP_MJ_SET_INFORMATION                 0x804f354a ntoskrnl.exe
   7 IRP_MJ_QUERY_EA                        0x804f354a ntoskrnl.exe
   8 IRP_MJ_SET_EA                          0x804f354a ntoskrnl.exe
   9 IRP_MJ_FLUSH_BUFFERS                   0x804f354a ntoskrnl.exe
  10 IRP_MJ_QUERY_VOLUME_INFORMATION        0x804f354a ntoskrnl.exe
  11 IRP_MJ_SET_VOLUME_INFORMATION          0x804f354a ntoskrnl.exe
  12 IRP_MJ_DIRECTORY_CONTROL               0x804f354a ntoskrnl.exe
  13 IRP_MJ_FILE_SYSTEM_CONTROL             0x804f354a ntoskrnl.exe
  14 IRP_MJ_DEVICE_CONTROL                  0xbafa3424 hxdefdrv.sys
  15 IRP_MJ_INTERNAL_DEVICE_CONTROL         0x804f354a ntoskrnl.exe
  16 IRP_MJ_SHUTDOWN                        0x804f354a ntoskrnl.exe
  17 IRP_MJ_LOCK_CONTROL                    0x804f354a ntoskrnl.exe
  18 IRP_MJ_CLEANUP                         0x804f354a ntoskrnl.exe
  19 IRP_MJ_CREATE_MAILSLOT                 0x804f354a ntoskrnl.exe
  20 IRP_MJ_QUERY_SECURITY                  0x804f354a ntoskrnl.exe
  21 IRP_MJ_SET_SECURITY                    0x804f354a ntoskrnl.exe
  22 IRP_MJ_POWER                           0x804f354a ntoskrnl.exe
  23 IRP_MJ_SYSTEM_CONTROL                  0x804f354a ntoskrnl.exe
  24 IRP_MJ_DEVICE_CHANGE                   0x804f354a ntoskrnl.exe
  25 IRP_MJ_QUERY_QUOTA                     0x804f354a ntoskrnl.exe
  26 IRP_MJ_SET_QUOTA                       0x804f354a ntoskrnl.exe
  27 IRP_MJ_PNP                             0x804f354a ntoskrnl.exe
---------------------------------------------------
```

Figure 13-73 *Volatility revealing IRP.*

60. This reveals to you the driver's IRP chain.

61. You have just analyzed a kernel mode rootkit.

62. Please feel free to experiment further with WinDbg. WinDbg allows you to investigate a lot of Windows structures. You can learn more about this in Microsoft TechNet and by Googling.

63. To continue your learning and to get a deeper level of understanding of rootkits and other techniques, please research further about the Windows kernel and Windows driver development.

Automated Sandboxes

In previous chapters, I discussed how to build your own malware analysis system. In this section, you will delve more into making an automated malware analysis system.

There are lots of automated sandboxes available. Some of them are software based, and some are hardware based. Some are free, while some cost a lot of money.

When it comes to open source automated sandboxes, my personal favorite is Cuckoo. It is completely open source, which means that aside from looking at its internals, you can modify and customize it as you want. Plus, you can use the skills you have learned in previous chapters to create the guest OS that will run the malware.

When Cuckoo processes a binary, it produces the following output:[4]

► Native functions and Windows API call traces

► Copies of files created and deleted from the file system

► Dump of the memory of the selected process

► Full memory dump of the analysis machine

► Screenshots of the desktop during the execution of the malware analysis

► Network dump generated by the machine used for analysis

These outputs can be presented in the following formats to make it more consumable to end users:

► JavaScript Object Notation (JSON) report

► Hypertext Markup Language (HTML) report

---

[4] Cuckoo Sandbox: http://www.cuckoosandbox.org/.

▶ Malware Attribute Enumeration and Characterization (MAEC) report

▶ MongoDB interface

▶ HPFeeds interface

You can learn more about Cuckoo at http://www.cuckoosandbox.org/.

LAB 13-9: *Installing and Configuring Cuckoo*

In this lab, you will install and configure Cuckoo 1.1 on a host running Ubuntu 14.04 LTS. It will also explain the process of installing a Cuckoo agent on a guest virtual machine running Windows XP with Service Pack 3.

This lab is divided into the following major steps:

1. Preparing the host

2. Installing Cuckoo

3. Preparing the guest

4. Installing the agent

5. Configuring Cuckoo

6. Running Cuckoo

What You Need:

▶ System running Ubuntu 14.04

▶ Windows XP with SP3 virtual machine (you will be using VirtualBox as your virtualization software)

Steps:

1. Prepare the host.

   A. Install Python on your Ubuntu machine. This is necessary because all the components of Cuckoo are written in Python.

   ```
   $ sudo apt-get install python
   ```

   B. Install mongodb. This is needed to use the web interface.

   ```
   $ sudo apt-get install mongodb
   ```

C. Install SQLAlchemy and Python BSON packages.

```
$ sudo apt-get install python-sqlalchemy python-bson
```

D. Some dependencies used by modules and utilities within Cuckoo are optional, but their installation is recommended. For an explanation of the role of those dependencies, please refer to the requirements section of the Cuckoo sandbox documentation located at http://docs. cuckoosandbox.org/en/latest/installation/host/requirements/.

```
$ sudo apt-get install python-dpkt python-jinja2 python-magic
python-pymongo python-gridfs python-libvirt python-bottle
python-pefile python-chardet python-django
```

E. Install Yara by following Lab 13-1.

F. To add fuzzy hashing capabilities to your sandbox, first you need to download and install ssdeep. Get the latest source from http://ssdeep. sourceforge.net/. As of this writing, the latest version is ssdeep-2.12.

```
$ tar -zxf ssdeep-2.12.tar.gz
$ cd ssdeep-2.12
$ ./configure
$ make
$ sudo make install
```

G. Download and install pydeep. Get the latest source from https://github. com/kbandla/pydeep/archive/master.zip.

```
$ wget https://github.com/kbandla/pydeep/archive/master.zip
$ unzip master.zip
$ cd pydeep-master
$ python setup.py build
$ sudo python setup.py install
```

H. If you encounter an error while building pydeep, make sure to install the necessary libraries for python-dev using the following command:

```
$ sudo apt-get install python-dev
```

I. A network sniffer such as tcpdump is necessary to capture the network traffic while malware is running.

```
$ sudo apt-get install tcpdump
```

J. Set Linux capabilities to tcpdump to avoid running it as root.

```
$ sudo setcap cap_net_raw,cap_net_admin=eip /usr/sbin/tcpdump
```

2. Install Cuckoo.

   A. Start by creating a new user dedicated to your sandbox. Make sure to add the new user to the group of users running VirtualBox. In this lab, you will make the user cuckoo and the group vboxusers.

   ```
   $ sudo adduser cuckoo
   $ sudo usermod -G vboxusers cuckoo
   ```

   B. Add the new user to the list of sudoers on the host. The visudo tool lets you edit the /etc/sudoers file.

   ```
   $ sudo visudo
   ```

   C. Once the sudoers file is opened, add the following line at the end:

   ```
   Cuckoo ALL=(ALL) ALL
   ```

   D. Save your changes to /etc/sudoers and quit.

   E. Log out and then log in as the newly created user. This is important because the guest VM has to be created under the new user account so the sandbox can have access to it.

   F. After logging in, extract Cuckoo.

   ```
   $ tar -zxf cuckoo-current.tar.gz
   ```

3. Prepare the guest.

   A. Install Oracle VirtualBox in Ubuntu by following the instructions in Lab 8-3.

   B. Create a Windows XP SP3 virtual machine. It is important that the VM has to be created while you are logged in as the newly created cuckoo user.

   C. It is advisable to enable sharing between the host and the guest VM to move the necessary files between the two machines. To enable sharing, you need first to install the Guest Additions on the guest VM. To do so, from the VM menu, choose Devices | Insert Guest Additions CD Image and then follow the wizard. See Figure 13-74.

   D. Next create a shared directory on your host. In your lab, you will name the directory sharedvb.

   ```
   $ mkdir sharedvb
   ```

   E. From the guest VM settings, choose Shared Folders. Right-click Machine Folders and select the option to add shared folder. Click OK to exit the wizard and restart the guest VM. See Figure 13-75.

Figure 13-74 *Install guest additions in VirtualBox.*

F. Python 2.7 or later is required on the guest VM for the analyzer component of Cuckoo to run properly. Since you are using Windows, download the Python installer from https://www.python.org/downloads/windows/.

G. You can also install the Python Imaging Library from http://www .pythonware.com/products/pil/. This is used to take screenshots of the Windows desktop during the analysis process. Install the library that matches the Python version you installed on the guest VM.

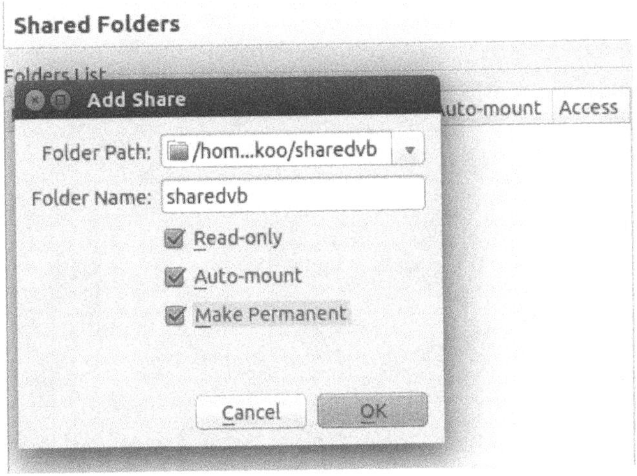

Shared Folders

Folders List

Add Share

Folder Path: /hom...koo/sharedvb

Folder Name: sharedvb

☑ Read-only

☑ Auto-mount

☑ Make Permanent

Cancel   OK

Figure 13-75 *Shared Folders settings.*

H. Make sure to disable the Windows firewall and automatic updates on your guest VM. This is necessary to get the most of your malware analysis and reduce the noise in your network dump. You can turn off those features from Windows Control Panel and then click Security Center. Within the Windows Security Center, there are options to modify the settings.

I. Check out Chapter 8 on how to make your host malware friendly to increase the success of malware running in the guest VM.

J. Configure the network for your Ubuntu host and the guest VM. The goal is to create a host-only network between the host and the guest VM and then to give Internet access to the guest through the host. From the VirtualBox menu on Ubuntu, choose File | Preferences | Network and then select the Host-Only Networks tab. Make sure that the virtual interface is listed on this tab. If it is not already there, then click the little plus (+) button on the top-right side. The virtual interface will show up automatically. Click OK to exit the wizard. See Figure 13-76.

K. Go to your guest VM setting and choose Network. Change the network settings to Host-Only Adapter, as shown in Figure 13-77. Click OK to close the wizard.

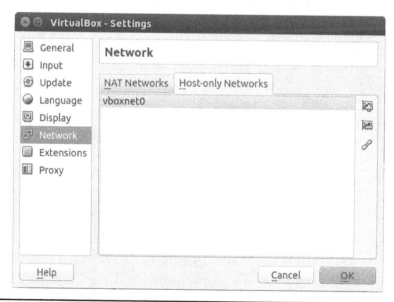

Figure 13-76 *VirtualBox network settings.*

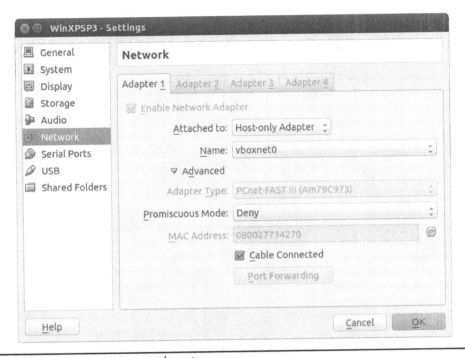

Figure 13-77   *Guest VM network settings.*

L. Check the IP address assigned to the virtual interface on the host machine by running ifconfig, as shown in Figure 13-78.

M. Assign a static IP address to your guest VM so it belongs to the same subnet mask as the host, as shown in Figure 13-79.

```
cuckoo@ubn: ~
cuckoo@ubn:~$ ifconfig vboxnet0
vboxnet0  Link encap:Ethernet  HWaddr 0a:00:27:00:00:00
          inet addr:192.168.56.1  Bcast:192.168.56.255  Mask:255.255.255.0
          inet6 addr: fe80::800:27ff:fe00:0/64 Scope:Link
          UP BROADCAST RUNNING MULTICAST  MTU:1500  Metric:1
          RX packets:0 errors:0 dropped:0 overruns:0 frame:0
          TX packets:401 errors:0 dropped:0 overruns:0 carrier:0
          collisions:0 txqueuelen:1000
          RX bytes:0 (0.0 B)  TX bytes:58344 (58.3 KB)
```

Figure 13-78   *Check the IP address by running ifconfig.*

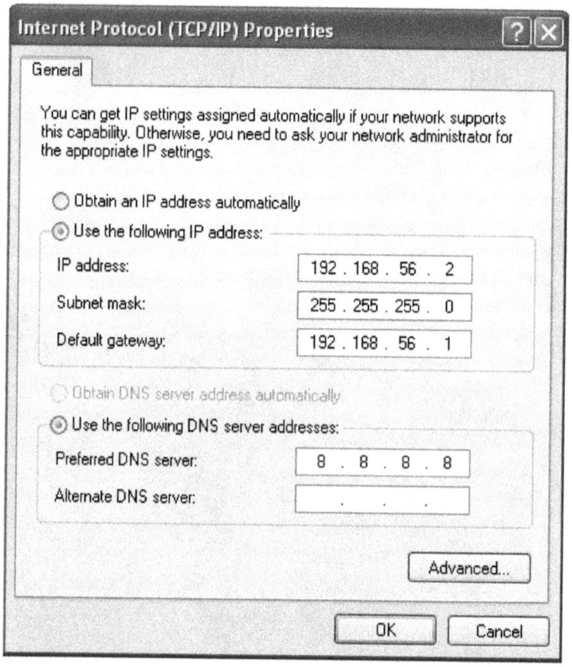

Figure 13-79   *TCP/IP properties.*

N.   You can test the connectivity between the host and the guest CM by making them ping each other, for example.

O.   To give the guest VM Internet access through the host, you need to modify the iptables on the host. Assuming the host has a physical interface eth0 and a virtual interface vboxnet0 with subnet mask 192.168.56.0/24, add the following rules to your iptables:

```
$ sudo iptables -A FORWARD -o eth0 -i vboxnet0 -s
192.168.56.0/24 -m conntrack
--ctstate NEW -j ACCEPT
$ sudo iptables -A FORWARD -m conntrack -ctstate
ESTABLISHED,RELATED -j ACCEPT
$ sudo iptables -A POSTROUTING -t nat -j MASQUERADE
```

P.   Finally, add IP forwarding.

```
$ sudo sysctl -w net.ipv4.ip_forward=1
```

Q.   Your guest VM now has Internet access. Test it by browsing to a popular search page.

4. Install the agent.

   A. Copy the file cuckoo/agent/agent.py from the host to the guest VM. You can do so using the established shared folder.

      ```
      $ cp cuckoo/agent/agent.py sharedvb/
      ```

   B. Copy the agent.py file to the Startup folder on your guest VM. On a Windows XP machine, the location of the Startup folder is typically at C:\Documents and Settings\<user>\Start Menu\Programs\Startup. This will ensure that the agent is launched every time the guest VM is booted. When you execute the file, it spawns a Python window informing you that the agent started on the guest VM, as shown in Figure 13-80.

   C. Now is a good time to take a snapshot of the guest VM and to make a backup of the whole virtual machine.

5. Configure Cuckoo.

   A. Before running Cuckoo, you need to configure some files on the host machine. All the configuration files are located under cuckoo/conf, and they are self-explanatory. You need to review the following files and make sure the settings match your environment:

      ▶ cuckoo.conf

      ▶ auxillary.conf

      ▶ machinery.conf

      ▶ reporting.conf

Figure 13-80   *Cuckoo agent running in the guest VM.*

    B. For this installation, the configuration settings are as follows:

        ▶ Here is cuckoo.conf:

```
machinery = virtualbox
[resultserver]
ip = 192.168.56.1
port = 2042
```

If you do not plan on using the default SQLite DBMS, you need to specify the connection string to your database in cuckoo.conf. For example, if you have MySQL installed on your host, your string will look like this:

```
[database]
connection = mysql://cuckoo:{pass}@localhost/cuckooDB
```

    where:
cuckooDB is the database name.
cuckoo is a user who has full privileges on cuckooDB.
{pass} is the password for the previous user.

    ▶ Here is auxillary.conf:

```
[sniffer]
enabled = yes
tcpdump = /usr/sbin/tcpdump
interface = vboxnet0
```

    ▶ Here is virtualbox.conf:

```
[virtualbox]
mode = gui
path = /usr/bin/VBoxManage
machines = cuckoo1
[cuckoo1]
label = WinXP
platform = windows
ip = 192.168.56.2
```

WinXP is the name given to the guest VM, and 192.168.56.2 is its static IP address.

    ▶ Here is reporting.conf:

```
[mongodb]
enabled = yes
```

This is important for the web interface to be able to pull data from the Mongo database.

C. As for the rest of the configuration files, there are no changes necessary.

6. Run Cuckoo.

A. Start Cuckoo by navigating to its directory on the host machine and running the following command:

```
$ python cuckoo.py
```

B. You can submit a file for analysis using the following command line:

```
$ cd cuckoo/utils/
$ python submit.py <path to file>
```

C. The submission Python script has many options. Please refer to the Cuckoo documentation to get more information on the usage of the submission tool.

D. For every file analyzed by the sandbox, Cuckoo assigns a task ID to it. Analysis reports are saved in cuckoo/storage/analysis. Use the task ID to find the corresponding subdirectory of the analysis files.

E. You can also submit samples using the web interface. First you will need to start the web server.

```
$ cd cuckoo/web
$ python manage.py runserver
```

F. Now open a browser and navigate to http://localhost:8000/. The dashboard, as shown in Figure 13-81, gives you an overview of all the samples analyzed by the sandbox.

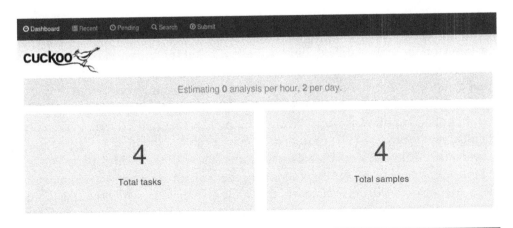

Figure 13-81 *Cuckoo dashboard.*

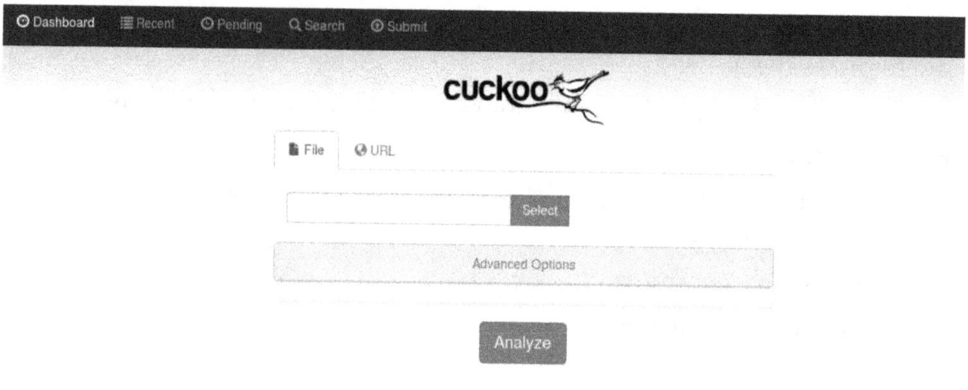

Figure 13-82 *Cuckoo submit page.*

> **G.** You can add more samples to the queue from the Submit page, as shown in Figure 13-82.
>
> **H.** To view the analysis report of a certain file on the web interface, you can use http://localhost:8000/analysis/<task_ID>/, where <task_ID> is the ID assigned by the analysis job upon file submission. Figure 13-83 shows an overview of an analyzed file.

7. Have fun playing with Cuckoo. You can also consult Cuckoo's documentation for more features.

Free Online Automated Sandbox Services

Setting up your own sandbox requires a lot of effort, research, and trial and error, but once it is finished, the happiness and excitement you feel when you see your creation working is unmatched. But for those without the time and resources to set up their own sandbox, there are automated sandbox services that are offered online for free. Of course, there is a catch. Everything you submit may become property of these free services, so read carefully the terms of use and privacy policies of these services. Avoid sending files that may contain personally identifiable information (PII) or information that can be classified as intellectual property (IP). These services may also share this data with other third-party entities.

Free online automated sandbox services offer a quick and easy way to analyze a file. Some services will determine whether a file is malicious, while some will only give you a report, and it is up to you to deduce whether it is malicious.

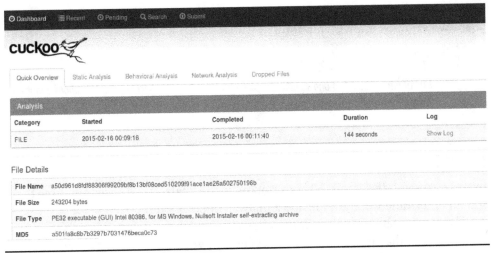

Figure 13-83 *Cuckoo analysis overview.*

The following are some of the more popular online automated sandbox services available for free:

- ▶ **Anubis** http://anubis.iseclab.org/
- ▶ **Comodo Instant Malware Analysis** http://camas.comodo.com/
- ▶ **Comodo Valkyrie** http://valkyrie.comodo.com/
- ▶ **EUREKA Malware Analysis Internet Service** http://eureka.cyber-ta.org/
- ▶ **Malwr** https://malwr.com/submission/
- ▶ **MalwareViz** https://www.malwareviz.com/
- ▶ **Payload Security** https://www.hybrid-analysis.com/
- ▶ **ThreatExpert** http://www.threatexpert.com/submit.aspx
- ▶ **ThreatTrack Public Malware Sandbox** http://www.threattracksecurity.com/resources/sandbox-malware-analysis.aspx
- ▶ **VICheck** https://www.vicheck.ca/

> **NOTE**
> *MalwareViz is used in tandem with Malwr. MalwareViz accepts malwr analysis link as its input.*

Experiment on these different automated sandbox services and compare each of their outputs. You can see that some of them offer more information than others. Compare them also to the output of your Cuckoo sandbox. These free online automated services can be your benchmark when it comes to the effectiveness of your own sandbox implementation.

> **TIP**
>
> *Do not limit yourself to one sandbox implementation. Always collect information about a malware from other sandboxes and combine them to paint an accurate picture of the malware.*

Recap

In this chapter, I discussed the common malware analysis use cases and how they should determine what goes inside a malware analyst's toolbox.

I also noted that regardless of the use case a malware analyst is trying to satisfy, there are tools that are considered indispensable when it comes to malware analysis. I call them tools of the trade. They are as follows:

- Sysinternals Suite
- Yara
- Cygwin
- Debuggers
- Disassemblers
- Memory dumpers
- PE viewers
- PE reconstructors
- Malcode Analyst Pack
- Rootkit tools
- Network capturing tools
- Automated sandboxes
- Free online automated sandbox services

Combining these tools the right way gives analysts and researchers a potent weapon in tackling the most difficult malware. In this chapter, you combined these tools to solve the most challenging use cases analysts and researchers always face. They are as follows:

- Manually unpacking a packed malware
- Analyzing a user mode rootkit
- Analyzing a kernel mode rootkit

It is important to note that there are more tools out there; the main thing is to find a tool that you are comfortable with and that satisfies your use cases.

Tools

- **Sysinternals Suite**   https://technet.microsoft.com/en-us/sysinternals/bb842062.aspx
- **Yara**   https://github.com/plusvic/yara
- **Cygwin**   https://www.cygwin.com
- Debuggers
    - **OllyDbg**   http://www.ollydbg.de/
    - **Immunity Debugger**   http://debugger.immunityinc.com/
    - Windows debuggers
        - **WinDbg**   https://msdn.microsoft.com/en-us/windows/hardware/hh852365.aspx.
        - **KD and NTKD**   https://msdn.microsoft.com/en-us/library/windows/hardware/hh406279%28v=vs.85%29.aspx
- Disassembler
    - **IDA**   https://www.hex-rays.com/products/ida/support/download.shtml
- Memory dumpers
    - **LordPE by y0da**   http://www.woodmann.com/collaborative/tools/index.php/LordPE
    - **Volatility Framework**   https://code.google.com/p/volatility/wiki/VolatilityIntroduction
- PE viewers
    - **Hiew**   http://www.hiew.ru/
    - **Heaventools PE Explorer**   http://www.heaventools.com/overview.htm
    - **PEview**   http://wjradburn.com/software/
    - **Dependency Walker**   http://www.dependencywalker.com/
    - **Resource Hacker**   http://www.angusj.com/resourcehacker/

- ► PE reconstructors
  - ► **ImpREC by MackT** http://www.woodmann.com/collaborative/tools/index.php/ImpREC
- ► **Malcode Analyst Pack** http://www.woodmann.com/collaborative/tools/index.php/Malcode_Analysis_Pack
- ► Rootkit tools
  - ► **Rootkit Unhooker** http://www.antirootkit.com/software/RootKit-Unhooker.htm
  - ► **Rootkit Revealer** http://download.cnet.com/RootkitRevealer/3000-2248_4-10543918.html
- ► Network capturing tools
  - ► **Wireshark** https://www.wireshark.org/
  - ► **TCPDump** http://www.tcpdump.org/
  - ► **TCPView** https://technet.microsoft.com/en-us/sysinternals/bb897437.aspx
- ► **OSR driver loader** http://www.osronline.com/article.cfm?article=157
- ► Automated sandboxes
  - ► **Cuckoo** http://www.cuckoosandbox.org/
- ► Free online automated sandbox services
  - ► **Anubis** http://anubis.iseclab.org/
  - ► **Comodo Instant Malware Analysis** http://camas.comodo.com/
  - ► **Comodo Valkyrie** http://valkyrie.comodo.com/
  - ► **EUREKA Malware Analysis Internet Service** http://eureka.cyber-ta.org/
  - ► **Malwr** https://malwr.com/submission/
  - ► **MalwareViz** https://www.malwareviz.com/
  - ► **Payload Security** https://www.hybrid-analysis.com/
  - ► **ThreatExpert** http://www.threatexpert.com/submit.aspx
  - ► **ThreatTrack Public Malware Sandbox** http://www.threattracksecurity.com/resources/sandbox-malware-analysis.aspx
  - ► **VICheck** https://www.vicheck.ca/

Appendixes

A

Tools List

This appendix lists all the tools discussed throughout the book.

- ▶ Free online antivirus scanners
  - ▶ **Trend Micro's HouseCall** http://housecall.trendmicro.com/
  - ▶ **F-Secure Online Scanner** http://www.f-secure.com/en/web/home_global/online-scanner
- ▶ Free malware removal tools
  - ▶ **Microsoft Security Essentials** http://windows.microsoft.com/en-us/windows/security-essentials-download
  - ▶ **Comodo Cleaning Essentials** http://www.comodo.com/business-security/network-protection/cleaning_essentials.php
  - ▶ **Kaspersky Security Scan** http://www.kaspersky.com/free-virus-scan
- ▶ Rootkit detectors
  - ▶ **Rootkit Revealer by Microsoft** http://download.cnet.com/RootkitRevealer/3000-2248_4-10543918.html
  - ▶ **TDSSKiller by Kaspersky** https://support.kaspersky.com/us/viruses/utility#TDSSKiller
- ▶ Startup examination tools
  - ▶ **Autoruns by Microsoft** http://technet.microsoft.com/en-us/sysinternals/bb963902.aspx
  - ▶ **Autorun Analyzer by Comodo** http://www.comodo.com/business-security/network-protection/cleaning_essentials.php
- ▶ Boot analyzer tools
  - ▶ **Gmer's MBR.EXE** http://www.gmer.net
  - ▶ **MbrScan** http://eric71.geekstogo.com/tools/MbrScan.exe
  - ▶ **MBR Backup** http://www.trojanhunter.com/products/mbr-backup/
  - ▶ **Boot Sector Explorer** http://www.pendriveapps.com/boot-sector-explorer-backup-and-restore-mbr/
  - ▶ **Nate's MBR and Boot Sector Analyzer** http://www.aqfire.com/boot/
  - ▶ **WinHex, MBR/boot sector editor** http://www.winhex.com/disk-editor.html

- ▶ Process examination tools
  - ▶ **Process Explorer by Microsoft** http://technet.microsoft.com/en-us/sysinternals/bb896653.aspx
  - ▶ **KillSwitch by Comodo** http://www.comodo.com/business-security/network-protection/cleaning_essentials.php
- ▶ Honeypots
  - ▶ **Dionaea** http://dionaea.carnivore.it
- ▶ **Windows 7 USB/DVD Download Tool** http://images2.store.microsoft.com/prod/clustera/framework/w7udt/1.0/en-us/Windows7-USB-DVD-tool.exe
- ▶ **Secunia Online Software Inspector** http://secunia.com/vulnerability_scanning/online/
- ▶ Firefox add-ons and plug-ins
  - ▶ NoScript
  - ▶ Better Privacy
  - ▶ RequestPolicy
  - ▶ Web of Trust (WOT)
  - ▶ Adblock Plus
- ▶ Proxy servers
  - ▶ **Hide My Ass!** http://hidemyass.com/proxy/
  - ▶ **Proxy 4 Free** http://www.proxy4free.com
  - ▶ **Samair.RU** http://www.samair.ru/proxy/
  - ▶ **Public proxy servers** http://www.publicproxyservers.com/proxy/list1.html
- ▶ Virtual private network services
  - ▶ **Private Tunnel** https://www.privatetunnel.com
  - ▶ **VPNBook** http://www.vpnbook.com
  - ▶ **JustFreeVPN** http://www.justfreevpn.com
  - ▶ **VPNAccount** http://www.vpnaccount.org
  - ▶ **L2TP VPN Service** http://www.freel2tpvpn.com
  - ▶ **OkayFreedom VPN** https://www.okayfreedom.com
  - ▶ **VPNAccess** http://freevpnaccess.com

- ▶ **Hotspot Shield Ad Supported**   http://www.hotspotshield.com
- ▶ **CyberGhost**   http://cyberghostvpn.com
- ▶ **Free UK & US VPN**   http://www.ukusvpn.com
- ▶ **Free VPN for UK**   http://www.vpnforuk.com
- ▶ **Premium VPN with Public IP**   http://www.truvpn.com
- ▶ **Free ProXPN**   http://proxpn.com
- ▶ Online anonymizers
  - ▶ **Anonymouse**   http://anonmouse.org/anonwww.html
  - ▶ **Free Web Proxy**   http://www.vpnbook.com/webproxy
  - ▶ **Online Anonymizer**   http://online-anonymizer.com
  - ▶ **Hide My Ass! Web Proxy**   http://hidemyass.com/proxy/
  - ▶ **KProxy**   https://www.kproxy.com
  - ▶ **Megaproxy**   http://www.megaproxy.com/freesurf/
- ▶ **Tor, the onion router**   https://www.torproject.org/docs/documentation .html.en
- ▶ **VMware Player**   http://www.vmware.com/go/downloadplayer
- ▶ **VirtualBox**   https://www.virtualbox.org/wiki/Downloads
- ▶ **Clonezilla**   http://clonezilla.org/downloads.php
- ▶ Virtualization software
  - ▶ **VMware Player**   http://www.vmware.com/go/downloadplayer
  - ▶ **VirtualBox**   https://www.virtualbox.org/wiki/Downloads
  - ▶ **VirtualPC**   http://www.microsoft.com/en-US/download/details .aspx?id=3702
- ▶ Trusted Adobe download sites
  - ▶ **Adobe Reader**   http://get.adobe.com/reader
  - ▶ **Adobe Flash Player**   http://get.adobe.com/flashplayer
- ▶ **Deep Freeze Standard by Faronics**   http://www.faronics.com/products/ deep-freeze/standard/
- ▶ **Clonezilla**   http://clonezilla.org/download.php
- ▶ **Tuxboot**   http://sourceforge.net/projects/tuxboot/files/

- **Dependency Walker** http://www.dependencywalker.com
- **pefile** https://code.google.com/p/pefile/
- **pedump** https://github.com/zed-0xff/pedump
- **pedump online PE file submission** http://pedump.me/
- Compression tools
  - **WinZip** http://www.winzip.com
  - **WinRAR** http://www.rarlab.com
  - **7zip** http://www.7-zip.org
  - **p7zip** http://p7zip.sourceforge.net/
- **GnuPG** http://www.gnupg.org
- **MD5SUM** http://www.etree.org/md5com.html
- **Microsoft File Checksum Integrity Verifier** http://www.microsoft.com/en-us/download/details.aspx?id=11533
- **PEiD** http://woodmann.com/BobSoft/Pages/Programs/PEiD
- **ClamAV** http://www.clamav.net
- Sample submission online services
  - **F-Secure Sample Analysis** http://www.f-secure.com/en/web/labs_global/submit-samples/sas
  - **Sophos** https://secure2.sophos.com/en-us/support/contact-support/sample-submission.aspx
- Malware scanning services
  - **VirusTotal by Google** https://www.virustotal.com
  - **VirSCAN** http://www.virscan.org
  - **Metascan by OPSWAT** https://www.metascan-online.com
  - **Jotti** http://virusscan.jotti.org
  - **Dr. Web** http://www.drweb-online.com/en/online_check.asp
  - **Fortiguard Online Virus Scanner** http://www.fortiguard.com/antivirus/virus_scanner.html
- Packers
  - **Armadillo** http://www.siliconrealms.com/armadillo.php
  - **ASPack** http://www.aspack.com/aspack.html

- ► ASProtect32   http://www.aspack.com/asprotect32.html
- ► ASProtect64   http://www.aspack.com/asprotect64.html
- ► PECompact   http://bitsum.com/pecompact/
- ► UPX   http://upx.sourceforge.net/
- ► PE Explorer   http://www.heaventools.com/overview.htm
- ► Packers and unpackers   http://www.woodmann.com/crackz/Packers.htm
- ► Sysinternals Strings.EXE   http://technet.microsoft.com/en-us/sysinternals/bb897439
- ► Sysinternals Suite   https://technet.microsoft.com/en-us/sysinternals/bb842062.aspx
- ► System monitoring tools
  - ► InstallRite   http://www.softpedia.com/get/System/System-Info/InstallRite.shtml
  - ► Uninstall Tool   http://www.crystalidea.com/uninstall-tool
- ► Memory analysis tools
  - ► Process Explorer   https://technet.microsoft.com/en-us/sysinternals/bb896653
  - ► Autoruns   https://technet.microsoft.com/en-us/sysinternals/bb963902.aspx
- ► Network analysis tools
  - ► TCPView   https://technet.microsoft.com/en-us/sysinternals/bb897437.aspx
  - ► Wireshark   https://www.wireshark.org/
- ► Yara   https://github.com/plusvic/yara
- ► Cygwin   https://www.cygwin.com
- ► Debuggers
  - ► OllyDbg   http://www.ollydbg.de/
  - ► Immunity Debugger   http://debugger.immunityinc.com/

- Windows debuggers
  - **WinDbg** https://msdn.microsoft.com/en-us/windows/hardware/hh852365.aspx.
  - **KD and NTKD** https://msdn.microsoft.com/en-us/library/windows/hardware/hh406279%28v=vs.85%29.aspx
- Disassembler
  - **IDA** https://www.hex-rays.com/products/ida/support/download.shtml
- Memory dumpers
  - **LordPE by y0da** http://www.woodmann.com/collaborative/tools/index.php/LordPE
  - **Volatility Framework** https://code.google.com/p/volatility/wiki/VolatilityIntroduction
- PE viewers
  - **Hiew** http://www.hiew.ru/
  - **Heaventools PE Explorer** http://www.heaventools.com/overview.htm
  - **PEview** http://wjradburn.com/software/
  - **Dependency Walker** http://www.dependencywalker.com/
  - **Resource Hacker** http://www.angusj.com/resourcehacker/
- PE reconstructors
  - **ImpREC by MackT** http://www.woodmann.com/collaborative/tools/index.php/ImpREC
- **Malcode Analyst Pack** http://www.woodmann.com/collaborative/tools/index.php/Malcode_Analysis_Pack
- Rootkit tools
  - **Rootkit Unhooker** http://www.antirootkit.com/software/RootKit-Unhooker.htm
  - **Rootkit Revealer** http://download.cnet.com/RootkitRevealer/3000-2248_4-10543918.html
- Network capturing tools
  - **Wireshark** https://www.wireshark.org/
  - **TCPDump** http://www.tcpdump.org/
  - **TCPView** https://technet.microsoft.com/en-us/sysinternals/bb897437.aspx

- ► **OSR driver loader**   http://www.osronline.com/article.cfm?article=157
- ► Automated sandboxes
    - ► **Cuckoo**   http://www.cuckoosandbox.org/
- ► Free online automated sandbox services
    - ► **Anubis**   http://anubis.iseclab.org/
    - ► **Comodo Instant Malware Analysis**   http://camas.comodo.com/
    - ► **Comodo Valkyrie**   http://valkyrie.comodo.com/
    - ► **EUREKA Malware Analysis Internet Service**   http://eureka.cyber-ta
      .org/
    - ► **Malwr**   https://malwr.com/submission/
    - ► **MalwareViz**   https://www.malwareviz.com/
    - ► **Payload Security**   https://www.hybrid-analysis.com/
    - ► **ThreatExpert**   http://www.threatexpert.com/submit.aspx
    - ► **ThreatTrack Public Malware Sandbox**   http://www
      .threattracksecurity.com/resources/sandbox-malware-analysis.aspx
    - ► **VICheck**   https://www.vicheck.ca/

List of Laboratories

T hroughout the book, there are labs that are designed to help you in your quest to analyze malware. This appendix lists all the laboratories contained in the book.

LAB 6-1: Installing Dionaea

LAB 7-1: Extracting and Copying Drivers to the Windows 7 Installation Media

LAB 7-2: Creating a Bootable USB Stick Windows 7 Installer

LAB 7-3: Creating a Bootable USB Stick Windows 7 Installer Using the Windows 7 USB/DVD Download Tool

LAB 7-4: Protecting Firefox Using Built-in Options

LAB 7-5: Protecting Firefox Using Add-ons and Plug-ins

LAB 7-6: Creating a Virtualized Ubuntu Desktop Using VMware Player

LAB 7-7: Creating a Virtualized Ubuntu Desktop Using VirtualBox

LAB 8-1: Installing VMware Player in Ubuntu

LAB 8-2: Uninstalling VMware Player in Ubuntu

LAB 8-3: Installing VirtualBox in Ubuntu

LAB 8-4: Uninstalling VirtualBox in Ubuntu

LAB 8-5: Disabling Automatic Updates in Windows 7

LAB 8-6: Disabling User Account Control in Windows 7

LAB 8-7: Making Internet Explorer Malware Friendly

LAB 8-8: Making Mozilla Firefox Malware Friendly

LAB 8-9: Making Google Chrome Malware Friendly

LAB 8-10: Making Microsoft Office Malware Friendly

LAB 8-11: Making Adobe Reader Malware Friendly

LAB 8-12: Setting a Non-persistent Image in VirtualBox

LAB 8-13: Setting a Non-persistent Image in VirtualBox Using the Command Line

LAB 8-14: Creating a Non-persistent Bare-Metal System Using Deep Freeze Standard

LAB 8-15: Creating a Clonezilla Live in USB Flash Drive

Volatility Framework
Basic Plug-ins

This appendix lists basic plug-ins for the Volatility framework.

apihooks	Detects API hooks in process and kernel memory
atoms	Prints session and window station atom tables
atomscan	Is a pool scanner for atom tables
auditpol	Prints out the audit policies from HKLM\SECURITY\Policy\PolAdtEv
bigpools	Dumps the big page pools using BigPagePoolScanner
bioskbd	Reads the keyboard buffer from real mode memory
cachedump	Dumps cached domain hashes from memory
callbacks	Prints system-wide notification routines
clipboard	Extracts the contents of the Windows clipboard
cmdline	Displays process command-line arguments
cmdscan	Extracts command history by scanning for _COMMAND_HISTORY
connections	Prints a list of open connections (Windows XP and 2003 only)
connscan	Is a pool scanner for Transmission Control Protocol (TCP) connections
consoles	Extracts command history by scanning for _CONSOLE_INFORMATION
crashinfo	Dumps crash-dump information
deskscan	Is a pool scanner for tagDESKTOP (desktops)
devicetree	Shows device tree
dlldump	Dumps DLLs from a process address space
dlllist	Prints list of loaded DLLs for each process
driverirp	Is a driver for I/O request packet (IRP) hook detection
driverscan	Is a pool scanner for driver objects
dumpcerts	Dumps RSA private and public Secure Sockets Layer (SSL) keys
dumpfiles	Extracts memory-mapped and cached files

envars	Displays process environment variables
eventhooks	Prints details on Windows event hooks
evtlogs	Extracts Windows Event Logs (XP/2003 only)
filescan	Is a pool scanner for file objects
gahti	Dumps the USER handle type information
gditimers	Prints installed Graphics Device Interface (GDI) timers and callbacks
gdt	Displays global descriptor table
getservicesids	Gets the names of services in the registry and returns calculated security identifier (SID)
getsids	Prints the SIDs owning each process
handles	Prints a list of open handles for each process
hashdump	Dumps passwords hashes (LM/NTLM) from memory
hibinfo	Dumps hibernation file information
hivedump	Prints out a hive
hivelist	Prints list of registry hives
hivescan	Is a pool scanner for registry hives
hpakextract	Extracts physical memory from an HPAK file
hpakinfo	Displays information about an HPAK file
idt	Displays interrupt descriptor table
iehistory	Reconstructs Internet Explorer cache/history
imagecopy	Copies a physical address space out as a raw DD image
imageinfo	Identifies information for the image
impscan	Scans for calls to imported functions
joblinks	Prints process job link information
kdbgscan	Searches for and dumps potential KDBG values
kpcrscan	Searches for and dumps potential KPCR values
ldrmodules	Detects unlinked DLLs
lsadump	Dumps decrypted Local Security Authority (LSA) secrets from the registry

machoinfo	Dumps Mach-O file format information
malfind	Finds hidden and injected code
mbrparser	Scans for and parses potential Master Boot Records (MBRs)
memdump	Dumps the addressable memory for a process
memmap	Prints the memory map
messagehooks	Lists desktop and thread window message hooks
mftparser	Scans for and parses potential MFT entries
moddump	Dumps a kernel driver to an executable file sample
modscan	Is a pool scanner for kernel modules
modules	Prints list of loaded modules
multiscan	Scans for various objects at once
mutantscan	Is a pool scanner for mutex objects
notepad	Lists currently displayed Notepad text
objtypescan	Scans for Windows object type objects
patcher	Patches memory based on page scans
poolpeek	Is a configurable pool scanner plug-in
printkey	Prints a registry key and its subkeys and values
privs	Displays process privileges
procdump	Dumps a process to an executable file sample
pslist	Prints all running processes by following the EPROCESS lists
psscan	Is a pool scanner for process objects
pstree	Prints process list as a tree
psxview	Finds hidden processes with various process listings
raw2dmp	Converts a physical memory sample to a windbg crash dump
screenshot	Saves a pseudo-screenshot based on GDI windows
sessions	Lists details on _MM_SESSION_SPACE (user logon sessions)
shellbags	Prints ShellBags info

shimcache	Parses the Application Compatibility Shim Cache registry key
sockets	Prints a list of open sockets
sockscan	Is a pool scanner for TCP socket objects
ssdt	Displays SSDT entries
strings	Matches physical offsets to virtual addresses (may take a while, is very verbose)
svcscan	Scans for Windows services
symlinkscan	Is a pool scanner for symlink objects
thrdscan	Is a pool scanner for thread objects
threads	Investigates _ETHREAD and _KTHREADs
timeliner	Creates a timeline from various artifacts in memory
timers	Prints kernel timers and associated module DPCs
truecryptmaster	Recovers TrueCrypt 7.1a master keys
truecryptpassphrase	Is a TrueCrypt cached passphrase finder
truecryptsummary	Provides a TrueCrypt summary
unloadedmodules	Prints list of unloaded modules
userassist	Prints user-assist registry keys and information
userhandles	Dumps the USER handle tables
vaddump	Dumps out the VAD sections to a file
vadinfo	Dumps the VAD information
vadtree	Walks the VAD tree and displays in tree format
vadwalk	Walks the VAD tree
vboxinfo	Dumps virtualbox information
verinfo	Prints out the version information from PE images
vmwareinfo	Dumps VMware VMSS/VMSN information
volshell	Shell in the memory image
windows	Prints Desktop Windows (verbose details)
wintree	Prints Z-Order Desktop Windows Tree
wndscan	Is a pool scanner for window stations
yarascan	Scans process or kernel memory with Yara signatures

Index

Numbers

0x55AA setting, end-of-sector markers, 36–37
7zip, 272–274, 295
64-bit format, PE file, 267

A

access
  hardening static analysis lab, 171–172
  protecting transferred files, 271–272
  user dependency attacks on, 101–105
active rootkits, detecting, 113–114
ActiveX control (OCS) files, implemented as DLLs, 234
ActiveX settings, Microsoft Office, 211
Adblock Plus add-on, Firefox, 171
ADD EAX/3, Immunity Debugger, 393, 396
ADD EAX/3/JMP EAX, Immunity Debugger, 394, 397
added files, monitoring file system for, 323–325
add-ons, Firefox, 170–171, 185
admin access, hardening static analysis lab for, 172
Adobe
  Flash Player, 209, 227
  Flash Reader, 209, 212–213, 227
  trusted download sites, 227
ad-supported software, 46
adware, 46
anonymizing
  all malware research labs, 150–151
  dynamic analysis labs, 214
  with online anonymizers, 176–177
  with proxy servers, 173–174
  static analysis labs, 172–173
  with Tor, 177
  with VPNs, 174–177
Anonymouse, 176–177, 185
anti-AV scanning, dynamic malware, 83–84
anti-debugging, dynamic malware, 80
anti-decompilers, static malware, 79
anti-disassemblers, static malware, 79
anti-reversing, 78–79
anti-sandboxing, dynamic malware, 80–82

anti-virtualization, 82
antivirus definitions, 10
antivirus detection, static analysis, 306–308
antivirus scanners
  detecting malware code snippets, 9–10
  dynamic malware protection, 83–84
  early solutions, 325
  entry-point obscuring from, 72–74
  fake, 43, 45
  malware collection with, 112, 145
  malware disabling, 94–95
  as static analysis lab tool, 149–150
Anubis, 481
appending parasitic viruses, 34
application control, software vulnerabilities, 61
apt-get command-line tool, Unbuntu, 165
Armadillo, 310, 316
ASPack, 310, 316
ASProtect32, 311, 316
ASProtect64, 311, 316
asymmetric cryptography. *See* public-key cryptography
attack component, monitoring file system, 324
attributes, hiding malware via, 322
AUTOEXEC.BAT, malware modifying, 326
automated malware analysis
  event dependency challenges, 100
  overview of, 15–20
  weeding out non-supported file formats, 94
automated sandboxes
  automated malware analysis via, 17–20
  configuring Cuckoo, 477–479
  Cuckoo website, 484
  free online services, 480–482
  installing Cuckoo, 472–477
  output formats of Cuckoo, 469–470
  overview of, 17–20, 469
  running Cuckoo, 479–480
  setting up Cuckoo, 470–471
Automatic Updates
  disabling for Cuckoo installation, 474
  disabling in Windows 7, 198–199
Autorun Analyzer by Comodo, 114–115, 117, 146

Complete coverage of today's top

IT SECURITY

certification exams

0-07-176026-1 • $60.00

0-07-178174-9 • $80.00

0-07-179308-9 • $105.00

0-07-183557-1 • $70.00

0-07-183156-8 • $50.00

0-07-183976-3 • $60.00

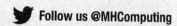 Follow us @MHComputing

Available in print and as an e-book.